St Matthew's Windsor

an Anglican Landmark celebrating 200 Years

St Matthew's Windsor, artist Greg Hansell, 15 cm x 20 cm, Schmincke pastels on Canson paper, *en plein air*, 2012. Courtesy of the artist. Photograph by Geoff Roberts.

St Matthew's Windsor

an Anglican Landmark celebrating 200 Years

Ian Jack and Jan Barkley-Jack
In conjunction with St Matthew's Anglican Church Windsor

ROSENBERG

Dedicated to all who have nurtured the spiritual growth and physical presence of St Matthew's Anglican Church in Windsor for over two hundred years; and to those who will do so into the future.

First published in 2016 by Rosenberg Publishing Pty Ltd
PO Box 6125, Dural Delivery Centre NSW 2158
Phone: +61 2 9654 1502 Fax: +61 9654 1338
Email: rosenbergpub@smartchat.net.au
Web: www.rosenbergpub.com.au

National Library of Australia Cataloguing-in-Publication entry
Authors: Jack Ian and Barkley-Jack, Jan.
Title: St Matthew's Windsor: an Anglican landmark celebrating 200 years/ Ian Jack and Jan Barkley-Jack.

Edition: 1st ed.

ISBN: 9781925078961(paperback)
ISBN: 9781925078978 (hardback)
ISBN: 9781925078985 (epdf)
Notes: Includes index.
Bibliography.

Subjects: Colonists-New South Wales-Hawkesbury.
Colonial chaplains- New South Wales- Hawkesbury
First contact of Aboriginal peoples with Europeans-New South Wales-Hawkesbury
Lachlan Macquarie, governor of New South Wales at Windsor
St Matthew's Anglican church, Windsor
St Matthew's burial ground, Windsor
St Matthew's rectory and stables, Windsor
St Matthew's glebes and Parish Centre, Windsor

Dewey Number: 283.9441

Front cover/jacket: St Matthew's Anglican Church Windsor. Photograph by Ian Jack, 2010.
Back cover/jacket: The apse with gold stars twinkling in the azure dome. Photograph by Chris Jones, rector of St Matthew's, 2016.

Printed in China by Everbest Printing Investment Limited

Contents

Foreword

When you remember your history, where do you start?

Many of us don't look much further back than two hundred years – a history of which we are mostly very proud. Truth is when we preach the crucifixion and resurrection of Jesus Christ we proclaim an event centred in the Middle East amongst an Aramaic-speaking population two thousand years ago which claims relevance to every tribe, language, people and nation.

And so when the British Empire landed on the shores of 'The Great Southland' it carried with it a message from the Middle East born with an Iraqi nomad called Abraham four thousand years before, and climaxing around two thousand years ago in the person and work of Jesus Christ.

This colonization and with it the Christian gospel would impact the Aboriginal inhabitants of Australia in ways which are being felt both negatively and positively today. The Aboriginals of Australia had their own history of thousands of years along the Deerubbin – what we today call the Hawkesbury–Nepean River. Their history was both ignored and forgotten and is only in recent days being rediscovered and given its rightful place.

The Anglican Church (Church of England) found its way to Australia on the back of the power of the British Empire and its colonizing impact around the world. Anglicans have worshipped since 1795 in the region around Windsor, which was the third area settled on the Australian mainland.

The St Matthew's Anglican Church Windsor has stood for two hundred years as an icon in the Hawkesbury, within its precinct of a rectory and stables, and an even older cemetery and glebe. It has grand buildings which hold their own in terms of age, significance and grandeur against other icons like St James' King Street in Sydney and the Hyde Park Barracks which are likewise the fruit of Governor Lachlan Macquarie's colonial building projects. Macquarie himself had a particular interest in St Matthew's Windsor and that forms part of this history. Today this precinct is an item of high heritage significance, listed as item SHR 00015 on the State Heritage Register of NSW.

The Anglican Church had a privileged place in European history. It was established by government and was seen as a key part of civil and military society. Despite such an advantage, and handicap, Anglican ministry began with evangelical fervour and zeal.

The great British hymn writer and converted slave trader Reverend John Newton's authorized biography says of the first chaplain, Reverend Richard Johnson, in the time prior to St Matthew's establishment:

> He was appointed chaplain for Botany Bay (or, as Newton regarded him, Bishop of New Holland), accompanying the first settlement of convicts to New South Wales in 1787. His appointment was achieved through the efforts of William Wilberforce and John Thornton who approached Pitt as the First Fleet was on the point of sailing. His departure prompted Newton to write these lines to William Bull:
>
> Go, bear the Saviour's name to lands unknown,
> Tell to the southern world His wondrous grace;
> And energy divine thy words shall own,
> And draw their untaught hearts to seek His face.
>
> Many in quest of gold and empty fame
> Would compass earth, or venture near the poles;
> But how much nobler thy reward and aim
> To spread His praise and win in immortal souls.

Well-known local place names such as Pitt Town and Wilberforce were called after famous figures of the late eighteenth-century in England. These men were instrumental in determining the nature of Christian ministry which was exercised in Windsor under the leadership of the Reverend Robert Cartwright and the principal chaplain, the Reverend Samuel Marsden, who succeeded the Reverend Richard Johnson.

God's church is always a living body of people committed to proclaiming the Lordship of Jesus Christ. A church can be a very lively church without a set of buildings to meet in, and yet St Matthews' Anglican Church Windsor has now met in a fine set of buildings closely associated with some of the formative names of early colonial society for two hundred years: names such as Andrew Thompson (the first ex-convict magistrate in Windsor and New South Wales) and the first burial in the cemetery. Together with Francis Greenway, Lachlan Macquarie, Samuel Marsden and William Cox their efforts and interactions form a rich part of our history and give a glimpse into early Australian colonial society.

Our congregation is deeply and gratefully indebted to the work of Dr Ian Jack and Jan Barkley-Jack in writing this exciting work. They have brought the details of buildings and structures to life with some of the stories of success and struggle to lead a church where convicts were compelled to attend and the well-off committed themselves when it suited. I have only grown in a sense of appreciation for their efforts as I have previewed their work and read the stories. They have shown us the past similar struggles for Christ's church that we experience even today.

I am new to St Matthew's. Our current struggles include finding an opening to minister in the name of Jesus Christ in a society that has moved Christianity to the margins. It is a society where for many the church seems largely irrelevant. Others have been deeply hurt. Some say we have entered a post-Christian era, although the church of Jesus Christ has had the habit of re-manifesting itself in fresh ways around the world at many times and in many different cultures.

My own vision for St Matthew's in this present time is that we be *A Credible Presence of Jesus Christ in the Hawkesbury.* For me it speaks to the nature of the life and the behaviour of the people of God who meet in these buildings. It also says to the people of the Hawkesbury that we are unashamed to continue to proclaim the goodness and relevance of Jesus Christ to men and women and boys and girls in our community. We want to do that in the most believable way that we can.

I think this is a wonderfully written history. I am proud to be the rector at the time of its release.

I am very appreciative of the efforts of the Repair and Restoration Committee members who raised funds for the publication of the soft copy edition. I am also thankful to the generous benefactors who gifted the $4000 to allow the very fine hard copy history to be published.

Reverend Chris Jones
Windsor Rectory
6 May 2016

List of Illustrations

Chapter 10

Acknowledgments

Authors in a book such as this are only facilitators to keep a history alive. The story's countless custodians, who have never worked for financial returns, the congregations and ministers past and present who created the spiritual and physical environment, the helpers who worked to forward it, the community which has so willingly taken the historic buildings, both grand and humble, to its keeping, and the descendants of those buried in its cemetery who have taken the precinct to their hearts, are those who have created the layers that make this history so compelling.

The many builders in the past who have worked with dedication to ensure that the fabric has survived over the years, using techniques approved at the time, and the experts in today's conservation practice which proceeds more scientifically, have all demonstrated the need for us to continue their work. It is a recognition that the inspiring fabric of the church reminds us not only of the presence of God, but of our forebears who met the challenges of keeping the fabric they had worked so hard to get.

In 1924, just after the centenary conservation work was completed, the Reverend Norman Jenkyn, who had led the renewal, exhorted the wider community with words which are still extremely relevant today. In thanking his congregation for providing the funds to that point, he enunciated the belief we hold today, that: 'St Matthew's does not belong alone to Windsor – it is more than a parish church. It is a national asset. It belongs to Australia, to the Commonwealth ... we cannot allow this historic church to grow shabby.'

How greatly this applies today when costs escalate rapidly and the skills of ordinary tradesmen are no longer sufficient to carry out the specialized work. The State Government Architect diverted some of the Public Works Department's facilities to help address the large problems of the tower, nave and rectory in 1962 and the following year the National Trust of Australia (New South Wales) came to the church's aid, launching a successful Restoration Fund Appeal throughout Australia. Individuals and a specially formed community group, the Stables Task Force, succeeded in the late 1990s in saving the important rectory stables.

Today we acknowledge that the National Trust has again taken on this role, as part of our bicentenary celebrations, to launch such an appeal for conservation funds to assist the parish. As in the past, private donations have already begun, and thanks are expressed for all who have donated or will in the future donate. National Trust Hawkesbury Branch is also assisting. Our thanks go to all who contribute to the task of conserving the St Matthew's precinct.

In compiling this book, much appreciation goes to Chris Jones, the current rector of St Matthew's, for making the gathering of the illustrations and information from the records and church artefacts so easy and enjoyable. Chris assisted personally also by supplying some stunning photographic angles of the church and its surrounds for use in this book.

Current church groups and parishioners went out of their way to tell us relevant and interesting facts about church life and routines, and very kindly lent their own personal copies of photographs and church magazines. The Ladies Guild, in particular, has inherited from Marj Noble an important set of the parish magazine which they are tending carefully, and have made the volumes available to us. Their hospitality and generosity of time at one of their meetings is also recognized with appreciation, along with the help of the parish councillors; the church wardens too have been helpful, and extra acknowledgment goes to John Barnard, Graeme Hunt and Margaret Fennell for a variety of help.

Former members of these groups, too, have assisted by giving willing interviews that enlarged perspectives and offering glimpses of the evolution of the church functions over time, like Tony and Fay Cragg, Kath and Peter Griffiths and Joyce Edwards. Together with help from Kerry Jones, Yvonne Soper, Margaret Terry, Wendy Dunstan and Kay Ryan, the story became more complete.

Without other extended interviews over many weeks, and welcome provision of photographic, information and proof-reading exchanges, of a group of particularly dedicated parishioners as well as descendants of those previously closely tied to St Matthew's Anglican Church, Windsor, this history could never have taken on the necessary depth. For this we recognize the Reverend John Butler and Dorothy Butler, Beverley Hunt, Carol and Geoff Roberts and Kim Alderton, while Kathleen Cobcroft, who cares for Elen Ferguson's wedding gown of 1839, has helped good-naturedly through very convoluted attempts to get an illustration.

Rebecca Turnbull, Museum Curator, Ruth Maittlen and other staff of Hawkesbury Regional Museum, Michelle Nichols and Hawkesbury City Library, the Powerhouse Museum staff, Donna Newton from the Royal Australian Historical Society, the State Library of New South Wales, Land and Property Information, National Library of Australia, State Records NSW, Sydney Living Museums, Macleay Museum and St Andrew's College both at the University of Sydney, former mayor of Windsor Wendy Sledge, Trevor Bunning from Canberra, Lorna Campbell and Joan Cobcroft have all been exceedingly helpful.

A special, personal touch has been added to the illustrating of this book by the wonderful artwork of Hawkesbury's most famous artist, Greg Hansell, who has allowed three pastel works generously to grace these pages: *Off Burralow Road*, Greg Hansell, painted *en plein air* in 2014, *St Matthew's Windsor*, Greg Hansell, painted similarly in 2012 and another work painted while the stables restoration work was under way. Thanks again to Carol and Geoff Roberts for providing the high-resolution copies on Greg's behalf.

Chris Burgess and Aleks Pinter, previous ministers at the church, kindly gave information about their years working at the church, and the Repair and Restoration Committee, established by Joyce Edwards, and now consisting of Helen Williams, Wendy Dunstan, Margaret Fennell and Fay Cragg, has been instrumental in preliminary fund raising and organization for the Bicentenary celebrations, including this book.

Professionally involved in keeping St Matthew's well conserved, Graham and Carol Edds have been generous with their time, discussed and lent us photographs from their extensive collection, and provided expert text about the latest works they have supervised on site. We are indebted to their help and ongoing interest. They also make great pumpkin soup!

A special thankyou needs to be extended also to Doug Minty, Cornelis Sondermeyer and Don and Jill Mills, all of whom were willing to talk about past contributions to the church life, and in the case of Don, still superintend the clock.

The Royal Australian Historical Society acting for Arts NSW awarded the church a substantial contribution under the Cultural Grants Program which made this book feasible.

Daphne Kingston, a long-time painter of Hawkesbury buildings has contributed a charming sketch of the church.

We have enjoyed enormously getting to know this remarkable church complex and its people and are grateful for the opportunity to share the story.

Ian Jack and Jan Barkley-Jack
Windsor, 8 June 2016

Conversions

(figures rounded)

Weight

Ounce (oz.)	28 g
Pound (lb; 16 oz.)	454 g

Length

Inch	25 mm
Foot (12 in.)	30 cm
Yard (3 feet)	91.4 cm
Mile (1760 yards)	1.61 km

Liquid measure

Pint	568 mL
Gallon	(8 pints) 4550 mL

Area

Acre	0.4 ha
Perch (1/160 acre)	25 m2

Money

Penny (d.)	1 c
Shilling (s.)	10 c
Pound (£)	$2
Guinea (21s.)	$2.10

Part One: A Ministry and a Chapel

1. Detail of the central section of the settlement of Mulgrave Place adjacent to the civic Square (left), James Wallis, engraved by W. Preston 1817, published 1821, 'A View of Hawkesbury and the Blue Mountains'. The thirty-acre farms at Cornwallis can be seen in the background, and the new wharf at Windsor is shown severely damaged by floodwaters. St Andrew's College, Sydney.

1 A Chapel for Hawkesbury

A Clergyman Visits the New District

> I am going to preach at the Hawkesbury Settlement on Sunday next, twenty miles distant from Home, and I know no more where I shall sleep, or perform Divine Service than you.[1]

These were the words spoken by the Reverend Samuel Marsden to a friend in Parramatta in October 1795. Marsden was the Assistant Chaplain in the colony of New South Wales, a member of the Church of England.[2] The upper Hawkesbury River settlement was approaching two years old when Marsden became the first minister to preach there.[3]

Although commonly known as 'The Hawkesbury', the settlement was officially named Mulgrave Place. It had been farmed by Europeans from around January 1794. All the earliest residents took up cultivation on the flood-prone lowlands,[4] their farms stretching along the river and creek banks over eight reaches from today's North Richmond to Sackville by 1795, scattered thinly in the landscape in some places, densely clustered in others.

The early farms occupied a central part of the tribal lands of the local Aboriginal people of the Boorooberongal clans of the Darug tribe, living where Indigenous peoples had roamed alongside the Hawkesbury River for at least 15,000 years. Some studies suggest their residence in the district has spanned 40,000 years.[5] The Aboriginal clans fished from their bark canoes, and hunted on both banks of the Hawkesbury River, which they called Deerubbin. On the lowlands they set traps for birds and small animals and hunted larger prey, as well as gathering grubs, yams and berries. The lands were revered by the tribes, and year by year the clans had ensured that the river's lowland bounty continued, whilst valuing the uplands, and mountainous areas downstream, as places where traditional carvings and ceremonies were safe even in flood times.[6]

Suddenly the clans were being forced to vie for their locations with the farms. The Europeans' immediate farming needs had directed their attention to these flats, regardless of clear signs of severe flooding.[7] Relationships between the two cultures soon deteriorated as they were forced to interact.

Access to the district's waterways, lagoons and food sources was increasingly denied the traditional owners. It was a problem common to any frontier shared by two vastly different cultures, despite King George III's instructions to the settlements to 'live in amity and kindness' with the local clans.[8]

Because of European ignorance of tribal law and the Aboriginals' growing dismay, as wave after wave of new settlers arrived and blocked off more of their lands without sharing the new crops, it was predictable that tensions would grow. An Aboriginal was believed to have been shot by a settler or his government servant as early as April 1794. Just five months later a settler and his labourer were wounded by the clans. The attack had been in retaliation for the death of an Aboriginal boy shot by settlers at what is today Cornwallis. Other injuries were inflicted on the tribespeople, and a few Aboriginal women cohabiting of their own free will with European men caused friction as it was done without the permission of the Elders.[9]

The deaths of three more Europeans made Acting Governor William Paterson take fright. In late May 1795 he sent a detachment of the military to 'drive the natives to a distance' to attempt to secure the colony's essential food supplies and to protect the more isolated settlers. More deaths on both sides ensued and the soldiers who had so inflamed the situation were deemed necessary to remain in the fledgling district.[10]

The conflict was in a temporary lull when the newly arrived Governor Hunter took over the colony in September 1795.[11] European officers and other gentleman from Sydney and Parramatta rode to visit the Hawkesbury settlement on business or out of curiosity. Captain John Macarthur gave written orders from Parramatta to the troops at Hawkesbury.[12] He and his wife, Elizabeth, visited the Hawkesbury on horseback, spending three days there, taking advantage of his ownership of no less than twelve of the 37 horses in the colony.[13] The couple would have ridden from Parramatta along the only track, which wound through Toongabbie Government Farm, following from there roughly the route of what is today called the Old Hawkesbury Road. In the short space of seven years, this road network was to be described by surgeon and magistrate James Thomson:

> About twenty miles west from Parramatta lies the Hawkesbury settlement, and on the road, about four miles from Parramatta, is Toongabbie, a small settlement where the government keeps its chief flock of cattle and a number of convicts, who cultivate between two and three hundred acres on account of the Crown ... On the Hawkesbury road there are several Farms of very good land.[14]

2. Aboriginal group beside the Hawkesbury River, James Wallis, engraved by W. Preston 1817, published 1821. The Aboriginal people do not appear in Wallis' original 1815 watercolour. From 'A View of Hawkesbury and the Blue Mountains'. St Andrew's College, Sydney.

The government supplies for the district had been delivered in January 1795 by the colonial vessel, the *Francis,* along with the Surveyor, Charles Grimes, the Commissary, John Palmer, and possibly the Deputy Judge Advocate, David Collins. Immediately Grimes began surveying the second batch of farms, and Palmer had come personally to assess the investment potential of the district, as much as to supervise the first of the infrastructure.[15]

About eighteen hectares of Crown land had been set aside as a Government Precinct among the farms on the southern side of the river. The area was where the government wharf, the government store, and a small granary had been built, and a barracks was being constructed for the soldiers near the store which was already in place by late 1795. In March, as the first maize crop in the district had been collected, the government took the excess grain into the granary to be shipped to Sydney to feed the older settlements. In his journal, Deputy Judge Advocate David Collins recorded how inadequate was the size of the public granary, where 'great quantities were left lying before the door, exposed to, and suffering much by the weather'.[16]

The store building and soldiers' barrack near the wharf, and the granary opposite, together with the open ground between them, was already forming into a community square, where locals met in 1795. The officer in charge of the Mulgrave Place settlement was Captain Edward Abbott who, with his detachment, was to be found in the civic square, along with the government-employed storekeeper. The settlers and their families and government labourers attended to pick up provisions, deliver their excess maize, call upon the military if uneasy about the Aboriginal clans near their farms and attend the compulsory annual muster. John Palmer had ridden to the Hawkesbury settlement in October 1795 to supervise the muster, around the same time that

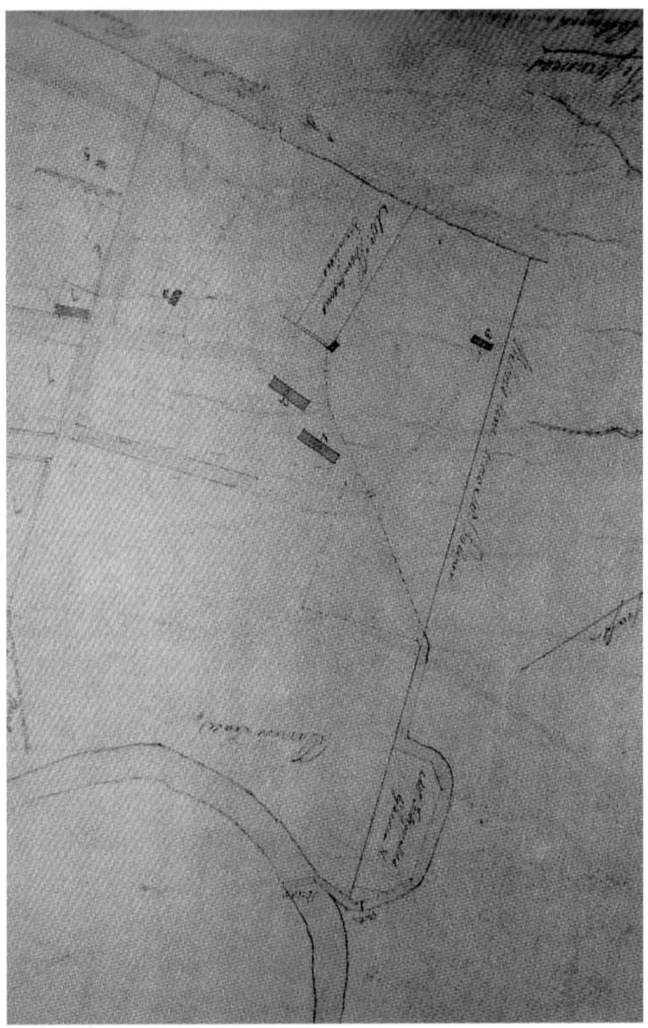

3. The area within the parallel lines stretching from the river (top north) to the South Creek (bottom) is the Government Precinct, and the curtilage of the cluster of government buildings shown in the centre and centre left mark the civic square of 1800 (now called Thompson Square). The lower of the two rectangles in the middle of this detail is the schoolhouse and chapel building of 1804. The Hawkesbury River is at the top and South Creek at the bottom of the map. Detail of Meehan's map of Windsor, 1812. State Records of New South Wales, Map SZ529.

Marsden was visiting the settlement to conduct its first religious service. Today this same civic area is known as Thompson Square, Windsor, and it is the oldest remaining civic square in Australia. The square was 1.2 kilometres from the site where St Matthew's Anglican Church was to rise two decades later from the virgin bush.[17]

Most of those other than the officers and gentlemen venturing to the Hawkesbury had to walk the eight-hour track from Sydney,[18] but for communications and transporting supplies, the river was the transport link. After her 1795 visit, Elizabeth Macarthur wrote about the lack of boats at a settlement which so relied on the river, commenting that, 'having no vessels, there is at present much difficulty in transporting the produce to Sydney'[19] This problem was soon to be rectified with settlers like James Webb constructing small vessels for their neighbours.[20]

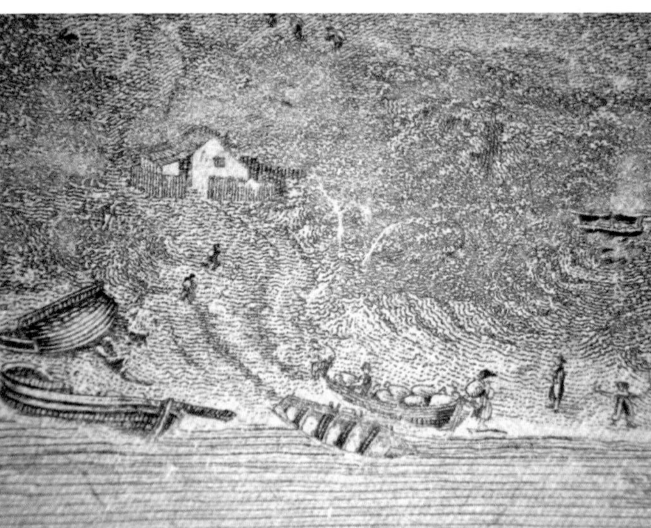

4. Small vessels, typical of those at Hawkesbury in the eighteenth century, beached at Thompson Square. Etching, 1812–1813, detail of 'A View of Part of the Town of Windsor', drawn and engraved by Philip Slaeger, published by Absalom West, Sydney, 4 June 1813.

5. Thompson Square today, taken looking north-west towards the site of the first store and barracks commenced in 1795. The Hawkesbury River is below the buildings. Photograph by Jan Barkley-Jack, 2015.

Crops grew easily in 1794 and 1795 on the fertile flats, and granting of the uplands began only in 1795 when James Whitehouse and Joseph Smallwood were promised land to the west beside the civic square, although neither of them registered his ground that year.[21] Whitehouse's grant was separated from that of Samuel Wilcox by the Government Precinct with its civic square, and Whitehouse's grant was later to be bought by an ex-New South Wales Corps soldier, William Baker, the man who was once Governor Phillip's orderly sergeant.

6. Drawing *c.* 1795–1796, Thomas Watling, 'Baker's Farm. High Land on the banks of the river', Mulgrave Place, at present-day Cornwallis. Engraving by William Lowry. Collins, *An Account of the English Colony in New South Wales,* Vol. I, 1798, taken from the original printing, Royal Australian Historical Society, Sydney.

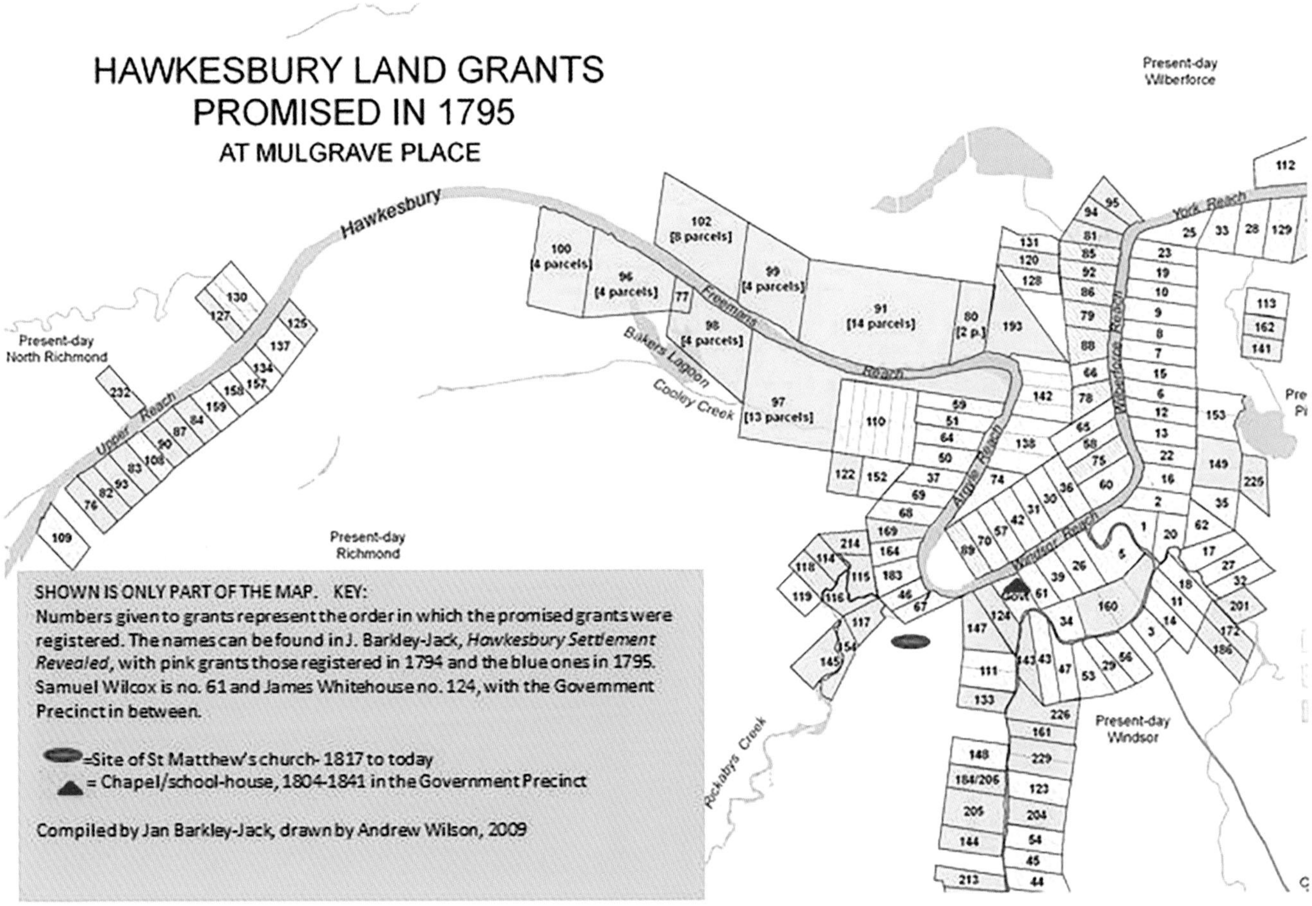

In mid-1795 Baker was living in the Government Precinct as the only civil officer in the settlement. He had been sent as a permanent commissariat superintendent, generally referred to as

HAWKESBURY LAND GRANTS PROMISED IN 1795
AT MULGRAVE PLACE

SHOWN IS ONLY PART OF THE MAP. KEY:
Numbers given to grants represent the order in which the promised grants were registered. The names can be found in J. Barkley-Jack, *Hawkesbury Settlement Revealed*, with pink grants those registered in 1794 and the blue ones in 1795. Samuel Wilcox is no. 61 and James Whitehouse no. 124, with the Government Precinct in between.

=Site of St Matthew's church- 1817 to today
= Chapel/school-house, 1804-1841 in the Government Precinct

Compiled by Jan Barkley-Jack, drawn by Andrew Wilson, 2009

7. Map of lands promised at Mulgrave Place around Windsor by late 1795. The owners, possibly their government men, employees and families constituted the congregation at the first sermon conducted at Hawkesbury. The Government Precinct is marked 'Govt'. The site of the later church of St Matthew was on the ungranted land between nos 67 and 147. Map compiled by Jan Barkley-Jack, drawn by Andrew Wilson, Archaeological Computing Laboratory, The University of Sydney, 2009.

storekeeper, for the district. His job was to issue the supplies and purchase the grain from the settlers, after the total lack of any government infrastructure or support during the first year of Hawkesbury settlement had been remedied in 1795. A guard of ten soldiers (which predated the force that arrived mid-year after altercations with Aboriginal people) was sent to stop any looting of government articles.[22] That year Baker had purchased a farm at Cornwallis two river reaches to the west of the Government Precinct, but lived adjacent to the government store of which he had charge.[23]

This then was the Hawkesbury settlement into which the 30-year-old Samuel Marsden rode in October 1795.[24] Marsden would have been acutely aware of the volatility of the respite achieved by the military attempting to force the clans away from the settlement. The doings at Hawkesbury were avidly discussed in Sydney and in Parramatta, on account of the officers believing, from their ideas of class, that an isolated settlement where 95% of the initial farmers in 1794 had been transportees, must be unruly. They were already looking for signs of poor behaviour there, deriding it as an inferior settlement and predicting that trouble could be expected.[25]

Unlike the gentlemen's predictions, however, the figures within a damning 1796 report compiled by the magistrates Samuel Marsden and Thomas Arndell actually proved the Hawkesbury settlers' industry. On average a settler at Mulgrave Place cultivated 3.38 acres, equal to that of settlers in the Prospect district and around Kissing Point, and whilst below that of the farmers closer to Parramatta, the Hawkesbury efforts are above that of those near Sydney, who were those the magistrates had rated as having a 'majority industrious'. Moreover, the average per capita numbers of small stock like pigs at the Hawkesbury ranked above those of the free settlers around Sydney, and there were over three times as many fowls as anywhere else in the colony.[26]

As a result, Marsden's potential congregation on that visit in October 1795 would have been drawn from those mainly ex-convict farmers, together with their partners and wives, a good number of children and the government servants allowed to each farm, and paid employees, clustered in the reaches around the South Creek mouth, or near the present-day towns of Windsor, Pitt Town and Wilberforce, or on the Richmond flats and the banks opposite. As well there was a small group of farmers who had come to the colony free as sailors, soldiers or seamen, in addition to the military detachment, living at Mulgrave Place.

8. The Reverend Samuel Marsden, 1833, Richard Reid jr, watercolour. State Library of New South Wales, Mitchell Library.

The preacher would have spent time in the civic square during his stay, talking to commandant Abbott, and storekeeper Baker, who were the only gentlemen in the district at that time and who

9. The barn of Daniel Smallwood on the banks of the Hawkesbury River, one reach downstream from the Government Precinct to the right of the photo. Detail from, 'Saunderson's Farm. Looking Down the River', *c.* 1795–1796. Collins, *An Account of the English Colony in New South Wales*, Vol. 1, 1798, taken from the original printing, Royal Australian Historical Society, Sydney.

already knew him. On returning to the colony in 1794, William Baker had resumed friendships with the military and civil officers, including Collins and Palmer.

It is not known where Marsden preached on that first visit, as no church building or any sizable public building existed in the settlement. The sermon would likely have been delivered either in the open air in the civic square as the most central and only official location in the district, or else on a farm close by, possibly in one of a few large timber barns completed by late 1795. Marsden's wife complained in 1796 that 'he had to preach sometimes ... in a Convict hut, sometimes in a place appropriated for Corn and at times does not know where he is to perform it, which often makes him quite uneasy and puts him out of temper both with the place and the people'.[27]

The military detachment had been at Hawkesbury only a few months and no separate accommodation had at that time been built for the commandant, let alone visiting governors or a rare visiting clergyman in 1795. Marsden would then have been forced to sleep in the small, crudely built barracks in the square, or in one of the farmers' huts nearby.

After his initial visit, Marsden was to make many trips to the Hawkesbury as assistant chaplain and magistrate based at Parramatta, but serving also the Mulgrave Place district. Governor Hunter's Order of July 1796, which required magistrates to visit their distant jurisdictions regularly to allow any disputes to be settled quickly, was taken seriously by Marsden. He purchased a small property of his own on South Creek just around a kilometre south of the civic square. Like most of the gentlemen at that time he had bought the land at Mulgrave Place from soldier grantees.[28]

By 1797 Marsden Farm, comprising 50 acres, had been formally transferred to Marsden by privates Thomas Westmore and William Anderson, the original grantees. Marsden could now feel comfortably settled when staying in the district. On the western side of South Creek, the farm was located between that waterway and where the present Day Street joins Mileham Street.

In high floods, the farm was inundated with water, and a natural waterway ran across Marsden's land spilling water across the adjoining ridge, sometimes joining up temporarily with the Hawkesbury River. The first of such floods experienced in the district was in 1799. Marsden's house was one or two metres deep in water when this happened. The rectangular dwelling with a central door flanked by a window either side, and surrounded by a wide verandah, can be seen in this state in a panorama painted in 1816.[29]

10. The home of the Reverend Samuel Marsden at Mulgrave Place on South Creek at present-day Windsor. Anon., 'Sketch of the inundation in the neighbourhood of Windsor … 2 June 1816', showing Marsden's house marked 'k' in the lower right. State Library of New South Wales, Mitchell Library, PX*D 264.

Marsden was often amongst the Hawkesbury farming community in the 1790s, mediating disputes and dealing with problems before they reached court if possible. For example, John Stogdell, John Palmer's powerful agent in the district, in August 1798 had charged George Cook with 'neglect of Duty and being of loose Manners' but agreed to forgive him, whereas, when Anthony Malone behaved in a 'riotous disorderly manner' and assaulted Stogdell's employee, Marsden sentenced him to four months in the gaol gang.[30]

One settler, John Harris, the ex-convict licensee of the Cross Keys Inn in the Government Precinct (who had been allowed the rare privilege of a lease and inn there beside South Creek in January 1798), believed Marsden was a fair investigator who kept everyone, regardless

Preaching in the Open Air

of rank, answerable for improper conduct.[31] As Senior Chaplain of New South Wales from 1800, Marsden's preaching at Mulgrave Place is more difficult to document. His surviving later sermons perhaps can suggest the themes he might have chosen and the type of wording he may have used. Marsden in real life had been stingingly critical of the colonial settlers, and had supposedly said of Hawkesbury dwellers that most were 'oftener employed in carousing in the fronts of their houses, than in laboring themselves, or superintending the labour of their [government] servants.'[32]

The latter at least was demonstrably incorrect. The maize harvest alone in 1795 at Hawkesbury had been sufficient for the small settlers to sell in excess of 2,200 bushels, after reserving sufficient seed for the next planting. This was equal to the productivity accepted at Parramatta as evidence of industriousness.[33] The gentlemen continued to see those who were lazy and drank publicly to excess as representative of all, so Marsden's words at the Hawkesbury perhaps resembled the sermons he gave at a later date about vice:

> Let me then exhort you at this solemn season as you value your souls, to cast off the works of darkness, and not dare to celebrate the birth of the Saviour in rioting and drunkenness, in chambering and wantonness, for this will be a great abomination unto the Lord. By such sinful conduct you will do all in your power to frustrate the gracious design (of God) ...[34]

> Nay many of us have lived in the open and avowed violation of his laws. In Sabbath breaking, in profanation of God's name, in theft, in adultery, in drunkenness and every vice that would render us obnoxious to an holy God. His laws have had no more effect upon our hard and impenitent hearts than if they had never been made known to us ...[35]

Services Move Indoors

Residents of Mulgrave Place remained isolated from regular services, and visiting clergymen felt distant from their congregation too. A political exile from Ireland, the Reverend Henry Fulton, conducted services in the district from 7 December 1800, after being appointed at the end of October

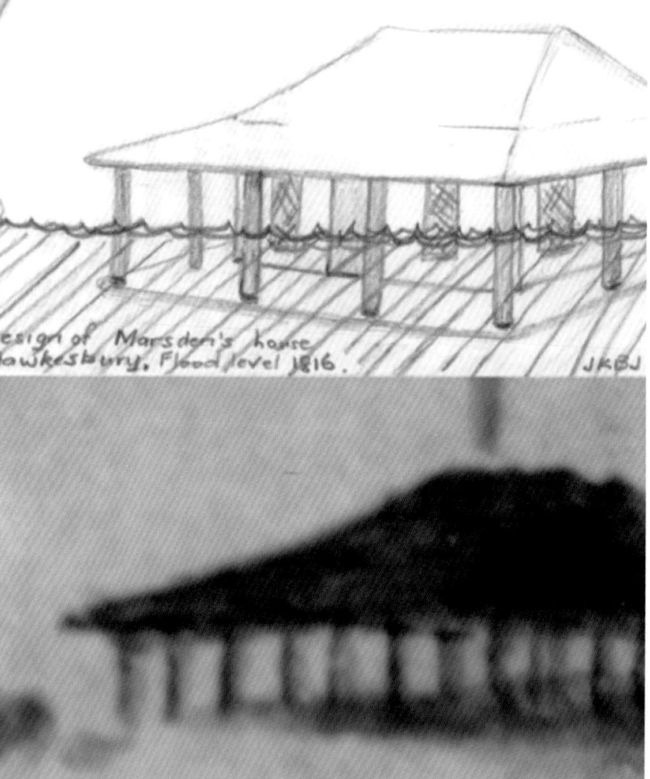

11. The Reverend Samuel Marsden's house, detail of the 'Sketch of the inundation in the neighbourhood of Windsor ... 2 June 1816', showing the house to have been a whitewashed, traditional dwelling with a central door, flanked by a window either side, surrounded by a verandah with four posts on at least three sides. (above top) sketch by Jan Barkley-Jack, 2009; (below) State Library of New South Wales, Mitchell Library, PX*D 264.

by Governor Philip King. He was soon awarded a conditional pardon on the grounds of 'having conducted himself with great propriety and in a most exemplary manner since he has been here.'[36]

Tom Melbourne, writing about Fulton recently, believes that:

> the fact that Fulton's ministry was restricted to the Hawkesbury region makes it clear that his appointment was not meant as a replacement for the just-departed [Reverend Mr] Johnson, which would have necessitated Fulton taking up work in either Sydney Cove or Parramatta. Rather, it instead points to a recognition by King that the outlying settlement of Hawkesbury was in need of leadership/ministry, and that the growing Irish population in that area would respond well to a fellow Irishman working amongst them.[37]

However, in February 1801 Fulton was appointed to Norfolk Island, where he received a free pardon in 1805. He returned to Sydney in Marsden's temporary absence from the colony as Acting Chaplain. The Reverend Fulton returned to Britain in 1810 to give evidence in support of Governor Bligh at the court martial of the leader of the rebellion.[38] The early period Fulton spent at Hawkesbury 'had given him a particular burden for the mainly Irish settlers there', Melbourne believes.[39]

It is said that services were held for a short while in the private house rented by John Harris, a missionary who became the schoolteacher and preacher at Hawkesbury.[40] There is no evidence as to where that school was located, despite it often being said to have been below the courthouse. This mistakenly hinges on an interpretation of the 1827 map of Windsor which shows that an unidentified school was there by that date, which, melded with the Meehan map of 1812 showing that as 'Harris's Lease', gives rise to the idea. This lease near South Creek was given to the ex-convict John Harris, not the missionary of the same name.

Other Pacific Island missionaries like William Crook, the Parramatta schoolmaster from 1804 and Pastor of Castle Hill, and Rowland Hassall who preached around that wider district, are said to have occasionally visited Hawkesbury.[41] Hassall gave services at Portland Head on the Hawkesbury River.[42] All were encouraged by Samuel Marsden.

The building of the separate dedicated chapel and schoolhouse got under way once the bricks were burnt at Hawkesbury by Governor King in 1803.[43] The building began to rise abutting the busy civic square on the Green Hills ridge.

This spacious two-storey construction measured *c.* 100 feet by *c.* 24 feet.[44] When the brickwork was finished in August 1804 its walls were some 24 feet high. On the upper storey, one end was reserved for the schoolmaster's living accommodation, separated from the schoolroom by a partition. The roofing was under way and almost complete. The *Sydney Gazette* reported that:

> Its situation is such as to form a street behind the new Store. The design of the edifice must interest every person ... it also illuminates the infant mind by the inculcation of moral principles and the help of such useful branches of instruction as are absolutely necessary to rescue the rising generation from the morbid glooms of ignorance.[45]

12. The brick schoolhouse/chapel (centre back) was built in the Government Precinct at the Green Hills in 1804 by Governor King. It sat between the brick granary (right back) and the timber Government House (left) where Governor Macquarie stayed on his visits to the Hawkesbury, as had governors before him. The chapel was downstairs, the schoolhouse and teacher's residence upstairs. Detail from 'Settlement on the Green Hills', watercolour, G.W. Evans, *c.* 1809. State Library of New South Wales, Mitchell Library, PXD 388, Vol.3, fol.7.

With most of the upper storey for a schoolhouse, the lower storey was to be the settlement's only chapel. Harris' home classroom had moved to the new schoolhouse in 1805.[46] Many of the district's first generation of children were reaching school age, so Harris was welcomed as both tutor and preacher. As a teacher he must have been interesting, for he had diverse experience as a lowly cooper, a missionary traveller amongst the Pacific Islands and teacher on Norfolk Island. In looks he was 'dark and swarthy' and in mannerisms reserved. He was an intelligent, religious man, with strong views.[47]

Spelling books, testaments and Bibles were difficult to procure in the colony, so lessons must have relied on ingenuity a great deal. Perhaps tales of the Pacific Islands were just the thing to banish the 'glooms of ignorance'. However, strict as Harris was as schoolmaster, the Hawkesbury school was a decidedly better learning environment than the school at Toongabbie, described by Rowland Hassall as 'having no floor, walls, windows, or shutters; and [in winter] ... the hearers tremble with cold.'[48]

Yet attending school at the Green Hills, as the area around the Government Precinct was becoming known, held special challenges, for, in two floods during 1806, Harris' pupils had difficulty getting to school, and those who did arrive had to share the building with the many ragged families whose homes had been washed away. The chapel was also used for the ensuing court sessions.[49]

Harris remained as pastor-teacher at Green Hills throughout Bligh's governorship, and Bligh viewed him favourably, having new cedar pews constructed for the chapel under the supervision of Andrew Thompson. The governor occupied pew number one on his visits.[50] Harris had been recruited by Samuel Marsden in Sydney to come to the Hawkesbury, and with Marsden in England, and with no encouragement from the illegal military government which deposed Bligh in January 1808, Harris left the district to return to Britain.[51]

After Harris' departure, the schoolhouse had been taken over as an extra granary and the chapel forced to share the downstairs area, barely functioning at all during the time of the military junta. The schoolhouse/chapel building was prominent on the ridge, well under the eye of the governors when each was staying in Mulgrave Place, and as visible on the road from Sydney as from the river, which was constantly plied by settlers in their small craft landing in the civic square. On the south-eastern side of the square, on the very peak of the ridge, the chapel sat between the Government House and the three-storey brick granary in the upper part of the square.[52]

During the period when Marsden was in Britain from 1807 to 1810, more clergy had reached the colony, and occasionally some, like the Reverend John Youl, who had preached at Hawkesbury around 1801, returned to the district. During his tenure as preacher at the Ebenezer church at the Portland Head settlement, Youl complained that the chapel at Windsor continued to be used as a courthouse. However, after the military seized control of the colony early in 1808, generally 'the churches ... [were] neglected and Sabbath devotion ignored.'[53]

Samuel Marsden's visit to Britain in 1807 bore considerable results. On his return to Sydney, Marsden announced that he had convinced two Anglican religious men to come to New South Wales to minister in the colony. They were the Reverend William Cowper, afterwards Dean of Sydney, and the Reverend Robert Cartwright.[54] Cartwright and his family proceeded to the Hawkesbury, where he became the first resident clergyman in the district of Mulgrave Place.[55] Although the building of the future St Matthew's Anglican Church was planned during Cartwright's incumbency and, although his portrait hangs in St Matthew's today, the church was still incomplete when he left the district.

13. From left to right, the Government House, the schoolhouse and chapel, the 1803 Stores, civic square (the buildings and open area in the centre, now called Thompson Square) and Whitehouse (Baker's) Farm, commencing at the far right. G.W. Evans, watercolour, 1807, image courtesy Hordern House Rare Books, Sydney.

Part Two: The Nineteenth-Century Church Building and Precinct

2 Seeking a Church

A Resident Clergyman

When the Reverend Robert Cartwright was appointed resident chaplain at Mulgrave Place in March 1810, he was almost 40 years of age. Cartwright was well-educated, had travelled in eastern Europe, was comfortably off, settled and well-respected in an English parish after fourteen years as an evangelical curate. When he met Samuel Marsden in 1808, he had needed persuasion to come to a penal colony on the other side of the world.[1]

Travel to New South Wales was in a convict transport with his wife Mary and their six children. On arrival he was sent by Governor Macquarie to Mulgrave Place to preach in a wide and diverse district and, though Anglican, he ministered to all religions. The Anglican church, known then as the Church of England, was the established religion in England and in New South Wales since the colony had been founded. The governor, as the King's representative, was bound to uphold Anglicanism as the established religion, and to worship according to its liturgy. Whilst small groups of people following other denominations gradually began to gather together on occasions, in 1795 there were no other churches or their leaders officially operating in New South Wales. Free or freed residents of religious persuasion other than Anglican had a stark choice: attend Anglican services or have no spiritual guidance at all. Prisoners, if compelled to attend church, worshipped the Anglican way regardless of their beliefs, until Roman Catholic, Presbyterian and Methodist ministers came to the colony. The early Anglican ministers carried heavy responsibilities.[2]

The ship *Ann* which carried the Cartright family and their two servants to the colony arrived in August 1809. A seventh child, William, died at three months and was buried in the new cemetery at the future location of St Matthew's, Windsor in 1812. Further children arrived later.[3] Like most gentlemen, the Reverend Cartwright brought a suitable library to the colony. One of these books, bearing his signature, *Pocket Sermons for Families and Village Readings*, printed in London in 1801

14. The Reverend Robert Cartwright, Anglican minister at Windsor from 1810 to 1819. The anonymous portrait in oils, which today hangs at the back of the nave under the organ gallery, was given to St Matthew's by his granddaughter, Mrs Hansard. Photograph by Chris Jones, rector of St Matthew's, 2016.

by the Philanthropic Society for the Promotion of Industry and the Reform of the Criminal Poor, is at St Matthew's today.[4]

As a government employee, Cartwright was an assistant chaplain to be 'under the immediate Control and Superintendance of the Principal Chaplain', by then Samuel Marsden. Cartwright's life was a busy one, ministering to a far-flung farming community just beginning to form the new towns established by Governor Macquarie in 1810. It included the districts of Castlereagh (Evan) and Richmond, until Fulton took the two over in 1814, and Windsor, Pitt Town and Wilberforce, stretching from Mulgoa down river for 70 or 80 miles.[5] In September 1810, it became even more demanding, for in every sphere of colonial life, the new governor required written reports, and the clergymen were no exception.

Cartwright may have been stationed out in the country, but Macquarie announced he had to report occasionally to the Reverend Samuel Marsden respecting his clerical duties as well as to fill in quarterly returns. These regular returns needed to be transmitted annually to England detailing the population of the colony, so, for the first time, all births and deaths were required to be recorded in registers kept with an emphasis on exactness by the chaplains in their districts. Prescriptive as ever, Macquarie insisted that 'care must be taken to specify whether the Deceased was Free or a Prisoner, as well as the Name of the Ship, and what Year he arrived in the Colony ... Mr. Marsden, the Principal Chaplain ... will make up a general one therefrom for the Governor'.[6]

Next, Macquarie decreed that all the male and female convicts employed by government, as mechanics or labourers at Parramatta and the Hawkesbury, were in future to be mustered by the chief constable every Sunday morning and marched to attend divine service, as happened in Sydney. This meant an increase in Cartwright's congregation. Matthew Lock, as Chief Constable at Mulgrave Place, was responsible for the arrival at the chapel by delegation, and the magistrate, at that time Andrew Thompson, was responsible for the orders being 'strictly obeyed and enforced'.

Since at that time Thompson was desperately ill and died the next month, that duty soon fell on William Cox, the next of Macquarie's appointees to the position of Mulgrave Place magistrate.[7] Cartwright himself was to become a magistrate in the district in 1811 and, together with the local medical man, Dr James Mileham, he joined Cox to form the Hawkesbury Bench.[8]

Robert Cartwright Makes a Call

On arrival, Robert Cartwright faced up to the fact that his church was a temporary chapel, but he was dismayed to find that the upper storey was still being used as an additional government granary, necessitating the chapel to share premises with the school on the lower floor.[9] John Ritchie has summed Cartwright up as 'energetic and popular, but one who avoided controversy, trying to focus on his ministerial duties'.[10] In the case of the use of the chapel, the minister felt justified at taking a stance for religious good. The new minister was adamant that the schoolhouse/chapel's extra use as a place for grain storage was to stop and he succeeded in having the grain removed. The upstairs room again became the schoolhouse.[11]

The ground-floor chapel was the only religious facility in the district on Cartwright's arrival around March 1810, except for Ebenezer chapel, which free settlers of Presbyterian and other communions in the farming area down river at Portland Head had constructed without government aid. The Ebenezer chapel was also

15. The schoolhouse/chapel at Green Hills (later Windsor). Detail from 'Settlement on the Green Hills', watercolour by G.W. Evans, c. 1809. State Library of New South Wales, Mitchell Library, PXD 388, Vol.3, fol.7.

a schoolhouse for that area from 1809, located a significant distance downstream from the Government Precinct. Thus, a dedicated religious presence in Windsor remained a government priority.[12] Governor Macquarie had announced he would visit the Hawkesbury soon after the time of the minister's arrival, but with the pressures of an entire colony to be relieved, it was December 1810 before Lachlan and Elizabeth Macquarie arrived in the Mulgrave Place district. Macquarie noted in his journal that the couple had just attended divine service in Cartwright's chapel, where he 'gave us a most excellent discourse and read prayers extremely well indeed'.[13]

Forced to support large families in many cases, the ministers of the colony needed to turn to additional pursuits. Henry Fulton, for example, commenced a school of classical learning at Castlereagh, and Marsden and Cartwright were both practising farmers. The commissioner sent from Britain in 1819 to gather evidence about Macquarie's governorship remarked that their efforts in this regard 'afforded more occupation to their time than augmentation to their fortunes'. With a large family, Cartwright urgently needed to supplement his salary of £20 per month.[14] The surplice fees paid to provide essentials for the church's running, at £4 12s. a year, were, according to Cartwright, 'very little more than half the amount of what I had expended'.[15]

Cartwright's family residence after 1815 was a parsonage house, the forerunner to that provided by government for the next minister at Windsor beside the new church. The location of this earlier parsonage, whilst obviously near Windsor, is not known. It may even have been a new use for some existing government property. The initial family's lodgings are also unknown, but the Cartwright family may have lived at Sutton Cottage between 1813 and 1815, for Cartwright had need of a farm to supply his family's food. In 1813 he had rented one for £30 per annum on high land behind the present Royal Australian Air Force base in today's Percival Street, overlooking Cornwallis and the town of Windsor. The family gained extra income from this land on the ridge between Windsor and Richmond, and whilst not a great deal is known

16. The farm of the Reverend Robert Cartwright between Windsor and Richmond, marked 'd' to the right of the exposed dry land on the left. Anon., 'Sketch of the Inundation in the neighbourhood of Windsor ... 2 June 1816', watercolour in four panels. State Library of New South Wales, Mitchell Library, PX*D 264.

of this farm, its location is shown on a painted panorama of the Hawkesbury in flood in 1816, as close to William Cox's Clarendon.[16]

The farm was a 'very eligible and pleasant Residence, called Sutton Cottage, situated within One Mile of the Town of Windsor'. The lands were fertile and allowed for a large agricultural concern, with a dwelling suitable for a 'genteel Family'. Cartwright cultivated and fenced into paddocks.[17] It appears to be part of either the property originally granted to William Nash or to Neil McKellar, with the house, outhouses and barn on high land. Lieutenant Thomas Hobby had added Nash's land in 1802 to his own grant registered in June 1800 nearby as Sutton Farm,[18] before heading to Evan district on the Nepean. The naming of the farm Sutton Cottage may suggest a connection with Hobby and the Nash Farms, which Hobby sold to Captain John Brabyn in 1810.[19]

At first, 'being much distressed by 1815', Cartwright applied for 'lodging money' and received the 8s. per week available from the government to government employees like himself and Richard Fitzgerald, the storekeeper, who had first told Cartwright of the assistance available for renting property.[20] Like other reasonably successful farmers in the colony, by 1817 Cartwright appears to have built up a herd of long-horned cattle, and was selling significant amounts of meat to the government. For example, he tendered for 2,000 units of beef late that year, and in the following January another 1,000.[21] It was, however, not a return sufficient to provide easily for his large family and the causes a minister and magistrate was called upon to support, particularly as the initial help provided by government, in the form of food, clothing, firewood and 'other indulgences' for his whole family and servants was withdrawn as the farm became more profitable. Cartwright estimated that this was equivalent to cutting his income in half, and was 'such a loss as I have not been able to bear'. Cartwright maintained that he, like many other ministers, had been forced 'to grazing or cultivation to keep our families from starving'.[22]

Like Marsden, Cartwright also set about acquiring a flock of sheep of the best breed in the colony.[23] These he may have pastured on the 400 acres of the church glebe given by Macquarie in 1811, although, since the glebe was not fenced,

17. Long-horned cattle of the kind owned by the Reverend Robert Cartwright by 1817. Cartwright also kept a flock of sheep and farmyard animals to supply his family's food. Detail of etching drawn by Philip Slaeger, 1812–1813, and etched by Slaeger as 'The Red House Farm', Windsor in New South Wales', published by Absalom West, Sydney in 1814. State Library of New South Wales, Mitchell Library, PX*D65

Cartwright found that difficult, or on the two grants he received in the district of Evan, which together totalled 1,100 acres on the Nepean to the west of Mulgrave Place.[24] Supervising part of Cartwright's property was the Reverend Thomas Hassall, and the improved quality of the wool was a topic of conversation in their correspondence. This was lodged and entered to the credit of Cartwright's account in Sydney with retailer, merchant and ship owner, James Birnie.

Birnie was one of the major players on the Sydney retail scene during the Macquarie period. He sent cargoes of sealskins and oil and other items to Britain, dealing in goods and generally being called on to play a gentleman's role in the colony by serving on committees and juries, whilst being a major vender of beef to the store.[25] Hassall was acting as Cartwright's agent in arranging the sale of Cartwright's wool and purchasing goods from Birnie or Henry Marr, shown in a record which survives from 1815. The goods he purchased for Cartwright on that occasion were general items like sugar, iron bars, rope, materials and glass window panes amounting to the value of £16 19s.[26]

A stable on his property was a necessity for Cartwright, as he needed a means of travelling between the towns and out into the countryside to preach at Wilberforce and Pitt Town, so was 'obliged to keep a Horse for duty'.[27] In December 1810, not many months after his arrival at Mulgrave Place, this duty had included accompanying Macquarie and his party, including William Cox, riding for hours across the commons to seek a suitable site for the towns when they were being created.[28]

Ministrations by Cartwright varied between services in the chapel, supervising the school and working to aid the poor and those in special need. In October 1810, Cartwright had been called upon to conduct the funeral service of Hawkesbury's richest and most esteemed citizen. Andrew Thompson had been a merchant, property owner, chief constable, and in the time since January that year the first ex-convict magistrate in the colony.[29] The district's current magistrate, William Cox, and many distinguished officers and gentlemen from Sydney and Parramatta were present at the funeral service, which was held in the chapel in what was soon named Thompson Square. Thompson was the first burial in the new Windsor cemetery under Cartwright's care, and his death had necessitated an early decision on the location of the future St Matthew's.

Cartwright told how the largest attendance at any of his services was at a funeral and Thompson's was the biggest of them all. Nonetheless, the bonds that had been made in enduring the convict lifestyle, and the hardships of a frontier existence encouraged friends to make a great effort to attend the last farewell of a person they respected, even before the arrival of either Cartwright or Macquarie. When Sarah Woolley, who had been sent to the colony for a stealing offence worth 8s. died in 1809 in a chaise accident, the funeral was 'numerously and respectably attended, many persons travelling from ten to twenty miles to pay this last tribute'.[30]

Settling In

Like the chapel, the town which became Windsor had its beginnings in the area around the government square, where the official wharf, store, soldiers' barracks and granaries were to be found. The small dwellings of the government employees sprang up around their work places, a house for the commandant of the settlement, which became the Government House, the new brick stores and granary, a watch-house, and gaol, which together with Andrew Thompson's lease gradually gave the appearance of a small hamlet. In turn this village grew as Thompson built a brewery and a retail store, and small allotments for housing and businesses on private property began to be subdivided off the rural acreages for almost a kilometre along the main George Street.[31] This hamlet was remarked on by Macquarie who reflected that:

> Thompson ... may justly be said to be the father and founder of the village hitherto known by the name of the Green Hills; there being hardly a vestage [*sic*] of a single building here, excepting the Government Granary, when he first came to reside on the Green Hills ten years ago.[32]

For this reason, along with the fact that the government infrastructure had remained solely at Windsor, when Macquarie came to form the township he incorporated the existing hamlet, and so it had already built fabric and a bustling civic square when the town was laid out in 1811. All the other towns set up by Macquarie commenced on ground with no infrastructure, housing, industry or commerce whatsoever. It was always, therefore, planned that Windsor would naturally, from starting as the largest of the Hawkesbury–Nepean towns, develop as the major town.

Combined schoolhouse/chapels were gradually built in each of the towns. Richmond, was the first completed. Castlereagh and Wilberforce followed and, rather later, Pitt Town. Each was built on the same lines as the schoolhouse/chapel at Windsor, which had been operating for around a decade when the others began. The one at Wilberforce is the only survivor. Windsor chapel remained the major religious centre, although the Reverend Cartwright rode around to give services at each place.

Windsor was the self-evident choice as Macquarie's major centre on the Upper Hawkesbury, because of its existing village. So the first

18. The town of Windsor in 1811, as seen from the river bank opposite Thompson Square. Andrew Thompson was buried on the ridge behind the trees on the far right, just over a kilometre from the chapel (the pink building towards the left). Attributed to G.W. Evans, 'Windsor, Head of Navigation, Hawkesbury'. State Library of New South Wales, Mitchell Library, SV1B/Wind/6.

19. View from the site of the Government House, looking south-west towards the site of the first schoolhouse/chapel at Hawkesbury, the forerunner to St Matthew's. The chapel was where the Reverend Robert Cartwright preached, and was located on the left approximately where the modern double-storey building can be seen on the south-eastern side of George Street. Thompson Square and the village of Green Hills were beyond. Photograph by Jan Barkley-Jack, 2009.

dedicated church was to be located there. In the meantime, before the church was built, the chapel at Windsor continued to serve its many purposes: chapel, schoolhouse, courthouse, refuge in floods and schoolmaster's residence.

Another feature of each of the towns was to be its burial ground, to be situated near the church or chapel. Marsden consecrated the new burial grounds not only in Windsor, where the body of Andrew Thompson had already been laid to rest beyond Green Hills, but also those in Richmond, Wilberforce, Pitt Town and Castlereagh early in 1811. From then on funds were sought throughout the colony to lay out the new burial and other facilities. The government gave start-up funds to all the appeals, as on 1 July 1812, when the colonial Police Fund, which was set up to finance public expenditure, gave Cartwright £10 to enclose the Wilberforce burial ground.[33] Just eight days later, the governor and his wife journeyed again to the Mulgrave Place district to see progress for themselves, as they did on numerous occasions.[34] Like other earlier governors, Macquarie stayed in the Government House, which had previously been the commandant's cottage overlooking the square.

Public philanthropy was relied on in the colony to supplement the government's contributions, as a great many new facilities were needed at that time, and Lachlan Macquarie was determined that they would be of a standard above any seen in New South Wales previously, both in quality and taste. The magistrates like Cartwright were expected to lead the way in giving contributions and collecting from others. This was not restricted to funds needed at the Hawkesbury, and in 1813 the minister found himself as a local collector for the Sydney Court House Fund.[35]

Subscriptions were urged for the Hawkesbury town projects, the first being the schoolhouse, and the enclosing of the burial ground at Richmond. Macquarie on behalf of the Government gave £35 in that instant. Two of the three magistrates of the district, Cartwright and Cox, pledged five guineas each, along with Marsden, and prominent citizens like Austin Forrest who was married to Jemima Pitt of Richmond, his brother-in-law T.M. Pitt, surveyor George William Evans, William Faithfull, boat-builder Jonathan Griffiths, John and William Bowman, Thomas Spencer, Archibald Bell and Robert Fitz. Richard Rouse gave six guineas, and a great many other locals and people from elsewhere gave amounts from £5 down to six shillings.[36] With Windsor and Pitt Town burial grounds to set up as well, and schoolhouses in all five towns, canvassing for donations took up Cartwright's time.

Another cause received Cartwright's support in early 1819 when he was one who organized and subscribed to the Fund for the Relief of the Poor at Hawkesbury. Subscriptions promised amounted to donations of £300 and upwards in wheat, and also 60 head of breeding cattle.[37]

The third magistrate in the district, James Mileham, the district's doctor, was well-known to Cartwright, and also of strained means. In 1814 the chaplain had reason to summon Dr Mileham to his own residence between Richmond and Windsor when Cartwright was the good Samaritan. A Castlereagh settler called John Lees, formerly a soldier in the New South Wales Corps, had stumbled faint and terrified into his home. Lees had been bitten on the wrist by a snake earlier that evening and had walked miles in a state of increasing desperation to Cartwright's house. James Mileham was sent for, and as in many of the cases of snakebite Mileham treated, the doctor saved Lees' life. Lees went on to promote religion zealously, and founded the first Methodist chapel in Australia at Castlereagh in 1817.[38]

Cartwright settled into the routine of life on the upper Hawkesbury River, and gradually built up his congregation as religion became an integral part of the development of the towns urged by Macquarie. All the while, Cartwright attended assiduously to the affairs of the chapel and the school, as well as the new burial ground on the site of the future church. In 1813 'sundry Alterations, Additions and Repairs' were carried out on the chapel with Cartwright given the substantial amount of £126 15s. by the government to pay for them.[39] Two years later Cartwright had the seating capacity of the chapel increased, with 'Benches and Forms purchased by him for Use of the Church at Windsor', amounting to £8 18s.[40]

This work was needed since Macquarie had reasserted that it was compulsory for prisoners within three miles of the town to attend service on Sunday under the supervision of the constables. Windsor was the largest town in the district of Mulgrave Place and so it housed a gaol gang from 1814, as well as other prisoners working for government, and the many government men assigned to the farmers in the area.[41] It was Cartwright who had reminded the governor in 1813 about 'the propriety of obliging the convicts to attend divine service'.[42]

The chapel was used by Cartwright to forward humanitarian causes too, as a letter written from the 'Vestry Room, Windsor' shows. William Cox, Dr Mileham and the ministers Cartwright and Fulton had co-authored the letter to inform the governor of a meeting they had convened to aid flood victims by raising money for those affected by the 1817 inundations. The Hawkesbury was in a sorry plight with much of the belongings, stock and grain again washed away, even as some had not yet recovered from their losses and subsequent debt after the 1816 flood devastated their farms. The seed loaned by the government had not yet been repaid, and again lack of food, shelter and bedding was felt throughout the district. The plea for subscriptions went out yet again, led by the magistrates, with Robert Fitz dealing with all communications. 'We have not less than 150 persons whom we shall be under the absolute necessity of victualling until the ensuing harvest, and our funds are not adequate,' they announced, and the merchants and retailers, affluent farmers and others in the colony to whom they appealed, like Samuel Terry, Henry Marr, Thomas Rose, Charles Thompson, Charles Armytage, James Chisholm, Joseph Underwood and Robert B. Hazard, of Sydney, some of whom had property in the Hawkesbury area, all responded generously and launched the appeal there.[43]

The donations flowed in from nearly 450 persons. Such benevolence was led by the Governor who gave £50. William Cox gave £3, and his sons also forwarded amounts of £2, £2 and another £1. The Reverend Robert Cartwright subscribed £3, whilst Mileham forwarded £2, and the former magistrate Thomas Arndell, £2. Other inhabitants of Mulgrave Place who had not been affected by the floods gave amounts ranging down

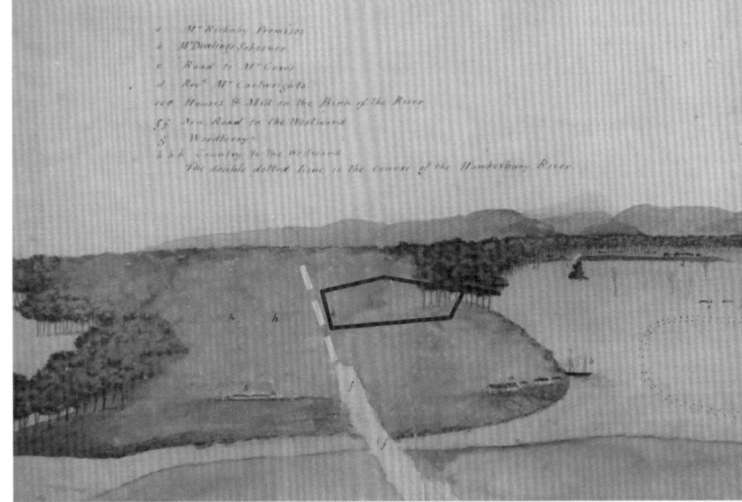

20. The high ground known as Windsor ridge in the 1816 flood, looking south-west towards the land on which the foundations of St Matthew's Church were to be laid in the following year (beyond the letters 'h', near the beginning of the trees to the right). The burial ground there had been in use for almost six years but is not visible in the panorama behind the trees. Detail from 'Sketch of the inundation in the neighbourhood of Windsor … 2 June 1816', watercolour by an unknown artist, panorama in four panels, State Library of New South Wales, Mitchell Library, PX*D 264.

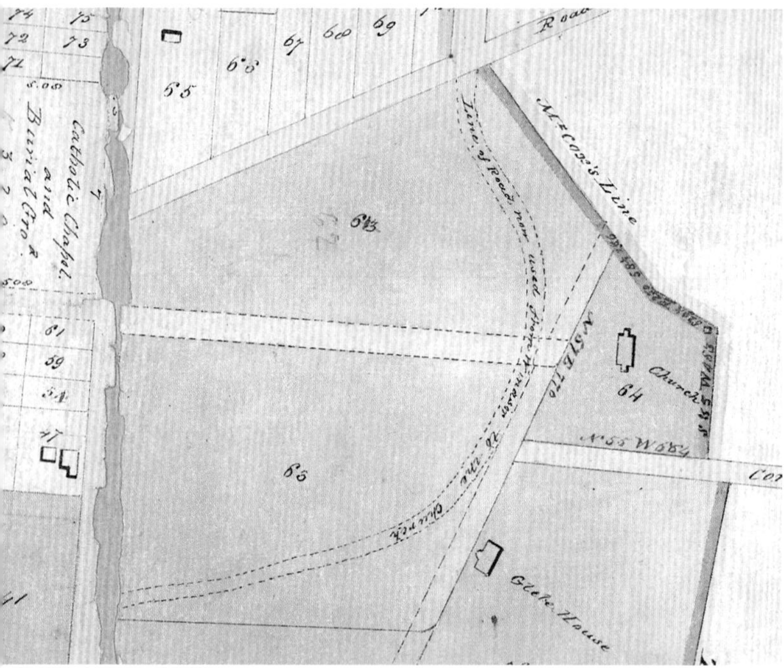

21. St Matthew's Church and cemetery in relation to Windsor's new town square (later McQuade Park), 1828. 'Georges Street' is a continuation of the road shown in the previous illustration, passing through the land marked 'h'. Surveyor J.J. Galloway, 1840, SRNSW Map 5966.

from £3.[44]

Cartwright's community duties were intensive. He officiated at many marriages in the Windsor chapel, including the wedding of James Gordon and Thomas Arndell's daughter,[45] while in 1819 Dr Mileham was married to the daughter of the merchant, Henry Kable.[46]

In some ways, however, Cartwright had an uphill battle. He felt that the Hawkesbury population did not appreciate his religious ministerings, unlike the Macquaries, who praised his sermons.[47] Throughout his duty at Mulgrave Place he felt keenly the disinterest of the population at large to religion, and 'frequently had to complain from the pulpit of their backwardness' to attend services on Sundays, despite his hard work.[48] In 1819 he forthrightly told Commissioner Bigge that 'I should have been sometimes without a congregation' but for the enforcement of Macquarie's order in 1814 for convicts to attend church.[49] Another problem was that Cartwright had little faith in the trustworthiness of many transportees. He had been robbed several times while at his church and he was convinced that property owners remained at home because of the likelihood of being robbed.[50]

In the late 1810s convicts constituted the larger part of the congregation. Between 50 and 100 others, a sixth of them women, attended the Windsor chapel. Cartwright claimed that 'no doubt many more would have attended if their families could have been accomodated [*sic*] with separate pews, or a comfortable Sitting in the Church; but there was no room'. Ever hoping to reach the lowlier population, Cartwright saw the need for a larger church building.[51]

Planning for a Church

When Governor Macquarie declared the new town of Windsor in December 1810, he immediately told the surveyors, Meehan and Evans, where the first church would be sited. Alone of all the new towns, the general location of the new place of worship had been effectively decided two months earlier by Henry Antill, the governor's aide-de-camp, when, on the governor's bidding, he chose the burial place of Andrew Thompson. The previous burial ground which lay close to the chapel, but on the western side of Bridge Street overlooking South Creek, was to be closed, except for criminal burials. As a mark of respect, Thompson's body had been laid to rest in the new cemetery on the green hillside, overlooking a valley canopied by a blue haze of mountains across on the horizon.

Lachlan Macquarie's pattern of placing the church close to the burial ground and commanding the best views is also evident in the burial grounds at Richmond and Wilberforce, proclaimed, like Windsor, late in 1810. The level area to the west of Thompson's grave was the natural site for the church, centrally located on the highest land. On 12 January 1811 Macquarie was again in Windsor and confirmed the location. With the minister, Cartwright, and the magistrate William Cox, the governor had the surveyors erect a 'strong post' with the name of Windsor 'on the scite of the intended new church, fronting the north face of the great reserved square [now McQuade Park]'.[52]

The site of the future St Matthew's overlooked Rickabys Creek just before it joins the Hawkesbury on the great bend between Windsor and Argyle

Reaches. In 1804, this land was part of the Richmond Hill Common which Governor King had declared along with two other commons in the district to enable small farmers to graze stock communally. Windsor was formed in the eastern-most section of the Common centred on the area which had already become known as the Green Hills, while Richmond was being set up to the west.[53] Placed on the highest part of the ridge, the church would overlook the land gradually sloping down to the farms on the lowlands along Rickabys Creek.

The boundaries of the land of the future church had been established by 1798. The southern boundary line of Thomas Rickaby's second grant, Catherine Farm, defined the easterly boundary, ending at Twyfield's 1794 grant which was to be the church's northerly neighbour, with Charles Thomas' grant on the north-west.[54]

The lands between the church and Rickabys Creek were already totally in private hands by 1796. Twenty acres with a short frontage to the creek had been granted to ex-convict Charles Thomas on the opposite side of the creek to Roger Twyfield, and twenty acres was given to Thomas' partner Sarah Verender as a grant in her own right.[55] These lands were partly on the first upward slope of the ridge, and partly lowland acres.[56] Thomas' Line, running north–south formed the church's south-western boundary.[57]

Today Greenway Crescent, leading to Cornwallis Road (the early road to Richmond), forms the northern boundary of the combined church and burial ground. The rest of the land originally allocated for the church to Greenway Crescent's east was later nominated a second church glebe, and now accommodates a modern parish hall beside the 1825 church rectory and its stables. Immediately beyond to the south-east of Rickaby's boundary, in front of the church was the Crown land which Macquarie designated the site of a 'great square' to supplement the pre-existing Thompson Square.[58]

Macquarie used the 'great square' and the church building as a means of joining the old Green Hills ribbon development along George Street, stretching almost to Rickaby's Line, with the allotments he had planned for the farmers as their refuge in flood time. Macquarie, born and educated in Scotland, had visited Edinburgh in 1804 and been impressed by the planning features of the New Town, which featured such a 'grand square' as an elegant junction between Edinburgh's Old Town and the New Town laid out below in rectangular allotments as Macquarie planned for his New South Wales towns. The new town of Windsor was part of this vision of the Scottish Enlightenment and St Matthew's was its centrepiece.

In 1813 the Windsor schoolmaster, Matthew Hughes, was transferred to Richmond. Cartwright had no worries with his replacement, Joseph Harpur, who remained as the Windsor schoolmaster after Cartwright had gone to Liverpool and worked under the supervision of the Reverend John Cross at Windsor until 1826, four years after the new church had been consecrated.

Like Hughes, Harpur had been transported, arriving from London in 1800, but he was well-experienced in colonial teaching at Sydney, and was also made the parish clerk, giving his signature

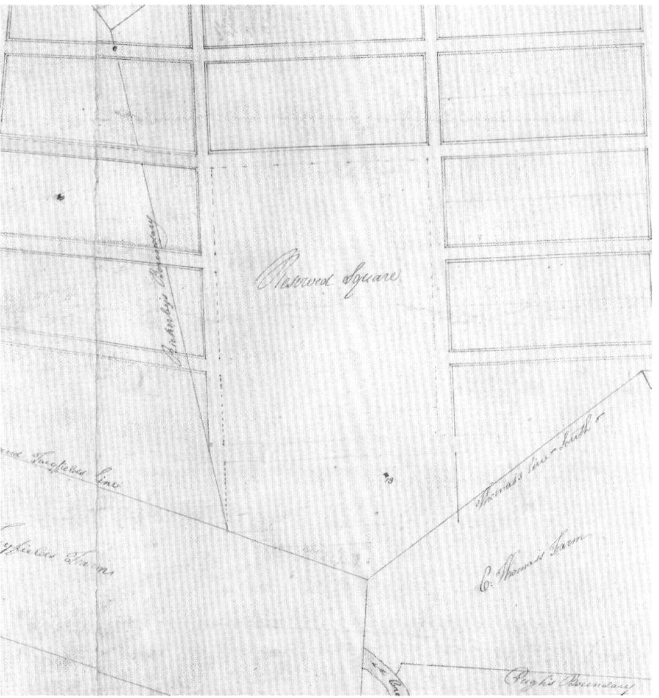

22. The 'great square' (reserved square) and the v-shaped land below reserved for the St Matthew's complex bounded by Twyfield's and Thomas' boundary lines, are clearly shown. The position of Andrew Thompson's grave established in October 1810 is marked. Map of Windsor, 1812, signed by Governor Macquarie, State Records NSW, Map SZ529.

23. Vista of the 'great square', now McQuade Park, Windsor taken from vicinity of St Matthew's Church. Photograph by Ian Jack, 2010.

to the ceremonies recorded in the Registers at St Matthew's over many years. He was an effective clerk and annotated his registers with some invaluable historic comments. His marriage to another convict, Sarah Chidley, the year following his arrival at Windsor, led to a large family. Harpur, like most of the regional public schoolmasters, appears to have followed the 'old' system of education in his classroom, unlike the master at the Sydney school. At least by mid-1822 Barnabas Rix appears as an assistant schoolmaster. Rix was paid by the Trustees of the Orphan Institute until March 1823, earning £16 per year. In 1825, just before he left Windsor, Harpur had 70 pupils enrolled, almost as many as the Parramatta school.[59]

St Matthew's Anglican Church Begins

With many pressing calls on the colonial revenue, it was not until 1816 that Macquarie began the process of commissioning a new church at Windsor. The governor's first recorded action was to order bricks. Although tenders for building the church were not invited until August 1816 and although no contract was finalised until June 1817, William Cox had in May 1816 been paid a first instalment of £200 for supervising the making of 220,000 bricks for the Windsor church.[60]

These bricks were made on John Jones' farm adjacent to the church site. In 1809 or thereabouts Jones had exchanged his previous house in what became Windsor for the 25-acre [10 hectares] farm owned by an ex-marine, John Pugh.[61] Pugh Farm lay a short distance to the west of the later St Matthew's, running from today's Richmond Road northwards to the area around the bridge which takes Cornwallis Road over Rickabys Creek, beside Charles Thomas' land.

Jones later reminded the governor that he had:

> allowed upwards of 200,000 Bricks (exclusive of what he made by Contract) to be made off his Land for Government use being the best earth for Brick that this part of the Colony can furnish.[62]

Henry Kitchen, the architect, later claimed that only 171,319 bricks were actually delivered by Cox for the project at the cost of £1881 8s., but the number is still very substantial.

The general location of the brick pit used at Pugh Farm is not in doubt. The brickmakers working for Jones are said to have been John Skinner and John Linton, working in 1817 'on ground along the Richmond Road'.[63] In 1817 the road to Richmond followed the line of Cornwallis Road today and crossed Rickabys Creek in the northern part of Pugh Farm. A reliable water-supply was essential for brickmaking, so the site of Jones' brick pits is likely to have been close to the present Cornwallis Bridge. Both Skinner and Linton, along with Elijah Cheetham, are independently known to have been brickmakers for government projects in Windsor around this time, under the direction of Richard Fitzgerald.[64]

Richard Fitzgerald was not only the owner of the Macquarie Arms, the most genteel inn in the district, but also Supervisor of Public Works and government storekeeper in Windsor, in succession to Baker. He had arrived in the colony as a convict on the Third Fleet and had shown himself to be managerial material at Toongabbie Government Farm and rose to be in charge of operations there and at all the government farms, including Hawkesbury.[65] John Macarthur rarely praised ex-convicts but, like Macquarie, he held Fitzgerald in esteem and regarded Fitzgerald as a man of 'remarkable activity and regular conduct', and employed him to act as his agent generally and at Mulgrave Place after Governor King dismissed Fitzgerald for neglecting his public duties in favour of his own farming activities.[66]

While William Cox was the contractor responsible for providing the bricks and getting the church built, using skilled government labourers, it was Fitzgerald who was responsible for all convicts employed on government projects, their work, their attendance and their rations. He was efficient, and 'the kind and faithful' friend of Elizabeth and Lachlan Macquarie, but in disgruntled evidence given to Commissioner Bigge, Fitzgerald was accused by some as rorting the system like others and forcing employees to accept payment the old-fashioned way in goods, rather than wages.[67] The work on the church building, like any major project, was not immune to comments and opinions from the various factions in colonial society, just as the architects involved were themselves sniping at each other.

The contract for the construction of the Windsor church had been given on 6 June 1817 not to Greenway, the Acting Civil Architect, but to Henry Kitchen, who was Greenway's only colonial rival. Unlike Greenway, Kitchen had arrived as a free settler, and set up in private practice, gaining many high profile New South Wales customers.[68]

A piece in the *Sydney Gazette* had noted his arrival in December 1816 on the ship *Surrey* from Cork: its passengers included 'Mr. Kitchen ... who as an architect intends at the same time to render himself professionally useful to the Colony'.[69] James Broadbent, an architectural historian of note, said of Henry Kitchen:

> He remains one of the most obscure and enigmatic of architects to have practised in early colonial New South Wales. While the promise of his architectural training and the striking designs of the buildings and plans attributed to him are lures to modern architectural historians ... there is not one building, extant or demolished, that can, with surety, be ascribed solely to Henry Kitchen.[70]

Henry Kitchen had been trained in the office of James Wyatt, who had prestige from his winning design for London's Pantheon. Kitchen's reference from Lord Bathurst was an informal one, and any hopes he had held of being appointed the government's architect were dashed when he found Greenway already appointed to the position. Kitchen often felt he had reason to criticize Greenway's designs, and sometimes submitted alternative plans for Greenway's commissions. Greenway in return had little time for Kitchen.[71]

By February 1817 Kitchen had an advertisement for his architectural and surveying business in

24. The approximate location of the brick pits for St Matthew's marked with a red oval on the northern part of John Pugh's 25 acres in the middle of this detail from the parish map. Today's Richmond Road runs along the southern boundary of Charles Thomas' land, but in 1817 the road to Richmond was the Cornwallis Road in the vicinity of the brick pits. Map of St Matthew's parish, county of Cumberland, 1st ed., Lands MN05 14076801, 1830s.

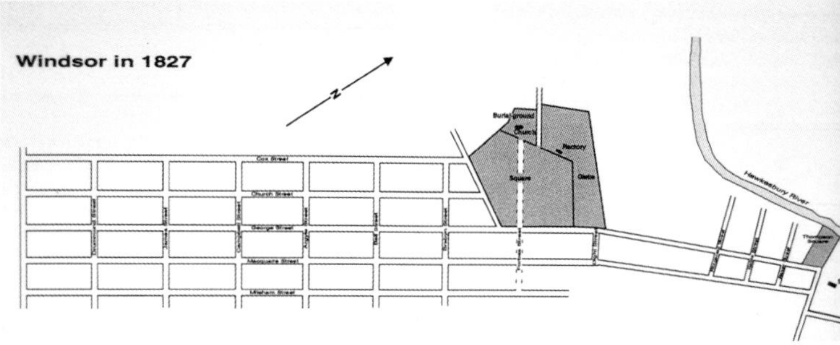

25. Schematic map showing the original plan of Windsor, which extended to Ham Street, South Windsor, as signed off by Lachlan Macquarie in 1812. The church and new square, along with the Rectory and the Rectory glebe, were located centrally between the old village of Green Hills and the new allotments. Map, Jan Barkley-Jack, drawn by University of Sydney Cartography, 1994.

the *Sydney Gazette*.[72] In 1821, in a letter, Kitchen stated that:

> With regard to my own affairs I am happy to say that my health is now so much improved that I am able to pursue my professional avocations with renewed activity, prospects here in private practice are daily becoming brighter, and I have no doubt but my exertions will ultimately he crowned with success. I am now employed in erecting a Dwelling House for Mr McArthur at the Cowpastures, where we have succeeded in burning a quantity of Lime-stone for Cement.[73]

The rivalry that had ensued between the pair of architects in the meantime meant the competitiveness and ill-feeling between them spilled into the work on the church at Windsor. Tenders were called on 17 August 1816 and the job was awarded to Henry Kitchen. Both the Windsor church and new parsonage house were noted in Macquarie's 'List of essentially necessary Public Buildings' issued on New Year's Day 1817. The invitation to tender was made in the *Sydney Gazette* in mid-August 1817, with a closing date of 9 September.

Macquarie announced that:

> I this day approved a Contract I have made on the part of government with M[r] Henry Kitchen Architect and Builder for erecting a church and tower at the town of Windsor ... for the sum of Two Thousand Two Hundred Pounds Sterling ... William Cox and John Piper, Esquires, having gone Security for M[r] Kitchen.[74]

Although Greenway did not see the contract in advance and although Kitchen was the supervising architect and builder, Greenway claimed to Commissioner Bigge in 1819 that he had drawn the elevation of the church before building began, which could be interpreted to imply that the initial design was his, not Kitchen's.[75] As discussed below, the fact that the foundations for the apse are shallow, in sharp contrast to the excavation to bed-rock for the nave and tower, suggest that the distinctive apse may have been an afterthought by Greenway, whoever designed the nave.[76]

The evidence of the Acting Chief Engineer, John Gill, claimed that Greenway had drawn the plan and the specifications.[77] Gill's later testimony was disturbingly vague when he was asked to recall Kitchen questioning the wall's thickness to him. Gill had questioned Greenway at the time. Greenway's reply to him when he raised the matter was that if Kitchen followed the specification he 'could not Err'. But in writing to Commissioner Bigge, Greenway also claimed that 'before a Stone of the Foundation had been laid I protested against the thickness of the Walls as being insufficient'. It seems unlikely, when Kitchen was bound to follow exactly the contract, and his very colonial reputation rested on the build being successful, that he would compromise it in any way deliberately; if Greenway were the architect and the walls were not well planned, it would be Greenway's fault that the building was inadequately drawn. Yet he always blamed Kitchen. The rights and wrongs of the abortive first build remain mired with contradictory and ambiguous statements.[78]

When the corner-stone was laid by the governor himself on 11 October 1817, Macquarie declared the dedication: 'His Excellency, in a very impressive tone of voice, said – "God prosper St. Matthew's Church"'.[79] Watching on were the Lieutenant Governor, James Erskine, the Acting Chief Engineer Captain John Gill, William Cox and Henry Kitchen. Cartwright was too ill to attend.

Reciprocal gifts were exchanged when the architect handed the governor a symbolic silver trowel, and the skilled and labouring men employed by Kitchen were rewarded with a five-gallon gift of spirits, an encouraging present from Macquarie.[80]

Later that night, the stone was disturbed and the holey dollar beneath it was stolen. The stone was re-laid by Macquarie over another holey dollar on 13 October, but again the stone was moved and the money stolen. Presumably the stone was put back, without a third silver coin, and work commenced, to be completed within eighteen months.[81]

The church building continued, with Henry Kitchen advertising in April 1818 that lime burners were wanted at Windsor, to supply 'about 2500 Bushels of well burnt Lime. –Whosoever is willing to contract for the supply of the same to be delivered at the above Place, are requested to send in their terms addressed to Mr. Henry Kitchen, Windsor.'[82] Kitchen received the payments from the government in instalments as stipulated in his contract. The second instalment came in two parts, one in February 1818 and the next one in

26. Lachlan Macquarie, governor of New South Wales from 1810 to 1821. The portrait, *c.*1822, was paid for by the residents of the Hawkesbury, painted in England and hung in the Windsor Court House until recently. M. Wymark, *The Court House Portrait*, n.d.

June, both for £200.[83] In all Kitchen was paid £600 for his work on the construction of St Matthew's.[84]

As Civil Architect, it was Greenway who went to inspect the work as it progressed, and who declared it wanting. If Gill's evidence to the Bigge Commission four years later is to be believed, Greenway's protest that he had made before the foundation was laid against the walls being too narrow, was hollow.[85] It was supposedly workmen at the site who started the rumours, which had reached an eager Greenway, and then the governor. Macquarie reassured Greenway that the whole works would be subject to the approval of the Colonial Architect. After Greenway's survey of progress, he recommended an inquiry.[86]

A government committee was composed of three bricklayers named Thomas Legg, John Jones and William Stone, and a builder by the name of James Smith. Smith and Legg had been nominated by Kitchen, Jones and Stone by the government.[87] It reported in July 1818 that the mortar was 'of a very bad quality' and that, although 74,000 of Cox's

27. A colonial Spanish silver dollar from Lachlan Macquarie's period of government, commonly called a 'holey dollar'. The imported dollar coins had the centre cut from them, and the small coin thus formed was called a 'dump'. A similar dollar coin was placed by Macquarie under the foundation stone of St Matthew's Church.

bricks already used in the church and tower were 'of the best quality', the remainder were 'of a very inferior kind'. The committee also condemned the quality of mortar joints and the workmanship.

The report ended: 'Upon the whole we consider the building as unfit to stand ... it ought to be taken down'.[88] As a result Kitchen was removed from the project and government workmen were engaged or re-engaged under Greenway's total supervision. The walls were taken down.

Once the walls were dismantled, the bricks were sorted. Presumably those better quality bricks were kept for use in the rebuilt walls. The defective bricks were acquired by Richard Fitzgerald, the Superintendent of Public Works at Windsor, and used to build a wall around his Macquarie Arms

28. The 1925 plaque attached to the original foundation stone laid in 1817. The chiselled arrow, which identified the stone in 1817 as government works, can clearly be seen immediately to the left of the plaque. Photograph by Ian Jack, 2016.

Inn in Thompson Square, only one hundred or so metres from the old chapel which was still being used while the church was in progress. The original wall can still be seen along the Thompson Square frontage, although along the side behind Howe House, the wall has been rebuilt using a besser brick interior with a skin of the old bricks from St Matthew's.[89]

Joseph Harpur wrote in the church register on 4 June 1819 that only the foundations still remained and that a new church 'is now in building on its site by Government of much larger dimensions and of the very best materials.'[90] But Greenway was rebuilding over the foundations which he claimed to have designed. The 'much larger dimensions' claimed by Harpur may have required some foundation removal and replacement, but it also possibly refers to the spaciousness of the high-ceilinged interior of the new church on the original foundations and to the addition of the apse. The evidence that the apse was an afterthought is entirely physical. The shallow foundations for the apse are different to the rest, which are excavated to bedrock at 1.5 metres. The balance of probability is that the original plan, whether by Kitchen or Greenway, was retained, with the addition of the tasteful apsidal chancel. It is thus likely that the foundation stone of 1817 is still in its original position. What is not in question is that the church which was finally erected on these foundations is a lasting masterpiece of Australian architecture, a worthy tribute to the foresight of Macquarie, the abilities of Greenway and the power of religion.

29. Lionel Lindsay, 1919, The Macquarie Arms (Royal Hotel), showing part of the eastern side of the wall which Richard Fitzgerald built around his inn with the condemned bricks from St Matthew's. This was the inn to which Macquarie and the party rode to celebrate after the foundation stone of St Matthew's was laid (the first time). Etching, Lionel Lindsay, 1919, 'Royal Hotel, Windsor' [now Macquarie Arms], National Library of Australia, PIC DRAWER 8840 #S5501.

3 St Matthew's Church

30. St Matthew's church from Greenway Crescent, ink and wash by Daphne Kingston, 1977. Courtesy of the artist.

Francis Greenway, Colonial Architect

Although Francis Greenway died in obscurity, full of bitterness, he had brought distinction to Australian building. The most tangible evidence today of Macquarie's vision of a better colony lies in Greenway's architecture: the Hyde Park Barracks and St James' Church in Sydney, the Female Factory at Parramatta, the (reconstructed) lighthouse at South Head, the Court House and St Matthew's Church at Windsor all attest to his qualities.[1]

The English city of Bristol was Greenway's home, London his education, before conviction for forgery led to his transportation for life to New South Wales. Arriving in February 1814, Greenway had a personal recommendation from the founding governor, Arthur Phillip, so he had not been in the colony long when Lachlan Macquarie, bereft of a trained architect, summoned him. A ticket-of-leave allowed him to begin a private practice in George Street, Sydney.

31. Francis Greenway, unknown artist, possibly a self-portrait, pencil sketch. State Library of New South Wales, Mitchell Library, ML 482, a1528291h.

At that time he was undertaking a design for the staircase in Dr John Harris' Ultimo House in Pyrmont, Sydney. Greenway's appointment as

Acting Colonial Architect in March 1816 was to take professional charge of drawing the plans for public buildings and supervising their erection. Governor and Mrs Macquarie had an interest in creating grand buildings that while useful, made aesthetic and architectural statements, and in this Greenway believed that his superior skills could add further grace and tasteful ornamentation, and he did not disappoint.

The resultant St Matthew's Church at Windsor was in earlier times rated by the Sydney Architects' Association as:

> a superb piece of work … [which] must rank as one of Greenway's best, if not his masterpiece. It is perched on a knoll of high ground that looks over the broad rich plains of the Hawkesbury Valley, and to approach the church from the lowlands and see it towering above one is a fortunate experience. The fine sturdy proportions, the delightful mellow rosiness of the brickwork, and the soft texture of the wood shingle roof make a picture of architecture that is scarcely equalled in Australia.[2]

The difficulties encountered in building the Windsor church between 1817 and 1822 are uncommonly well-documented by the Windsor schoolmaster, Joseph Harpur, a highly literate ex-convict. Harpur was also a good Anglican, who taught in the Sunday school and was Cartwright's parish clerk.[3] He had a sense of history and in 1817 he had written to the Reverend Thomas Hassall asking for information 'towards the writing of a History of New South Wales'.[4]

Sensitive to the importance of the saga of St Matthew's as it unfolded from 1817 to 1822, Harpur used two blank sheets in Cartwright's Register of Births, Marriages and Burials to record some of the critical events which would otherwise have been lost.[5]

Harpur's chatty and fascinating testimony has become very familiar. It was printed in full in the *Windsor and Richmond Gazette* on 29 January 1894, reprinted by James Steele in 1916 and again by D.G. Bowd in 1969, while in the 1960s (and later editions) the Reverend W.F. Carter used the material in *The Cathedral of the Hawkesbury*.[6] The printed versions are not entirely accurate and all quotations used in the present study have been checked with the original manuscript. Harpur wrote on 4 June 1819:

> The walls of the church, to which the above memoranda refer, have been taken down to the very foundation, through some defect in the building, and another is now in building on its site by Government, of much larger dimensions, and of the very best materials; it is, I believe, to retain the name of St. Matthew given to the first building.[7]

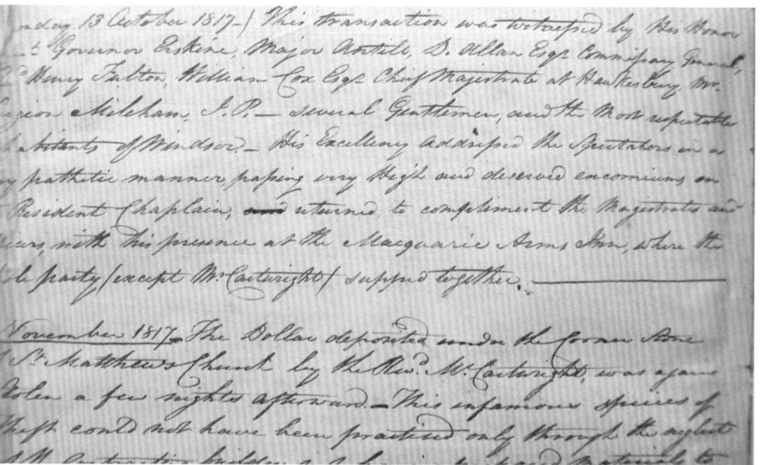
nday 13 October 1817.) This transaction was witnessed by His Honor
Lt Governor Erskine, Major Antill, D. Allan Esqr Commissary General
Henry Fulton, William Cox Esqr Chief Magistrate at Hawkesbury, Mr
geon Mileham, J.P. — several Gentlemen, and the Most respectable
habitants of Windsor — His Excellency addressed the Spectators in a
y pathetic manner, passing very High and deserved encomiums on
Resident Chaplain, returned to compliment the Magistrates and
ers, with his presence at the Macquarie Arms Inn, where the
le party (except Mr Cartwright) supped together. ——
November 1817. The Dollar deposited under the Corner Stone
St Matthew's Church by the Revd Mr Cartwright, was again
Stolen a few nights afterward. — This infamous species of
Theft could not have been practised only through the neglect

32. An 1817 entry in the Register of Births, Deaths and Marriages of St Matthew's Anglican Church, in which the parish clerk recorded extra events critical to the church's history. St Matthew's Anglican Church, photograph by Ian Jack, 2016.

Harpur's story is supplemented by evidence to Commissioner Bigge between 1819 and 1821[8] and by the regular government archives, but its singularity is striking.[9] Harpur was as close to the creation of St Matthew's as the ministers, Cartwright, Cross and Marsden, and gives a rare glimpse of those watching anxiously as the drama unfolded between 1817 and 1822.

Whilst commencement of the church at Windsor gladdened the heart of the long-suffering first resident minister, Robert Cartwright, who had been there throughout all the planning stages of the town and the church, its commencement came at the end of his chaplaincy at Windsor. Cartwright had supported Macquarie throughout, and preached in a chapel that was inadequate in size and content. It had been so when he arrived in 1810, and had had little improvement made to it, especially as work swung more and more into construction of the new church. During the final years the Cartwrights spent at Hawkesbury, the district was racked by floods in 1816, 1817 and again in February 1819, which must have impacted on the brickmaking and general building activity amid a general despondency among the afflicted community.[10]

The *Sydney Gazette* recorded the Hawkesbury's plight in 1817:

> Without food, fire or light, of any kind, sadly listening to the howlings of the angry storm that threatened ... then suddenly aroused to greater terrors by the crashing of immense trees that carried all before them ... and at length driven to the extremity of climbing their own roofs, there to endure ... until the morning should bring to their relief some vehicles ...[11]

When Mary Cartwright had visited England in 1818, it had been without Robert, as Governor Macquarie had refused him permission to return at that time, and it must have been with mixed feelings that Cartwright requested a transfer to the new parish church of St Luke at Liverpool, also still under construction in 1819. This was a full year before the church at Windsor was expected to be finished. Possibly motivated by his financial problems, and partly because of his enjoyment of new horizons, which was apparent at other times during his life in New South Wales, Cartwright left no indication of his reasons behind the request for transfer at that critical stage. Friction with the magistrates of the bench was, however, claimed as a problem for all the early rectors at Hawkesbury in a letter written by the Reverend Joseph Docker in 1833.[12] This is a very serious claim and casts a new light on the problems encountered by the first resident ministries at Hawkesbury.

Cartwright's Reflections

The ministry at the Hawkesbury had held bright spots, Robert Cartwright admitted. Sometimes he had found that men forced to attend church when convicts 'attended through inclination after they have become freemen'.[13] The ministering had been particularly taxing for the first four years, and from 1814, even after he had been relieved of the Castlereagh part of the parish by the Reverend Henry Fulton, it still tired the Windsor chaplain, for Cartwright continued to need to ride considerable distances. He was holding services at Windsor every Sunday, as well as one at Pitt Town and another across the river at Wilberforce, and attending to other duties throughout these far-flung settlements. There was, on and off, a direct punt crossing from Pitt Town to Wilberforce from 1812, and another river crossing at Thompson Square from 1814, and these together with the advent of the schoolhouses, built centrally in the Pitt Town and Wilberforce districts to be used also as chapels, meant Cartwright gradually enjoyed better travelling facilities. But visits to parishioners beyond the townships were still long horse rides.[14]

It was the 'regular families' at Wilberforce who maintained a 'good attendance' at the Sunday service there, and Pitt Town was similar; whilst the largest of the congregations, at Windsor, was 'chiefly composed of Convicts'. They were generally orderly, and no doubt magistrates Cox and Bell and others saw to that, watching from their family pews, ready to issue punishment if necessary the next day. Archibald Bell saw himself as the most righteous of the parishioners, boasting to Commissioner Bigge that he and his family were almost the only regular churchgoers in Cartwright's congregations – a fact which seems belied by Cartwright's own perceptions. At a meeting called to form the Windsor Bible Society, one of the first public forays of Cartwright's successor, John Cross, Bell continued to see himself as society's moral guardian, and was the mover of the motion that the meeting was 'deeply affected by the sinful condition of many of their fellow creatures around them'.[15]

It was the youth of the district, however, that warmed Cartwright's heart. He found them attentive, commenting that:

> I think that the younger classes, and the children of settlers are the most punctual and observant of religious duties. So great was the attendance latterly at the Lecture I delivered on a tuesday [*sic*] evening at the church [chapel] in Windsor, that I could not help remarking it from the pulpit.[16]

Despite all his comments, predictably bound up in the cultural beliefs of the inferiority of the poorer and criminal classes of the time, the minister remained optimistic that the most 'moral and respectable' of his flock were the free emigrants to New South Wales. They may not yet justify this belief, but he was sure that they 'would attend more regularly Divine Service if they had the means of doing so'.

The big surprise was the minister's conviction that the 'cornstalks' (children born in the colony) were in this category of the most moral. Overall, he held out little hope of converting most of their parents, the freed and poorer parishioners, or current criminals whose swearing and public drinking he objected to vehemently: 'The most striking contrast between them and their parents is the aversion that the former uniformly shew to drunkenness, the principal vice of their parents'.[17]

33. John Frederick Cobcroft, one of the children born at Wilberforce in 1797, the son of John and Sarah Cobcroft, photograph *c.* 1850s. John Cobcroft was one of those 'cornstalks' described by the Reverend Robert Cartwright. Courtesy of Joan Cobcroft, Jerrabomberra.

It was this passion for the potential of the youth of the colony that had kept him many a time from returning to England. The one feature of the ex-convict population that gave Cartwright pause to think was that, despite the 'irregularity of their own lives', they were keen for their children to better themselves and receive an education.[18] In 1815 and 1817 the government put part of a shipment of Prayer Books, Testaments and Bibles in the hands of Cartwright to distribute from his residence at Hawkesbury, and the governor expressed the hope that 'Fathers of Families, and Persons having Servants' would purchase them or be given them, to forward this aim.[19]

The evidence Cartwright gave to the Bigge Commission about his beliefs was presented at the end of his term in the district, and is insightful as to the needs of his successor. For instance, he believed that the duties a minister was expected to enact at Mulgrave Place were 'impossible'. This was because of the distance of the residents down river at Wiseman's Ferry and especially beyond, urging that another clergyman was needed there.[20]

Just before his transfer, Cartwright was appointed to Governor Macquarie's Committee of the Native Institution.[21] The official notice of Cartwright's transfer which appeared in the Government and General Orders, published on 18 December 1819, makes clear that the move was 'On the personal Request of the Reverend Robert Cartwright'. The chaplaincy at Liverpool was vacant at the time from the move of the Reverend John Youl to Port Dalrymple in Tasmania.[22]

The Notice in the *Sydney Gazette* announced:

> The Reverend John Cross, lately officiating at Parramatta during the Absence of the Reverend Samuel Marsden now returned, is to perform the Duties at Windsor, in the Room of the Reverend Robert Cartwright.- These Appointments to take Place from Wednesday next, the 22d Instant [December 1819]. The Reverend Richard Hill is to continue to do Duty at Sydney, in conjunction with the Reverend William Cowper, Senior Chaplain at that Place. By His Excellency's Command, J.T. Campbell, Secretary.[23]

John Cross at Windsor

Cartwright's replacement, John Cross, was an equally enthusiastic minister, ten years Cartwright's junior. Well educated, with a high reputation as a Greek scholar, he was an assistant tutor in a boys' school in London before becoming a minister. Like Marsden, Cross had a leaning towards the teachings of the Methodist Charles Wesley, and had applied for missionary work overseas. John Cross became the fourth Anglican clergyman to be resident in New South Wales, arriving in 1819 aboard the *Baring* with his wife, Ann, and their three children.[24]

Cross came to Windsor before the Hawkesbury church's completion, in a colony totally changed from ten years back when Cartwright had come to the district. The mountains had been crossed and settlement extended west beyond Bathurst, north to the plains beyond the Hunter River, and south to what would later be Melbourne. Russian ships of exploration were preparing to visit Port Jackson,[25] and the governor was under attack from disgruntled gentlemen residents, including the Reverend Samuel Marsden, who had been at odds with Macquarie almost since their arrival together in the colony in early 1810.

Cross's eldest daughter later described Cross as wearing the typical minister's garb of the period, and one that is still closely associated with ministers of the time, especially Samuel Marsden. Her father, she said, had been:

> clean shaved and he wore a long black coat, almost to the ankles, stockings and buckled shoes, a low crowned beaver hat, the rim on each side turned up and held with black ribbon rosettes, wide flaps on the front of his white collar.[26]

The summation of John Cross's ministry in the *Australian Dictionary of Biography* rates him as holding

> broad and liberal views, but was a strict disciplinarian and would allow nothing to stand before his duty. He was a good friend to the poor, and sensitive and tender-hearted to those in trouble. He was uneasy about his position among the military and the convicts.[27]

Marsden left Sydney in July 1819 with the seven missionaries who had voyaged to the colony with John Cross, bound for the Bay of Islands as missionaries, and Cross was appointed to relieve at Parramatta for the four months of Marsden's absence. Cross was then sent to Windsor.[28]

The family probably moved into the parsonage house, which Cartwright had occupied after 1815. Its location has not been identified. Cross's family later were to become the first residents of the new rectory beside St Matthew's Church.[29]

Cross owned a farm near Windsor, with excellent soil, bounded on the south by Ridge's Farm of 50 acres near South Creek and on the west by the common.[30]

Most people living at Mulgrave Place, particularly those with Sydney contacts in business, work or pleasure, travelled to and fro between the towns with greater regularity than is generally realized, and Cross was no exception. On one occasion, according to his family, Cross on his return visit from Sydney met a bushranger, a common threat on the roads. Unwisely Cross was travelling after dark when suddenly, into the middle of the road in front of him, stepped a man. Thinking it was a minister friend he was expecting to meet, Cross addressed him calmly. On seeing who it was he had bailed up, the bushranger bid him continue unmolested because he knew Cross 'to be a good fellow'. On another occasion, Cross was returning to the parsonage from a service in the country, when again he was held up. A similar scene played out, once the would-be bandit recognized Cross. Not one to miss an opportunity Cross is supposed to have 'severely lectured him ... at the same time giving him a few shillings'.[31]

34. The Reverend John Cross, *c.* 1820–1830, artist unknown. State Library of New South Wales, Mitchell Library, P1 / 1328, http:/acms.sl.nsw.gov.au/item/itemLarge.aspx?itemID=893527.

Before 1815 those whose calling was to do missionary work for the Church of England, were the first ministers to come to New South Wales, because they were more willing to journey across the world into the unknown. The Establishment church in New South Wales had been expanded by the sending of such ministers who had sympathies with its Methodist and evangelical roots.[32] It was only later, under Lord Bathurst in the Colonial Office, that there was a deliberate move to send ministers firmly within the conservative side of the Church.[33]

All the early ministers of the Anglican church at Hawkesbury had evangelical leanings including John Cross. Archdeacon Scott, appointed in late 1824, on the other hand, 'lacked any understanding of the Evangelical purpose of Marsden and Cowper, his senior chaplains, deeming it "enthusiastic" and ill-disciplined'.[34]

Cross was friendly towards other denominations in his eight years at Windsor, particularly the Wesleyans, and although bound not to attend services of other faiths he sent his family to Wesleyan services if no Anglican ones were available when travelling, and invited travelling Wesleyan preachers to stay at his house overnight.[35] Cross supported the charity and Bible societies of his day. He preached at least one charity sermon in St Matthew's on the ninth anniversary of the commencement of the church in October 1826, and later donated generously to the endowment of a school in his next parish. John Cross was not an Oxford scholar, like the ministers of St Matthew's either side of his tenure, but like them he had wide leanings and a strong sense of duty. As he had no experience as a curate in Britain before coming to the colony, Windsor was his first cure of souls and he had fitted well to his ministry, being sensitive and kind.[36]

Music played a part in Cross's services, which was to become increasingly frowned upon by those with more conventional beliefs. Macquarie had prohibited the new versions of the psalms and singing in the service, which Marsden had introduced.[37] At Windsor, John Cross was pleased with the children at his church being taught to sing by John Newsome, under a contract organized by Magistrates Cox and Brabyn. At Port Macquarie, his next posting, Cross's services were accompanied by a violin and a flute.[38]

John Newsome had arrived in his early thirties as a convict aboard *Atlas* with a seven-year sentence, charged with stealing books in October 1819. His sentence was served by March 1826, mostly at Parramatta. He was a tall, brown-haired young man who was to replace Joseph Harpur as the Windsor schoolteacher after Harpur retired in 1826. Newsome had been sent to Parramatta on arrival and had been one of the overseers to the male factory there, before being one of the government men with Samuel Marsden between 1822 and 1824. Literate and trustworthy convicts were much valued, and Cross would have been able to sum up Newsome's worth when relieving minister for Marsden at Parramatta between July and November 1819. Newsome then married Cordelia White and later came to Windsor, probably at the behest of Cross, continuing at the school until 1829, beyond Cross's departure for Port Macquarie.[39]

The Bricks and Foundation Stones

Greenway was at work on the church even before Cross's arrival. The architect had stipulated that he would need four bricklayers, four masons, two carpenters and some labourers. Two of the four bricklayers were the convicts, Skinner and Linton, who had already been William Cox's brickmakers for Kitchen's church and, like Cox's convicts on the Western Road in 1814, they got a ticket-of-leave on completion.[40] Jack Skinner died in 1827, aged 38, and is buried in St Matthew's cemetery.[41] All this was still well remembered in Windsor at the end of the century, though perhaps it improved in the telling, because their trainee brickmaker, Duncan McKellar, known as Duke, was still a local identity in the 1890s. McKellar maintained that some of the bricks for the first St Matthew's came from the Brickfields, a nineteenth-century site at Fairey Road, South Windsor.[42]

During the rebuilding of the church, Cox's wife, Rebecca, fell ill and died in March 1819. Cartwright had another major funeral to conduct, as Rebecca was 'universally ... lamented' and had shown much 'Christian fortitude' in the weeks leading up to her death, while Cartwright was no doubt called upon to sustain her faith.[43] By 1820 William Cox had won other government contracts, and had moved on to organize the building of a schoolhouse at Castlereagh and a watch-house at Richmond, extensions to the Windsor Gaol and repairs to Pitt Town School. He was an effective entrepreneur who 'was very well organised, reported regularly on progress ... and took care in finishing buildings and their grounds'.[44]

As supervisor of the brickwork Greenway chose John Jones, the man responsible for the making of the original bricks and probably also of the replacement bricks in 1819. Jones received a payment of £33 from the Police Fund, for 'Bricks for the new Church at Windsor' in January 1820. In January 1819 at a meeting of clergy, magistrates, and principal inhabitants, John Jones was one of the four chosen to represent Windsor on the committee for 'conducting a Subscription and raising a permanent Fund for the Relief of the Poor in the local districts.'[45] Jones would have known William Cox well in a work capacity.

At the end of the operation, Greenway wrote of his supervisor that:

> in consequence of the attention of Mr Jones not only in making Bricks for the Front but in carrying into effect the Brickwork of Windsor Church such workmanship has been produced that would be no discredit to the Metropolis of England.[46]

As a reward in 1821 Jones received a grant of 500 acres of land just south of Bathurst, where he intended to run more stock than he could on Pugh Farm and where 'a part of his Family is also about to settle'.[47]

35. William Cox as Captain in the New South Wales Corps, *c.* 1803. Cox was the magistrate at Windsor from 1810 until 1837. State Library MIN382 a1087003h.

The handover from Cartwright left John Cross in charge of services at the old chapel in 1820, as the building of the new church progressed. It was Cross who first viewed the grand plaque or founding stone which Macquarie had prepared for the church in 1820, very similar in design to the one for his hospital at Windsor, which is also dated 1820.[48]

The sandstone block for St Matthew's features the capital letters 'G' and 'R' for King George IV (Georgius Rex). Between the raised letters is a stylized crown beneath which are the name of the church and the date of 'A.D. 1820'. The final line displays the name of the governor of New South Wales who had commissioned the church, 'L. Macquarie Esq., Governor'. The church plaque was attached to the south wall in the early 1820s: Harpur does not mention it all, and when the south porch was added in 1857–1858 this founding stone was hidden behind it and forgotten. Only when the church fabric was being conserved in 1919 was the stone rediscovered and attached to the porch.

36. Brickwork on St Matthew's, showing the Flemish bond, a repeated pattern of a short end of a brick with a longways laid brick, on the main part of the Church, the method chosen in the nineteenth century to apply a sophisticated finish to a building, and a fancy version of this on the decorative pillar work on the corners. Photograph by Chris Jones, rector of St Matthew's, 2016.

37. The carved founding stone attached to the south wall of the church over the entry by Governor Macquarie in 1820. Photograph by Chris Jones, rector of St Matthew's, 2016.

The foundation plaque attached to the foundations, on the other hand, had been quietly re-laid in earlier times, and this is the stone bearing the government broad arrow visible today at the south-west corner of the tower: the marble plaque attached to the stone was commissioned only in 1925 and claims that the stone was laid on 11 October 1817.[49] It is likely, but not certain, that this stone remained in its original position when Greenway started to build again on the exposed foundation in 1819.

In March 1820 Governor Macquarie escorted officers from visiting Russian ships on a full day's trip to Windsor. It so pleased the visitors that other Russian ships visited Sydney in November. Macquarie recorded in March:

> We Breakfasted at the [Macquarie Arms] Inn, and afterwards went to see the New Church now Building, and the rest of the Town of Windsor, including the Govt. Cottage and Domain ... We then went to attend Divine Service in Church [the old Chapel] – the Revd. Mr. Cross having preached – After Church, we went down the River for about Two miles in the Govt. Pleasure Boat. – Took some refreshment at the Inn on our return – and set out for Parramatta.[50]

38. The view coming into Windsor of the area around the old chapel and schoolhouse at Windsor at the northern end of the township, much as Macquarie and the Russian visitors would have seen it in 1820. The actual chapel building is out of sight behind bushes. Detail of 1824, 'View of Windsor upon the river Hawkesbury, New South Wales', looking north-west, by Joseph Lycett, 1824. The bridge, nearer the township, crosses South Creek, with the civic square (now Thompson Square) directly beginning above it at the top of the ridge, and falling away out of sight to the river beyond. State Library of New South Wales, Mitchell Library, MRB/F980.1/L.

'Three months away from completion'

Lachlan Macquarie could not stay away long, and was back at Hawkesbury in early September 1820. In particular he continued to have a special interest in the progress of St Matthew's. With the Acting Chief Engineer, Major Druitt, Macquarie arrived by carriage and inspected both the current government construction works in the town, first the church and then the convict barracks (now part of the old Hospital Building in Macquarie Street). Significantly, the governor revealed the cause of such keen interest, for beyond his own inclinations, the pressures of avoiding a mishap under the critical eye of Commissioner Bigge loomed large. The following week the governor was out in the Liverpool area with the Reverend Robert Cartwright but not before Macquarie had summed up that both the church and convict barracks were only three months away from completion.[51]

William Cox did not win every contract for the district's considerable number of new buildings. For example, Richard Fitzgerald supervised the construction of the new military barracks opposite the start of Macquarie Street, Windsor, and John Brabyn the schoolhouse and chapel at Wilberforce. But Cox was successful in gaining many of the other lucrative deals.

A purpose-built Court House in Windsor was Cox's next construction. The governor had announced the desire for tenders, to follow the design of Francis Greenway. Cox went back to having bricks burned, and signed the Court House contract in October 1821. Unlike the church, the Court House was completed in fifteen months, for a modest £1,800.[52] Richard Fitzgerald also supplied unspecified 'Materials' for the new church and the Emu Plains Government Farm.[53]

With so much building work under way by the government throughout the Mulgrave Place district, and after such a long wait for his new church, the rector, John Cross, tried to accelerate the use of the church, believing that the Windsor church building was largely completed when the contract for the Court House was signed in 1821, a year after Macquarie's hopeful prediction of an 1820 completion.[54]

'Now so far completed as to admit of Divine Worship'

Cross told Marsden in a surviving letter on 10 September 1821 that the building 'is now so far completed as to admit of Divine Worship being performed there' and that Governor Macquarie had directed that it should open on Sunday 16 September. The governor was anxious not to miss the event with his departure looming.[55]

Marsden refused to consecrate the church then because of the shortness of notice and because of the solemnity of such a service.[56] Funerals, like that of Thomas Arndell, the ex-magistrate of the district, continued to be held in the old chapel, with Marsden officiating and Cross having his eyes opened to the vehemence of colonial wranglings. What took place at that funeral was an unparalleled act of 'turpitude and atrocity', according to the newspaper, when settler, Andrew Doyle from Portland Head, interrupted Marsden's proceedings. At first just an annoying disturbance to those seated with him in the pew, Doyle's louder interruption of the service accused Marsden of telling lies. The magistrates, always handy attenders in church ready to keep order, had Doyle arrested. Taken before the Windsor Bench the next day, he was convicted to imprisonment in Sydney in solitary confinement on bread and water for three months. For good measure, to ensure he stayed in gaol, the release security was set at £1,000 for Doyle to pay with two sureties needed to produce £500 each. An almost audible sigh of relief reaches us today from Cross, that the incident had not taken place in the new church, and marred its early religious life.[57]

The rivalry between Kitchen and Greenway and now Doyle and Marsden would have been enough for any new curate to handle, but to make things worse, the conflict between Macquarie and Marsden appeared to be surfacing again. Macquarie was deeply committed to St Matthew's. He had visited the district on at least twelve occasions, and over the last few years he had personally inspected the work. With Cross indicating that the church was ready for use, it is hard to escape the conclusion that Marsden was flexing the power he had, to exclude Macquarie and his wife from the ceremony of consecration that he knew they so wanted to attend before they left the colony. The replacement governor arrived and took over the colony soon afterwards in December 1821.

There is no evidence that any service was actually held in the new church in 1821. The only event reported by Harpur in his memoranda for the whole of 1821 was that early in September 'some sheet lead was blown off the dome of the new church by a violent gust of wind; a large sheet was lodged in the scaffolding, and another fell to the ground torn into holes, the lead having been nailed down only, and not sodered [soldered]'.[58] So when Cross wrote to Marsden, the scaffolding was still in place and quite serious damage had just been done to the structure.

Macquarie's frustration at the delay increased as his departure from the colony approached. By early 1822 as he and his family prepared to leave the colony, the church at Windsor had been being planned for twelve full years, and under construction for over five. After its false start, part demolition and modified design, work had progressed smoothly, if slowly, but although Macquarie technically had control of the chaplaincy as head of the church in New South Wales and because the colony was a military establishment, even Macquarie was not in a position to argue too much if Marsden objected. This was because, as most governors had found, the peace was fragile so far from Britain, and the last public uprising had led to Bligh's being deposed.[59] The governor had the power to order that civic decrees be made from the pulpit, and that magistrates serve with exceptional reformed ex-convicts like Andrew Thompson and Simeon Lord, but Samuel Marsden had continually snubbed the governor's fair-minded requests when they involved him working with transportees, no matter how worthy and industrious such men had proved themselves to be. Likewise, although a great missionary to the New Zealand and South Seas Indigenous peoples, Marsden had given only lip service to Macquarie's well-meant plans to help the Aboriginal peoples. Finally, Samuel Marsden had written to England to agitate for Macquarie's removal, which added to Macquarie's distress.

After the new governor, Sir Thomas Brisbane,

was installed and governing late in 1821, the Macquaries undertook final tours of the various settlements to say goodbye to their many friends. The Hawkesbury district was among the last places to which Macquarie journeyed on his round of goodbye visits. There was genuine sorrow at the couple's departure along the upper Hawkesbury River districts, and settlers there had raised the money for Macquarie to have his portrait painted to hang in the district. Macquarie noted in his diary on Friday, 4 January 1822:

> The deputation, with the address from the inhabitants of the Hawkesbury waited on me, consisting of the magistrates, chaplain [John Cross] and eight other respectable inhabitants and the address was read by their chairman, William Cox, Esquire, to which was added a request that I should sit for my portrait on my arrival in England and to be hung up in the new Court House at Windsor – for defraying the expense of which they had entered into a subscription. I made a suitable answer, acquiescing in their request for my sitting for my portrait in London.[60]

When the portrait finally arrived back in New South Wales, it was consigned to old friends, not the new clergyman. William Cox and Richard Fitzgerald acknowledged its arrival, and had it hung in the Court House, where it remained until recently when the Justice Department decided that it needed greater security than the building could provide, as its court use was being scaled back.[61]

Governor Macquarie left the colony early in 1822.[62] In January that year the Reverend Samuel Marsden wrote, perhaps feeling the pressure for justification:

> I admit there is one church in the colony in which the litany is read and not furnished with pews and that is at Liverpool. The Rev. R Cartwright, without due consideration, entered that church with[out] Pulpit, Desk or Pews, when I was sent to New Zealand, but he has repented much, ever since for doing so ... Mr. Cartwright has been obliged to carry his chairs out of his own house to the church for the accommodation of his people to this very day.[63]

Writing to Bigge in January, Marsden used a similar reason, claiming that he refused to consecrate the church 'before there was a pulpit or desk, or the pews' but then added a third and totally new reason: 'until I get the Grant of the Glebe.'[64]

As a result, the ceremony was delayed for over a year. Marsden did not come to Windsor to consecrate St Matthew's until 18 December 1822. Although Marsden was on much better relations with the new governor, Thomas Brisbane, than he had been with Macquarie, he took a very firm line over declaring new churches ready for services. Earlier in 1822, he had refused to allow St James' in the city to open because it lacked pews or pulpit and had no instrument of endowment: Marsden delayed its consecration by two years.[65]

The consecration service at Windsor was conducted by Marsden as Principal Chaplain for the colony, assisted by three other ministers, Cross, Cartwright and the young Thomas Hassall, Marsden's son-in-law.[66] The Parish Register notes:

> This day the new Church of St Matthew's, Windsor, was consecrated and opened for divine service, by the Rev. Samuel Marsden, Principal; Chaplain of the Territory ... After the ceremony the Holy Sacrament was administered to a goodly company from various parts of the colony. Scarcely an individual was observed but what appeared deeply attentive during the whole service, and the church was nearly filled before the Communion Service was commenced. (Signed) J. Harpur, Windsor, Wednesday, 18th December, 1822.[67]

The *Sydney Gazette* reported the consecration, calling the church an 'elegant and commodious place of public worship' and noting that 'In such a colony as ours, nothing can tend more strongly to evidence moral and religious prosperity than the opening of Churches and Chapels.' The congregation, it noted, was 'far from uninteresting.' The journalist was obviously aware of the pitfalls of naming attendees on second-hand information. The Eucharist was administered and a sermon by Marsden was from the words to be found in the 87th Psalm: 'Glorious things are spoken of thee, O City of God!'[68]

Andrew or Matthew

One uncertainty seems to have remained for a while. To which saint should the new church be dedicated? Although the dedication to St Matthew had been declared by Macquarie in 1817 and although Harpur had commented in 1819 that the church 'is, I believe, to retain the name of

39. Watercolour, 1824, Detail of 'View of Windsor upon the river Hawkesbury, New South Wales', lithograph by Joseph Lycett, looking north-west. St Matthew's Church is in the top left-hand corner. The bridge, nearer the township, crosses South Creek, with the civic square (now Thompson Square) directly beginning above it at the top of the ridge, and falling away out of sight to the river beyond. The site of the church, amongst the hills to the left of the square, is distant about 1.2 kilometres from the chapel. State Library of New South Wales, Mitchell Library, MRB/F980.1/L.

St. Matthew given to the first building', a dedication to St Andrew, the patron saint of Macquarie's Scotland, seems to have been considered as an alternative. As Steele shrewdly noted long ago, there is a hint of uncertainty in Harpur's phrase 'I believe' in 1819.[69]

Harpur himself is said, in a well-informed secondary source, to have officiated at the 'Windsor Chapel, St Andrew's', though this is more likely to refer to the schoolhouse/church in Bridge Street where Harpur taught.[70] However, the *Sydney Gazette* in 1823 published an official proclamation by Governor Brisbane appointing a committee of John Cross, William Cox and John Brabyn 'for the Church of St. Andrew, Windsor'.[71]

Finally, the communion chalice and paten, made by Garrard, the leading London silversmith, presented by King George IV in 1822, is inscribed 'St. Andrew, Windsor'.[72]

This fine Georgian silver is said to be superseded by the purchase of a new set (not inscribed to St Andrew) from Richard Lamb for £35 in 1851 or 1852. Since this was largely financed by a special appeal among the congregation, 34 of whom contributed a total of over £28, it was a very deliberate act to acquire new communion silver.[73] This may perhaps reflect some unease about the St Andrew's attribution of the earlier silver. The set by Lamb is no longer to be found.

40. The base of the Communion chalice, part of a set presented by King George IV in 1822, is inscribed to St Andrew, Windsor. Photograph by Ian Jack, 2016.

Royal patronage was reflected also in the gift of a large Bible, published in 1821, which was delivered in 1822 through the Society for the Propagation of Christian Knowledge. A Book of Common Prayer published in 1814 was probably already in use.

Unlike the silver gifted in the same year, 1822,

the Bible was used in St Matthew's until 1936, when it was honourably retired and replaced by a fine Bible given by the Marsden family. It takes a place of honour today under the gallery in the display cabinet donated for the purpose by Nurse Primrose in 1937.[74]

Two final signs of royal approval were installed in the church in 1822 under John Cross's supervision: the bell and 'a very good clock', both still in good order and accessible up the tower stair.[75]

The clock was manufactured in 1821 by Thwaites and Reed of Clerkenwell in London.[76] The firm had been established in 1740, and was the firm later selected to look after the clock on the British Houses of Parliament, known as Big Ben. From 1816 Thwaites went into partnership with George Reed.[77]

41. Communion paten which together with the chalice was given by King George IV in 1822. Photograph by Ian Jack, 2016.

In all there were five similar clocks gifted by King George IV to New South Wales. The turret-clock in the original Female Factory building was another, and Marsden's church in Parramatta also. The others are to be found at St Luke's, Liverpool, and in Hobart. Originally one of the clocks was in St David's Church there, but it is now in Government House.[78] The bell, cast in 1820, was one of at least two which came out to the colony in 1821 or 1822 from the English maker T. Meares, of

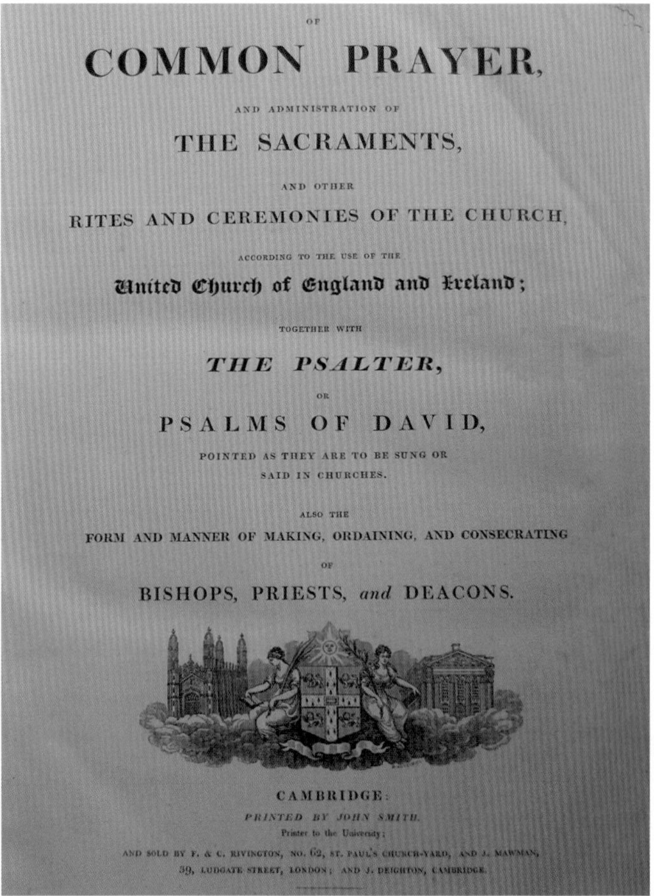

OF

COMMON PRAYER,

AND ADMINISTRATION OF

THE SACRAMENTS,

AND OTHER

RITES AND CEREMONIES OF THE CHURCH,

ACCORDING TO THE USE OF THE

United Church of England and Ireland;

TOGETHER WITH

THE PSALTER,

OR

PSALMS OF DAVID,

POINTED AS THEY ARE TO BE SUNG OR SAID IN CHURCHES.

ALSO THE

FORM AND MANNER OF MAKING, ORDAINING, AND CONSECRATING

OF

BISHOPS, PRIESTS, *and* DEACONS.

CAMBRIDGE:

PRINTED BY JOHN SMITH,

Printer to the University;

AND SOLD BY F. & C. RIVINGTON, NO. 62, ST. PAUL'S CHURCH-YARD, AND J. MAWMAN, 39, LUDGATE STREET, LONDON; AND J. DEIGHTON, CAMBRIDGE.

42. The first Book of Common Prayer used at St Matthew's Anglican Church, dated 1814. Photograph by Ian Jack, 2016.

the celebrated foundry at Whitechapel. The other was installed in St James' in Sydney in 1824.[79] No reference to the arrival of the bells can be found in any of the ships' manifests in the *Sydney Gazette*, but the Windsor information, first recorded in 1874, clearly comes from the rector, Charles Garnsey, who took the correspondent of the *Town and Country Journal* up the tower to look at the bell, the clock and the view. Garnsey was the son-in-law of Henry Stiles, who had become rector of St Matthew's in 1834 and who had displayed a keen interest in the history of his church, knowing many of those prominent in church affairs in the early 1820s.[80]

Over its half-millennium or more of existence the foundry has operated in London under several names. More often than not, these have been the name of the bellfounder who owned it at that time. The name 'Whitechapel Bell Foundry Ltd' did not come into use until the company was incorporated in 1968. It is still making bells today.[81]

43. Detail of the clock face on the St Matthew's Anglican Church tower, Windsor. Photograph by Ian Jack, May 1999.

The new Colonial Architect, Standish Harris, came out to Windsor and examined his predecessor's church in 1824. He agreed that the building was 'executed in a good and workmanship manner', but was critical of the mortar used, worrying that 'its permanency cannot be depended upon'. Internally the cornices and the plastering, 'tho' comparatively well done', were showing cracks and would, he feared, 'shortly give way'.

On the aesthetic front Harris was critical of the expensive 'ornaments' which remain an eye-catching feature of Greenway's tower. Harris judged the stone urns to be 'more suitable for a Theatre, or fancy dwelling'.[82]

There was no wooden cross and orb on the apex of the tower in the 1820s, although the lantern top and the dome capping and four tower ornaments were in place. The tower in this form did not please everyone.

When Jane, Lady Franklin, the wife of the Governor of Van Diemen's Land (Tasmania), saw it in June 1838, her opinion was harsh, and nothing like the *Sydney Gazette*'s evaluation that the church was 'elegant'.

44. The clock works, installed in St Matthew's tower in 1822. Photograph by Chris Jones, rector of St Matthew's, 2016.

Lady Franklin was out of sorts and enduring a severe headache while in Windsor, but she was no friend of Georgian architecture and declared that:

> The church is a large, ugly, red brick building, 6 windows & door in side tower at West, & with white cupola lantern, a frightful thing, above it – they talk of wanting globe and cross, but nothing can mend it.[83]

And she found the red-brick rectory no less ugly.

45. The bell cast in 1820 from the Whitechapel foundry of T. Meares in London. Photograph by Ian Jack, 1999.

46. View inside St Matthew's bell tower today. The bell cast by 'T. Meares of London' in what is today the Whitechapel Bell Foundry, dates to 1820. Photograph by Ian Jack, 2016.

47. The belfry dome at St Matthew's. Photograph by Chris Jones, rector of St Matthew's, 2016.

48. One of the four original tower ornaments carved in stone over two metres high. Photograph by Graham Edds, 2008.

4 The High Pulpit

A Congregation in Waiting

As James Steele, the historian of Windsor, observed, when Standish Harris, Greenway's successor as Colonial Architect, reported on St Matthew's to Governor Brisbane in 1824:

> there were but seven settled parishes in New South Wales—St. Phillip's and St. James's, in Sydney; St. John's, Parramatta; St. Luke's, Liverpool; St. Peter's, Campbelltown; Christ Church, Newcastle; and St. Matthew's, Windsor.[1]

49. St Matthew's Anglican Church, drawn by Standish Harris, 1824. State Library of New South Wales, Mitchell Library, C 226, reel CY 1035.

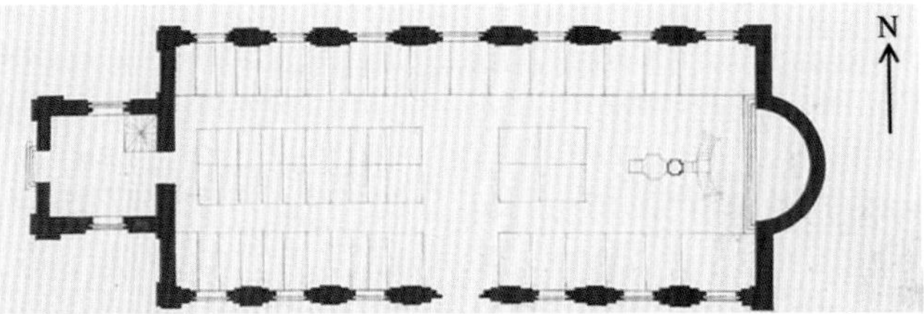

50. Standish Harris' plan of St Matthew's, 1824. Redrawn from Morton Herman, *The Early Australian Architects and Their Work*, Angus & Robertson, Sydney, 1954, after p. 104, in conjunction with the original plan, State Library of New South Wales, Mitchell Library, C 226, reel CY 1035.

Greenway's Windsor church had a simple interior, consisting of a nave, where the congregation sat, with a semicircular apse behind the altar, forming a sanctuary. A tower room at the west end of the nave had a staircase and ladders to the bell and clock. Although Greenway had laid foundations for a south porch, the door in the middle of the south wall of the nave opened directly onto the ground until the present porch was finally built in 1857–1858. This was the basic fabric of the church as the Reverend John Cross, his family and his parishioners had come to know it, after the church was finally consecrated on 18 December 1822.

The delay between Macquarie's requested date of consecration and the actual ceremony was fifteen months. This meant that during that period John Cross was forced to hold the funeral services of up to 40 more people at the old chapel near Thompson Square. The funeral procession then walked over a kilometre to the graveside beside a now externally completed church. The seventeen-year-old son of Richard Fitzgerald was one of those buried during this time.[2]

After such a prolonged period of waiting for the church to be in use, the congregation should have been beyond happiness. Certainly they were beyond words, for no detailed account of the service that Marsden conducted has come down to us from any of the congregation, after gazing in awe on the interior of their new church building for the first time.

The Church in Use

A note in the Register by the faithful clerk Joseph Harpur indicates that a further delay of almost two months took place after the church was consecrated, before it was used for burials. The first child presented for baptism was probably Sarah Deakins, the local brewer's daughter, on 2 March 1823, whilst the first marriage in the new church is unknown.[3] There is no doubt about the first burial service, for the Register says of Daniel Barnett (or Barney) that on 17 February 1823: 'This corpse was the first brought into the body of St Matthew's Church, attended by many of the oldest inhabitants of these parts, Barney being one who came out in the First Fleet'.[4]

Barnett had lived in the upper Hawkesbury area since he was granted his 30 acres of land there as one of the first group of 22 settlers to the district early in 1794. His farm was near the mouth of South Creek, beside what is today the road to Pitt Town.[5]

51. Daniel Barnett's farm on South Creek. Barnett's grave is in the north-western quadrant of the burial ground at St Matthew's. Barnett died on 15 February 1823, and was buried two days later by John Cross. Barnett was a First Fleeter, aged 68 years at his death. His was the first corpse brought into the church for a funeral service. Photograph by Jan Barkley-Jack, 2009.

The Reverend Elijah Smith

Elijah Smith may have served the shortest term of all the ministers of St Matthew's, remaining only one year in Windsor, but he led an interesting life. On 4 February 1828 when John Cross left Windsor he was replaced at once by Smith, who was 28 years old.[6]

Smith's father was an English clergyman who was by far the most connected with academic life of any of the forebears of the previous ministers. Smith sr served as headmaster of English grammar schools and had been at St John's College, Cambridge, whilst Elijah Smith himself had been ordained in 1827. He came to the colony very soon after ordination in England.[7]

Elijah Smith had married Martha Lucas in London in 1821 and arrived in Sydney on 25 November 1827 with his wife and son, Elijah Basil. He came to Australia as assistant to the chaplains and was appointed by Archdeacon Scott to Windsor as from 4 February 1828.[8] He set to the work of the parish, being called upon first to bury just a week later, to baptize on 17 February 1828, and to perform a wedding three days after that.[9]

Smith apparently soon caused a stir in Windsor where he welcomed a 'lady of the night' into the church 'as a sinner returning to the flock'. This created a commotion, according to a descendant, but does not seem to have harmed Smith's reputation generally. Smith had plans to establish a grammar school at Windsor and had made a formal request to the Archdeacon. Martha Smith, however, did not like the Hawkesbury summer heat and the family contemplated a return to England.[10]

When it was wrongly reported in October 1828 that Elijah was to be appointed to Launceston in Tasmania, swapping with the temporary minister there, the *Sydney Gazette* had remarked: 'We can ill spare to the sister Colony a man of such solid acquirements as a scholar, and such respectable talents as a preacher, as the present clergyman of Windsor undeniably is'.[11]

Smith spent eleven months in Windsor. He remained officiating there until the end of the year. His last official service to St Matthew's parish was to bury nineteen-month-old Charlotte Cross from Lower Portland Head on 30 December.[12]

In Sydney before he left the colony, Smith performed a marriage in St James' Church in March 1829, during the incumbency of Richard Hill.[13] Although Smith had declared an intention to return to England around this time, he was initially dissuaded and strongly encouraged instead to open a 'classical seminary of the very first respectability' in Parramatta.[14] But this school does not seem to have eventuated either.

Once back in Britain, Smith continued as a minister, fitting in travel to Archangel in Russia, returning to England in 1840, and an appointment as chaplain to King's College Hospital. In 1848 he went to St Petersburg, and there he established a British school for the English Factory. By 1851, however, he was once more in New South Wales, and in 1863 he was appointed incumbent of St Stephen's at Penrith, conjoined with St Mary's at South Creek.

Smith's obituary in 1870 states:

> Besides being well acquainted with the Hebrew, Greek, Chaldaic, and Syriac languages, he was familiar with many of the languages of Northern Europe, and, in the course of his life, had translated some works from the Swedish, for which he gained great commendation and reward. Up till very recently he displayed all the energy and zeal of his early years in his sacred calling.[15]

Elijah Smith was buried in Balmain cemetery, but when that ground became a public park in the 1940s the obelisk erected over his grave in October 1870 was re-erected beside the entry porch of St Stephen's.[16]

52. Obelisk for Elijah Smith in the grounds of St Stephen's Church, Penrith, after it was moved from Balmain cemetery. Photograph by Ian Jack, 2016.

The Reverend Joseph Docker

Joseph Docker, the next clergyman appointed to St Matthew's, had come from school-mastering in England to New South Wales. He had arrived in June 1828, with a wish to start a school in Sydney.[17] The Archdeacon, however, sent Docker to Windsor. He was to remain at St Matthew's until what some saw as 'a local campaign to undermine his position' forced him to resign in 1833.[18]

Docker, like Smith, was selected in a process different from that for the early ministers at St Matthew's. He had been an official appointee in Britain, sent to be a chaplain in New South Wales, and directed once here to Windsor and Richmond, as opposed to being a volunteer or missionary pastor coaxed to the colony by Samuel Marsden. The Government Order announcing his nomination was issued on 6 February 1829:

> His Majesty having been graciously pleased to nominate the Reverend Joseph Docker, Clerk, to a Chaplaincy in New South Wales, His Excellency the governor, upon the Recommendation of the Venerable the Archdeacon, has been pleased to appoint him to take Charge of the Parishes of Windsor and Richmond.
>
> By Command of His Excellency the Governor,
> Alexander McLeay ... Colonial Secretary's Office.[19]

Joseph Docker and his wife, Sarah, arrived at the parsonage in Windsor with a six-month-old daughter, Mary Jane, who had been born at sea in June 1828.[20] Mary's baptism was Joseph Docker's second official duty at St Matthew's, eight days after he had buried John Cliffe, a prisoner, on 6 January 1829.[21] The Dockers' second child, a boy, baptized Charles William on 1 September 1831 when he was sixteen months old, was the first child born in the Windsor Rectory. In November 1831 Stanley Horricks Docker arrived, and like the other two, was christened by his father.[22]

After Docker had left the ministry, another son, Frederick George, was born in May 1835. Although Henry Stiles was then shown in the Register rightly as the minister, he wrote a note there that the christening had been carried out elsewhere, and that he was recording a certificate that 'Docker transferred to him in March 1838'. It is not known who baptized Frederick.[23] Matthew Docker was christened by Stiles in 1837.[24] Joseph Docker officiated from January 1829 until 23 March 1833, but had a final church service at St Matthew's and a baptism at Kurrajong in July 1833 just before he resigned.[25]

Docker seems to have made more use of the church's glebe land than former ministers who had complained that the Clarendon glebe remained unfenced, making full-time carers for the animals essential. By mid-1829 Docker's glebe workers included John Cooper, the stockman, and Michael Barry, a convict shepherd responsible for Docker's flock. Barry remained with the sheep during the day as they grazed and was responsible for counting them into a moveable pen at night, even then remaining close by.

53. The Reverend Joseph Docker, from a daguerreotype in the family collection in Victoria, *c.* 1850. J. McMillan, *The Two Lives of Joseph Docker*, Spectrum Publishing, Melbourne, 1994, p. 73.

A correspondence with the Church and Schools Corporation began almost as soon as Joseph Docker arrived in Windsor. He confronted them on being told that the quotation for work he had obtained was too high. Docker had conformed to regulations, obtaining a competitive quote for the necessary job of fencing the glebe. Without hesitation when he received a negative reply he wrote back in his practical, forthright manner, explaining that the price was determined by there being 'no timber fit for fencing nearer than five miles' and that it could not be made cheaper. Such a reply was not what the Corporation wanted to hear.[26]

The farm hands were James Riley, William Hodges and Thomas Cobner (who was later murdered in 1836). Other government men included John Shipton, a stockman and Thomas Clemson, a gardener. All of Docker's workers were important for the smooth operation of his establishment, but the rector had three in particular whose services were extremely valuable in a time where almost everything within a household had to be made to keep costs down. William Bennet was the essential blacksmith who made all fittings from door latches to hinges, and also made and mended all the farm tools. Then there was a cabinetmaker, James Nelson, and the other specialized government servant was a tailor, Frederick Langtry, who made clothes for the household and the workers on the farm and glebe. The workers were provided with clothes, and with their wages could buy rations for themselves from the store that the minister ran for the purpose.[27]

The Dockers cared well for their government servants but expected loyalty in return. Alice Trelly or Wafer was the washerwoman. She had received on arrival a new pair of shoes, a handkerchief, gloves and 'cap ribbons (a present from Mrs Jones)'.

The next year she was given '12 shillings and a week's holiday', perhaps as in that year, 1830, aged 32, Alice was listed as one returned to government.[28] Ex-convict William Sinclair was their footman, supplied with shirts and waistcoats and stockings as befitted a servant working in a busy rectory, where it was he who would greet visitors at the door.[29] Sinclair probably lived in a men's quarters, responsible for his own food like the other servants.[30]

Keen to help all his faithful servants, as well as to forward the church services, Joseph Docker appointed Sinclair to become the sexton, or parish clerk, when the job became vacant. Sinclair, like Newsome before him, was able to improve the singing in the services, having a good singing voice. When Sinclair found the job of collecting the pew rents too onerous – for he was able to do it only in his spare time after he had completed his assigned tasks – Docker recommended another of his servants, James Connor, a brickmaker.[31] A further appointment as parish clerk when the position fell vacant had been given by Docker to the schoolmaster Matthew Hughes, although it was then given to John Wood as someone 'on whom I can depend'.[32]

Tension built up between the local magistrates and the rectors at St Matthew's. The minister's activities were largely controlled by the Church and Schools Corporation, after it was set up in 1826 with control of the minister's spending, but the Windsor Bench, with William Cox its long-time leader, had aspirations to exercise its extensive civic powers.

Cox had been the contractor for building the church and in this role would often have had to act perhaps even against the wishes of the

54. The front doors of the Rectory at St Matthew's at night. Photograph by Chris Jones, rector of St Matthew's, 2016.

ministers. One instance of the conflicting roles and controls between church and magistrates can be found later in the records of employment of the Windsor teacher, John Newsome, when Cross and Smith were rectors. A letter shows that, although the Corporation paid his wages, the bench had required a binding contract, under the auspices of the magistrates, whereby Newsome had to teach singing to the children at the Windsor church for two and a half years. The agreement was specifically 'made with Messrs. Cox and Brabyn.'[33] Disagreement between the Bench and the minister also arose from time to time from the severe sentencing sometimes handed down in the court.[34]

Despite the Church and Schools Corporation struggling and being dissolved in 1829, the winding-up period was protracted until 1833,[35] so Docker remained the local contact for the Church Corporation when the building of a schoolhouse at Kurrajong, with accommodation for the schoolmaster, was being advertised in 1832.[36]

In the 1820s the Colonial Office began to take a closer interest in the recruitment of clergymen, which may explain Docker's and Smith's more formal appointment. The shift in New South Wales can be seen in the appointment of an archdeacon in the mid-1820s and closer modelling on the English church, whilst the arrival of six more clergy and the establishment of a branch of the Society for the Propagation of Christian Knowledge showed that 'more aggressive Anglicanism had arrived.'[37] However, in New South Wales at that stage, the politics was less absolute, as the missionary clergy were still a big part of the colonial church, and had membership of the Church and Schools Corporation, along with government representatives like the Colonial Secretary Alexander McLeay and Cowper's son Charles. Archdeacon Scott was at their head. The Corporation had been set up to fund the Anglican Church in New South Wales alone, and to have control of every minister's expenditure. The Church and Schools Corporation had been controversial throughout its life, even drawing letters in the *Times* newspaper in London. Archdeacon Scott, replying in 1833, indicated that 'the sum expended on the Episcopal Clergy, never never did, in any one year, exceed £11,000, which sum includes stipends, buildings, repairs, rent, etc. and second, that the sum set apart for the support of the Schools, has been expended, on that object, and on that alone' by the Corporation.[38]

As Archdeacon Scott had been told by the Colonial Office to forward the 'Anglican design' and 'not

55. The entrance to the Rectory, Windsor. Visitors to Joseph Docker would have been greeted by footman William Sinclair. Photograph by Chris Jones, rector of St Matthew's, 2016

give any additional ... authority to Mr. Marsden' as he was considered 'turbulent', the way forward during the late 1820s and early 1830s was fraught, threatening the 'unity of the clergy'. Scott's heavy-handed style offended the new ministers.[39] When Archdeacon Broughton took over in 1829 he was even more determined to forward the British agenda of using only the 'forms of the Church of England'.[40]

One of the six new rectors, all of whom still seem somewhat of the missionary style, was Joseph Docker. Another was Elijah Smith. Both resigned, along with three other clergymen in New South Wales, during Scott's or Broughton's time as Archdeacon.[41]

56. St Matthew's nave was well lit with seven large windows, as seen on the northern side. Photograph by Chris Jones, rector of St Matthew's, 2016.

Church and Rectory Repair

Docker was generally patient with the bureaucracy and at first his troubles seemed localized and minor. He clearly was not afraid to act in small matters of urgent repair. The fabric of the church and the Rectory was only some ten years old, and the buildings were still considered more than sufficient for the needs of the rector and his parish at Hawkesbury, although defective workmanship was already evident. Docker may have had dreams of an organ for his church,[42] but his early dealings with the various corporations through which the money for improvements would flow obviously convinced him that no new major projects for his church would be possible. Besides, for Joseph Docker it was the welfare of his parishioners that was important. Many in the district were struggling on the land, many still lacking access to a school. Education drove Docker. He saw it as the path forward for his flock, and he devoted much time and effort to achieving schooling for all ages throughout the furthest corners of his pastoral district.[43]

Docker was deeply involved with education and his parishioners, while not neglecting maintenance of the buildings. After only a decade the fabric of the church needed repair rather than refurbishment, and in his usual, earnest manner, Docker fiercely attempted to attend to the upkeep of the buildings. Indeed, it was the cause of his drawing letters of 'please explain' from the committee when he first arrived in 1829. He was a man who believed in ministers of religion having enough control over their daily lives to keep things around them running efficiently. He had no intention of endangering his young family or congregation by unhealthy living conditions, while he waited for the seemingly endless clearances needed to fix the urgent problems.

Docker's difficulties with the church authorities were exacerbated because of his determination to get his rectory and church fixed so they were actually liveable. This may have been the beginning of the previous problems referred to by Broughton in 1833,[44] for where he thought repairs justified Docker was prepared to act decisively so that situations did not drag on. Some wooden fabric on both buildings was in need of replacement from water damage, despite being reasonably new, with urgent repairs required to the wooden window frames of the church.

Docker stated:

> I had no authority from the trustees for 'Wilson's repairs to the church' but they were absolutely necessary. If the window frames had not been repaired immediately the greatest part of the church windows would probably have been broken by the high winds which at that time prevailed.[45]

The Reverend Thomas Reddall, also new to the colony, independently confirmed that this problem was almost universal to the colonial churches,

57. The drawing room of the Rectory at Windsor today. The fireplace, still in need of a grate when the Docker family arrived, can be seen on the right. Photograph by Chris Jones, rector of St Matthew's, 2016.

since the woodwork had never been painted properly. Docker did the church a great service by not allowing the woodwork to decay further, but this is not how his practical approach was viewed by the Corporation. It apparently saw nothing except a lack of proper respect for the committee itself and for its somewhat ponderous procedures.[46]

Though only four or so years old, the parsonage roof leaked. Docker's biographer gives a valid surmise of the effect on the building: water-stained walls in the drawing room of the Rectory and a smell of dankness, necessitating fires to be lit in the grates throughout to make the building liveable. The rain had been getting in through breaks in the wooden shingles, and upstairs the damage would have been more severe where some of the lathe and plasterwork of the ceilings had crumpled or fallen in. The Docker family, including baby Mary, was forced to live in just a couple of the least affected of the downstairs rooms, along with all the furniture stored there until the problem could be fixed. They had to eat in an inn because of the state of the rectory kitchen.[47]

It was clear that the building needed immediate attention, and Docker regarded ongoing maintenance as essential, also hoping for internal whitewashing to be included in the works he quickly applied for. Two weeks into their stay, the rector had provided the Corporation with the three quotations necessary to have expenditure on the repairs approved. His requests to rectify the family's difficulties were accompanied by a list of immediate needs: 'a large boiler, bells and a good [grate] for the living room', although 'common grates might do for the rest'. The rector was also a humble man, able to distinguish between what was essential and what was not, as evidenced by his letter in regard to the whitewashing where he added:

> As to the Whitewashing I have only to say that to keep a building in decent order an annual Whitewashing is necessary; but if it is not done for the other Chaplains I by no means expect it for myself.[48]

Even the proposal to dig a necessary well was postponed by the committee of the Corporation so that Docker might 'consult with someone conversant with the situation' and obtain the probable depth and cost.[49] With regard to the ceiling, the committee responded with warnings of the need for economy and suggested replacement of the plaster with wooden boards instead of repairs. Docker, undeterred, wrote back that he had employed 'Collison the plasterer' to look at the situation. Collison had advised, Docker informed the committee, that in several rooms the plaster could be mended as it was unlikely to shrink further, and that wooden boards would 'cost twice as much as those of mortar'.[50]

Always firmly practical and polite, Docker later wrote defensively in reply to the committee's queries of unauthorized expenditure:

> when I was appointed to Windsor the Parsonage was in a state of dilapidation, which I attribute in great measure to the want of timely attention to the roof, and now that the ceilings are good, I think it would be mistaken economy to suffer them to fall into the same state through neglect.[51]

Schooling as a Priority

Education of all types occupied Joseph Docker, and here too he liked to get things done and to achieve his goals. On matters of the payment of salaries for church and school, he tried to be subservient as required, but he never wavered in his support for schools. It is little known that at Windsor Joseph Docker achieved his long desired goal of establishing a respected private school, which he described as 'one of the first Boarding Schools in the Colony' from around 1829 soon after he moved to the district. Its location is unknown, but may have been in the Rectory.[52] By 1830, one of the pupils was William, the son of a wealthy widow, Maria Cope, but William drowned 'while bathing in the Hawkesbury'.[53] The boy was buried near the graves of Rebecca Cox and Thomas Arndell in St Matthew's cemetery in the south-western sector of the burial ground by Docker on 6 March 1830.[54]

It was not until several years after William's death that Maria Cope bought land in the middle of the town of Windsor from the wealthy businessman Samuel Terry. It was then basically farm land, and the house built there which is still standing facing George Street is today known as Cope's Cottage. Maria subdivided much of her northern lands, which abutted the Glebe area around the Rectory.[55]

58. Marker of eight-year-old William Cope's burial on the side of the family altar monument in the south-western corner of the graveyard at St Matthew's. The recutting has mistakenly altered the date of death from February 1830 to 1856. No Cope was buried in that year. Photograph by Ian Jack, 2016.

Docker was moved by his pupil's death. The sermon he wrote on the occasion of the Sunday's service following eight-year-old William's burial, was based around 2 Samuel chap. 12 verses 22 and 23, the declaration of a father's grief, which Docker described as 'one of the most beautiful and affecting narratives which the sacred volume contains'.[56]

Joseph Docker superintended carefully the public schools in his parish, as well as starting an infants' school in the old schoolhouse/chapel at Windsor. Mrs Sommers was added to the school staff as infants' mistress later in the same year, with an enrolment of 60 by 1833.[57] Docker's arrangements that Mr Sommers take the senior pupils and Mrs Sommers the infants and sewing classes at Windsor were dismissed in a directive from Archdeacon Scott, who advised that Sommers was to take only the boys of all ages upstairs and Mrs Sommers all the girls, downstairs, so that the sexes were separated. Forthright as ever, Docker informed the Archdeacon that:

> I am afraid the division of the schools you have suggested would not answer as the infants ought *All to be in the one place* under the care of Mrs Sommers and the senior boys and girls could not be separated without an additional teacher.[58]

Giving help to children in the outer Richmond area was important to the clergyman too. He was working towards setting up a school of industry for the older children, visiting every household to gain subscriptions towards it. The school at Kurrajong, about which prospective builders were directed to contact Docker for details of the building contract in 1832, had been Docker's initiative too. The struggle began in 1829 to educate children in the remote parts of the Evan and Richmond districts, estimated to be about 20 to 30 pupils. The residents were too poor to pay a teacher themselves, so Docker maintained that subsidization from the Church and Schools Corporation would be necessary. Disagreement by the Corporation with Docker's experience-based suggestions about payment, about who would be an appropriate teacher and whose land would be suitable, proceeded back and forth, until the 'Curryjong schoolhouse' became three years in the making, and even then criticisms surfaced that the school was 'hastily put together'.[59]

Judy McMillan, Docker's biographer, believed:

> [Docker] ... saw too that justice in the colony tended to be a commodity, useful to exchange for some form of

59. *Off Burralow Road*, at Kurrajong Heights. Artist Greg Hansell, 2014, 20 cm x 20 cm, Schmincke pastels on Canson paper, *en plein air*. Greg Hansell, photographed by Geoff Roberts, 2016.

> power or prestige or with some end in view instead of being a simple right. With severe penalties being meted out daily for any lapse of good behaviour and no-one to stand up for them, Docker increasingly found his role was that of a champion to the poor, the unemployed and the uneducated ... Inevitably there were clashes with those whose views did not coincide with his own, both within the church and outside.[60]

Colonial developments meant new laws began to be considered. The committee was abolished in 1829, and Broughton replaced Scott as archdeacon. A wave of more sympathetic feeling regarding other denominations was sweeping the colony, even more quickly than in Britain. Yet at the same time Broughton was even more determined than Scott to bring the Church of England back to conservative ways. Much of this pressure played out in small things, and it would be quite easy to see the difficulties that Docker began to experience as a personality clash, were there not the deeper underlying tensions of previous disagreements with the church authorities on the everyday running of the churches and schools. The historian A.G. Austin comments that before Archdeacon Scott 'had been long in the colony he had contrived to antagonize his own Clergy, the Press, the members of every other sect, the Judiciary and even the Governor'.[61]

There were also the pressures of Broughton's own agenda of which Docker may not at first

60. The Rectory and its stables with St Matthew's in the background, from the east. Etching by Sydney Ure Smith, 1917. *The Rectory Stables,* booklet by Stables Task Force, 2003.

have been aware.[62] Marsden for instance was later to declare that: 'The Archdeacon is a very high churchman. He will not countenance the smallest deviation from the rules of the established church.'[63] Broughton, who became bishop in 1836, was not one to tolerate insubordination, on even the smallest of issues, and it was inevitable that those of practical and independent mindset like Docker would clash with the administration during the 1830s.

Political changes in Britain, like the movement to allow free worship for Catholics, became reflected in the colony and there was increasing support for the rights of other denominations. Here the political agendas of reformers seeking more egalitarian changes to colonial life intersected with those seeking greater church freedom. The reformers thought that: 'Archdeacon Scott's authoritarian style ... was regarded as the natural support of Governor Darling's oppressive regime: indeed Scott had been one of the chief supporters of the press censorship which Darling introduced in 1827.'[64]

Joseph Docker Strikes Trouble

For all his involvement in minor written disagreements with the Archdeacons, the surviving evidence does not put Docker in the midst of the political or reformist melee. He appears a quiet man, involved only because of his concerns for his church, home and others' welfare. In fact, Docker's immediate problems in 1833 were with the Windsor magistrates. When they deliberately involved Archdeacon Broughton in their moves against Docker, this was the catalyst for his resignation, although it is clear from the documents which survive that there was some pre-existing animosity between the Archdeacon and the Windsor minister, or else some favour owing the magistrates.

For example, Joseph Docker expresses himself unfairly treated in a:

> very hasty and precipitate manner ... for you must allow that to supersede me in the performance of all my clerical duties to suspend me for all intents and purposes unheard, for a period of four months, is contrary to reason, and repugnant to every principle of justice.[65]

Unlike those before him, except perhaps Smith, Joseph Docker had received his appointment to New South Wales from Lord Stanley.[66] After an impoverished childhood, both his school education and his entry into the ministry had been unorthodox. All this affected his ministry. Docker's descendants were exceptional recorders of the detail of the family's life in the colony and they believed that the dispute that overtook Docker's life came because he, over many years, stood up to Broughton. As well there was his dislike of the pomposity coming from the local magistrates, who were significantly powerful members of the congregation.[67]

A later memorial from his parishioners stated the 'high sense' of Docker's merits, and praised his 'kind and charitable disposition, evinced in promoting whatever may tend to the comfort of the poor and destitute'.[68]

One revealing point made by Docker himself

61. Old Inns at Windsor at the bottom of Baker Street, numbers 12 and 14 Macquarie Street, perhaps similar to the White Hart Inn in George Street. Ink and watercolour by P. Mulray, 1950. State Library of New South Wales, Sydney, online, record no. 35709.

was that all the early incumbents of St Matthew's had experienced difficult relationships with the magistrates of the Windsor Bench, and from the information Docker's parishioners told him, it was particularly William Cox and Archibald Bell who 'influenced the other magistrates'.[69]

Such an insight is interesting. Cartwright had requested a transfer just when he had his finances under control and his new church within reach; Cross had headed for a distant parish; and Smith remained for only one year. Joseph Docker stated forthrightly that:

> The conduct of Messrs Bell and Cox has been actuated by a hostile, persecuting, unchristian spirit. All the Clergymen who have preceded me at this station have been driven away by them. The Revd Mr Cartwright, the Revd Mr Cross and the Revd Mr Smith all received the same treatment, all shared same fate.[70]

It is hard to avoid the inference from the evidence in total that a loose connivance between the local civil powers and the Archdeacon, together with the Colonial Secretary, each for his own reasons, was opportunely and deliberately orchestrated against Joseph Docker. For Docker, wishing only to minister quietly to his parish and to help his parishioners, the whole situation developed in a way he could never have conceived, at the White Hart Inn in Windsor, where a now infamous dinner party had been hosted by the Windsor magistrates on 21 January 1833. The ensuing record of accusations and reprisals is recorded in a long series of surviving letters which reveal Windsor's community leaders sharing in normal human flaws.[71]

The magistrates, William Cox, Samuel North, Archibald Bell, William Cox jr and W. Richardson, with eleven other men, were at the inn, farewelling the military commander, Captain Chetwode. Cox and Bell were ex-military, and were conservative church parishioners, who held heightened views of their position in colonial society. Bell, for instance, revealed this overtly in his answer to Commissioner Bigge some years before.

Despite having been complicit in the deposition of Governor Bligh, Bell still held somewhat unreasonable expectations of power and complained: 'I have been at Government house in the uniform of my Corps where Mrs. Macquarie had passed me by without notice & has held out her hand to persons who had been convicts & who were present'.[72]

The dinner in Windsor had curious features from the outset. Docker was deliberately excluded from the farewell party dinner, which is odd as the Reverend Matthew Devenish Meares from Pitt Town and the Reverend John Cleland from Ebenezer Presbyterian chapel were invited. The sending for Docker just as the military-style toasts were beginning can only have been calculated to irritate, as was proposing a toast to the Reverend Mr Meares, the other Anglican minister in the district. The tradition of toasts at such gatherings involved downing an entire glass for each one of the very many toasts, and meant that everyone became rapidly affected by the alcohol, especially those like Docker who were not used to this military tradition. Judy McMillan commented on this when she published the letters for the first time, echoing the words of Captain Scarvell of the Veteran Company, at the time.[73]

The allegations of the magistrates are two-edged, for they do none of the participants credit. Docker admits he did become intoxicated, but that so too did Cox and Bell and the others. This is not an unusual occurrence, for alcohol was widely and excessively consumed in the colony, but the deliberate goading of Docker's increasing passions and feelings of grievances is obvious in the events related, until Docker was fuelled to tell a few home truths to the gathered company.[74]

William Cox sr decided that 'as heads of families' the magistrates were obliged to give the Archdeacon a report on the intoxication of Joseph Docker and his 'most intemperate and abusive' language, which allegedly included profane oaths.[75] Broughton asked Docker to stand down until he could complete an investigation.[76] Understandably, Docker's reply was tinged with 'surprise and astonishment' at his suspension without the immediate chance to reply, since Broughton was away in Tasmania. The fact he had not been given a copy of the accusations was protested by Docker, who made the point that he had not been any more intoxicated than the others at the dinner, referring to his belief that his accusers had 'all far exceeded the bounds of moderation'.[77]

Docker, wounded, continued:

> Have I not on all occasions ... supported ... [the colony's] various charitable and benevolent institutions? The Revd Mr Threlkeld's praiseworthy exertions for the conversion of the native blacks ... the Sydney and Hawkesbury Benevolent Societies ... the School of Industry ... for the last of which I procured a larger collection than had ever been obtained ... owing to the pains I took in visiting every house in the Parish.[78]

Docker's defence was strong, also including reference to the high standard he had achieved in the last four years conducting a private school at Windsor, an impossibility, he contended with plausibility, if he was a drunkard; not to mention his years of conscientious fund-raising, supporting those needing charity and the firm testimony of his visits to those in need and in gaol, to which his parishioners testified. Written proof of his worthiness was supplied with Docker's letter of reply: a letter from Captain Scarvell, the petition from parishioners who fully respected their minister, along with the support of a former magistrate, John Brabyn, who signed the petition. All was ignored in the face of Archdeacon Broughton's assessment of 'the heinousness of the offence'.[79]

Counter-claims by Docker alleged that William Cox himself had forgotten decency and decorum in his own actions that night at the inn, quarrelling with his brother-in-law, and using 'a very imperious tone', calling 'turn him out, turn him out': and actually ordered constables to remove his wife's relative. Docker referred to other instances recorded in documentary evidence whereby the good name of others had been injured by William Cox. In one letter to Broughton Docker referred to 'the mysterious and unaccountable suppression of the original charges'. Docker added that if he followed on from Bell's example, he:

> might ransack the private and public history of Mr Bell of Belmont ... I might refer to his interview with General Darling [the governor] who denounced his proceedings in the affair of Colonel Johnston[e], caused his dismissal from the office of Police Magistrate, designated the Windsor Magistrates as 'Banditti' and stigmatised the Windsor Bench as being one of the worst conducted in the Colony.[80]

There are instances in records separate to Docker's case where others did complain about the unjustness of the decisions handed down by the Windsor Bench. For instance, John Rush, a convict who was sentenced to seven years hard labour at Port Macquarie in 1823, maintained that he had been wrongly convicted to protect Bell's illegal practice of employing government clearing gangs for his personal advantage. Cox, too, had been accused of similar offences in evidence to Commissioner Bigge, although this never came before a court.[81] As with his dislike of the Corporation and Broughton, the animosity Docker generated with the local civil authority in his duties as rector had also been brewing for some time, probably over a plethora of small injustices, fuelled by the fact that the minister spoke out when he did not agree with magisterial process.

Quite innocently, the seventeen-year-old daughter of the Reverend John Cross gives proof of this. In a letter to her father, she shows that the idea to act against Docker had been festering prior to the fateful dinner.

Louisa Cross was on a visit to friends in Windsor early in January 1833 when she wrote to her father effusing that they had heard Mr Docker preach and that it had been a 'pleasure'. She commented, knowing it would be of interest to her father after his own difficulties with the same group:

> It is reported he is going to leave, the Magistrates cannot

agree with him. I know they have had fine work at Windsor, but I am not sure it is true, he is going to be removed, mind, that is only a report ...[82]

Docker's biographer points out tellingly that this letter was penned thirteen days before the date of the supposedly incriminating behaviour of Docker at the farewell dinner, proving that animosity was already simmering.[83]

By 1833 the distinction between the terms 'high' or 'low' church to describe the strictness of adherence or otherwise to the Church of England's prescribed worship was beginning to cut more clearly between the clergy, although the terms themselves were little used. A situation very different from what had previously been only a manageable difference between two views of policy within the church was being created. Those of evangelical bent disliked the terms, and they were never specifically used in the extensive evidence remaining of the later Docker letters, yet the distinction is there, unspoken and powerfully played out by the Archdeacon using his rank. Moreover, if Broughton's judgment seemed to be harsh and his supposition of guilt preconceived, it would lack procedural fairness, not just in Docker's case but in other disputes as well.[84] Broughton referred to 'such measures as would be necessary to vindicate religion and the Church from the discredit thrown upon them.'[85]

Broughton's response was driven by his zeal to maintain the authority of the Church. Moreover, the Archdeacon had returned to Docker his supporting evidence, including the petition. It is hard not to agree with Docker that the non-consideration of Docker's character witnesses, the decision to hold a private hearing where Docker was outnumbered by his accusers and the giving of the original complaint to Docker only after the appointed time of the hearing would have led to an unfair enquiry.[86]

In August 1833 Governor Bourke read the two initial letters and the stream of correspondence between Broughton, Docker and others that had followed over the next five months. Bourke had, however, determined to stay neutral, and like Macquarie saw the pitfalls of interfering in the Church's governance. Broughton knew this, which only points more strongly to the power that Colonial Secretary McLeay's deliberate manipulation of the governor's reply carried, as explained by McMillan. In conveying Bourke's reply to Docker, McLeay left out the governor's words insisting that 'his character would go with him', by which the governor had meant to prevent an ongoing slur on Docker's good name.[87]

Making an historical judgment on the true degree of seriousness in the charge made by the magistrates against Joseph Docker would be fraught, were it not for two telling pieces of independent information. The first was never given the weight it deserved, for no less than 56 of the parishioners signed a petition in support of Docker.

From later events in the Stiles period it is clear that at least some of these men who signed supported the concept of a parish where lay people had a greater say in the conduct of their church. The wishes of the 56 parishioners were totally disregarded, along with Docker's previous years of toil, all in the interests of 'good church governance'.

The petition contained very specific support for Docker, stating:

We the undersigned being respectable inhabitants of Windsor and Richmond and having had full opportunity of observing your life and conversation for a period of Four years and upwards, during which you have officiated as our respected Minister, feel it to be our duty publicly to avow the high opinion we entertain of your private as well as your public character and to assure you of your unalterable esteem for you as a man, a Christian and a Clergyman.

In this voluntarily acknowledging our high sense of your merits, and of your kind and charitable disposition, evinced in promoting whatever may tend to the comfort of the poor and destitute ... we offer an effectual antidote to the charges made against you, and even if they could be substantiated believing as we do that the occurrences ... have taken place at a moment of excitement when anyone, but more especially a man of your well-known retired habits might exceed the bounds of moderation, are of the opinion it would have been more creditable to all parties and more in accordance of the wishes of your parishioners if the affair had never been brought before the Public.

We cannot help flattering ourselves that the Venerable the Archdeacon ... will ... honourably acquit you.

The former magistrate John Brabyn, Captain

Scarvell of the Veteran Company, J.R. Rouse, government officials Richard Fitzgerald and George Loder, constable James Bullock and the well-known district identity and storekeeper, Thomas Tebbutt sr, were among the signatories to the petition, which included others at the heart of the community: several of the school-teachers, along with the millers, farmers, innkeepers and tradesmen of the districts.[88]

His Only Alternative: The Reverend Joseph Docker Resigns

Docker's resignation, though predictable in the circumstances, especially when he did not attend the hearing forced by Broughton, meant that Windsor was left without a resident minister. The duty on Sundays and baptisms from the end of March 1833 were shared by various clergymen: Samuel Marsden, Robert Forrest, William Yate, William Simpson and Robert Cartwright. Marriages and burials from April to August, and baptisms in August, within the parish were undertaken by Matthew Meares of Pitt Town.[89] All this time, Docker had been denied a copy of the original accusations.[90]

Finally the whole dispute, with recommendations by Broughton, had been referred to the Governor. Docker continued to maintain that if he 'had the misfortune to disagree with a small number of the leading men of my district, I have lived and still do in the esteem and affections of a great majority of my parishioners.'[91]

Such drama unfolding in Windsor had one more climacteric before it had completely run its course, and that took place, not in a pub, but in the church itself. By 28 July 1833, when he still had had no real consideration of his complaints and after he had deemed the supposed face-to-face meeting called to resolve the accusations as unfairly short notice for him to submit a case, Docker could take no more. He had decided to resume his Sunday duties to force the issue. He strode into the church and began the service, whereupon Cox and Bell and a few others left the church.

The high pulpit with its prayer or reading desk and clerk's desk, which had been part of the church since its consecration, became an element in the unfolding conclusion between Docker and the magistrates. In the lowest section of the high pulpit the parish clerk sat to lead the singing of the psalms, and above him sat the minister. The highest tier was the place where the sermon was delivered, a dominating and formidable space towering over the congregation below, representative of the moral power of the preacher. The military band probably reinforced the dramatic scene. Docker brought before the congregation his deep commitment to his parishioners.[92]

Those who attended church that 28 July 1833 saw a remarkable exchange between the two ministers Meares and Docker. When Docker informed Matthew Meares of his intention, the Pitt Town minister began to protest, in front of the congregation. What happened next is told by Docker in his clarification to the Archbishop:

> to avoid further discussion I proceeded to the reading desk for the purpose of performing divine service. Mr Meares followed me and again entered into a discussion which induced me before I commenced the services of the day to explain my conduct for the satisfaction of my hearers. Mr Cox, Mr Bell, and one or two more ... left the church. I then proceeded with the service without further interruption.[93]

Samuel North took up the story with appropriate righteous indignation:

> In consequence of my servant being rather later than usual with the carriage it was six minutes past eleven o'clock when I arrived ... at the church gate when I saw the principal part of the congregation coming out of church and on enquiring of the cause I was informed that Mr Docker had forcibly prevented Mr Meares from entering the Reading desk and acted in such a manner that all the respectable portion of the congregation left the church in disgust ... I think with the exception of myself, Captain Brabyn and the Military there were not three free persons remaining in the church.[94]

Docker throughout the entire saga had remained respectful to the Archdeacon, although his determination to argue the case and to justify his behaviour seemed to Broughton worthy of an admonition. The Archdeacon accused him in writing of 'adopting a tone which nearly borders on disrespect, and which I shall not permit to be continued.'[95] In his letter of resignation, Docker maintained politeness:

> I can easily conceive the disappointment which my refusal to comply with your repeated solicitations for my attendance at the Court House at Windsor on 30th ult. [30 July 1833] must have occasioned you. Whatever impressions have been made on your mind by the events of that or any antecedent day I beg leave to assure you, that as I never questioned the authority vested in you as Archdeacon, or the right you have to exercise it in the maintenance of order and discipline in the Church so I never meditated any opposition to it ... I now tender my resignation of my appointment as one of His Majesty's Chaplains provided you are of the opinion, upon a full and impartial consideration of my conduct, that my services could not henceforth be beneficially employed in another part of the Colony.

To the end, Docker was employing a polite irony, to show the Archdeacon and anyone else who read the letter, that he still believed Broughton had not given him a 'full and impartial consideration.'[96]

The preaching platform or reading desk, symbolic of power over the service, had originally, 'stood opposite the chancel [i.e., sanctuary], where it obstructed the view of the communion table.'[97] A century later, the *Windsor and Richmond Gazette* described the original pulpit:

62. The high pulpit, with reading desk and clerk's desk, and the box pews with doors in St James' Church, Sydney, in 1831. There is no comparable illustration of the initial interior of St Matthew's. Kenneth Cable and Rosemary Annable, *St James', 1824–1999*, Churchwardens of St James', Sydney, 1999, p.10.

> In the centre passage and opposite to the southern door was the old-fashioned three-decker pulpit, then quite the usual thing. Later on this pulpit was removed to another position in the church. It was abolished altogether in 1878.[98]

The Reverend Joseph Docker resigned on 1 August 1833. He had been an active minister, conducting 133 baptisms, around 70 marriages and 184 burials throughout the wider district of Windsor Parish, and was respected by his parishioners.[99] After he left the ministry of St Matthew's in 1833, Joseph Docker bought the Clifton property from John Brabyn, possibly the farm once lived on by his predecessor Robert Cartwright on the ridge land beyond Cornwallis, overlooking the church. Remaining at Clifton as a farmer for four years, Docker's next venture was a squatting run, Bontharambo on the Ovens River near Wangaratta in Victoria, where Docker's support to the Indigenous people included allowing corroborees to be held on his land.[100]

Two contemporary comments help to sum up this tumultuous episode in the history of St Matthew's. Captain Scarvell's compassion and unprejudiced actions to help Docker are striking, for he had no knowledge of any of the players in the Docker saga, since he was newly arrived to the district and lived in a retired manner. Scarvell, from a sense of fairness, had made enquiries of 'persons of respectability long resident in the neighbourhood' to allow him to hold an informed opinion. He took pleasure in telling Docker that:

> I have it from them that they never heard any individual speak of you but in the most respectful terms that they know you to be a man of most retired habits and that your general deportment was such as to deserve the respect and best wishes of all your Parishioners.[101]

Finally, the words of Joseph Docker himself, because by implicating his three predecessors at St Matthew's in his explanations, he was less likely to be improvising to suit his needs or to make excuses for his behaviour. In one of his more introspective moments and responding to his claim that

Cartwright, Cross and Smith had all 'been driven away by them [the Windsor magistrates]', Docker wrote:

> Is it enquired why a Clergyman cannot be on terms of friendship with these men [Cox and Bell]? The answer is at hand. He is generally, as all clergymen ought to be, honest and conscientious and therefore cannot at all times conceal his disapproval of their actions.[102]

63. View of part of Docker's parish from the upper window of the Rectory. Photograph by Chris Jones, rector of St Matthew's, 2016

5 A Life's Work

From Orphan School to Windsor

On Joseph Docker's resignation, the master of the Female Orphan School at Parramatta, Henry Tarlton Stiles, became the replacement minister. Stiles conducted his first duty as rector of St Matthew's on 25 August 1833 by presiding at Richmond at the burial of Samuel Craft, who had arrived on the Third Fleet.[1]

Stiles was aware of the perils of disagreeing with his archdeacon, after the very public resignation forced upon his predecessor, Joseph Docker. He adjusted to the 'high' forms of service favoured by the Anglican church in the colony at that time in his life at St Matthew's. More and more Stiles supported Archdeacon Broughton who, in turn, involved him in the broader church work, on the recommendation of influential citizens who were strongly conservative members of the faith, like Sir William Burton, one of the judges of the Supreme Court.[2]

Burton's major book, *The State of Religion and Education in New South Wales*, was published in England in 1840. It gave details of Stiles' ministry:

> The duties of the Rev. Mr. Stiles extended at the commencement of the year 1839, not only over the town and hundred of Windsor, but also over the adjoining town and hundred of Richmond, the Curryjong, which is in the County of Cook, and the Cornwallis, which is on the banks of the Hawkesbury, between the towns of Windsor and Richmond.[3]

According to Burton, around Kurrajong there were 'about eight hundred persons ... scattered up and down in the gullies of the Blue Mountains Range'. As Docker had found previously, it was, in Burton's words, 'a very wild and mountainous country'. An interesting light is cast on how fatiguing was the travel in a colonial minister's life, and just how important was the clergyman's horse, for Burton's book describes the poor state of the local roads and the unreliability of the punt at Windsor, which

64.The Reverend Henry Stiles, minister of St Matthew's, 1833–1867. J. Steele, *Early Days of Windsor*, original edition, Tyrrell's, Sydney, 1916, facing p. 88.

in 1840 'scarcely ever is used, so that the river must always be forded, which is just practicable, though far from agreeable'.[4]

Momentous Times

Stiles was an impressive and caring minister who served Windsor well throughout his 34-year incumbency. William Walker, a prominent local solicitor, who was keenly interested in ecclesiastical affairs, himself a Presbyterian, thought well of Stiles: 'a true specimen of an English gentleman and clergyman. He was a quiet, unobtrusive man, of cultured habits – a beautiful reader, and though not brilliant, a pleasing preacher'.[5]

Born in Bristol in 1808, the new minister had come to the pastoral care of the upper Hawkesbury district at the age of 25 years, younger than any of his predecessors. Early in his career in England he had had strong evangelical leanings and was a scholar, tutoring the children of Colonial Office staff. He had trained at the Church Missionary Society's college and accepted appointment as the master of the Female Orphan School in Parramatta before he left Britain on the understanding that he would be given a chaplaincy or a parish as soon as possible. His bride, Jane, came to the colony with him.[6]

The Stiles family had arrived in Windsor with their first baby in August 1833. The household grew till it consisted of eight children, although three of these died young. The eldest in the family was Henry (born in April 1833) along with sons George (1835), Charles (1839), Samuel Marsden (1840), William (1842), Clement (1847), and the two girls Mary Emma (1837) and Annie Jane (1849). Samuel had died at six months in May 1841, William died in December 1842, aged six weeks, and Annie died when she was just eight days old in 1849.[7]

65. The grave of William Cox in the south-western section of St Matthew's burial ground (left front). Cox died in 1837 and was buried by the Reverend Henry Stiles. Photograph by Ian Jack, 2016.

During the first five years of his ministry at St Matthew's, Stiles witnessed the greatest upheaval in the rhythms established for the district over 40 years, for not since the death of Andrew Thompson and the departure of Governor and Mrs Macquarie had the district's religious and civil organization been so altered. In both cases Henry Stiles was part of the history in the making.

The first occurrence was the death at the age of 72 of Magistrate William Cox sr at his new Windsor residence Fairfield. Cox was buried by Stiles on 20 March 1837 in St Matthew's cemetery in the vault with his first wife, Rebecca.[8] Stiles does not seem to have experienced the lack of cooperation hinted at by the previous ministers and their families with the magistrate, but Cox had been ill before his death and possibly not so active as in his earlier years when undertaking his renowned feat of building the road over the Blue Mountains and contributing more Hawkesbury buildings than any other contractor, very efficiently and profitably for his family. His control on the affairs of the district and the bench was lessening. On the other hand some had continued to complain of his self-interest, rather than professionalism, in dealings with them, and in his employment of the government resources at his disposal.[9]

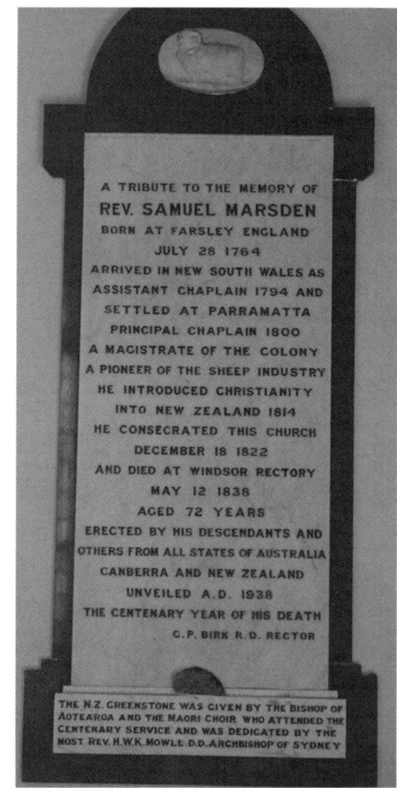

66. Memorial to the Reverend Samuel Marsden on the northern wall inside St Matthew's Church. Photograph by Chris Jones, rector of St Matthew's, 2016.

The second occurrence was the death the following year of the Reverend Samuel Marsden whilst on a personal visit to Stiles in Windsor. Marsden died in an upstairs room of the Rectory on 12 May 1838 having gone to the country to rest in his recent ill-health. Marsden's body was taken back to Parramatta and buried in St John's cemetery.[10]

Marsden, like Cox, was a complex character, who achieved much in his lifetime, but aroused controversy for many of the same reasons. William Cox was at times criticized, and Marsden more so, being branded by Commissioner Bigge as 'stamped with severity'. Both were officious and self-serving in their civil roles, and both Marsden and Cox had made the most of opportunities in the colony and, while contributing in return, had nonetheless hugely benefitted materialistically. On the other hand, there is evidence that in personal life they extended a gentler treatment to their families and their workers.[11]

Whatever history's final view of Marsden, he had contributed much to the religious life at Hawkesbury, particularly in the earlier years, and a memorial plaque hangs in the church, making particular mention of his outstanding missionary work over many years in New Zealand.

Parish Duties

Routine for Stiles and St Matthew's continued after the loss of two of the most powerful men in shaping the district. Before he had buried Cox, Stiles had said a service over the grave for a lowly prisoner, and ten days later officiated at the burial of four-year-old Sophia Wood at Windsor. The St Matthew's Register notes them all equally, continuing in the manner Macquarie had decreed.[12]

Around the time of William Cox's funeral St Matthew's was able to accommodate about 450 persons, although, according to Burton, the number attending normal service was usually closer to 320.[13] Each Sunday until 1842 Stiles conducted services at Richmond as well as at Windsor. On week-days he, like Docker, was busy. Burton lists his routine as: 'a full service at the schoolhouse, in the Curryjong ... every alternate Wednesday'. He remained responsible for the children attending Docker's school, and 'from this place, as the headquarters, he makes ... pastoral visits to the people round'.[14]

In Windsor, in addition to church services, Stiles conducted

> a service every fortnight at the Public Hospital, and another at a like interval in the Town Gaol, in both of which places he converses with the men individually Three schools were under his supervision at Windsor, Richmond and at Curryjong, where he regularly visits and examines the children.[15]

After the services had moved to their new, much awaited church site, the school in Windsor remained in the same building close to Thompson Square until 1841. Then another school building was constructed in Bridge Street, a little to the south-west between the former schoolhouse and the military barracks. The site is now occupied by the Federation-style home in Bridge Street built for the policeman George Boyd.[16]

Edward Quaife was its first teacher from 1841 until 1865. John Tebbutt, later a world-renowned astronomer and church warden at St Matthew's, was among the scholars, after having attended Stiles' own school.[17] Few records of the school remain but the photograph below shows its location just above the South Creek bridge.[18]

67. Location of the schoolhouse in Windsor between 1841 and *c.* 1870. The post and rail fence on the left marks the school grounds in Bridge Street. Photograph looking south-east towards the Sydney road entry into the town. Macquarie Street enters on the right below the two barns. Postcard Kerry & Co. from Macleay Museum, University of Sydney.

The Rector's Personal and Social Surrounds

Like the rectors before him, Stiles had government servants issued to him and employed others to help run the household. When the children were older, the Stiles family had taken into service a boy, aged between thirteen and fourteen years, the common age in Britain for rural youth to seek employment, but the arrangement did not prove satisfactory. Late in May 1862, the servant absconded, and Henry Stiles had the Windsor Bench issue a warrant for the apprehension of this short dark-haired boy with dark eyes, last seen wearing a brown Holland full shirt.[19]

On a visit to the Windsor Rectory in 1839 Jane Franklin, the wife of the governor of Tasmania, warmed to her hosts, describing them sketchily in her journal as:

> nice people – he quite clerical & clever looking, fine grey eyes – he preached the visitation sermon – his [wife] has pleasant & good & earnest countenance – Bishop spoke highly of her – said she had some talent but thought her now rather out of spirits – maid said she'd given her mattresses away to the poor or to servants going away – for first time I slept in the same bed as Sophy [Jane's companion], there being no second mattress, no sacking to bedstead, nor sofa.[20]

Lady Franklin seemed to be rather out-of-sorts generally as she and her companion, the Tasmanian governor's niece, Sophy, stayed at the Rectory on 19 June 1839 on her way to Wisemans Ferry, and she must have provided both interest and difficulties for Jane Stiles. From her diary entries, Jane Franklin appears to have very definite and negative views of the merits of country life in New South Wales at the time.[21] On the page in her diary relating to her Windsor visit she spoke of many aspects of the trip, and found almost everything wanting.

The weather was 'a misty damp drizzling day', the drive into town from the Cox property was through 'open, ugly, hard & fenced country' (that today we would call paddocks and scrub), Macquarie's 'great square' was an 'open space … very ugly', and having Mr North and Mr and Miss Betts to dinner she found 'heavy and fatiguing'. The church design too fared no better in Jane Franklin's opinion (see Chapter 3).

The struggle that Stiles, like the other rectors before him, was having financially to make ends meet is borne out in Franklin's sniffy appraisal of the Rectory, which was home to the family of six:

> The house they live in was built for clergyman with design of having school … Though the house is large, the rooms are scarcely furnished and miserable looking. Stiles could not accommodate our servants who went to public house.[22]

Church Duties

Generally the 1840s were extremely difficult for both Henry and Jane, with the death of three of their children, and Henry Stiles' increasing concentration on church doctrine caused friction with the parishioners over the form of the service. Like his predecessors at Windsor, Henry Stiles carried out many varied duties within the Hawkesbury community and the life of the parish went on, full of bitter-sweet contrasts. Only a month after the family buried son Samuel, Henry Stiles presided at a marriage between two families of schoolmasters in the district both of whom Stiles knew well. Margaret, daughter of Matthew Hughes, the teacher at Richmond, wed Edward Quaife of Windsor, by special licence.[23]

Over three decades, the minister saw two generations educated and marrying. He followed them through the births of their own children and buried them, their parents, their offspring. The Alcorn family is a good example. Richard Alcorn, a convict who arrived in 1803 with his wife, a free arrival, with their two children, Richard jr and Edward, had more children in New South Wales, before Stiles knew the family, and before Richard died in 1812. All had been known to the

68. Mrs Alcorn's house (marked 'f') on South Creek, sketched from Windsor looking south-east across to today's Mulgrave. Alcorn's entire farm and those of her neighbours can be seen submerged, not for the first time, almost to the roofline by the flood waters in 1816, four years after her husband died. Anonymous artist, 'Sketch of the Inundation in the neighbourhood of Windsor … 2 June 1816'. State Library of New South Wales, Mitchell Library, PX*D 264.

earlier ministers at the chapel and some may have attended school there.

In 1833 John Alcorn, the youngest son, and Mary Ann Cross were the first people whom Stiles married at St Matthew's. Their son John married Isabella Strachan there on 9 July 1857 and Stiles again officiated. Possibly the minister baptized their first son John two years later only to bury him later in the same year. Three years later another son was baptized with the name John.[24] The family had also been back in church with Stiles between 1838 and 1857 for the burial services of members of their wider family: 4½ year-old William Richard Alcorn, 3½ year-old Richard Alcorn and then John sr himself were laid to rest by Stiles.[25]

Stiles prepared the parish's first candidate for confirmation on 11 October 1836. The service was presided over by William Broughton,[26] as the first Bishop appointed in New South Wales.[27]

Broughton noted in his diary other confirmations at Windsor in 1844:

> *January* 6.—Held a Confirmation at St. Matthew's Church, Windsor: extremely well attended; and appearance of the candidates quite as satisfactory and pleasing as before described.
>
> *January* 7.—Attended morning service at Windsor; preached on the text, John vi. 50. Administered the Holy Sacrament, assisted by the Rev. H.T. Stiles. The table well attended; and by several confirmed yesterday. After service proceeded to Richmond; where the Rev. J.K. Walpole is stationed. Preached at St. Peter's; and held a Confirmation.[28]

Baptisms, funerals and weddings continued under Stiles. One marriage in particular, celebrated in February 1839, remains vivid for us today, although at the time the special day of Elen Ferguson and her groom, Joseph Suffolk who was a widowed English immigrant, was just one of fifteen conducted by Stiles that year. But 177 years later Elen's beautiful wedding dress has survived. Handed down from family member to family member to female descendants living in Canberra, it is now part of the Australian Dress Register. Elen and Joseph Suffolk had moved to the South Coast, where they farmed, cut cedar and raised six children.

The wedding dress that Elen wore as a twenty-year-old bride was a blue-green silk gown. It had been lovingly made by hand, as shown by the slight pucker and unevenness in the piping around the plunging waistline. The sleeves are narrow and have a band of ruffled blue silk and cord braiding on either side of the elbow. It has a central bone inserted in the bodice, and two diagonal pleats from sleeve to waist, with braid repeated round the neckline, and a full gathered skirt. It was lovingly cherished, and kept in its original form, not remodelled after going out of fashion. It is probably representative of many of the wedding dresses of the young women of the parish at that time and gives an enchanting glimpse into the world of a young Windsor girl on the day Henry Stiles married her.[29] Now faded to a grey-green, the much-loved dress nevertheless is also a powerful reminder of the minister's importance to each of his flock, and how Stiles participated in all his community's most important personal occasions.

Stiles had attended a public meeting held in the schoolhouse at Richmond in October 1835, with Samuel Marsden in the chair. Richmond had grown to comprise over 1,300 persons making the current chapel (also the schoolhouse) inadequate, as it was able to house only one hundred. Stiles seconded the motion of William Cox sr that a church should be erected in Richmond 'on the ground ... originally set apart for that purpose'. Stiles was to be on the Committee, and in the way of all progress, subscriptions were no longer sought door to door as Docker and the other ministers had painstakingly been constrained to do, but lists were to be drawn up 'at the several Banks' along with the usual media appeal. Here again progress had ensured that not just one newspaper but four newspapers existed by 1835, and were employed to advertise the appeal. Stiles gave the considerable amount of £10 and St Peter's Richmond was consecrated in 1841.[30]

Wider Interests

Henry Stiles served the Anglican Church in a much more general and varied manner than the rectors of St Matthew's before him, whilst at the same time keeping up the parish business.

A firm friend of Samuel Marsden, Stiles went on two short missions to Norfolk Island for him in

1834 and 1835–1836, after being suggested by Mr Justice Burton and requested by Governor Bourke in a letter dated 21 August 1834. Burton had just been to Norfolk Island and had sentenced thirteen prisoners to death, and it was thought that Stiles' ministering might ease the men's last hours, while later he would conduct the burials of the six Protestant convicts. The Roman Catholic priest, Dr Ullathorne, was sent also to minister to the other condemned men. Stiles' short visits to the island allowed him to conduct ten baptisms there. On his return to Windsor Stiles recorded both these burials and births in the St Matthew's Register.[31] In his absences, Jane had tended the Rectory and looked after the children, while pastoral duties were carried out by Thomas Hassall, Robert Forrest, Robert Cartwright, Matthew Meares and Samuel Marsden.

Governor Bourke's words to Stiles in 1834 seem to sum up the minister's life: 'I know well your disposition to do good whenever an opportunity offers'.[32]

This simple statement probably does much to explain a request passed on by Bishop Broughton in January 1840 from William Cox's son, George, regarding a female Aboriginal woman from Mudgee whom one of his employees sought to marry. Bishop Broughton wondered if there was anywhere in or near Windsor where she could stay to be tutored by Stiles in the necessary preparation for baptism before the marriage. Although Stiles' answer to this new challenge is unknown, the episcopal plea reflects his standing within his church community.[33]

Henry Stiles involved himself in wider causes willingly. In 1835 he wrote with evidence to the Commission on Transportation, to plead for reform of the penal system. Later he was a member of the committee set up to oppose the formation of National schools. In 1843 eighteen questions were posed to each of the clergy in New South Wales 'upon the condition of the Aborigines and the best means of promoting their welfare'. Stiles' reply was outstandingly sympathetic to the plight of the '*two* [Aboriginal] men in Windsor, *three* in Richmond, and *five* in Curryjong' remaining from the original inhabitants of the area. He indicated that these survivors were forced to live by begging from the settlers, 'who are generally kind to them indeed', and that he had had no opportunity of learning more about the Aboriginal race.[34]

69. A surviving wedding dress, now on the Australian Dress Register, was worn in February 1839 by Elen Ferguson when she wed Joseph Suffolk in St Matthew's Church. Photograph supplied by Kathleen Cobcroft, Canberra, now on Australian Dress Register.

Stiles had gradually come to support openly the revival of conservative church principles of worship espoused by Bishop Broughton, following the Oxford Movement which sought to return greater emphasis on ceremony and ritual. This meant the opportunities available for participation by Stiles' congregation were lessened, alienating him from many of his parishioners who still worshipped according to the missionaries' legacy of lay involvement.[35]

Stiles had not in general been ill-disposed to other reformed denominations. In his funeral sermon for Samuel Marsden in 1838 he compared the Principal Chaplain to Martin Luther and John Knox as well as to Thomas Cranmer. He praised Marsden for having 'no narrow and sectarian mind' and, like Marsden, supported the London Missionary Society, although he came to the view that it was 'in hands, for the most part, of dissenters from the English Church'.[36]

With Marsden dead, and his bishop pushing for change, Stiles adopted the 'high revival' doctrine and railed strongly from the pulpit against Methodism, which had a solid following at Hawkesbury. He complained about the way the Wesleyan Methodists went about inaugurating their new chapel in Macquarie Street, Windsor. The new Methodist preacher at Windsor, the Reverend Samuel Wilkinson, had arrived in mid-1838 and had been quick to denounce Windsor as 'this ungodly town'.

The old Wesleyan chapel, built in 1818–19, had outlived its usefulness, and the foundation stone of its replacement was laid in October 1838.[37] As the completion date approached late in 1839, invitations to the opening were sent out 'not only to Methodists but also to members of the Church of England'. Anglican ministers were not allowed to attend the services of other denominations, but there was no such constraint on ordinary members of the Anglican congregation. Nonetheless, while professing 'no animosity to the [Methodist] body or to individuals', Stiles felt strongly that Wesleyans 'have separated, and are now separating, to all appearance more widely than ever, from the Church of England' and on 1 December 1839 he delivered a vigorous sermon at St Matthew's, declaring that Anglicans should not have been invited to 'a schismatic church'.[38]

Stiles preached that day to 'a large and mixed congregation – mixed as regards strangers and regular attendants'.[39] Despite this thundering sermon, the inauguration of the Wesleyan chapel two days later was attended by a 'large and respectable' congregation, 'among whom [the Methodist clergy] observed many of the members and hearers of the Church of England'.[40] A group of leading Methodists called on Stiles at his rectory the following day to discuss his sermon, part of which Stiles read out to them.

The Methodists found the tone of the sermon 'much more severe than had been reported'.[41] Undeterred, Stiles proceeded to publish his sermon early in 1840. This in turn provoked a 22-page printed riposte from a highly articulate local, calling himself 'A Friend to Truth and Peace', who wrote more in sorrow than in anger. He addressed Stiles directly:

> Will you bear with me, if I tell you an unpleasant truth? You have created a prejudice against you in Windsor, that I fear you will never be able to remove. Your talents for usefulness will be, to a large extent, buried. And many of those, to whom you have hitherto been an angel of mercy, will look upon you with suspicion, coldness, and indifference. This will weigh down your spirits and distress your heart. You will become, in fact, an unhappy man.

The anonymous letter advised Stiles to leave Windsor, but not Australia, conceding: 'You have much work to do in this wicked Colony, and we cannot dispense with your labours. But elsewhere learn, from the things you will suffer, never to begin such strife as you have done in Windsor'.[42]

Eventually theological disputes seemed to lose their appeal for Stiles, and five years after his altercation with the Methodists he delivered a very differently worded sermon from the high pulpit to welcome the Oddfellows to their first Windsor lodge. On 18 April 1845, a fortnight after the inauguration of the benevolent association, towards the end of his substantial sermon, Stiles spoke directly to the lodge-members:

> [Christ's] love to you requires you to love your fellow men. Admitting this, whether you belonged to your Brotherhood or not, you would still be bound to fulfil the law of Christian kindliness. May the establishment of your Lodge in this town be the means of uniting together in a bond of peace men differing in many points, and too frequently allowing such difference to interfere with the high duty, incumbent upon all, of living in unity and mutual forbearance.[43]

A quietly spoken man, Stiles nonetheless continued to be able to arouse opposition amongst the Low Church members of his congregation when he felt strongly enough. Introducing Chope's *Hymnal*, on 2 October 1864, in place of the Metrical Psalms of Tate and Brady, provoked a meeting of parishioners in May 1865.[44] A signed petition in opposition by 41 men of the congregation (fewer than Docker's supporters in 1833) led to the Metrical Psalms being reinstated by the Bishop. John Tebbutt, the astronomer, was the most articulate of those opposed to Chope's *Hymnal*.[45]

Tebbutt had been a pupil of Stiles from 1845 to 1849, but in adulthood found himself opposed to the minister.[46] For many years Tebbutt was the honorary secretary and treasurer of the St Matthew's Parochial Association, which had been formed in 1856. At first the society raised almost £1,000 for Sydney-wide church activities since it was connected with the Sydney Church Society, although after the conflict with Stiles and Garnsey their proceeds diminished. Other members were locals Richard Dunstan, Samuel Edgerton, John Dawson and James Ascough.[47]

Upgrading of St Matthew's Gets Under Way

St Matthew's Church building was a crucial centre to all the pastoral work, and remained a continuing focus for Stiles for the rest of his life. The local load on Stiles marginally lessened when Richmond was formed into a separate parish, after St Peter's Church was built in 1841. The first resident clergyman at Richmond was the Reverend A.W. Wallis, appointed in 1842.[48] It may be no coincidence that refurbishment at St Matthew's began in earnest when Stiles was relieved of much of his arduous travel in the greater Richmond area and had more time to concentrate on his physical surroundings nearer home.

Initially there was no music at church services. Macquarie was not alone in feeling that parishioners were there to hear the word of the Lord. The organ of which Docker had dreamed had not eventuated before he resigned, and no musical instrument was installed in the church before 1840. Instead the 'magnificent band' of the 80th Foot Regiment, which was first stationed at Windsor in 1838, marched to the church every Sunday and sat in the back three rows of the centre block of pews, accompanying the hymns. The bandmaster was Samuel Edgerton, a long serving member of the regiment and church. It is likely that earlier regiments had also supplied band music.[49] The regiment had left Windsor in 1845, but in 1916 James Steele reported that in 'the three back centre pews ... [a] portion of the old music stands may still be seen', and they apparently survived until 1963 when the cedar pews were sanded back or removed.[50]

In 1840 Stiles presided over the installation of a pipe organ at the cost of £320. This celebrated two-manual instrument, still in use today, had been made in England and was reassembled in the colony by the recently established Sydney firm of Johnson and Kinloch. William Johnson, who emigrated in 1836, had married the daughter of the poet Charles Tompson in St Matthew's in July 1838. The new organ was shown off in Sydney in 1840 prior to its installation at Windsor and was advertised, a shade misleadingly, as 'the first specimen of organ building in the colony'.[51]

70. 'Richmond looking West' depicts the main street, looking towards St Peter's church. Artist F.C. Terry, published in *Landscape Scenery, Illustrating Sydney, Paramatta, Richmond, Maitland, Windsor and Port Jackson, New South Wales*, also known as *Australian Keepsake*, Sands and Kenny, Sydney and Melbourne, 1855, plate 38. Original steel engraving by Arthur Willmore, second impression, courtesy Royal Australian Historical Society.

A gallery was built to accommodate the instrument and the choir at the west end of the church.[52] It was criticized for providing insufficient spaciousness for the instrument: a correspondent to the *Sydney Morning Herald* at the time complained that:

> When the Church at Windsor was laid out, an organ was not contemplated, and, as a consequence, there is not proper height in the gallery, and the instrument has necessarily been squatted down to suit its place. ... But deficient height was not the only obstacle this instrument had to contend with: the contract [price] had been taken too low to allow of the best remedies for confined space being exhibited, and ... the bass of the instrument has suffered miserably in consequence. The larger pipes (and they are truly noble ones) which have necessarily been ranged at the sides below the wind chest, for want of height above it, being fed from this, in the old fashion, by conveyances, instead of being furnished with the more modern improvements of a separate wind chest to themselves, (this, with the necessary additional mechanism, might have cost an extra £20). Although these pipes speak well, yet they actually do not give out nearly the quality of tone, nor above one-fourth of the power, which, from their fine proportion and very liberal size, they are calculated and intended to produce.[53]

Nonetheless, the installation of the fine two-manual organ in 1840 gave St Matthew's real distinction and over the next 175 years the capacity for mounting a significant organ recital has been a recurrent source both of pride and revenue.

The organ's arrival was part of a larger reorganization by Stiles, whereby the pews were rearranged around the same time. Although 59 pews are shown in Standish Harris' plan of 1824, in his accompanying census of the contents of the church Harris identified only seventeen pews, valued at £5 each and one 'large pew' valued at £10. The pews had been made of 'very good quality' cedar, but in Harris' view were 'miserably executed'.[54]

One of the ways the church was able to raise funds was by pew rental. The *Sydney Gazette* had carried an advertisement in 1824:

> St. Matthew's Church, Windsor.- Persons desirous of renting pews or seats in this church are desired to make applications to the Chaplain in writing, stating the quantity of accommodation that may be required and where situated, that the same may be delivered to the committee for their inspection.[55]

The pews were high walled, box-like structures which enveloped the occupants. The main seating in the church was apportioned to those who rented. Those pews in the main nave in 1840 were reduced in number so that there were 47 pews downstairs (instead of the original 59), facing the communion table at the east end, still arranged along two aisles. The eight large pews at the east end along the north and south walls (2–5, 33–36) were the most desirable and expensive, costing £5 a year in 1841; the fourteen central pews cost £4 and the 'single' pews, the narrow ones at the west end (6–17, 37–47) cost £3.

Three rows of new pews capable of seating 50 people were also installed in the organ gallery: the front row cost £4 a year, the middle row £3 and the back row £2 10s.[56]

The large square pews right at the east end of the nave, numbers 1 and 32, were presumably reserved for the clergyman's family and for the churchwardens or distinguished visitors.

This is in contrast with the earlier arrangement,

71. The organ gallery built to house the organ and choir in 1840 in the western end of the church. In 1896 the organ was moved to the front of the church and the gallery used as seating. Photograph by Geoff Roberts, 2014.

where in 1830 William Cox sr, the powerful magistrate who had supplied the bricks, occupied pew 1 on the south side. The adjacent pews on the south side were held in 1830 by the influential John Brabyn, Archibald Bell and James Hale, while Richard Fitzgerald was on the north side. The pew status was an important physical manifestation of rank in society.

Cox's son, William jr of Hobartville near Richmond, with his family, rented pew number 1 on the north. The Cox servants had pew 5 and six other pews were also rented. It is not possible to marry all the pew numbers given in 1830 with the plan drawn by Standish Harris six years earlier.[57]

The Wardens' Accounts show that in June 1840 Peter Adamson was paid for 'removing pulpit' as well as other 'alterations in the interior of the church', presumably including the reordering of the pews.[58] Adamson also made the wooden font which sat among the pews until 1845 when it was made 'more conspicuous' in some unspecified way.[59]

It is uncommonly useful that a plan of the interior of the church survives from this period, sketched on the back inside cover of the Wardens' Accounts. Although the plan shows the disposition of pews as they were rearranged in 1840, it cannot be earlier than 1845 because of the presence of the stone baptismal font, which was installed late that year.[60] The plan cannot be later than 1857 because of the relocation of the pulpit and the changes in the pews in 1858 discussed later.

The plan can, therefore, be dated to between 1845 and 1857. It shows that in 1840 the high pulpit had been moved, along with its curving stairs and two lower desks, to a position on the north wall directly opposite the entry door. 'Interior doors' (possibly between the tower and the nave) were erected at this time but are not shown on the plan.[61]

The communion table was in the apsidal sanctuary, the pulpit in the nave. It was only after pews were removed from the east end of the nave, at the time the pulpit was moved in 1858, that the present chancel might be deemed to have been created, incorporating both the apse and the eastern nave. This chancel area was not differentiated architecturally for another century, because it shared the nave's stone flagging and its ceiling. The seven stained-glass windows straddled the two areas. It was not until 1958 that the chancel area within the original nave was marked out by a tiled floor, while the abbreviated nave remained stone-flagged.

72. High walled, box-like pews somewhat similar to those cedar pews which were in St Matthew's originally. The illustration is of a pew in St Beuno's Church, Culbone, Somerset, England. http://www.britainexpress.com/attractions.htm?attraction=2391, accessed 16 March 2016.

Late in 1845 Stiles acquired the present stone octagonal baptismal font from Mulgoa and had it lined with lead. The font was placed in its present position, in the midst of the nave, between the entry door and the pulpit, superseding the wooden font.[62]

The link between Windsor and Mulgoa was presumably the Cox family, who held extensive properties in Mulgoa Valley by the 1830s. The land for St Thomas' Anglican church at Mulgoa was donated by the Coxes and the stone for that church was quarried on Edward Cox's Fernhill between 1836 and 1838. William Cox sr had organized the acquisition of the Mulgoa properties in the names of his sons.

The stone font now in St Matthew's was either newly made in a Mulgoa quarry, probably at Fernhill, or it was an existing font donated by St Thomas' in 1845.[63] Since the old font at St Thomas' is wooden, replaced only in recent times by a marble and sandstone font formerly at Greendale church,[64] it seems likely that the St Matthew's

73. The arrangement of the pews in St Matthew's Church before 1840, drawn in 1824 by Standish Harris. Of the two large pews flanking the pulpit at the east end, that marked 1S was occupied by William Cox, the magistrate in 1830, pew 1N by his son, William Cox of Hobartville. The high pulpit is at the east end of what is now the chancel, and the pews are shown as boxes on the plan. The outline of the south porch, built in 1857–1858, has been added in later pencil. North is to the left. Redrawn from Morton Herman, *The Early Australian Architects and Their Work,* Angus & Robertson, Sydney, 1954, after 104; Steele, *Early Days of Windsor*, p. 82.

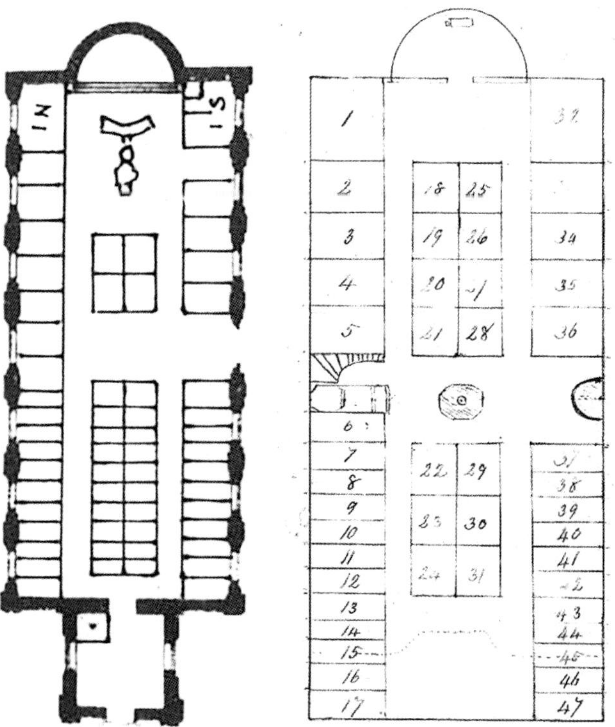

74. The interior layout of St Matthew's between 1845 and 1857. The dotted line shows the front of the organ gallery. The other features are the communion table in the sanctuary, which is separated from the nave by a step; the pulpit now on the north wall of the nave (on the left side of the plan); and the stone font of 1845 in the middle of the nave, opposite the south door, the only door shown. North is to the left. Wardens' Accounts, 1837–1882, inside back cover.

stone font was a gift from the Cox family which went unrecorded: the only cost to the church was the cartage from Mulgoa.[65]

Attention to the Exterior Begins

Over time, once Bishop Broughton had died in 1853 and the new bishop, Frederic Barker, had arrived, Stiles found himself increasingly isolated doctrinally. Bishop Barker came to New South Wales, a graduate of Cambridge full of missionary zeal. Although not reformist, he was firmly convinced that a less traditional form of service was the answer for the colony. He pushed for many new ministers of like beliefs to come to the colony, added graduates of the new Moore Theological College in Liverpool and found allies amongst the older Calvinist Evangelicals to balance the metropolitan clergy, who were almost all High Church. Stiles was out of step with the new bishop and, marginalized within his own church community, began to concentrate on the exterior fabric of his parish church.[66]

His first renewed energies went into achieving the orb and cross mooted for the dome from at least the 1830s.[67] In 1844 Stiles supervised their construction and erection atop the church tower. On 23 July 1844 George Panton, a local merchant and parishioner, had donated £14 10s. specifically 'for Ball and Cross on Steeple': six days later, he was appointed the Rector's Warden. Although no expenditure is itemized for the purpose of making and erecting the cross and orb, it is likely that the various sums paid that year to one of the James Atkinsons, father or son, covered the cost of hoisting the cross.[68]

The model is said to have been similar to the cross on the dome of St Paul's in London.[69] The orb and cross have been a defining feature of St Matthew's ever since, although the cross had to be replaced in 1963. The cross was used as the government trigonometrical survey mark for the Windsor district.[70]

In 1855 an iconic view of the church with its embellished tower was published. Frederic Terry's steel engraving is the only surviving detailed image of the church before the next suite of changes which took place in 1857.

Setting up his easel in the south-east corner of the churchyard, Terry captured the Windsor church at a critical time, just before the south porch was added in 1857 and the shingle roof was replaced with slate in 1858. The moonlit scene is atmospheric. A well-dressed couple stand to the right of the simple path to the south door. There is no sign of the elaborate oval driveway to the church door shown in maps of the previous decade. The six windows and the doorway on the south side of the nave are elongated and narrow, the belfry similarly slimmed in bulk, by artistic licence.

Terry did not sketch a precise topographical view of all the building details. But the two stone steps into the main doorway, introduced in 1834, are clearly articulated. This earliest southern entry had remained temporary and somewhat difficult. Today the porch leads straight into the nave without any step. However, the single stone at the threshold of the western external door into the porch, though now obscured by later paving, may be one of the steps put in place in 1834 at the southern entry and which were removed in the twentieth century.

In 1834 the new rector, Henry Stiles, had complained that two feet (61 cm.) was 'a most inconvenient height for some persons to ascend or descend as one step' and he engaged James Hunter to construct two stone steps 'on each side' at a cost of £4 10s.[71] The second set of steps was presumably at the tower door on the west end.

In 1854, Stiles and the wardens asked a local builder, Matthew Sharpe, to inspect the shingled roof of the church and report whether the roof-beams were 'sufficiently strong to bear the weight of slates'. At the same time Sharpe was commissioned to advise on the condition of the tower and the sanctuary dome.[72] Sharpe reported back early in 1855 and was paid £3 8s.[73]

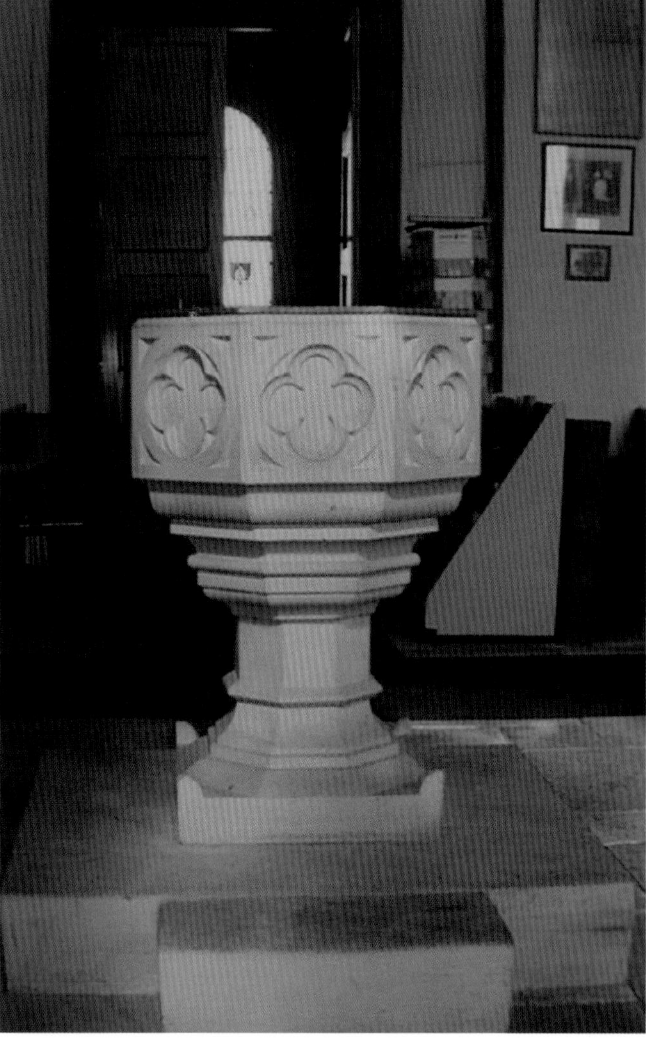

75. The stone font brought from Mulgoa in 1845, caught with colour reflections from the stained glass. Photograph by Ian Jack, 2009.

As a result of Sharpe's report, the Vestry Meeting decided to remove the shingles on the church roof and replace them with slate, while at the same time repairing the tower.[74] In April 1855, Edmund Blacket, the architect of the University of Sydney and formerly Colonial Architect, was invited to undertake the superintendence of slating the roof, while a Richmond builder called Long was asked to inspect the tower and its turrets, particularly estimating the amount of lead which would be required.[75] Long declined the contract and Blacket agreed in May to superintend the work on the tower as well as the roof. Blacket visited St Matthew's in mid-May and reported that the ceiling of the church was 'in a dangerous condition', urging urgent work. The wardens asked Blacket to give an estimate for a wooden ceiling to replace the damaged plaster one.[76]

The church officers moved very decisively. A contractor, William Hudson, was employed under Blacket to rebuild the ceiling for £350 and he began work on 5 November 1855. Later that month Hudson's proposal to repair the turret with lead for £110 was also accepted. After an inspection by Blacket in December, Hudson completed the repairs to the tower early in January 1856. Stiles kept a keen interest in all these changes to the fabric and he wrote informative notes about developments in the minute-book in addition to the formal minutes.[77] The wooden ceiling is that still in use, although the present colour scheme was chosen in 1958.

76. The cross and orb added to the church in 1844. Both were replaced in 1963. Photograph by Chris Jones, rector of St Matthew's, 2016.

Because of these additional expenses, the shingled roof was given a reprieve and was repaired late in 1855, with a ridge-capping of the new and trendy corrugated iron, costing over £9.[78]

The first work that changed the exterior after Terry's drawing was published was to add the porch which had been foreshadowed from the church's inception. Greenway had laid the foundations for a porch around 1819.[79] The porch was intended to shade the entry in the middle of the south side of the church, and without it the main door opened directly onto the forecourt.

A sketch of the long-awaited porch on the Greenway foundations prepared by Weaver and Kemp was approved by the Vestry Meeting at Easter 1857. James Atkinson jr, a prominent builder in the Hawkesbury–Nepean area, tendered successfully in September and completed the work for £143 on 18 January 1858. The cost was more than covered by subscriptions from fifteen of the congregation amounting to £212 10s. £100 of this was given by Robert Fitzgerald, the wealthy pastoralist and son of the prominent citizen, Richard. Robert used his father's Macquarie Arms in Thompson Square as his stately country residence. Another £50 came from 'the late Miss Roxburgh', a member of a newly arrived Hawkesbury family.[80]

The impulse for these two large donations seems to have been the death of Fitzgerald's daughter in a fall from a horse and the death of Captain Roxburgh's daughter, Catherine, at the age of 24 in October 1853.[81] Stiles had presided at the funerals of both Louisa Fitzgerald and Catherine Roxburgh.

Rather surprisingly, the new porch was built over Macquarie's wall-plaque, with the connivance of Stiles, who disliked 'placards'. The large marble plaque, bearing the royal arms and GR (for George IV), with the governor's name and the date 1820, was revealed again only when the porch was dismantled before reconstruction in 1919. It had been protected by plaster in 1858, and since 1919 it has been restored to public view on the south pediment of the rebuilt porch.[82]

Once the porch was completed, repairs to the roof and ceiling became pressing, although money had to be borrowed to finance the extensive works. James Atkinson jr again was successful and the contract was signed in April 1858. Blacket was no longer involved. Instead William Kemp, formerly in Blacket's firm, now of Weaver and Kemp, who had already been advising the church over its pew

77. The threshold stone at the western door into the porch, possibly one of the two stones placed at the southern door of the church in 1834. Photograph by Ian Jack, 2009.

arrangements and was the designer of the new porch, was the supervising architect. Kemp is best remembered today for his work as the New South Wales schools' architect from 1880 to 1896, the designer of Sydney Technical College and the old Museum of Applied Arts and Sciences in Pyrmont in 1891 and 1892.[83] It was Kemp who signed off on Atkinson's work on the new slate roof in June 1858. Atkinson had also boarded the eaves of the church roof with pineboard for an additional £62. His final bill in 1858 came to £681 15s., while his father did some minor repairs in the belfry.[84]

In June 1858 the wardens also commissioned John Adams to 'paint' the church ceiling erected by Blacket and to 'colour' the walls to specifications drawn up by Kemp. These specifications are not available. This cost a further £110 8s. 6d. between July and September, as well as architect's fees totalling £38.[85] All this indicates that the fabric of the wooden painted ceiling was the work of Blacket, but its original colour scheme was chosen by Kemp. Kemp's choice does not survive and the present colours were chosen by Professor Leslie Wilkinson in 1958.

Meanwhile, also in 1858, the pews and other church furniture were being drastically rearranged to a plan devised by Kemp three years previously. The pulpit, which had since 1840 been in the centre of the north wall, directly opposite the main entrance, along with the reading-desk and clerk's desk, was moved to the south-east corner, where pew 32 had formerly been located, closer to the communion table in the sanctuary. The old high-backed pews were either cut down or replaced and their doors were removed. Whereas there had been only 47 pews downstairs, after 1858 there were at least 85. Pews against the north or south walls commanded an annual rent of £3: the central pews were only £2.

The Bishop had decreed that one sixth of all the seating should be free. As a result, the entire seating in the gallery was free, as were five pews numbered 72 to 75 and 85, probably under the gallery.[86]

This flurry of renovation over the late 1850s left the church in debt to one of the parishioners, Robert Dunston, to the tune of £400 in 1860 and priority was given to the annual payment of 8% interest and the gradual reduction of the capital sum before further improvements were contemplated. The debt and interest were not fully repaid until 1862.[87]

An Ailing Minister's Final Act of Generosity

St Matthew's church and its rectory lay above the great floods of the 1850s and 1860s. These floods caused widespread distress. In the 1864 inundation, walls of houses in Bridge Street, Windsor,

78. The two stone steps at the south door of the church installed in 1834. Detail of artist F.C. Terry, published in *Landscape Scenery, Illustrating Sydney, Paramatta, Richmond, Maitland, Windsor and Port Jackson, New South Wales,* also known as *Australian Keepsake,* Sands and Kenny, Sydney and Melbourne, 1855, plate 30. Original steel engraving by Arthur Willmore, second impression, courtesy Royal Australian Historical Society.

79. Dress of the late 1850s and early 1860s, around the time Terry was painting St Matthew's Church. The fashions of the St Matthew's parishioners were similar but less ornate, more everyday versions worn with bonnets. Vintage Victorian, Massachusetts, atQuery@VintageVictorian.com, accessed 27 April 2016.

80. Artist Frederic C. Terry's famous view of St Matthew's taken from the south-east, published in *Landscape Scenery, Illustrating Sydney, Paramatta, Richmond, Maitland, Windsor and Port Jackson, New South Wales,* also known as *Australian Keepsake,* Sands and Kenny, Sydney and Melbourne, 1855, plate 30. Original steel engraving by Arthur Willmore, second impression, courtesy Royal Australian Historical Society.

had given way, and a house near them had been washed away. Bridge Street itself was choked by 'broken furniture, hay, pumpkins, household and farming effects' and reports of 60 destitute people stuck in the upper part of a lowland barn in Richmond brought prompt rescue. The earthwork preparations for the railway sank. The parsonage at Pitt Town had four feet of water inside it.

People and animals were seen floating perilously downriver on haystacks.

The clergy of the district were engaged in helping the Benevolent Society give rations to all in need. At 15.05 metres, it was the highest flood to that time experienced along the Hawkesbury River since settlement, and a month later there was another only marginally less destructive flood. Several families who had lost their homes were taken in by Henry and Jane Stiles and lived for a while in the rectory.[88]

The district was in a state of shock. The *Sydney Morning Herald* gave special mention to the efforts of the Reverend Charles Garnsey (Stiles' assistant), Samuel Edgerton, and others.[89]

By 1867 the Windsor district was producing over 20,000 bushels of wheat, over 315,000 bushels of maize and 16,000 bushels of other grains, as well as potatoes and grapes. Around 26,000 stock of various sorts grazed on the farms and commons. The population was close to 10,000 people, so the losses were catastrophic.[90]

None of the horror of 1864, however, prepared either the family at the parsonage or the rest of the population in the various districts along the Hawkesbury River for what was to happen just three years later.

In 1867 the river rose to an unimaginable four and a half metres above that of June 1864, reaching a height of 19.68 metres above normal river level at Windsor. The district became a series of small islands within a sea of churning water. Three churches were destroyed, and the enormous body of water rushing downstream continued relentlessly. Along the Wilberforce–Freemans Reach side of the river only eight dwellings were

81. The 1820 plaque now exhibited on the pediment of the 1857–1858 porch as rebuilt in 1919. Photograph by Chris Jones, rector of St Matthew's, 2016.

reportedly left standing. People had to be rescued from their roofs.[91]

It was estimated that 100 houses in Windsor were extensively damaged, and the correspondent movingly described what he saw for the farmers around him

> returning ... to the spot where a few days before it [his house] stood, to find his stock all destroyed ... slimy mud, or stagnant water, all around him; no food, no fuel, no clothing, not even a bed to lie on; unable to commence the necessary work on his land. The feeling of bitter anguish expressed – not in words but in the blank look of utter despair – would move the most hardened.[92]

The list of persons driven from their homes in Windsor and its immediate surrounds numbered 200,[93] and twelve people died, including ten children.[94] Many years later one of the survivors, a Miss Templeton (later Mrs Neilson), remembered fondly how St Matthew's had been made available to survivors. She had been rescued from a swamped butcher shop.[95]

Samuel Edgerton, John Tebbutt, one of the Norths, George Harpur, Edward Quaife, a Doyle, and their families were amongst those displaced in Windsor – all names familiar to the Stiles family. The *Windsor and Richmond Gazette*, in an article taken from the *Sydney Mail*, recorded:

> The School of Arts is crowded, with houseless sufferers, so too are the Court House, the Anglican, the Roman Catholic and the Wesleyan churches. Nothing can exceed the, hospitality – shown by the inhabitants – whose houses are above the flood line towards their less fortunate townsfolk. They have been up night and day during the latter part of the week and have spared no trouble or expense to rescue the endangered and to mitigate their sufferings. Though worn out by anxiety, fatigue and exposure; their generous sympathy is not repressed, and they are now relieving the necessities of the more wretched as best they can ... At a place at Pitt Town there are thirty-five children in [the] charge of one lady. Other houses are crowded, in similar proportion ... The only bake-house left is that of Mr: Moses [at the corner of George and Bridge Streets].[96]

82. 1867 flood illustration. *Illustrated Sydney News,* 16 July 1867, State Library of New South Wales.

Fairfield, previously the second home of William Cox, where Stiles' son-in-law Charles Garnsey had been running a school since 1865, was out of flood reach, close to the church to its south-west. During the 1867 flood, the Garnseys took in many people.[97]

In the time of direst need by their community, the Stiles family was also drawn into personal mourning. Henry Stiles had suffered increasing ill-health in 1866 and 1867 and could not be actively involved in caring for those sheltering in his church, but his last act, on his deathbed in June 1867, had been to order the doors of St Matthew's to be flung wide to give sanctuary to all who were fleeing the floodwaters.

Those who came into the church to shelter included the Methodist minister who was an early arrival, along with those who had the previous night sheltered in the Presbyterian church on the corner of George and Christie Streets before water entered there. Also amongst the temporary inhabitants of St Matthew's of that time were Thomas and Elizabeth Cupitt who arrived after they were rescued from the roof of their home at Cornwallis with five of their sons.[98]

Henry Stiles died on 22 June 1867, the day before the floodwaters peaked.[99] He left a legacy of £200 to the church. Jane Stiles moved to stay with her minister son George in the goldmining town of Sofala and died at that rectory about eight months after her husband's death. She is buried in St. Matthew's alongside Henry. Their grave inscription at St Matthew's reads:

83. The view of floodwaters, probably taken from Fairfield, the home of the Reverend Charles Garnsey looking north across the Richmond Road to the site of the brickfields where the bricks for St Matthew's Church were made. St Matthew's Church is several hundred yards across to the top right of the photo. Powerhouse Museum, 85/1284-334.

The Rev. HENRY TARLTON STILES, M.A.,

Born June 24th, 1808, Died June 22nd, 1867.

Him that overcometh will I make a pillar in the temple of my God, and

he shall go no more out.— Rev. iii., ver. 12.

Lovely and pleasant in their lives. In their deaths they are not divided.

JANE STILES, Wife of the Rev. Henry Tarlton Stiles, M.A.

The rector had been buried close to the sanctuary apse. The unusual design of the marker was replicated nearby in the cemetery in 1868 for the grave of Stiles' younger brother, John, who had been Clerk of Petty Sessions at Yass.

84. The gravemarker of Henry and Jane Stiles, 1867. Photograph by Ian Jack, 2016.

85. (Left) Stiles' grave is located within the graveyard of St Matthew's, close to the sanctuary apse. Photograph by Ian Jack, 2016.

6 Late Victorian Slumber

86. The memorial window to the Reverend Henry Stiles, erected by his friends in 1869, two years after his death. The maker was Wailes and Strang of Newcastle upon Tyne in England. Photograph by Ian Jack, 2009.

Charles Garnsey, Rector 1867 to 1876

From 1855 until 1882, Bishop Frederic Barker brought an evangelical outlook to Sydney Anglicanism in contrast to his predecessor, William Broughton.

> The enduring legacies of Barker to Sydney diocese were the strong body of evangelicals amongst the ninety-eight clergy, the smoothly-functioning synods in which lay and clerical representatives of the parishes had an equal part in decision-making, the various organizations which gave richness and purpose to church life, and an evangelical culture which permeated the churches and homes of Sydney Anglicans.[1]

But at Windsor Henry Stiles' High Church convictions lived on under his son-in-law and successor, Charles Garnsey. A man of 38 when Stiles died in 1867, Garnsey had started his adult life in Britain as a lawyer, but soon migrated to Tasmania, where he became a private tutor to the local bishop's children. He had been born into an evangelical Anglican rectory and was ordained as a deacon in Tasmania in 1853, before he came to New South Wales to teach in a private Anglican school in 1858.[2] He was tempted to Windsor in 1860 and in September set up his own boarding-school, Everton College, a fine two-storey house built by Dr Dowe which still adorns the north-east corner of Bridge Street and George Street.[3]

The attraction of Windsor to Charles Garnsey was not least Mary Stiles, the rector's only daughter, nine years younger than her suitor. Henry Stiles had been a family friend of the Garnseys in England and had a few reservations about Charles, both as a new headmaster and as a prospective son-in-law.[4]

These reservations were quickly overcome, however. Charles and Mary were married in St Matthew's on 27 December 1860. Everton College was a success over the next four years, Charles was licensed to officiate in church in 1861, was ordained a priest in 1864 and put his father's evangelicalism

87. St Matthew's church in 1868, showing the new paling fence installed by Thomas Greentree in February 1867. Photograph by David Scott, by courtesy of Sydney Living Museums.

headmaster until a month after Stiles died during former Windsor home of William Cox and then of James Hale, which was conveniently close to the church, and transferred his school there from Thompson Square. Fairfield became home for the expanding Garnsey family in the next two years.[6] In 1866, when Stiles was unwell, Charles was officially appointed a salaried curate at St Matthew's, although one of the more evangelical members of the Parish Council, the prominent lawyer, Richard Coley, had dared to suggest that Garnsey was 'undesirable for the post'.[7]

Garnsey doubled in the roles of curate and headmaster until a month after Stiles died during the catastrophic flood of June 1867. Just as Stiles opened the church and the rectory to those dispossessed by flood, so Garnsey accommodated up to 200 distressed local people at Fairfield. He was soon appointed rector, closed his school and moved to the parsonage.[8]

Garnsey was heir to the substantial physical improvements which Stiles had achieved during his long incumbency, including the new fencing.[9] St Matthew's was, however, still lit by candle-light. The lighting became a problem for Garnsey, when one of his first initiatives was to increase the frequency of services at the small outlying church of St Philip at Clydesdale in what is now Marsden Park. Because these services were given on Sunday afternoons, Garnsey was obliged to conduct some services at St Matthew's in the evening. Virtually his first act as rector was to persuade the churchwardens to buy kerosene lamps for the substantial sum of £46 (over $5,000 in modern terms). The first oil-lit evening service was held in Greenway's church on 3 November 1867. The fitting of lamp-holders throughout the church was completed by February 1868.

Garnsey was responsible for the decision in 1870 to cut the high pulpit down to a less commanding presence.[10] At the same time the internal organization of the gallery was changed to accommodate the Sunday school. If these changes were completed in 1870 or 1871, they were done by voluntary labour, since no relevant payment appears in the Wardens' Accounts.[11]

Garnsey vigorously consolidated his father-in-law's tentative beautification of the church interior. In Stiles' last years, the church had been enhanced by the progressive installation of fine stained-glass windows, endowed by relatives of the individuals commemorated. Stiles had seen two windows installed, both in 1864, both on the north side, near the apse. One was erected

88. Interior of St Matthew's as it was after *c.* 1868 showing kerosene lamps attached to the north and south walls. The high pulpit is in the south-eastern corner. State Library of NSW, Mitchell Library, Government Printer, d1_18224r.

90. Detail of the window in memory of Edwin Rouse, by Hailes and Strang, installed by the widow, Hannah Rouse, in 1864. Photograph by Chris Jones, rector of St Matthew's, 2016

to remember John Terry, the stepson of Samuel Terry, the most successful of all transportees. John lived at Box Hill on the Windsor Road and married Eleanor Rouse from Rouse Hill House nearby. John Terry had died untimely in 1842, leaving Eleanor a formidably wealthy woman in her own right. She married again and lived with her second husband, Major Thomas Wingate, in a famous mansion at Potts Point. But she did not forget John Terry and it was she who in 1864 engaged the prominent English firm of William Wailes and Thomas Strang, based in Newcastle upon Tyne, to supply the first of St Matthew's great windows 'to the honor & glory of God & for the adornment of His House'. The scene depicting the call of St Matthew was exquisitely appropriate. Eleanor is identified on the accompanying plaque merely as E.W.[12]

In the same year 1864 a matching window, also from Wailes and Strang, showing the raising of Lazarus, was installed beside John Terry's in memory of Eleanor's brother, Edwin Rouse, who had died in 1862. This was endowed by Edwin's widow, Hannah.[13]

Garnsey soon saw the installation of two windows on the south side, directly opposite the Terry and Rouse windows. The first was

89.(Left) The window in commemoration of John Terry who died aged 35 in 1842 and is buried at St Matthew's. Made in 1864 by Wailes and Strang of Newcastle upon Tyne in England at the expense of Terry's widow, by then Mrs Eleanor Wingate, it shows the call of St Matthew. Photograph by Ian Jack, 2016.

91. Detail of the Gethsemane window dedicated to Major Wingate, 1869. Photograph by Chris Jones, rector of St Matthew's, 2016.

in memory of his father-in-law, Henry Stiles, showing the preaching of John the Baptist, while after Thomas Wingate's death in 1869, the twice-widowed Eleanor paid for a Gethsemane window in his honour. These windows were also imported from Newcastle upon Tyne.[14]

One more window, manufactured by Wailes and Strang, was erected in Garnsey's time, completing the southern suite. Anthony Hordern, the founder of the major Sydney store in 1855, had been married in St Matthew's in 1841, by Henry Stiles. His bride was Harriet, the daughter of the local tanner, Samuel Marsden. Harriet died in Genoa in January 1872 as she was preparing to return from a European holiday and her widower commissioned a window, showing the two Marys and Salome before the tomb of Christ.[15]

After Garnsey's time as rector, two more windows were installed, both on the north side, one to Harriet Elias who died in 1877 (along with Edward Robinson, who had died in 1874), the other to Lucinia Wood whose son erected a window after her death in 1888. Over the quarter-century since 1864, the church had indeed been adorned as Eleanor Rouse/Terry/Wingate had intended, and ever since coloured light has been liberally shed on the increasing number of marble plaques on the walls.

The significant suite of stained glass has been

92. Colour from the stained glass on two of the Fitzgerald plaques. Photograph by Ian Jack, 2016

well preserved. There was no recurrence of the hail storm of 1847 which had smashed eight of the tall plain windows.[16] Early in World War II, fearful of enemy bombardment, the church authorities, with the financial assistance of the families of those commemorated, dismantled the windows and took them to the cellar of Rouse Hill House. The empty fenestration was boarded up with fibro until the windows were reinstated in 1945.[17]

The creation of a fine corpus of matching coloured glass was the principal physical achievement of Garnsey's decade as rector.

Despite some unrest from members of the congregation about Garnsey's ecclesiology, he was a popular minister. Doctrinal feelings were, however, aroused when the marble tablet in memory of Captain W.H. Blake of the British navy was erected at the east end of the nave in 1874 by his widow and his father-in-law, the influential Robert Fitzgerald.[18]

Fitzgerald had already installed tasteful marble

93. Window in commemoration of Harriet Elias, who died in 1877. Photograph by Chris Jones, rector of St Matthew's, 2016.

plaques on the wall flanking the apse in memory of his wife, his daughter and his father, Richard, who had become one of the richest emancipists in the colony long before his death in 1840.[19] The Blake monument was of a different scale, with an uncommonly long inscription and, controversially, a substantial marble cross and anchor above. John Tebbutt, the astronomer, and a trustee of the church, published his objections in the Anglican press and consolidated them into a pamphlet in 1876, while Garnsey was still rector. Tebbutt wrote:

94. The marble plaque to Captain W.H. Blake, erected in 1874. Photograph by Ian Jack, 2016.

> I am informed that the introduction of the image of the cross is viewed with pain and alarm by many of the brethren. With this feeling I fully sympathize, but I believe I am utterly powerless in the matter, except to offer my own protest and moral influence, whatever that may be worth, against the introduction. I am fully alive, not simply to the danger which the introduction of such things presents to the souls of men, but also to the actual consequences which are already being reaped in some of the Churches of England. Some the finest Churches there are already the scenes of debasing idolatry.[20]

The genuine differences of opinion did not reach any climax and the Blake memorial remains under its intact cross today.

95. The Fitzgerald wall of plaques beside the apse. Photograph by Ian Jack, 2016.

The Reverend Charles Garnsey conducted the same services at the church as his forebears had done. One member of the congregation in January 1874 has left behind a rare and candid glimpse of the human side of the minister's zeal, after attending the funeral of one of the congregation, John Hoskisson. A member of an old Hawkesbury land-owing family[21] and a mill owner, Hoskisson was said to be worth half a million pounds, according to Thomas Champion a photographer who specialized in printing the last portraits of the deceased. Champion wrote in his diary that Hoskisson had been attended in his illness by Dr Selkirk and in the week before his death Charles Garnsey called to see him.

John Hoskisson's funeral was conducted with gravitas by Garnsey as was required, but secretly Champion had wished for a shorter sermon:

> Followers to meet at dwelling House ½ past 11 o'clock. Weather unpropitious. ½ [past] 11at Mrs H's a great meeting off to church ¼ past 12 after service in Ch a lengthy address or oration by Revd CΓ Garnsey. 1 pm before funeral was concluded. A heavy fine raining all this time.[22]

Garnsey's High Church principles had also involved him in some local politics. In 1871, for example, he was nominated unsuccessfully for the presidency of the Windsor School of Arts, where William Walker, a local solicitor and a prominent Presbyterian, had been influential for many years. The master-baker, William Moses,

> a political enemy of Mr. Walker, nominated the Rev. C.G. Garnsey, the High Church parson ... It was thought that Mr. Garnsey, a clergyman, would be the likeliest individual to defeat a person of Mr. Walker's general popularity – so he was selected.[23]

As well as his humanitarian work in the 1867 floods, the Reverend Charles Garnsey was part of the community response to a fire that raged for hours in 1874 in the centre of the town of Windsor. The townspeople worked amongst the fierce flames, hot westerly winds and clouds of smoke-filled, dusty air. With the fuel provided by timber blacksmith's shops and tanneries, a chemist, a grocer and other businesses and dwellings with dry shingled roofs and timber eaves, the fire raced in several directions.

The *Sydney Morning Herald* noted that by mid-afternoon 30 houses had been burnt down from the Oddfellows' Hall and the Wesleyan church and parsonage together with the Reverend Wilkinson's large library of books and his furniture (although the schoolhouse, a detached brick building in Macquarie Street, was saved) to small dwellings and granaries. The paper painted a graphic picture:

> The day was as disagreeable as can possibly be imagined ... along the whole width of this area, from George to Macquarie streets, the flames advanced northwards towards Fitzgerald-street ... For a considerable distance on either side of the fire men, women, and children were busily engaged in removing goods from their houses, and carts were in active requisition moving the household furniture and goods away ... Men were shouting, and of the women numbers were crying ... watering-carts kept

96. The fire damage in central Windsor after the fire of 1874. The contemporary photographs show the devastation between George Street in the foreground and Macquarie Street. Photograph in Hawkesbury Library collection, published in M. Nichols, *Disastrous Decade: Flood and Fire in Windsor, 1867–1874*, Deerubbin Press, Berowra Heights, 2001, p. 44.

> the two engines at work vigorously, and there was no want of willing hands to work them.[24]

Along with the mayor and many others, Charles Garnsey gave what support he could to those fighting the unpredictable blaze which destroyed several blocks of the town.

Garnsey understandably wanted to find a larger and more receptive congregation, but he had been appreciated. In 1873 he had been presented with a silver salver and in 1876 when he left to become assistant minister at St James' in Sydney he was given a gold watch.[25] In 1878 he moved on to Christ Church St Laurence, where he 'sought to link the sacramentalism of his later years to a positive social gospel'.[26]

Four Successive Ministers

Garnsey's successor at St Matthew's was Henry Archdall Langley, an Irish-born minister who had already been his invaluable assistant at St Philip's, Marsden Park. That small church had often been filled to capacity, with extra seating brought from the public school.[27] With his wife Elizabeth and five children, Langley moved into the St Matthew's Rectory in 1876. His son Henry and daughter Minnie were born there in 1877 and 1878, the sixth and seventh children in the family.[28]

Langley was moved on briskly in August 1878 to Victoria, where he later became Bishop of Bendigo, so he had little time to leave a mark on St Matthew's, except in one regard: he was the leader in acquiring the land in New Street on which a new school hall would be built in 1880.[29] The acquisition of the allotment in New Street, Windsor, was to be financed in part by the sale of the old Bridge Street schoolhouse but this sale was not finalized until 1902, so the church had to raise the money from other sources for the new school which opened in 1880.[30]

Only after accumulating more funds over some years could the parish renew its efforts to improve the interior of the church. The next minister was Frederick William Stretton, who came to Windsor from Mudgee in 1878. Although his health was not robust, Stretton did much for building the parish.

97. Anglican Church Hall in New Street, Windsor, built in 1880 as the new church school, the third in the town. Photograph by Jan Barkley-Jack, 2016.

A new church at Riverstone, St John's Church at Colo, and the church at Vineyard were all added to the parish. Vineyard was given a lectern made from part of the high pulpit at St Matthew's which Garnsey had cut down. There was also expenditure in 1880 on the new school hall in New Street.[31]

It is probable that the painting of the sanctuary dome in azure with gold stars was done around this time, although there is no positive evidence in the church archives, just as there is no confirmation

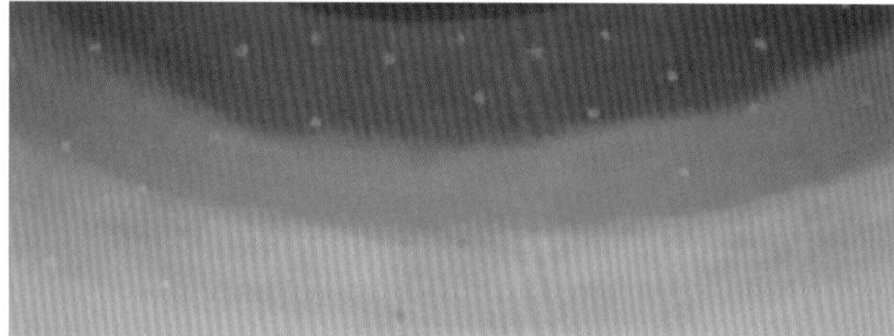

98. Detail of stars painted on the ceiling of the apse. Photograph by Chris Jones, rector of St Matthew's, 2016.

that John Tebbutt's fame as an astronomer is reflected in this characteristic late Victorian decoration.[32]

The largest change to the external environment of the church under Stretton was the building of the ostentatious monument which dominates the entry to the front porch. The McQuade monument, built of imported Carrara marble and carved in Italy by Antonio Caniparoli, was reassembled in Windsor in 1882 by the local stonemason George Robertson. It commemorated Amelia McQuade who died in 1875 and her parents, James Hale (died 1857) and Mary Hale (died 1866).

Both the Hales and the McQuades had risen to economic prominence from a convict background. James Hale had become part of the Anglican establishment, with a prestigious pew in St Matthew's, just behind William Cox's. When Cox died, Hale bought his Windsor house, Fairfield, where, like his political ally, Robert Fitzgerald at the Macquarie Arms, he entertained lavishly. Amelia was his only child, born in 1829. A talented musician, she married William McQuade when she came of age in 1850. The McQuades were Irish Catholics and the marriage was registered both at St Matthew's Catholic Church and at St Matthew's Anglican Church. The elder Hales were both buried in the Anglican graveyard and when Amelia died she was buried in their grave, but her burial does not appear in the Anglican register. When her McQuade husband died in 1887, he was buried in the old Catholic cemetery and none of the four children of the marriage was baptized at St Matthew's Anglican or buried there. It is noteworthy that the most grandiloquent monument in St Matthew's Anglican church grounds should have been erected by a Catholic with Catholic children in memory of his Anglican wife and his Anglican parents-in-law.[33]

99. The McQuade monument. Photograph by Ian Jack, 2016.

100. St Matthew's around 1880 while Frederick Stretton was rector. Royal Australian Historical Society, photograph 21779036.

In 1883 the Blacket firm (Edmund died in that year) was asked to move the vestry to the space under the south end of the gallery and to give an estimate of the cost of reseating the church to an 'amended plan', which does not survive.[34]

More substantial works, supervised by the two sons of Edmund Blacket, Cyril and Arthur, followed in 1884. The roof of the cupola on the tower was reclad in iron, gas lighting replaced Stiles' kerosene lamps in the church and ventilation was improved. This work was completed by November 1884 by Hannan and Lockyer at the total cost of £228.[35]

101. The wide sweep of road leading to St Matthew's gave a good view of the graveyard, with the more ostentatious Victorian monuments towering over the rest. The tallest at the front of the church was the marble monument to Amelia McQuade and her parents (centre right). Centre left is the tall grave of John Primrose. Photograph, 1901, by Mrs Foster, Royal Australian Historical Society, 22566004.

A proposal for extensive changes in the interior of the church had been before the parishioners on 21 January 1884. Stretton argued forcefully for the removal of the organ from the gallery:

> The organ would stand where the pulpit is now [in the south-east corner of the nave]. A smaller pulpit would be placed on the other side of the Church, and seats placed sideways would be useful to those whose infirmity of hearing rendered it necessary for them to be near the preacher. The Lectern with the Bible would stand in the middle. ... Seats for the Choir would be placed [in front of the organ].[36]

The plan of these changes drawn up by the Blacket brothers in 1883 was exhibited to the meeting, which accepted the proposal unanimously. But dissent was foreshadowed in another vigorous letter from the absent John Tebbutt, who argued that repairs to the tower and fencing should take precedence.[37] The organ remained in the gallery for another twelve years.

A curate was made available to Stretton, who was now also the Rural Dean, so that services could be held at Clydesdale, Riverstone, Vineyard, Wisemans Ferry, Freemans Reach, North Rocks (now Forrester), and at three places along the Colo River. But neither Frederick nor Mary Stretton was of robust health. Mary gave birth to two daughters in the rectory in 1879 and 1882, and then died in February 1884 at the age of only 30. Frederick Stretton died seventeen months later, in July 1885 at the age of 39. Like the Stiles, Frederick and his wife were buried in St Matthew's cemetery close to the church.[38]

Stretton's successor in 1885 was Arthur Blacket, a nephew of Edmund Blacket. He tried unsuccessfully to move the organ. He wanted to close the gallery altogether because of unsubstantiated fears about its safety, and he did manage to bring the choir down to the nave, in front of Garnsey's cut-down pulpit.[39]

Like Langley, Blacket was soon transferred to a Victorian parish and by 1895 he was a missionary in Persia.[40] The new minister at Windsor was Gerard d'Arcy-Irvine. He came from a clerical background. His father, who held a doctorate of divinity from Trinity College, Dublin, had emigrated to New Zealand in 1870 as a school headmaster, then came to Australia as a canon of Goulburn Cathedral. Gerard was not immediately called to the church, but became a bank employee, finally turning to theological education at Moore College in Liverpool. He was ordained an Anglican priest in 1886. After a short time as curate at St Stephen's in Newtown and at St John's in Parramatta, he was appointed to Windsor early in 1890 and soon became a Rural Dean also. But d'Arcy-Irvine stayed at St Matthew's for only three years, before moving on to Bowral and Wollongong and finally to Sydney where he became a canon of St Andrew's Cathedral and its first coadjutor bishop in 1926.[41]

Despite his short tenure, d'Arcy-Irvine took a keen interest in St Matthew's. Under his watch, the old school site in Bridge Street was at last sold, bringing some welcome capital to the churchwardens.

The continuing delay in moving the organ was occasioned partly by lack of funds and partly because the distinguished architect, John Sulman, advised in 1891 that replacing the pulpit with the organ would be aesthetically undesirable and would 'spoil' the stained-glass window on the south wall, which was a memorial to the Reverend Henry Stiles.[42]

Sulman's proposal to construct a new pulpit was accepted in 1891. The following year the present pulpit, made of American oak and designed by Sulman, was installed in the same south-east corner, near the Stiles window, with a new prayer-desk beside the choir stalls.[43]

The old pulpit was broken up in 1892, part of it going as a small lectern to the new Anglican church at Vineyard, while the rest of the local cedar was kept to repair pews at St Matthew's.[44] The unused part of this wood may have been part of the church's stocks of cedar later stored with a local builder called D'Emilio and sold off in 1952.[45] The Vineyard lectern is now on display in the Hawkesbury Regional Museum in Windsor.

102. Sulman's new pulpit, installed in 1892. Photograph by Ian Jack, 2009.

Substantial repairs were done to the Rectory, where the kitchen was reroofed, and the stables were renovated.[46] At the church, the top of the tower was in need of repair. Many years later, the minister's daughter recalled how d'Arcy-Irvine tried to persuade the three churchwardens to climb the tower to assess the need, but the first said 'Oh. I'm too old', the second demurred because 'I'm too fat' and the third said roundly 'I don't want to die yet', so the rector climbed the tower himself.[47]

In the final decade of the Victorian period the rector of St Matthew's was Sydney Fielding. In 1895 the organ was at last removed from the gallery and, after its action was overhauled, was rebuilt in the south-east corner of the nave, close to the Stiles memorial window. The organ was maintained by W. Blackburn and Son, the well-known piano and organ tuners of Parramatta, whose representative made visits to the Windsor and Richmond districts regularly, 'and also on receipt of letter'. The firm, established since 1876, was used by many residents of the district.[48] To accommodate the re-sited organ, the Sulman pulpit had to be moved across the nave to the north-east corner, along with the choir stalls.[49]

103. Interior of St Matthew's soon after 1895, when the organ was moved down into the nave. The lighting is still gas, introduced in 1884. The minister is Sydney Fielding, rector from 1893 to 1903. Detail of photograph in possession of St Matthew's.

A visitor to the commemoration celebrations in 1898 wrote his views about the church he saw:

> The second Church of St. Matthew's was and is staunch and solid; until a few short years since, the lofty stone-flagged vestibule, with its rough roofing and the lime-

104. The photograph of 1909 shows the gas fittings in the church. In 1884 gas lighting had replaced kerosene lamps in the church, and in 1895 the organ was moved to the south-east corner of the church. F. Walker, 'Windsor', Royal Australian Historical Society unpublished MS, Rare Book 991.3 WIN.

> stained cedar of the old vestry, the benches and the balustrades of the stairs leading up to the organ loft, struck one as chill and bare; but since that time much in the way of decoration has been effected, and there is now a greater warmth and a more genial appearance about the interior in consequence. As when built, the ceiling is flat and in square mouldings, and on either side of the communion table, according to the bygone wont are written the Lord's Prayer, the Creed, and the Commandments. The aisles are broad, and the pulpit ... made way for a more pretentious and modern piece of church furniture.[50]

Sydney Fielding, a Man of Many Parts

Fielding was a man of parts, who wrote poetry and novels, produced a treatise on *The Relation of Ancient Masonry to Modern Science & Religion* and whose published sermon on *Thy People Britain* is still retained by St Matthew's. In 1903 Fielding gave a public lecture on 'Wit and Humour'.[51] In 1886, he had married the daughter of a Central West solicitor and their six children who attained adulthood had distinguished academic and professional careers.[52] His interest in books prompted him to rebind the original St Matthew's Bible, printed in 1821, and presented to the church in 1822, which remained in liturgical use until 1936.[53]

Whilst in Sydney attending the Jubilee celebrations at St Andrew's Anglican Cathedral in August 1900, Fielding organised with William Brooks and Co. of Sydney the publication of his new children's book *Down to the Sea in Ships.* The *Windsor and Richmond Gazette* reported these doings:

> the story is chiefly laid in the South Seas. The book is to be nicely got up, with a number of full page illustrations by Mr. [David Henry] Souter, the well-known artist, and will be published early in October. Mr. Fielding is also arranging for the publication of another book in London, which will probably appear early next year.[54]

105. Inkwell and pen stand belonging to the Reverend Sydney Fielding. Collection of Hawkesbury Historical Society, housed in Hawkesbury Regional Museum, Windsor, accession no. 1977.323.1,2 and 3.

In 1922 an American silent romantic film was made with the same title.[55] Any relationship between the two is unknown, although both derive their title from Psalm 107:

> They that go down to the sea in ships, that do business in great waters;
>
> These see the works of the Lord, and his wonders in the deep.[56]

It became customary to hold 'an annual fund-raising event in mid-October, to celebrate Macquarie's first laying of the foundation stone on 11 October 1817', and it was reported in 1900 that the Grand Fair and Juvenile Industrial Exhibition lasted three days, from Saturday 10 October to the following Monday.

Visiting dignitaries included Sir Matthew Harris, the lord mayor of Sydney, who joined the rector, Sydney Fielding, for lunch at Brinsley Hall's Lilburn Hall in Thompson Square on the Saturday before Lady Harris, a Lane from Windsor, opened the fair, as she had done on previous occasions. The numerous stalls set up in the church hall, selling food, arts and crafts, were warmly patronized and the event concluded on the Monday with a grand concert by local artists.[57]

Other fund-raising events, like bazaars, were held in the grounds of parishioners' homes. The grounds and summer house of Glenroy, a grand townhouse located between George and Church Streets, were one venue. Just two blocks south of St Matthew's in the suburban hub of Newtown growing around the Windsor railway station, the event was hosted by Gertrude and Richard Cobcroft, whose tannery business was in Argyle Street. The bazaar featured an amble in Glenroy's renowned rose garden, croquet on the croquet lawn and stalls.[58]

The widow of John Hoskisson (whom Charles Garnsey had buried in 1874) had built the original Glenroy cottage as an investment, and sold it to the Cobcrofts a decade later. The Reverend Sydney Fielding and his wife were friends of the Cobcrofts, and were part of the wedding reception at an aggrandized Glenroy, given by widowed Gertrude for the marriage of daughter Olive to Walter Benson of Sydney. The ceremony was conducted by Fielding, and the wedding march played by St Matthew's organist, Mrs C. Eather, one of the best piano teachers in Windsor.[59]

The local newspaper gave the wedding an unusual amount of coverage, revealing aspects of the social life of the Fieldings in Windsor:

> the old church was well filled with sightseers and guests from all parts of the district, and also from Sydney. The bride's girl friends had been busily engaged during the morning at the church. The wedding bell and two hearts with initials were exceedingly pretty ... the choir sang 'The Voice That Breathed O'er Eden' ... During the signing of the register, Miss Carlotta Young sang 'O Perfect Love'.

The description the bride's dress shows it to be the centrepiece of an ornate, white wedding, with the bride in silk with lace trim and chiffon shirred bodice, and a train of tiny frills also veiled in spotted chiffon and worn with an embroidered veil and coronet of orange blossoms and jasmine. The bridesmaids also were dressed in white, with Paris lace and fashionable shirring. With cream straw hats decorated with lace and chiffon, and wearing gold brooches and carrying daffodils, they too were a picture of modernity.

The wedding breakfast was served at Glenroy in a billiard room 'beautifully draped with flags and wattle, the table having buttercup and white flowers, with maiden hair fern'. Fielding himself proposed the first toast, to 'Bride and Bridegroom', and other toasts followed. There were music and photographs. The Dunstons, Mr and Mrs Brinsley Hall (local member of parliament), the Tebbutts, McQuades and Moses families were all present, along with Mrs Eather, the organist, and many others from the district.

The townspeople were informed that Mrs Fielding was dressed in a 'black frock, with black bonnet and pink roses', and that the Fieldings' gift to the young couple was a silver and glass rose bowl. The rector and Mrs Fielding were then amongst those who wished the new Mr and Mrs Benson well as they 'left by the 4.20 p.m. train amidst showers of rice and confetti'.[60]

As with the wedding, large crowds were drawn from locals and visitors to a special series of community events. Evangelical religious missions were held around the district in Richmond, Windsor and Riverstone in a large tent specially pitched for the occasions in 1903. The meetings were totally undenominational and the audiences listened to stirring religious addresses, sometimes by visiting clergy. The newspaper reported that the services 'demonstrated more than once that the Christianity preached and advocated is a happy one, with a smile in it'. Sydney Fielding was a participant as *Hawkesbury Herald* told:

> one of the outcomes of the tent mission was held in Windsor last Sunday night in St. Matthew's school-hall, after the ordinary church services. There was a splendid attendance. The clergy present were Revs. Fielding, Dandie, Jones, and the visiting preacher, Rev. John Walker, who delivered a powerful, appealing, stirring address. It looks a big success. The second of the Wednesday-night united prayer meetings was well attended. It was held in the Church of England school-hall. Rev. S.G. Fielding presided, and gave a most impressive address. At the conclusion of the service, the rev. gentleman who, on account of other pressing engagements, had been unable to take much part in the tent mission expressed his sincere sympathy with the mission and his heartfelt gratitude for the good it had done.[61]

Sydney Fielding preached his last sermon at St Matthew's on Sunday, 29 May 1904.[62] The attitude of goodwill between religions under Fielding extended to the Roman Catholic priest, the Reverend Father McDonnell, who attended Fielding's farewell in Windsor, and told how, when he had first come to Windsor, 'Mr. Fielding came along and extended to him the right hand of fellowship'.[63]

The Fieldings went to Sydney, where the rector took up duties at the Garrison Church in 1904.[64] The *Hawkesbury Herald* reported that Fielding:

> hopes to do a good spiritual work among the waterside workers of the northern part of the city ... It is satisfactory to know that he has already received many expressions of goodwill from prominent churchmen, who welcome him to the city, where doubtless his acknowledged abilities will speedily place him in the front rank of city clergymen.[65]

106. The Reverend Sydney Fielding in the Rectory garden in 1899 with his wife and his children, Erica (born at Wellington 1890) and Una (born at Wellington 1888) on either side of their parents, Morris (born at Parramatta 1892) in the middle, Daisy (born at Windsor 1894) and Enid (born at Windsor 1896). Hawkesbury Historical Society's collection, housed in Hawkesbury Regional Museum, Windsor, accession no. 1977.84.9.

7 The Burial Ground and Surrounds

A New Burial Ground, October 1810 to 1817

Governor Lachlan Macquarie created a new place for dealing with death in the Hawkesbury. For most of the settlers in the earliest days at Mulgrave Place, the death of a loved one had meant a burial on the family property or from the early 1800s, acquiring a plot in the Green Hills burial ground beside South Creek to the north-east of Baker Street in Windsor. Only a few, like John Stogdell and Euphemia Lock, were taken to be buried in the Sydney or Parramatta cemeteries.[1]

When in the space of a few days the governor created the townships of Castlereagh, Pitt Town, Richmond, Wilberforce and Windsor in December 1810, his plans revolved around the location of the sites for the civic squares, the burial grounds and the churches in each place. Although the burial ground created by Macquarie at Windsor was the last to be formalized, the Windsor site was the first to be brought into use. In fact, the graveyard already had received a burial before the town was named and surveyed.

A single burial had taken place there because of the death of Hawkesbury's magistrate and one of the colony's wealthiest citizens, ex-convict Andrew Thompson. Judge Ellis Bent went so far as to comment:

> Mr Thompson ... is now, I may say, one of the first men, if not the first in the Colony. He possesses an amazing head of cattle, a most extensive property at the Hawkesbury ... Besides, he has to the amount of £50,000 engaged in different pursuits. He has established a Tanyard ... a Salt Works etc.[2]

Thompson's death had occurred two months before Macquarie's visit to create the towns, and the Macquaries had regarded Thompson so highly that they brought forward the implementation of the mooted burial ground. Indeed Lachlan and

107. Detail of the old Burial Ground at Green Hills, showing altar monuments, in anon., 'Sketch of the Inundation in the Neighbourhood of Windsor, June 1816'. State Library of New South Wales, Mitchell Library, PX*D 264.

Mrs Macquarie counted Thompson as a friend as well as Hawkesbury's leading citizen, well-known for employing his many boats to rescue those in the community in danger during flood times and using his other assets to aid various government initiatives and colonial growth. Macquarie decided that Thompson's body was to be the first placed in Windsor's new burial ground.[3] Captain Henry

Antill, Macquarie's aide-de-camp, was sent to Green Hills to finalize where exactly Thompson's plot was to be. It is obvious that in the months prior to Thompson's death, Macquarie had consulted Thompson about the town location and layout, Thompson having the most knowledge of the district.[4]

Thompson's honour of being the first ex-convict Macquarie appointed to one of the highest public positions in Australia, that of magistrate,[5] gives him a significance even beyond the distinction of his own many valuable and officially recognized contributions to the survival of both the Hawkesbury district and the colony generally in the earliest period. Macquarie's policy to rehabilitate former convicts has been a much debated feature of this country's early march toward nationhood, and its application, especially in this first instance, gives Thompson rare status in our historical record.

Thompson died of consumption in his residence in the village, probably atop the retail store, and the funeral on 25 October 1810 left from there:

> Between twelve and one in the afternoon, the remains of this much-lamented Gentleman were removed from his house on the Green Hills, which for the hospitality of its owner had been for many years proverbial, and conveyed to the Chapel on the Green Hills, whereat the Rev. Mr. Cartwright attended and delivered a very eloquent and appropriate discourse upon the occasion.[6]

The body was:

> Conveyed to the New Burial-ground, and there deposited in a vault in the presence of the multitude, who, it may be unexceptionally said, felt the most sensible regret in taking their last farewell ... In the funeral procession the Rev. Mr. Cartwright walked foremost, and was followed by Surgeons Mileham and Redfern who had attended the deceased during the long and painful illness ... Next followed the Bier attended by Captain Antill, as Aide-de-Camp to His Excellency the Governor, as Chief Mourner. The Paul (*sic*) Bearers were, Mr. Cox, Mr. James Cox, Mr. Lord, Mr. Williams, Mr. Arndell, and Mr. Blaxland. A number of Gentlemen followed as Mourners, and a long train, composed principally of the inhabitants of the settlement followed in succession.[7]

The Macquaries personally visited the new cemetery in early 1811:

> Mrs Macquarie and myself ... rode in the carriage to the new burying ground ... to view the tomb where the remains of our late worthy and highly esteemed good friend Mr. Andw. Thompson ... are deposited ... we took leave of our departed friend's tomb (which we intend to improve and render more elegant & conspicuous as a tribute of regard and friendship for his memory).[8]

108. The location of Andrew Thompson's grave (front) within today's cemetery, looking west, deep in the afternoon shadows. The slab was originally elevated on the four stone pillars now flanking the stone. When Macquarie first viewed Thompson's grave, it was alone in the cemetery. Photograph by Ian Jack, 2016.

True to their word, two years later, on Thompson's tomb, Macquarie laid a flat, extremely large and handsome tablet for which Macquarie himself had composed the words:

> Andrew Thompson Esquire, Justice of the Peace and Chief Magistrate of the Districts of the Hawkesbury ... distinguished himself by the most persevering industry and diligent attention to the commands of his Superiors. By these means he raised himself to a state of respectability and affluence which enabled him to indulge the generosity of his nature in assisting his Fellow Creatures in distress ... In consequence ... Governor Macquarie appointed him a Justice of the Peace. This act ... restored him to that rank in Society which he had lost.[9]

The thick sandstone altar stone with its finely mitred edge was originally laid horizontally, elevated in an altar design. The tomb was painted, probably repainted, white in 1821, and black paint was also used, presumably to pick out the letters of the long inscription.[10]

A 1916 transcription of Macquarie's words was used to restore the lettering in 1960 when Hawkesbury Historical Society raised the money for the conservation of the grave.[11] Further work was done to improve the legibility of the inscription in 2010.

In the week following Thompson's funeral, the settlers of Hawkesbury arranged a tribute to Thompson, who was extremely well-liked in the district for his hands-on approach and help he gave everyone from the lowliest to the governor himself. On 3 November, they presented an address to the governor:

> strongly expressive of their Regret at the late Event which deprived them and that Settlement at large of their common Friend and Patron, Andrew Thompson, Esq. and His Excellency is happy to receive so unequivocal a Testimony to the Rectitude of the late Mr. Thompson's general Conduct, both as a Magistrate and as a private Gentleman.[12]

Macquarie also announced that: 'The square in the present town I have named Thompson Square in honour of the memory of the good and worthy late Andrew Thompson.'[13]

The new Hawkesbury magistrate appointed by Macquarie was William Cox. This too met with approval from the district. William Cox, when still in the military had rented Argyle Farm from Captain Neil McKellar from 1802, and with his wife and family came to live in the district between Windsor and Richmond, on the grant he received in trust for his sons in 1804.

Cox had been called to England in February 1807 after speculating with regimental funds as paymaster (a usual occurrence) and being unable to repay the money. He had been declared bankrupt in the colony, and rather than face the military court he resigned from the regiment. On return to New South Wales in January 1810, Cox settled into his life as a gentleman farmer on his sons' grant between Windsor and Richmond, on what is today part of the Royal Australian Air Force Base, Richmond.[14]

Fronting the northern end of the newly created square opposite the graveyard, on the site of the intended church and at the front of the grounds, 'a strong post with the board on which is painted the name of the town [Windsor]' was erected in front of great numbers of the local inhabitants.[15] The governor's party then proceeded to the glebe land that was to be set aside for the clergyman of

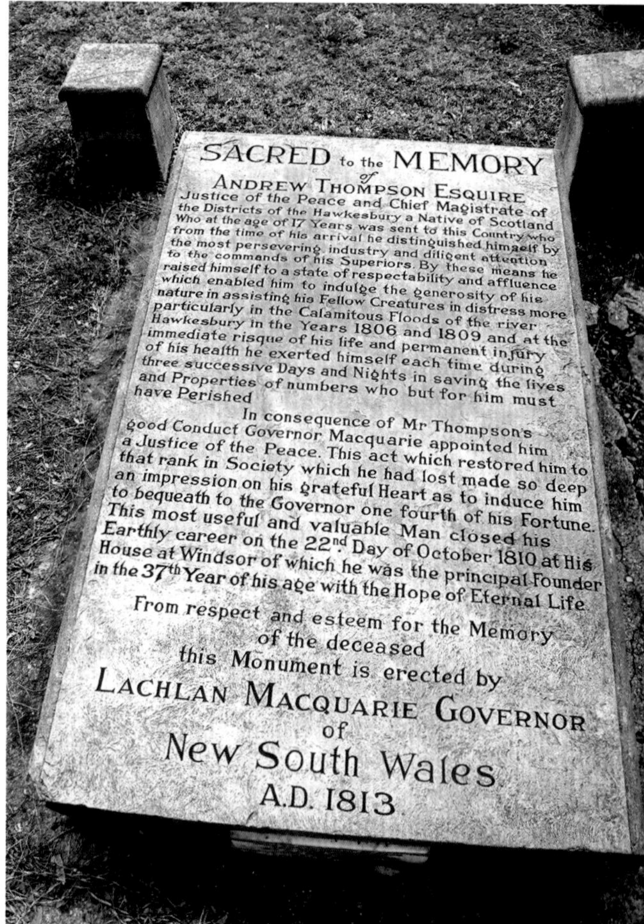

109. The gravemarker of Andrew Thompson, with the stone Elizabeth and Lachlan Macquarie personally laid to commemorate Thompson's regained respectability in the colony. Photograph by Ian Jack, 2010.

the district (see Chapter 8).[16]

James Meehan's fieldbook survives, showing him at work surveying the new churchyard in January 1811.[17] Along with George William Evans, Meehan had been instructed specifically to 'set apart 2 acres of Ground' (although the cemetery in fact contained just over three acres). J.T. Campbell, Macquarie's secretary, had informed the Reverend Samuel Marsden that he was to 'proceed as soon as convenient' to the new Hawkesbury towns and on to Liverpool to: 'consecrate the several burial grounds measured out and assigned for the use of those Townships – Mr Evans the Deputy Surveyor will be ordered to attend you on these occasions to point out the Several situations of the said Burial Grounds.'[18]

Macquarie informed the citizens of the colony on 11 May 1811 in a Government and General

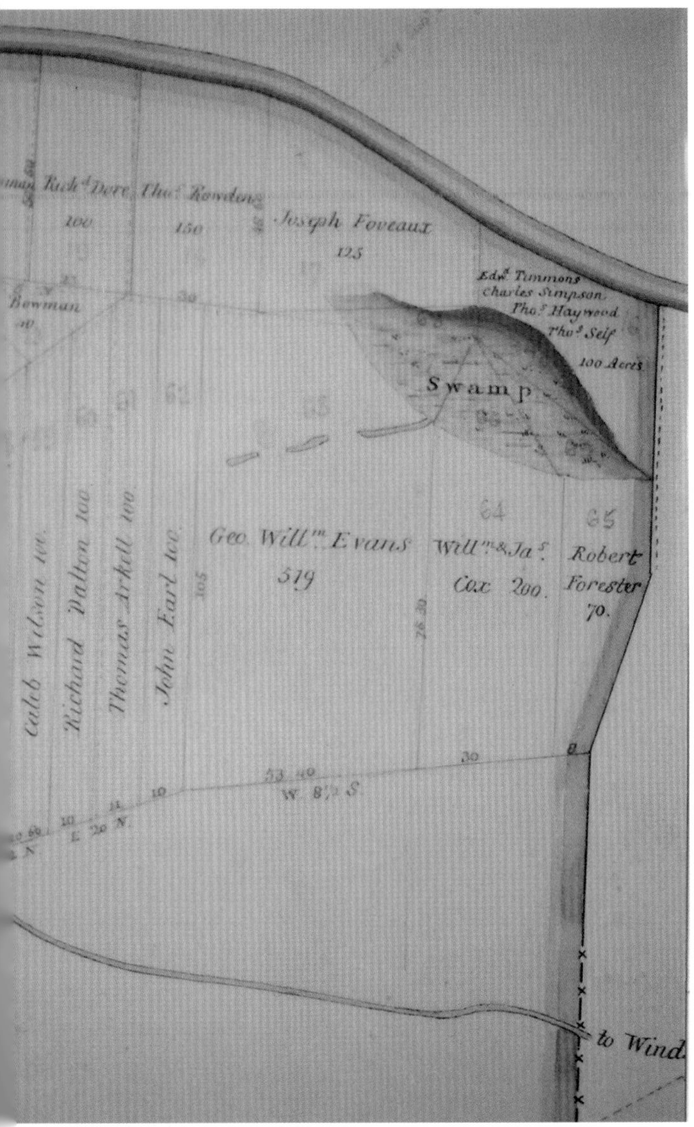

110. Map showing the grant of 1804 given to two of William Cox's sons. It is located between Windsor and Richmond and the lower part of the map from above the road through to part of the grants is today part of the RAAF Richmond Base. Adjacent to the Cox grant is one to Surveyor George William Evans of the same date. The 'swamp' became known as Bakers Lagoon. Map of Ham Common parish, county Cumberland, *c.* 1830s, SRNSW, Map 6216, n.d., photograph by Ian Jack, 2005.

Order that:

> The Respective burial grounds ... having been lately consecrated by the Principal Chaplain, His Excellency the Governor is pleased to give this public notice thereof; and at the same time directs and demands that in future all settlers and others resident in those townships, or in their respective vicinities, shall cease to bury their dead as heretofore within their several farms, and shall in a decent and becoming manner inter them in the consecrated grounds now assigned for that purpose in their respective townships.It is further ordered that when a death should happen, notice of the event shall immediately be given to the constable of the district wherein it has occurred; and the constable receiving such information is hereby directed to communicate the same with the least possible delay to the nearest resident chaplain, in order that he may attend and perform the funeral service. Any neglect of these orders will be severely punished. [19]

Only after the consecrations of all the new Hawkesbury cemeteries were completed by 11 May 1811, would burials be likely in the new grounds.[20] As a result, it appears almost certain that the four burials that took place after Thompson's interment and before the graveyard was actually marked out on 12 January 1811 were interred in the old Green Hills burial ground. They were recorded nonetheless in the St Matthew's Register because Cartwright officiated at the funerals.

It is highly likely that the next eleven burials, conducted between the survey of the cemetery on 12 January and its consecration on 11 May 1811, were also in the old South Creek cemetery. All eleven were from the Windsor area, four being ex-convict men, three in their fifties and one, James Rixon, aged 36 years. Two were ex-convict women, and one a colonial-born. One was a soldier attached to the 73rd Regiment, and three burials were of children aged between seven months and six years old who had been born in the colony.[21]

The Orders of 11 May 1811 marked a major change for colonists in how they managed the physical responses to death. From 1811 all burials within a twenty or so mile radius of a township were to take place in the public consecrated spaces Macquarie had set aside, not on their own property

111. Group of four early graves in the north-western corner of Macquarie's new burial ground in Windsor in place before the church was built and consecrated. The marker on the right is that for Phoebe Cussley, 1815. Photograph by Jan Barkley-Jack, 1998.

and not in the old South Creek burial ground.[22]

Thus any settler recorded in the St Matthew's Burial Register as buried after 11 May 1811 with no place of burial shown next to the name can be assumed to lie in the 1810 graveyard. Anyone buried in the burial grounds of one of the other Hawkesbury towns has the place listed specifically as 'at Castlereagh', 'at Pitt Town', 'at Richmond' or 'at Wilberforce'. Some residents who lived in another town were buried at Windsor in the new ground, presumably by request.

As an 'Act of Justice towards the Chaplains', for their increased work load, they were authorized to charge 'Surplice Fees, from Free Persons only' from 1 January 1811. Those costs relating to funerals were to be

> For all Marriages, Christenings, Churching of Women, and Funerals, the several Fees specified in the following Table; namely, £ s d ...
>
> Funerals... . Clergyman ... £0 3 0
> Clerk ... £0 1 0
> Bell ... £0 0 6
> Grave Digger £0 2 6 ...
>
> HIS EXCELLENCY further authorises the said Chaplains to dismiss or otherwise punish the Grave-diggers within their respective Parishes who shall demand or receive any larger Sum for the Digging of a Grave than that prescribed in the foregoing Table of Fees; or who shall neglect to make the Graves of a suitable Depth, as well for the sake of Public Decency as of preventing any noxious Effluvia arising from thence to the Offence or Injury of the Society. – HIS EXCELLENCY strictly enjoins the Chaplains to pay the fullest Attention to this very important object.[23]

Until a separate register was begun for each of the other towns, the burials in that town's cemetery continued to be recorded in the St Matthew's Burial Register. Similarly, until other denominations received grounds of their own and opened their own cemeteries in the 1820s and 1830s, their adherents continued to be buried in the Establishment Anglican ground. The exception was the nonconformist graveyard of Ebenezer where the church was opened at Portland Head in 1809: there the oldest remaining gravemarker was erected in 1812.[24]

In the first year after consecration of Macquarie's new burial grounds in the Hawkesbury towns, 28 burials were recorded at Windsor's new graveyard, along with three taking place at Richmond, one at Castlereagh, three at Wilberforce and one recorded as being in the Pitt Town burial ground.[25]

Ten of these Windsor interments in the first year after the graveyard was consecrated (up to 11 May 1812), almost a third, were young children, all born in the colony, whose ages ranged from three weeks to nine years, with most being babies up to four months. Five were girls: the oldest being Ann Smith, aged nine years. One who died aged three months was William, the son of the Reverend Robert and Mary Cartwright.[26]

All of the remaining nineteen adults interred at Windsor that year were men, fifteen of them ex-convicts. Ten of these transportees had arrived in the colony in the eighteenth century, but unlike the burials at Wilberforce, only a small percentage had been amongst the earliest grantees: Stephen Smith whose 25 acres had been promised in 1795 when he was a soldier in the New South Wales Corps; James Baker who received a grant in 1794, the first year of Hawkesbury settlement; and a farmer from Prospect, John Merriott or Merritt, who had purchased by 1800.[27] There were five drownings at Hawkesbury between May 1811 and May 1812, three of them being buried at Wilberforce and two in Windsor. Only Austin Forrest, who had married Jemima Pitt of Richmond, and James Thompson were free arrivals, from among the Windsor burials up to 11 May 1812.[28]

James Thompson had come in *William Pitt* in 1806 and was buried aged 53 years on 8 February 1812. His is thus the oldest original gravemarker remaining in the cemetery, as opposed to the oldest grave, which of course was Andrew Thompson, who was not related. The sandstone headstone belonging to James' grave is near the present church's low back northern line, further west than the grave of Andrew Thompson, and much lower down the slope of the hill, yet still in the north-eastern sector of the burial ground. Other members of his family are also buried there, the group of markers surrounded with a chain railing.[29]

John Merritt's intact, highly legible headstone nearby, dating from around May 1812[30] is an anthropomorphic sandstone marker, located

112. Gravemarker of James Thompson, the oldest known stone in the cemetery, dates from February 1812. It is on the left of the back row of this Thompson family group. Originally there were four stone pillars, three of which remain, holding a chain railing around the group. Andrew Thompson, the first burial at St Matthew's, had no marker until 1813. Marker stones, like most of those above, which imitate the human form, with curves representing the human head and shoulders, are called anthropomorphic. There are many variations within the genre. Photograph by Jan Barkley-Jack, 2016.

113. The gravemarker for John Merritt (Merriott in the church register), buried in the new cemetery on 9 May 1812. Merritt had come to the colony on the First Fleet and the small brass plaque was added to the stone by the Fellowship of First Fleeters. Photograph by Ian Jack, 2009.

amongst the group of earliest graves in the north-eastern corner of the graveyard, just a little south-east of James Thompson's headstone.[31]

Merritt (or Merriott) was a farmer. The age of 69 years shown on his tombstone is in conflict with the birth date of 1751 given in other information,[32] but all agree that he was a First Fleet arrival and his gravemarker now bears the small black plaque of the Fellowship of First Fleeters. He and James Sherrard had jointly purchased land granted to others on upper South Creek in 1795 and registered in 1797.[33] The partners had a large acreage sown and together kept 70 pigs, and a horse each by 1802, having purchased more land. The store of wheat and maize held in their barn was the second highest in the district, larger than even Andrew Thompson had in 1802. By 1808 Merritt was the sole farmer on Sherrard's land and had an allotment in the Green Hills village.[34] He had married Ann Taylor in 1792.[35]

Including Andrew Thompson, these 29 burials in the new Windsor cemetery by 11 May 1812, the first anniversary of its opening,[36] had all been conducted by the Reverend Robert Cartwright. Almost immediately in the same month, May 1812, three more men who had come to the colony as prisoners were buried in the new Windsor cemetery: Richard Burke, Edward Kelly and Richard Alcorn. Alcorn's grave is close by Merritt's in the north-eastern corner of the cemetery, also below Andrew Thompson. Richard Alcorn too has a sandstone anthropomorphic headstone marking his grave from around the time of his burial on 22 May 1812, recently found lying broken on the ground but now repaired. Of these three remaining original markers in the cemetery, the grave of Richard Alcorn is the closest to Greenway Crescent (the former Cornwallis/Richmond Road). The Alcorn grave is part of a large family plot retaining five of the six original markers.

Like many of the early Hawkesbury settlers, and as seen in Chapter 5, the Alcorn family continued to have close ties with St Matthew's through the continuity of many ministers. After the earliest Richard Alcorn was buried by Robert Cartwright, his son Richard was married there ten years later by John Cross, his youngest brother John married by Henry Stiles in 1833, and two of his sisters in between. One of these sisters, Elizabeth, the witness at Richard jr's wedding, was married there just nine months after Richard jr. Their mother Sarah continued farming on upper South Creek, and when she died in 1832 was buried in the family plot at St Matthew's by Joseph Docker.[37]

115. The graves of Richard Alcorn, John Merritt and others buried in 1812, taken looking towards the west. These anthropomorphic gravestones are in the lowest flood-free part of the north-eastern sector of the graveyard. The Alcorn family was part of the active St Matthew's congregation over many generations (see also Chapter 5) and Richard's wife Sarah is marked by the stone shown on the left. Photograph by Ian Jack, 2016.

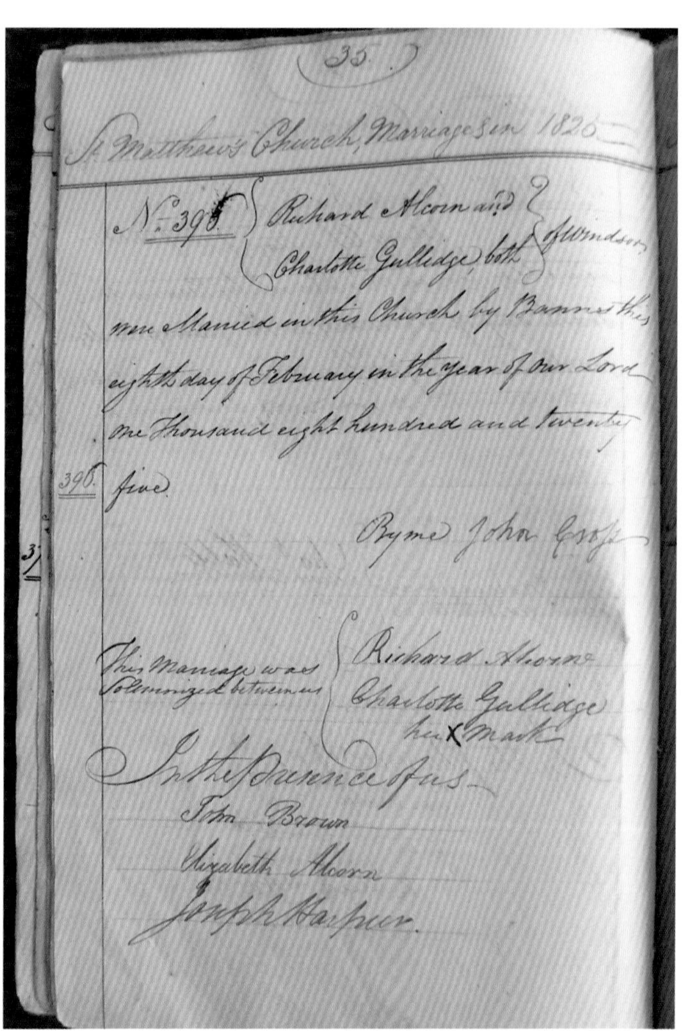

(35)

St Matthew's Church, Marriages in 1825

No. 398 Richard Alcorn and Charlotte Gullidge, both of Windsor were Married in this Church by Banns this eighth day of February in the year of Our Lord one Thousand eight hundred and twenty five

398.

By me John Cross

This Marriage was solemnized between us: Richard Alcorn, Charlotte Gullidge her X mark

In the presence of us — John Brown, Elizabeth Alcorn, Joseph Harper

114. The wedding details of Richard Alcorn and Charlotte Gullidge on 8 February 1825. The groom had been born in England in 1799, the son of Richard and Sarah Alcorn. The couple went to live at Jerrys Plains in the Hunter Valley. Page from the St Matthew's Marriage Register, 1810–1856. Photograph by Ian Jack, 2016.

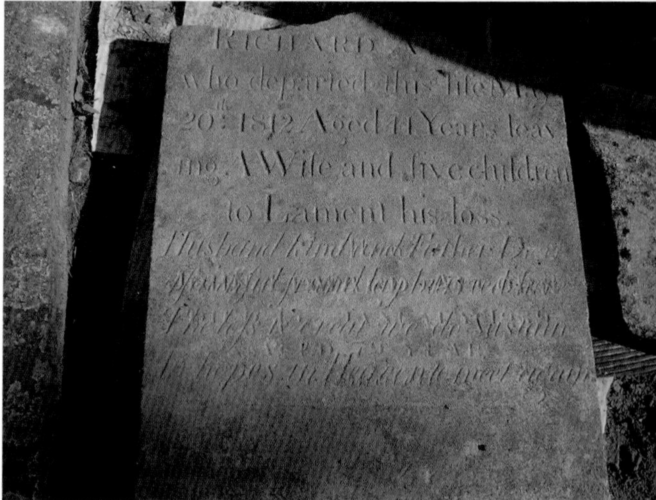

116. The gravemarker of Richard Alcorn (buried 22 May 1812), already once mended, had fallen and lay in two pieces within the large boundaries of the family plot of the Alcorn family in the lower north-eastern sector of St Matthew's graveyard. It has again been placed upright in May 2016. Photograph by Ian Jack, 2016.

The final burial in May 1812 was that of four and a half year old Edward Martin, son of John Martin and Mary Allen.[38] Like the stone of James Thompson, the gravemarkers of John Merritt and Richard Alcorn are also older than Andrew Thompson's.

For the rest of the year in 1812 there were ten

more male burials in the new Windsor cemetery. The nine adult men had all been transported to New South Wales, most of whom had served their sentence. The first ex-convict woman registered as buried in the new Windsor cemetery was Julianna Franklin, aged 24, buried on 16 June 1812. There is no marker for Julianna.[39]

During 1813, most deaths continued to be convict or ex-convict men (eight aged between 24 and 95). Five of the women who died in Windsor that year were buried in the new Windsor burial ground, and two of them, Mary Ralph (aged 36) and Elizabeth Waring (aged 52), had come free. Elizabeth Waring, half of a very successful early trading duo with husband William in Sydney, had settled in the area in 1794 first on South Creek, until the low-lying nature of their land saw the Warings relocate to a Wilberforce grant and then to land at Pitt Town.[40] Two of the Windsor burials in 1813 were children, John Smith (14 months) and Sarah Barnes (17 months).[41]

During the next three years from 11 May 1814 until 11 May 1817, the new Windsor graveyard saw 70 interments, more than any of the other burial grounds in Macquarie's towns. Of these, 29 had arrived in the colony in the eighteenth century, but only six had land in the district promised before 1801. The deaths followed much the same pattern as in the first two years, with drownings still common; but one of the most poignant deaths was that of Mary Ezzy, who died in 1816 aged only sixteen. Five days before she was to be wed, Mary had been struck by lightning while ironing. Her grave is unmarked, but the Ezzy family has since erected a generic monument to members of the family in the graveyard.[42]

In these fourth, fifth and sixth years of the Windsor burial ground's existence two convicts, Robert White and James Bennett, were killed in 1816 by falling trees, two others by snake bite and another two were murdered. Patrick Grady, a 30-year-old convict, was in April 1816 the first registered death at old Windsor Hospital. Charles Williams, a First Fleeter who held the second grant registered for the district, was buried in 1815, aged 52 years. Williams was the neighbour and friend of James Ruse on their early Parramatta farms, and it was this pair who had convinced Acting Governor

117. The area of some of the earliest burials in the north-east corner of the graveyard, dating from 1812, taken looking towards the south-west. The stone fence along Greenway Crescent, installed in 1961, is in the foreground. Photograph by Ian Jack, 2009.

Grose to let them be the very first farmers at the Hawkesbury, which action became the impetus for the entire Mulgrave Place district being set up as the third mainland farming area in Australia.[43] Williams' grave is today unmarked and unlocated.

Two early settlers who died before the church was begun were Thomas West and George Smith; as ex-convicts they had received their Hawkesbury land in 1794. They were buried by Robert Cartwright in 1814 and 1816 respectively but it is not known where. A settler from 1795, Benjamin Cussley lost his wife Phoebe, a transportee, and her headstone, located amongst the earliest graves in the north-western grouping, shows her aged 60 years when she died on 17 November 1815. This group of graves is in an east-west line with the James Thompson and Richard Alcorn grouping.[44]

A month later in December 1815, Pitt Town's John Benn, the most prosperous ex-convict to be buried since Andrew Thompson, was interred in a family vault in the area near to Thompson's grave on the north-eastern slope. Benn, along with Thompson, had been the two financers of the Hawkesbury's entry into the colony's first industry, that of whaling and sealing. The vessel built at Hawkesbury by neighbour James Webb and owned jointly with John Benn was the *Unity*, a cutter of 36 tonnes, which was launched near

118. Graves in the far north-western corner of St Matthew's cemetery, including the 1815 marker of Phoebe Cussley, second from the right, and the first within the enclosed area. The graves beyond are those of the Forrester family. Most in this area are burials from the 1820s. Photograph by Ian Jack, 2016.

Pitt Town in 1808. Although Benn's vault with its altar marker was probably erected in the 1840s, it marks the site of an earlier, simpler grave for the family, and an older marker is now the almost illegible stone covering the vault entry. The vault now contains the body of Benn's centenarian father-in-law, John Griffin who was born in 1733, the earliest birthdate in the cemetery, as well as Mrs Lydia Benn who died in 1846.[45]

The north-east lower slope soon received the son-in-law of the First Fleet convict merchants, Henry and Susannah Kable. William Gaudry, who had come to the colony free, had wed Diana Kable,

119. The entry to the vault under the altar monument where John Benn and his family are buried. The stone has part of the word 'McDonald' visible, and can thus be identified as an earlier gravemarker for the family. John McDonald was the second husband of Lydia Benn. Photograph by Ian Jack, 2016.

and the couple had later rented Blighton, once Governor William Bligh's property at Pitt Town, after William Gaudry's finances had been affected by the debt Kable found he owed Simeon Lord when their company split. Gaudry died in 1816 and his grave was to become the Kable family vault with altar monument.[46] The Andrew Thompson, Benn and Kable family vaults are almost in line ranging down the northern slope.

All these burials and many more in the new Windsor cemetery were made in a paddock devoid of any building on the ridge in the vicinity of Andrew Thompson's vault. Only three headstones survive intact from the first two years and only two from 1813–1815, but together with the other extant markers up to 1817, the spatial patterning of the earliest graves can be seen. The central position in the grounds was always intended for the church, and so by 1817 the lower ground to the north held the earliest graves of the poorer settlers, with the only other section apparently used by 1817 being the lower eastern side. The western side of the church, the south-western sector and the eastern area at the front of the church may well still have been unused for graves by 1817. The existing graves continued to be carefully placed so as to leave the central, section free for the church.

The Graveyard Becomes a Church Construction Site, 1817–1822

Construction work on the church began in 1817 and continued for five years until 1822. During this time burials continued around the building site. There is enough fabric surviving from before 1817 to see that the spatial arrangement of the graves appears to mirror the occupants' social status when alive. Those most lowly in the community in life were generally being buried on the lower slope of the northern side of the church. Most graves, however, now lack a marker and many of those may never have had a headstone. There is a degree of contrast with Wilberforce cemetery, where early families have substantial marked plots, because the families there tended to stay in closer proximity over the years.

After mid-May 1817 another fifteen burials had taken place before the foundation stone of the church was laid on 11 October. In the last months of 1817 another thirteen burials took place, all unmarked. Probably these were spreading along in the northern area below Thompson's vault, where there are surviving early markers. The burial of the ten-year-old Walker Fitz, whose father had property and status as clerk to the Windsor Bench, seems to have led to the opening up of the mid-western side of the churchyard as an area apart from the ex-convict families.[47]

During the next years, the church took shape and the exact space it would need became absolutely defined, although the workmen continued to toil on the church's exterior beyond 1819. It was then that the area to the south-west of the church came into use. Again it was the choice of a genteel family. The first burial there on the high ground at the front of the church was Rebecca Cox, the wife of William Cox, her position chosen by her magistrate husband. She had died on 3 March 1819 and was interred four days later. Another eighteen years elapsed before William was placed in the grave beside her in 1837.[48]

Two years later a second Hawkesbury family had a magistrate to bury and chose a location beside the Cox vault. Thomas Arndell of Cattai, a surgeon on the First Fleet and an early Hawkesbury magistrate, was interred in the south-western sector in a vault with an altar monument in May 1821.[49] Whilst there were other altar monuments in the graveyard by then, mostly on the eastern side, both the élite burials of Rebecca Cox and Thomas Arndell were on the opposite side of the church building, diagonally across, and as far away as possible, from the equally affluent markers of ex-convict merchants. These 1819–1821 decisions to bury in the south-western front corner appear to have been deliberate acts, a choice exercised as a social statement by the families of the departed, to retain in death the elevated place they perceived they occupied in life; for although the entrepreneurs on the east had won respect and wealth, those who set themselves up as colonial élite, having arrived free, met with them only in business or by necessity.

A distance away from the Cox and Arndell vaults on the western side, more graves of the respectable non-merchant, ex-convict community began to gather. A particularly well-known personality, Ann Bladdey (or Blady), was buried in 1820 just below Walker Fitz's grave. Ann was Lieutenant Considen's partner and the mother of his children in the early colony, and had then been married for twenty years to the constable and friend of Andrew Thompson, William Bladdey.

Ann Bladdey was commemorated with a handsome flat stone in the western part of the cemetery opposite and close to the tower entry to the church. Ann had been one of only a few women to receive a grant in her own name, and both William and Ann had been level-headed, solid citizens, coping with early colonial frontier conflict between the settlers and the Indigenous clans with humanity, even if fearful in themselves at times. She was a much relied-on midwife around Windsor, and was also the housekeeper at the government cottage at Hawkesbury for Lachlan and Elizabeth Macquarie on their early visits. It was Ann who arranged their first meal and stay in the Government House in December 1810.[50]

The area to the east of the new church, up the slope to the south of Thompson's vault, does not seem to have been used for burials until the 1820s. The lines of altar graves there show that this easterly position quickly become the preserve of the more lowly but not unsuccessful free arrivals and a few ex-convict merchants who died in the 1820s and 1830s.

George Loder's grandson died in 1820, aged one year, and the Loder plot seems to have been the first in this category. The altar monument may not have been added until 1834, or even until the

120. Gravemarker of Ann Bladdey or Blady (there are a number of variant spellings), 1820. Photograph by Ian Jack, 2009.

121. St Matthew's exterior looking east. The graves of Walker Fitz and Ann Bladdey are off to the right. Photograph by Wendy Dunstan, 2015.

original Loder in New South Wales had died in 1848, but the burial of the Loder baby was likely in this vault. The original George Loder had been a member of the New South Wales Corps, and then a settler and the Windsor gaoler.[51]

The vicinity of the Loder vault seems to have been an area favoured by the ex-military and ex-seamen: Thomas Dargin, originally a seaman, was, for example, buried close to Andrew Thompson in July 1824.[52] What this group had in common was their free background, less affluent lifestyle and later farming lives.

George Black, another soldier in the New South Wales Corps, was one of the few who did not sell his grant as part of a consolidation deal with other soldier grantees. He had been in the district 25 years. His burial took place on 14 September 1820, perhaps in this area.[53]

Below the vault of the Loders and to the north-west, there was already an altar monument for one of the best known and affluent families in the district, the Fitzgeralds. The need for a plot had become necessary when Richard Fitzgerald and his wife, Mary, needed to bury their teenage son Richard in April 1822. Having arrived in the colony at the age of seventeen, and having been sent to Toongabbie Government Farm, Richard Fitzgerald sr had soon begun to show the organizational and leadership qualities that made him one of the wealthiest ex-convict settlers in the colony at the time of his death in 1840.

From his first promotion as head of a convict work gang on the Government Farm, he had risen to hold powerful supervisory positions for the government on all the early Government Farms, to the charge of the Commissary's Store and convicts at Windsor and running the Government facility at Emu Plains.

The Fitzgeralds had moved to the district from Seven Hills (on Old Windsor Road), around 1806, just after Richard jr had been born. In the Hawkesbury, as well as at Parramatta and Seven Hills, Fitzgerald was for many years an agent for the powerful John Macarthur.[54]

Increasing Grave Density and a Working Church

The burial of Daniel Barnett (Barney) in the north-western sector nearer to the church is notable because on 17 February 1823 his was the first corpse to be taken into the church building for a funeral service.[55] Harpur noted that 'many of the oldest inhabitants of these parts' attended the service for Barnett, who had come on the First Fleet and been among the 1794 settlers on the Hawkesbury.

Barnett's original stone and footstone survive below Ann Bladdey's grave with a delightfully loving verse. Daniel had brought up his son after his wife's death, and the inscription includes the tribute: 'This stone was erected by his son Daniel as a lasting testimony of his filial love to a kind parent.'[56]

Daniel Barnet is the earliest of three initial grantees at Hawkesbury in 1794 whose graves are locatable in St Matthew's graveyard: the others were Robert Forrester in 1827, Benjamin Cussley in 1845.

122. The headstone and footstone of Daniel Barnett, the first corpse taken into the church building after it was consecrated in December 1822. The grave (in the foreground) is to the north-west of the church at the top of the slope, almost level with the line of the western end of the building. Photograph by Ian Jack, 2016.

John Brabyn, the magistrate who supported Joseph Docker in his struggle with William Cox and Archibald Bell, died in August 1835 and was buried in the south-western sector alongside Thomas Arndell and William Cox. As in life, competition was in evidence in this corner of the cemetery. Other families like the Tebbutts and Copes, similarly regarding themselves as élite, although not having magistrates amongst their family, chose this sector too. Wealthy widow Maria Cope buried her son there in 1830. The Cope altar monument uses several pedestals to raise it above the rest, striving to demonstrate that as in life the little boy was from an affluent family. The earliest Tebbutt burial was Ann, wife of free arrival and Windsor retailer, John. She had been

123. Plan of the churchyard. Photograph by Ian Jack, 2009.

buried in January 1837, aged 71 years. The present extremely large Tebbutt vault monument is a later addition, presumably including the plot in which Ann was buried.[57]

The eastern sector of the graveyard was particularly favoured by those of middling to high social status who could afford to erect an altar monument, many of them free arrivals in the colony, like James Raworth Kennedy, the son of an Anglican minister and a free settler of 1795. His daughter, Jane, was to marry Chief Constable John Howe in May 1811.[58] His sister married Andrew Hume: their son was Hamilton Hume, the well-known explorer.[59] A teacher in Windsor at York Lodge in later life, James Kennedy was buried close to the mid-point of the apse of the church in 1826.[60]

From then on around the eastern area more or less in a wide sweep south to north are the first burials and altar monuments of the Dunston, Hassall, Davies and Upton families who buried loved ones between 1827 and 1834. The line of vaults continues to merge with the early merchant vaults northwards with Charles Daley and Mary Beasley down to John Benn and below him Henry Kable and the Durham and Stewart families, amongst them members of established families like First Fleeter John Cross (no relation to the minister) who died in 1824.[61]

Both Susannah Holmes and her partner Henry Kable had, like Forrester, arrived as convicts on the First Fleet and had been amongst the first few couples married on Australian soil. The Kables prospered in Sydney through trading, farming, sealing and judicious lending of money on the surety of Hawkesbury farms but struggled after the partnership with Simeon Lord put Kable into enormous debt. When Susannah died in 1825, she was interred in the same vault as her son-in-law, William Gaudry, and her name was added to the altar stone. When in turn Henry Kable died in 1846, he too was buried there.[62]

Amongst the above swath of altar monuments, on the edge of the lower slope, are the two altar monuments built side by side which belong to the Fitzgerald family.

The two Fitzgerald vaults contain the bodies of at least seven family members who died between

1822 and 1865, including the original Richard Fitzgerald, whose body was brought from his large farming estate of Dabee near Rylstone in the Central West, to be buried in 1840. Around the earlier, most easterly of the two altar monuments, the metal fence is of fine blacksmith-wrought iron with twisted points all around, a rare survivor in cemeteries today. The later altar monument to the west has an iron fencing surround, but it is moulded and precast, not hand-made. Inside the church is a plaque commissioned by Richard's family and erected the following year.

The second altar monument with hand-wrought iron surround is at the southern end of the eastern side of the church, almost in a direct line south of the Fitzgerald graves to the front of the church. This vault contains members of the Rouse and Terry families associated with Rouse Hill House and Box Hill. It is shown in the Frederic Terry etching of 1855 of the church, which was

125. The ironwork around the earliest Fitzgerald altar monument is blacksmith-made, one of only two such wrought-iron railings in the cemetery. Photograph by Ian Jack, 2016.

124. The Terry-Rouse vault contains nine members of the family who died between 1833 and 1996. The wrought-iron railings are outstanding and were included in Terry's 1855 view of the church, shown in fig.126.

126. Detail of etching of St Matthew's, showing the Terry-Rouse altar monument and blacksmith-wrought railings in 1855, despite the monument being drawn as positioned across instead of more north–south. Artist F.C. Terry, published in *Landscape Scenery, Illustrating Sydney, Paramatta, Richmond, Maitland, Windsor and Port Jackson, New South Wales,* also known as *Australian Keepsake,* Sands and Kenny, Sydney and Melbourne, 1855, plate 30. Original steel engraving by Arthur Willmore, second impression, courtesy Royal Australian Historical Society.

discussed in detail in Chapter 5. There was, however, no relationship between the artist and the Terry family commemorated here.

The Terry vault today lists nine of the family buried between 1833 and 1996.[63] The family chose the front of the burial ground on the highest part of the ridge as the place of most respectability, on the eastern side of the church where all the earliest smart but non-élite burials were to be found in 1833.

Also in the south-east sector is Simon Freebody, who had arrived a convict with the First Fleet, had been convicted in the colony for murdering an Aboriginal boy, caught up in the frontier conflict with Robert Forrester and others at Cornwallis in 1799, but who became a successful farmer and died in December 1856 at the age of 103: he had been a resident of the Hawkesbury for 62 years.[64]

The Make-up of Society

In St Matthew's graveyard there are over twenty burials of men and women who arrived on the First Fleet in 1788 as convicts. Daniel Barnett, William Roberts, James Smith, Charles Williams and Ann Bladdey were amongst the earliest Hawkesbury grantees, while others, like John Merritt, John Anderson, John Cross and Henry and Susannah Kable acquired land in the district in the early nineteenth century. Some, like Thomas Arndell and William Goodhall, came free to the colony as surgeon and soldier respectively.

In the cemetery are at least another 150 eighteenth-century arrivals. Many of these were among the earliest Hawkesbury grantees or grantees' wives, including Rachel Burton, Stephen Smith, Elizabeth Waring, Thomas West, Edward Reynolds, Thomas Rickaby, William Aspinall, Mary Goodall, John Badlife, George Tilly, Ann and James Richards and Elizabeth Jackson. There are also many of the early Cornwallis farmers, like Thomas and Sarah Upton, William Duckett and Nicholas Crosby, along with other ex-convicts and free settlers who prospered, such as William Baker (*Neptune*), landowner and publican, William Ezzy, Andrew Doyle and William Roberts. Many other burials are those who died in the district whilst still serving their sentences as convicts.

'Paupers' as a group began to be identified in the registers in 1826, but the first to be buried in the cemetery was John Badlife, a 1794 settler, who died destitute in Windsor Hospital in May 1829 aged 93. He was followed three months later by John Burke, probably the 1795 Cornwallis ex-convict settler, aged 71. During the 1830s other men and women were buried as 'paupers', receiving some form of charity from the Hawkesbury Benevolent Society. The original convict barracks at Windsor was transformed into the Windsor Hospital in 1823. Among officials from the hospital buried at St Matthew's were two overseers, John Tunnicliffe in 1832 and John Benyson Hern in 1840, the gatekeeper William Roberts in 1833, and the dispenser of medicines John Taylor in 1839.[65]

Pauper burials in unmarked graves were numerous up to 1867. In the 1830s there were about 65, of whom 21 had died in the poor house, 29 in the hospital and fourteen at home. In the 1840s there were 80 such burials, almost all the paupers listed as dying in the Benevolent Asylum. By contrast, in the 1860s between 1860 and 1867 there were 58 such deaths, all at the hospital, but only one pauper death in 1868 and in 1869. During the 1870s there were nineteen such burials, all from the Benevolent Asylum, and in the 1880s 33, mostly from the asylum.

The large number of paupers and prisoners buried at St Matthew's is evident only from the registers since characteristically there were no gravemarkers. The story told by the extant gravestones today conceals the width of social inclusiveness in St Matthew's, and the cemetery's deep connection with the district's convict past. Buried in unmarked graves were convicts identified as serving in seven road gangs. Between 1830 and 1835 twelve men working in various road gangs who died in the area were buried in the cemetery. The age of ten of these convicts is given: three were in their early twenties, five in their thirties and the other two were aged 49 and 57. Five convicts who had reoffended in the colony and had been sent to work in iron gangs were also buried in St Matthew's between 1830 and 1835: their ages ranged between 25 and 63.

Most of the nineteenth-century burials were, from the nature of settlement composition, people of European descent, but there were a few exceptions. The first burial of another race was Black Benedict in 1820. A native of Tahiti, aged about 35 and known only as Charles, was buried in 1822. In January 1852 two Chinese labourers in the service of Mr Fitzgerald, known as Ong Khai and Chooing Hong, both of whom had arrived on the *Ganges*, were buried but had no ceremony, because they were 'Heathen'. On 14 September 1855 another Chinese man was buried at St Matthew's, one of the paupers who had died in Windsor Hospital. In the register his entry reads: 'Tuim-Tuim ... a Chinese. No service performed. The man being an unbaptized Heathen. H.T.S[tiles].'[66]

'Boyallie Sambo' or Sam Brown, who died in 1928 aged 101 years, was a native of the New Hebrides who is presumed to have remained loyally with the Brown family when they returned to live near Windsor,[67] and two Aboriginal people are listed as being buried. One, in 1887, was called Charles Porter from Queensland; the other, in 1888, Elizabeth Browne from Blacktown.[68]

The cemetery is a rich field for research with a rich array of stone markers (both headers and footers) from the early nineteenth century, and monuments of marble, sandstone, one of iron and others, more modern, of cement and granite. The pre-Victorian monuments are important as one of the most striking collections of vernacular carving in Georgian style. Above all the spatial relationships among graves reflect Hawkesbury society's variety and self-perceptions.

The long reign of Queen Victoria became marked by increasing detail and ornamentation in architecture, painting and daily life in the decoration within the home from antimacassars over armchairs to drapes in doorways and potted aspidistra plants on hall stands, in stark contrast to Georgian simplicity. In the cemeteries an enthusiasm for decoration changed the plain anthropomorphic gravemarkers. Decorative emblems appeared: woven stone wreaths of leaves and flowers, and the hour-glass symbol of death morphed into symbolic ropes (connectedness), anchors (a symbol of hope and steadfastness), wings and birds (peace), clasped hands (unity and togetherness), scallop-shells (a pilgrim's journey or resurrection) and lilies (returning the soul to innocence)[69] until the markers themselves became new shapes and elaborate, tall compilations. Marble became common for the well-to-do.

Winged cherubs were a popular symbolism of the late Victorian period in Windsor. They have engaged historians of necrology ever since two American scholars published a seminal article in 1966, which examined the transition from the winged death's-heads of the seventeenth century to the cherubs of the eighteenth and nineteenth centuries.[70] In St Matthew's the motif appears on four gravemarkers carved between 1872 and 1895.[71]

The prominent local stonemason, George Robertson, and his employee John Charles O'Kelly carved cherubs for the family of Henry Curtis, a small farmer who died in 1880 and probably for

127. The gravemarker at St Matthew's carved by George Robertson for farmer Henry Curtis who died of an accidental gunshot wound in 1880. Photograph by Jan Barkley-Jack, 1998.

William Townsend, the father-in-law of Henry Curtis, in 1895.

The Curtis and Townsend markers are to the west of the church and other examples of cherubs are in the south-east near Moses Street, commissioned for the Beveridge family in the 1880s. They stand at the front of the cemetery allotment towards Greenway Crescent, where the graves are closely arranged, rich in Victorian motifs.

Many of those buried in this location were professional people, or were the descendants of families long resident in the district. Included here are the graves of the Mullingers, a well-known local family of builders for several generations. Five-year-old James was the first Mullinger burial in 1856.

128. Carvings probably by George Robertson, of a cherub and deep lush foliage on the grave of William Townsend, died in 1895. Cherubim were the second order of angels who attended on God, and to be in the presence of a cherub brought one closer to God. Grape vines were a symbol for prosperity. William Townsend was related to the Curtis family. Photograph by Jan Barkley-Jack, 1998.

However, by the later part of the century 67 other members of the family were interred including James Mullinger who built Glenroy, a handsome villa at 465 George Street, South Windsor, between 1878 and his death in 1890. Another buried in this south-west sector in February 1858 had a more unusual profession: William Dettmer of Pitt Town was a piano maker from Marylebone, London.[72]

The Primrose gravemarker is a striking amalgam of popular motifs of the Victorian period, culminating in the top of the monument itself becoming a snapped-off tree branch, symbolic of a life cut short. It was erected for John Primrose, a successful ex-convict who ran the Bell Inn in Little Church Street, Windsor, on part of Maria Cope's subdivision.

After he died in 1856 his family erected a high, white marble monument with a variety of Victorian symbols: a broken trunk of loss, the anchor of hope, the extinguished torch of death and the shell of resurrection. The elaborate Primrose gravemarker, raised on a series of four stone bases, towered over all others in the 1850s and is a prime example of the wish to demonstrate increased wealth and social position. John Primrose's son, Thomas, became a magistrate and was four times mayor of the new municipality of Windsor which he did much to create in 1871.[73]

The most ostentatious monument in the cemetery is not a gravemarker but a memorial, discussed in chapter 6. It dominates the entry to the church, erected in 1882 in memory of Mrs Amelia Ann McQuade and her parents, James and Mary Hale.

For the church over two hundred years, the cemetery has at once been a consistent source of revenue for the church and a maintenance charge upon its physical and monetary resources. The cost of owning a plot was carefully controlled and was adjusted from time to time.

In 1863 a new system of charges was introduced, whereby a basic grave-enclosure was to cost one shilling per square foot, with a maximum of 81 square feet. If more land was needed, for example to build a vault, then it could be bought *pro rata*. Vaults incurred additional charges, depending on their capacity. Each space for a coffin would cost £1 10s., so that a nine-person vault would cost £13

129. The grandiose marble gravemarker of John Primrose, 1856. The symbols of death include the shell, the anchor and the broken tree trunk. Photograph by Jan Barkley-Jack, 1998.

10s. in addition to the cost of the land.[74]

With adjustments over the years, such revenues loom large in the church accounts. Although there was always paid assistance, the upkeep often fell upon parishioners. Throughout the great series of minute books, spanning a century and a half, working-bees among the weeds, scrub and ever-present prickly pear are a recurrent theme.

Paths, Fences and Buildings in the Graveyard

The grant of the cemetery land was not finally ratified until 19 June 1843, when the title was properly transferred to Bishop Broughton and four local trustees, Samuel North, John Panton, Francis Beddek and Thomas Tebbutt.[75]

The cemetery continued to fill up as population grew in the town and surrounding farming district. The early distinctions made among the various social positions of the families buried there continued to evolve, but became more complex, particularly as generation followed generation. In the main, the graves of ex-convict families continued to be situated in the northern, low-lying, periphery.

In organizing the layout of the St Matthew's and other burial grounds, Macquarie's earliest orders went further than just requiring residents to be buried there. They required the settlers to fence the new burial grounds. The governor called this their 'sacred duty' since this was the best means to protect the remains of their relatives and friends from roaming animals and other mishaps.

Prescriptive as ever, Macquarie required the fencing to be done immediately and securely, either by means of 'a good wall or strong palisades'. As an encouragement Macquarie pledged a government contribution of ten pounds sterling towards the ground's enclosure.[76]

This order was published in the *Sydney Gazette* on two occasions in May 1811, so settlers at Hawkesbury would have been well aware of its contents.[77] However, it would have been William Cox as magistrate who organized the construction team in Richmond and in Windsor. Cox was paid £40 for 'fencing the burial ground at Windsor' during the quarter July to September 1811.[78] The promised government subscription of £10 towards the cost was paid to Cox in the last quarter of 1812.[79] The specifications for the fence around the Richmond burial ground give some idea of what could be the expected fencing initially at the other cemeteries including Windsor's new ground: 'the Fence to be of split Posts, Rails, and Paling ... the Paling to be 5 feet 6 Inches long, the Pannels to be 9 Feet in length, and 2 Rails each ... The Nails will be found, and the Stuff brought in.'[80]

By 1813 the permanent fencing around the graveyard appears to have been completed, as Macquarie paid William Cox the government's share of the cost. Perhaps it was no accident that during that same year, 1813, Governor Macquarie went ahead with the new and impressive gravemarker for Andrew Thompson's vault that he and wife Elizabeth had promised that day in December 1810 when they paid their respects to their friend at his graveside. In July 1822 the former governor, Lachlan Macquarie, reported that all six of his graveyards were now composed of four acres and were all fenced.[81]

130. Hardy Wilson's famous drawing of St Matthew's looking from the north-east showing a romantic view of the graveyard with four massive altar tombs amid luxuriant vegetation to emphasize the church in what Wilson called his 'architecture of sunlight and shadow'. Hardy WIlson, 1919, published in his *Old Colonial Architecture in New South Wales* as plate 30.

In fact, however, St Matthew's cemetery, including the site of the church, consisted of only 3 acres and 23 perches, a measurement which was confirmed by the final appropriation of the ground in 1833.[82] The fencing, although duly erected under William Cox's supervision in 1811, kept falling into disrepair and remained a recurrent cost to the church. Wandering stock entering the graveyard through defective fencing was still a problem late in the nineteenth century.[83]

On the south-eastern side of the church the regular pattern of the later nineteenth century's mainly north–south grave orientation is interrupted by three graves at right angles to the others. One of these is a military grave of 1837 and it may be that this area near the eastern fence-line, previously unused, was expected to contain a group of soldiers' graves. Sergeant William Horton died in Windsor on 27 December 1837 almost as soon as his 80th Regiment was stationed in the barracks. The lettering of the inscription is idiosyncratic, with the guidelines still visible, and may have been done by another member of the regiment.[84]

The upkeep of the cemetery was initially the responsibility of the local magistrates, but from 1838 onwards wardens were appointed with responsibility for the finances of the church and graveyard. One warden was appointed by the rector, while the other three were elected by the Parish Council representing the congregation. This still continues, with the wardens being elected or appointed each March for the ensuing twelve months.[85] Secure fencing remained a perennial cost. The burial ground was systematically re-fenced in 1849 for over £47.[86] Although there is a good deal in the minutes of the parish meetings about repairs to the fencing around the cemetery, it was clearly ineffectual. As late as 1882, the wardens had to instruct the sexton to impound all trespassing cattle and in the following year it was decided to build a new fence along Cornwallis Road (now Greenway Crescent). Few things happened quickly at St Matthew's: tenders were advertised only in January 1884 and the work, costing £26 15s. was not completed until July.[87]

This fence is likely to be the simple wooden fence shown in an undated photograph, probably taken in the early twentieth century.[88] That fence is constructed of high vertical planks supported by strong upright posts and two cross-bars. It was in sharp contrast to the succession of paling fences along the Moses Street front of the church and cemetery land. In 1824 Standish Harris' report described how: 'The fence in front of the Burial Ground is a strong palisading on a base stone coping, well painted, and in good preservation, but the opposite fence is in a very bad state, and

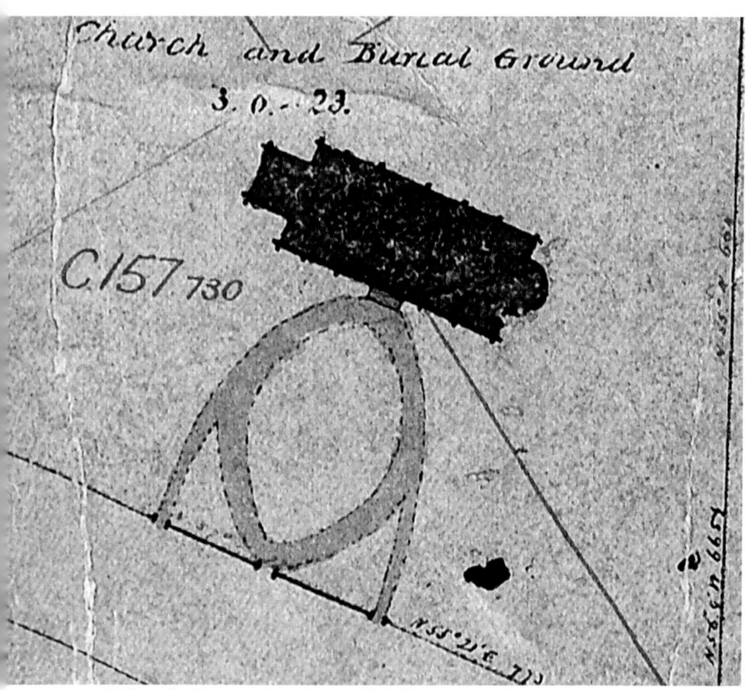

131. Galloway's plan of 1841, showing an oval driveway with three entrances at St Matthew's. There was no south porch at this time, but Galloway shows the foundations laid by Greenway. Land and Property Information, Crown Plan, W 443a.

132. Fencing along Greenway Crescent, to the right, and along Moses Street, to the left, probably in the early twentieth century. Hawkesbury City Library, photograph 006418.

requires to be made new'.[89]

A survey of the church allotment made by the surveyor Galloway in 1841 shows an elaborately conceived oval double carriageway from Moses Street to the south door of the church, with two pedestrian entries on either hand.[90] A triple entry of this sort is implied in Standish Harris's listing in 1824 of 'a pair of Palisade Gates painted, Hinges and Panels', which would be the carriage entry, along with '2 small do. [ditto]', which would be the side-gates.[91]

In Terry's famous etching, published in 1855, discussed in Chapter 5, there is only a plain single footpath extending to the church door. This could be regarded as artistic licence or perhaps Galloway was suggesting improvements.[92]

Nineteenth-century images show trees and scrub beyond the church on the west and north. The sparse tree plantings close to the south side of the church and beside the entry path did not survive. As the graveyard became planted to its limits with monuments and markers the shrubbery disappeared.

Care and sentimentality were lavished on the graves of relatives in the Victorian era. But many of the children and grandchildren of the early settlers at Hawkesbury had moved to properties across the Blue Mountains, in the Hunter Valley and in the Southern Highlands by the time Sydney Fielding's ministry at Windsor came to an end in mid-1904. This reduced the number of family members dedicated to caring for the early graves. Instead of well-tended family shrines, the graves in old churchyards like St Matthew's were gradually neglected as families thinned and memories dimmed. The upkeep of the cemetery became an increasing concern for the wardens and the parish council. Already by 1900 the impressive slab placed by Macquarie over the grave of Andrew Thompson lay 'prone amidst the long grass' beside its four original columns.[93]

8 Two Glebes and a Rectory

The Glebes

133. Looking east from the church tower across to the Rectory glebe and the Rectory and stable complex. Photograph by Graham and Carol Edds, 2008.

It was recognized in the early colony that an allocation of land and an initial loan of stock were necessary to sustain first the assistant chaplains and then, as Anglican churches increased in number, the parish ministers. At St Matthew's there were two quite separate areas designated as glebe land, though each of these contracted markedly in size in the 1830s. The original glebe of 400 acres, known as the old glebe, was at Clarendon nearly three kilometres from the church, but when it contracted in size it became known as the new glebe. The other glebe near the church lay immediately adjacent to the land on which the Rectory was built.

The old glebe consisted of 400 acres (160 hectares) laid aside for the use of the minister by Governor Macquarie on 12 January 1811. The governor described the site as 'very good both for tillage and for pasturage, and extremely well watered, having a lagoon forming the northern boundary.'[1] Although the glebe was treated as established, no official registration of the grant happened until 1822, when the church was completed, and then only at Samuel Marsden's insistence.[2] The land was part of Richmond Hill Common which had been declared by Governor King in 1804.[3] It was located in an irregular rectangle south and south-east of the present village of Clarendon, bounded on the south-east by the extension of the line of Cox Street in Windsor, crossing Rickabys Creek and incorporating the whole of the later Racecourse as its north-east sector. The 'lagoon' described by Macquarie appears as a 'swamp' on Felton Mathew's map 23 years later.[4]

A 31½ acre glebe survived the excision of 200 acres for the Racecourse in 1865 along with 21 allotments of five acres each measured for sale on the western side. The sale lots constituted a long narrow strip running right down to Rickabys Creek.[5]

The first rector, Robert Cartwright, who had his own house and farm on the east side of what is now Percival Street between Windsor and Richmond, complained that, since he already had grazing rights on the common and since the new glebe land was unfenced, he was gaining nothing by the declaration of a glebe.[6] In 1819 Cartwright denied that the glebe as an entity existed since it had neither title nor fencing. He blamed that as the reason he had been forced to rent a farm for £30 a year. Cartwright also thought it 'hard' that the governor would not purchase his farm 'on any terms' for a glebe.[7]

The principal chaplain, Samuel Marsden, had a comparable problem. He complained that his 400 acres of glebe, situated at Parramatta, were 'of bad & middling Land, unenclosed & not cleared' and gave him no benefit at all, but he begrudgingly admitted to Commissioner Bigge that, although it too was not adjacent to where he lived, he did make use of it because 'it is better so than if it were farther off.'[8]

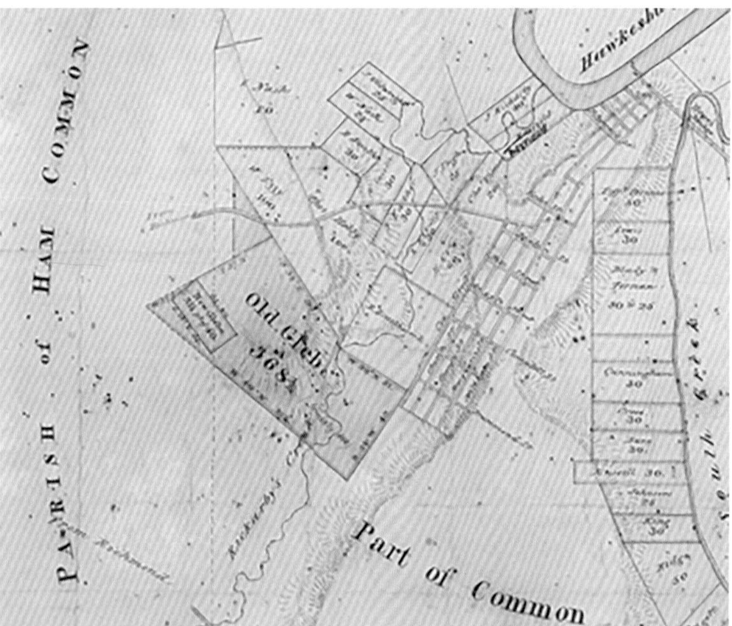

134. The old glebe and the subsequent, much reduced, new glebe at Clarendon. J. Armstrong, 'Plan of the New & Old Glebe adjoining the Town of Windsor', 1837, State Library of New South Wales, Mitchell Library, ZM2 811.1122/1837/1.

Cartwright left St Matthew's in 1819 and by 1822, when systematic records begin, his successor John Cross was leasing out twenty acres (8 hectares) of the Clarendon glebe for £20 a year and had on loan from the government six head of cattle to graze on the rest of the glebe, which was still unfenced.[9] In 1823 Cross returned the government stock but continued to have use of the glebe until 1827 when he was paid an annual sum of £100 in lieu of the glebe.[10]

Macquarie intended to build a parsonage house at Windsor and was conscious by 1817 that both Castlereagh and Liverpool already had rectories. He reported back to Britain in April 1817 that the Windsor Rectory would 'be commenced as soon as the Church at that Station has been Erected'.[11] The church itself took much longer to build than had been envisaged and plans for the Rectory do not seem to have been drawn until 1822, the year in which the church was consecrated. Macquarie confidently reported to London in July 1822 that a 'New Parsonage House near [St Matthew's] is now in progress', but no tenders had been sought, no foundations laid.[12] Only on 30 October 1823 was there a call for tenders in the *Sydney Gazette*, with a closing date of 1 December.[13]

At the same time the church land around the new rectory was surveyed. This was separated from St Matthew's church by Cornwallis Road, now known as Greenway Crescent. This land had apparently never been officially 'approved or confirmed' [14]

Around 1828 a survey showed this land extending eastwards as far as George Street and encompassing just over fourteen acres (5.6 hectares), but five and a half acres of this was 'considered by the Inhabitants as belonging to the Town'.[15]

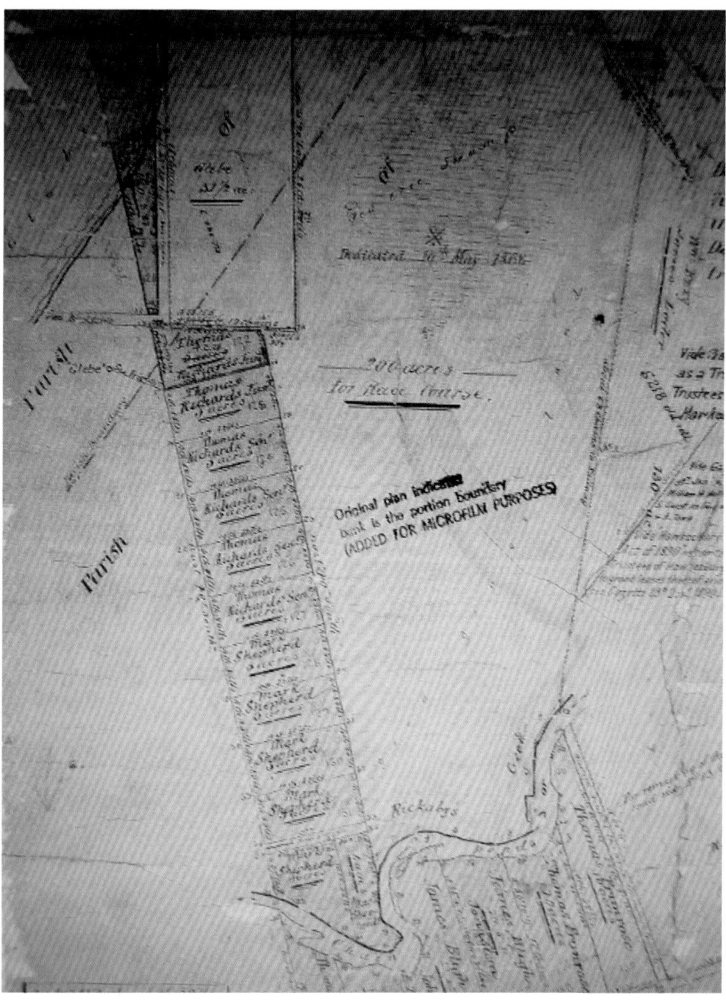

135. (Left) The subdivision of the 400 acres of the St Matthew's Clarendon glebe in 1865. Land and Property Information, Crown Plan, C909 .690.

136. Photograph taken from St Matthew's belfry around 1910 looking east towards the Rectory and what remained of the Rectory glebe. Originally much of the area in the top right-hand corner had also been part of the glebe for two blocks through to George Street, Windsor. Cutting supplied by Kim Alderton.

Work Begins on the Rectory

The successful tenderer for the building of the Rectory was William Cox, the local magistrate who had supplied the bricks for the church.

Cox began work briskly, perhaps before 1823 was out. The returns of the colony for 1823 claimed, optimistically, that the Reverend John Cross's parsonage was 'nearly finished'.[16] The main rectory building seems to have been largely well advanced in 1824, when in October further tenders were sought 'for the Building of Office-houses, to be attached to the Parsonage-house at Windsor'.[17]

These 'Office-houses' must be the kitchen, attached to the rear of the Rectory, and the detached stables. The whole was completed in 1825. Cox received payment in four instalments, two in 1824 and two in 1825. The total amount paid to Cox was almost Spanish $10,000. The fourth and final payment was for the 'parsonage house at Windsor etc.': the 'etc.' must refer to the kitchen and stables.[18]

There is no reasonable doubt that the contractor for the rectory complex was William Cox. The identity of the architect is a more vexed question. Long before the tenders for the parsonage and its stables were issued, William Cox had received a plan for stables. He got this on 9 May 1820 from Henry Kitchen, who had been displaced by Greenway in the building of St Matthew's. Kitchen also gave a signed copy of the design to John Macarthur, for whom he was to build Hambledon Cottage at Parramatta in 1821. This copy survives in the Macarthur archives, but it is clear that the original plan was given to Cox.[19] Although Cox's copy of Kitchen's plan seems to be lost, the Macarthur copy shows that there were similarities and dissimilarities with the Windsor stables. There is no proof that Kitchen gave Cox a plan for a parsonage as well as for a stable.

Kitchen died on 8 April 1822 and Greenway was removed from the position of Civil Architect the following November. The tender advertisements say clearly that the plans and specifications for the Rectory in October 1823 and for the outbuildings in September 1824 were available at the Chief Engineer's office in Sydney: the outbuildings plan was also available from John Howe, the Chief Constable at Windsor.[20] It is highly unlikely that these plans had been conceived by Kitchen. Much later, in 1835, Greenway claimed that he furnished plans for 'a parsonage house at Windsor', which must refer to St Matthew's.

Greenway may have drawn up plans of the Rectory for Macquarie before they both left their offices in 1821–1822. Commissioner Bigge, despite his general hostility to emancipists, had in 1820 approached Greenway about designing the Rectory.[21] The rectory building itself is compatible with a Greenway design. On balance, therefore, it seems very likely that Greenway was the architect of both the church and the parsonage.

The kitchen wing and the stables, for which there were separate plans, are less straightforward.

Greenway did not claim the stables, but this is inconclusive. His successor as Civil Architect, Standish Harris, held the position over the key period, 1822 to 1824. Architectural historian James Broadbent describes Harris' two-year tenure as 'ignominious' and it is true that it was not distinguished: not a single building has been plausibly attributed to Harris.[22] But the Windsor stables may just possibly be by Standish Harris.

The parsonage was occupied by the Reverend John Cross from 1825 onwards[23] and all subsequent rectors have normally resided there. Joseph Docker, the fourth rector, ran a boys' school in the Rectory for three years from 1829. James Dowling, one of the students, who was the son of a future chief justice, later wrote in his memoirs that the boys learnt very little and that the rectory building was 'ugly'. In hindsight, Dowling thought that it was the sort of place which 'Dickens would have peopled with "queer characters"'.[24]

Docker's correspondence with the Committee of the Clergy and School Corporation showed that the lack of painting of the woodwork of church buildings, the lack of maintenance of the shingles on the roof of the Rectory and the protracted negotiations and high level of proof of economy required in the quotes for work to be done, all worked to cause early deterioration of the fabric of the parsonage, as detailed in Chapter 4. The saga over the essential item of a well for drinking water, illustrates well the justness of his complaints. The Minutes of the Committee of the Clergy and School Corporation for 12 August 1829, signed by Archdeacon Scott in Sydney, show:

> Present: The Venerable Archdeacon T.H. Scott, the Hon. Alexander McLeay, the Revd. Samuel Marsden, the Revd. William Cowper, the Revd. Richard Hill.
>
> The Archdeacon submitted the Revd. J. Docker's request to have a well sunk at the Windsor Parsonage, and the Clerk was desired to inform him that prior to the Committee sanctioning the expense, they requested he should consult with some person conversant with the situation and ascertain as nearly as possible the probable depth required or probable cost of the undertaking.[25]

Although Docker resigned in March 1833, he continued to live in the parsonage and left only at the end of February 1834.[26] Henry Stiles had been appointed to the charge on 1 September 1833.

137. South elevation of St Matthew's Rectory, as it was in 1931. Helen Baker, *Historic Buildings: Windsor and Richmond*, State Planning Authority of New South Wales, Sydney, 1967, p. 13. The elevations and plans were drawn by John L. Browne for Professor Wilkinson and were used by the Public Works Department.

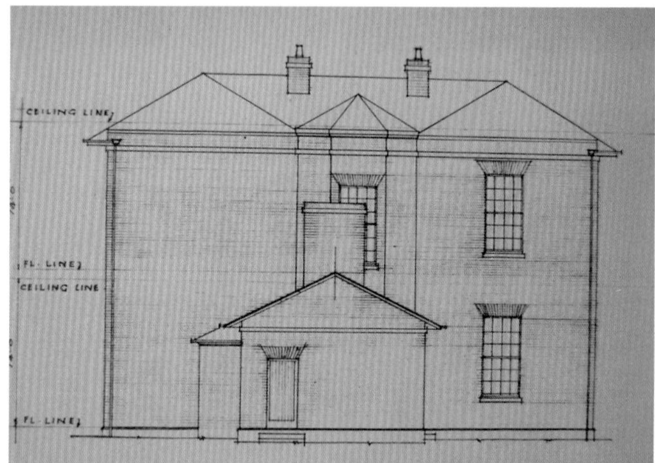

138. West (back) elevation of St Matthew's Rectory, as it was in 1931. Helen Baker, *Historic Buildings: Windsor and Richmond*, State Planning Authority of New South Wales, Sydney, 1967, p. 12. The elevation was drawn by John L. Browne.

He was given an allowance of £60 a year to lease accommodation until the Rectory was vacant and he seems to have moved into the house at the beginning of April 1834 after repairs had been done.[27] Stiles was uneasy about the expense of maintaining so spacious a rectory. While Docker was still in residence, Stiles had written to the Colonial Secretary in February 1834 complaining that: 'I now find that to keep in repair so large a house will be more expensive than I anticipated and than I can afford'.[28]

The Colonial Secretary conferred with the Archdeacon and scribbled a judgment of Solomon on the back of Stiles' letter:

> I concur with [the Archdeacon] ... that the size of the Chaplain's House at Windsor is disproportioned to the Chaplain's Stipend, and that it would be a hardship on Mr Styles to insist on his occupying it and keeping it in repair. It will be perhaps be found advantageous to dispose of this House hereafter tho' I apprehend it can not be done at present without loss, and it must at all events undergo some immediate repair.
>
> Let Mr Styles therefore be informed that on the House being put into tenantable condition he will be required to occupy it and his lodging allowance will cease, but that he is to understand that he is to surrender the House when called upon ... so to do in which case he will either be provided with a more suitable House which he will be required to keep in repair, or he will return to the allowance for lodgings. In the mean time whilst he occupies the larger House it will be kept in repair as heretofore.
>
> The Col. Architect has I believe been already desired to inspect the House when Mr Docker is leaving it & to report what repairs are required.[29]

The Stiles family remained in the Rectory during the whole 34 years Henry Stiles remained rector at St Matthew's. Visitors like Jane Franklin, and servants like the washerwoman, Alice Trelly, came and went, children grew up and moved away to their own lives. Stiles' daughter Mary was the one who remained the longest at the Rectory, for as wife of the next minister, Charles Garnsey, she was to return between 1867 and 1876.

During her 1839 visit with Bishop Broughton Lady Franklin claimed: 'It is an ugly red brick house, said to be the best parsonage in the colony – it is probably the ugliest also.'[30]

Warm appreciation of the architecture had to wait for the twentieth century. Rachel Roxburgh (who played a major role in the National Trust conservation of the church in 1963–1965)[31] saw the Rectory as a fine exemplar of eighteenth-century virtues:

> A gentle, well-mannered background to living, with ample space, yet manageable in size, and with detail that is decorative but without ostentation. ... The front door is accented with charm and elegance; the carved wooden cornice above the semi-circular fanlight is welcoming, not intimidating.[32]

Echoes of the correspondence of an ungrateful

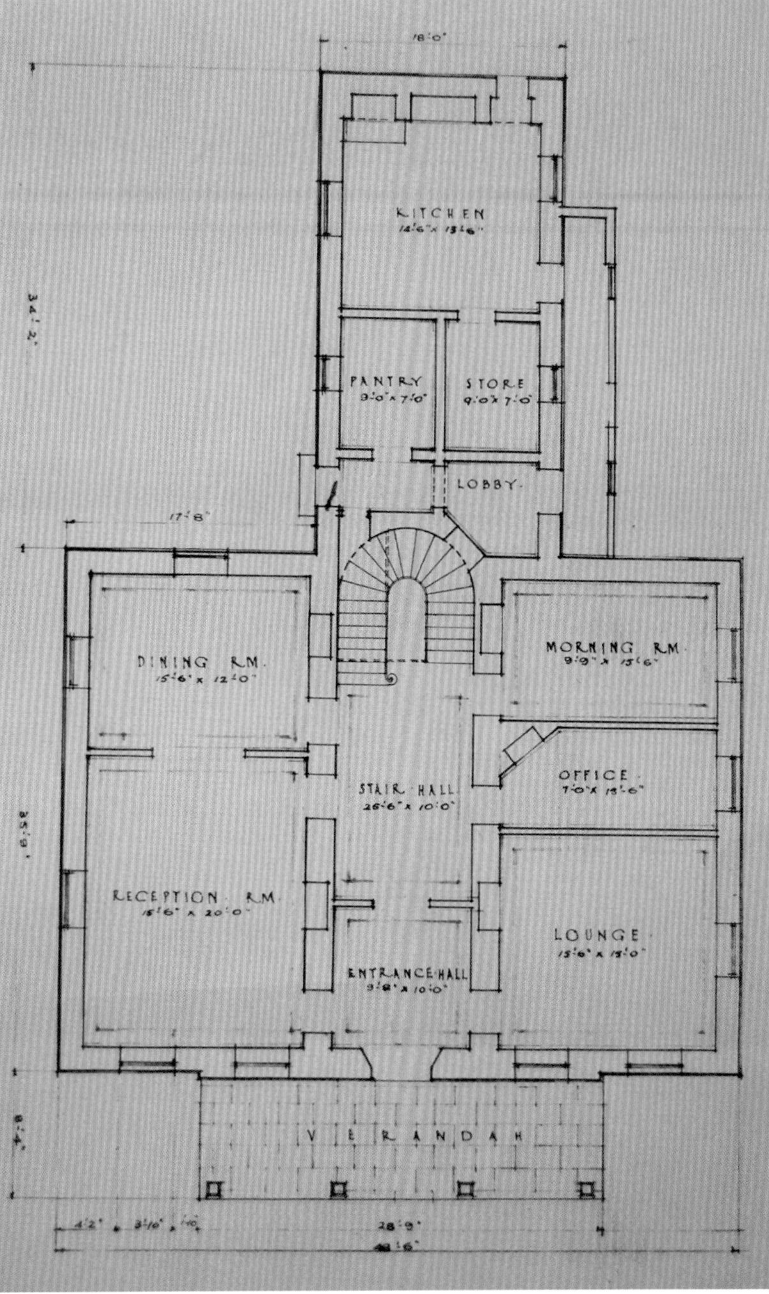

139. Plan of the ground floor of St Matthew's Rectory, as it was in 1931. Helen Baker, *Historic Buildings: Windsor and Richmond*, State Planning Authority of New South Wales, Sydney 1967, p. 12, plan by John L. Browne.

rector from 1829 can be heard in the twentieth century, when other ministers did not appreciate the Georgian rectory and when there were moves to replace it 'with a more suitable House' or even to demolish it altogether. It survived as the Rectory in the Victorian period because Stiles and the church hierarchy did not pursue the course of action suggested by the Colonial Secretary in 1834.

140. The front façade of the Rectory today. Photograph by Chris Jones, rector of St Matthew's, 2016.

141. St Matthew's Rectory, 1901, taken by Mrs Foster. Royal Australian Historical Society.

142. Detail of Mrs Foster's photograph, the group of figures shown outside the Rectory in the right-hand corner of the above photo. Royal Australian Historical Society.

Changes to the Glebes

When Henry Stiles became rector in 1833, the current provisions were noted in the Annual Returns: 'Each chaplain is allowed a Glebe of 40 acres (16 hectares) and two men clothed and rationed by government for the purpose of cultivating etc.'[33] This 40 acres was defined as lying in two separate locations, with 31 acres 1 rod 34 perches (12.5 hectares) in a rectangle excised from the north-west corner of the former 400 acres in Clarendon. The reduced Clarendon glebe had been fenced on all four sides by the middle of 1834.[34] Its shape had been redefined as a straightforward rectangle. A hut had been erected in the northern part of the glebe. This land was regularly let and during the mid-Victorian period £15 a year was paid by the lessee.[35] Although the sum was not fixed, it was reaffirmed as £15 in 1926.[36] Despite the church being entitled to appoint trustees for the Clarendon glebe, in 1882 it was decided to vest ownership in the Diocesan Property Trust under the archbishop.[37] In 1898 Hawkesbury Agricultural College made a complaint about the problem of additional water over Richmond Road at the Rickaby Creek bridge caused by the draining of the Clarendon glebe. The water continued to lie there for a considerable time.[38]

The second location defined for the St Matthew's glebe was the remaining land around the Rectory. By 1834 the original fourteen acres around the Rectory had been reduced to eight and a half acres ending at The Terrace instead of George Street. The eastern five and a half acres had been subdivided around Little Church Street. The Catholic church, also dedicated to St Matthew, was built in this eastern part of the former Anglican glebe between 1836 and 1840.[39] The eastern section along The Terrace had been occupied by a 'garden' at that time, while a small area was fenced off at the north end of the garden paddock, hard against Twyfield's grant of 1794. The boundary is shown as Twyfield's Line in Macquarie's survey of 1812 and some later maps.[40] By 1843 the eastern paddock had been enlarged, with a different fence line, bounded on the east by Rickaby's grant of 1798. This boundary is shown as Rickaby's Line in 1812.

Again by 1843 the garden had contracted to the

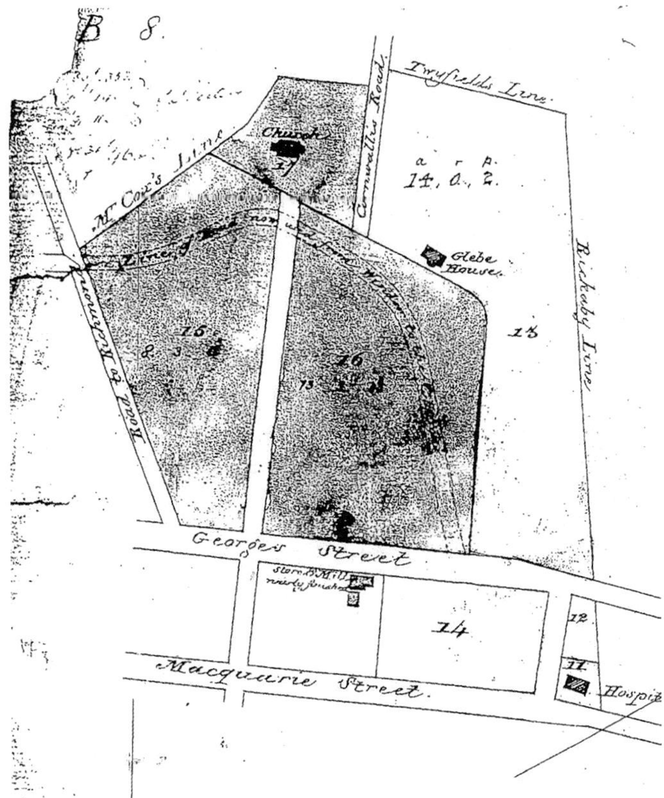

143. The Rectory shown within its glebe at its fullest extent shown in a map of 1828. State Records NSW, Surveyors' Sketchbook, Reel 2778, vol. 1 B8, X 750 A53.

area immediately beside the Rectory. The house and its stabling now lay within a fenced square, internally divided into four separate areas. The glebe proper lay beyond this square, fenced into three paddocks of unequal size. The largest paddock had its western boundary along Cornwallis Road and then along the old Twyfield's line. On the east the garden of the mid-1830s had been incorporated into an irregularly shaped paddock, with a new small enclosure at the north end.[41]

The Rectory had a kitchen garden to the east in the 1830s separately fenced off from the glebe-land. The principal gate into the property was made of palings in the 1840s.[42] Work on the various fences around the Rectory grounds are recurrent items over the rest of the nineteenth century but the details are rarely supplied in the Wardens' Accounts. In 1899 some bold and heartless thieves stole the fence around the Rectory, and later came back for the entrance gates. The local paper commented wryly that 'Later on they will probably steal the house itself, brick by brick'.[43]

A Focus on the Whole Precinct

Presumably the Rectory was renovated before Stiles moved there in April 1834 and the church, not the rector, then took responsibility for keeping the building in repair. Samuel Marsden had died in the upstairs bedroom on the east frontage of the Rectory in 1838, but this did not impede works, for immediately after Marsden's death, Charles Clifford was paid £10 for unspecified repairs to the parsonage.[44] This was also the time that the church roof was re-shingled and the churchyard fences and gates were repaired.[45]

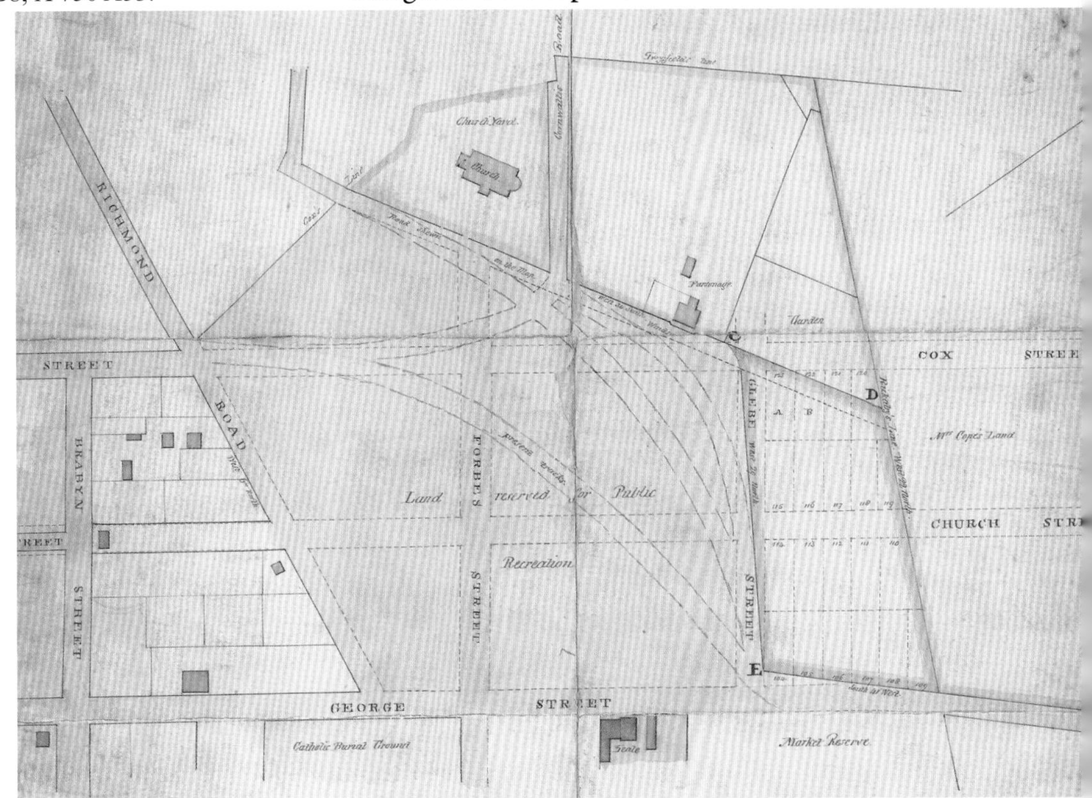

144. The church and Rectory glebe land in relation to the later McQuade Park, 1835. State Records NSW, Surveyors' Sketchbook, Reel 2778 vol.3 part 1 between 0498 and 0499

145. The Rectory of St Matthew's today, facing Moses Street, Windsor. Photograph by Chris Jones, rector of St Matthew's, 2016.

146. The kitchen, with its massive chimney, attached to the back of the Rectory in 1825, and its later built-in verandah. Photograph by Chris Jones, rector of St Matthew's, 2016.

Unspecified repairs to the Rectory are recurrent items in the Wardens' Accounts in the 1840s. The shingles on the Rectory roof required attention in 1842. The sum involved, £12 15s. 2d. suggests that about half of the roof was re-shingled: five years later nearly £6 had to be spent on more shingling and a final £21 in 1849.[46] The interior rooms were plastered and painted, with recurrent reworking. The most extensive works were done in 1847 and 1848, when the wardens had to find over £112 for the Rectory, as well as £80 for the church.[47] All aspects of the Rectory, internal and external, including stonework, presumably in the foundations or in the flagging, were addressed in these years. A new privy was constructed in 1847. Familiar local tradesmen were employed, including one of the two James Atkinsons, James Marra, James Hunter and Joseph Mortley.

In the 1850s much of the focus was on the fabric of the church and only the most routine work was done at the Rectory, like the renewal of the lead in the guttering to alleviate leaks.[48] In general the church continued to take priority in maintenance. So even the Rectory itself had had to wait in line for repairs at this time. Not until the summer of 1862–1863 and the autumn of 1865 was there substantial activity in the parsonage, by James Atkinson, John Johnson and Thomas Collison. The details are not known and the costs were rolled in with church repairs, under Henry Stiles.[49] Once again when fund-raising begun in 1872 the rector found that although donations had been sought to assist with repairs to both the parsonage and the church, in the subsequent years all the expenditure was on the church.[50]

Docker and Stiles, and probably Cross, had a resident groom, who by the 1840s had his own rooms in the stables: the southern carriage entry was converted into two small rooms for the groom, at the other end from the small toilet projecting from the north-west corner.[51]

Petty crime was nothing new in the barns of the Hawkesbury, and the rectory stables were no exception. A newish bridle with 'polished steel snaffle bit' belonging to Henry Stiles was stolen from the stable in March 1865, along with a bushel of corn.[52] Repairs to the rectory stables were rare over the years, especially when the church building received such a major overhaul in the 1840s–1860s.

In 1891, however, the seven doors on the front of the stables were externally painted with lime and copperas for £4 10s.[53] The rector, d'Arcy-Irvine, took a particular interest in the stables, because he had been obliged to supply harness out of his own pocket: the 'old set of "parish" harness' in the stable was still too dangerous to use even after repairs in 1890.[54]

A rare glimpse of the domestic arrangements is given in the Wardens' Accounts in 1877, when three iron tanks for water storage and a second-hand kitchen range were bought at an auction for the Rectory. The expenditure was the not insubstantial sum of £19 2s. 6d., but the stove lasted until 1921.[55]

In 1881 £30 was spent on painting the outside woodwork and the verandah at the parsonage, along with work on the guttering again,[56] but other than that a new fence along what is now the Moses Street frontage of the land between the rectory and Greenway Crescent was the most substantial maintenance in the 1880s. It was constructed in 1886 by Edward Mellish for £17. It was five feet high, made of hardwood palings with cut-off corners, and there was a small gate at the corner of Greenway Crescent.[57] Since the roof continued to give trouble at the Rectory, and also at its stables, the profits of the Flower Show in 1890 were earmarked to re-roof both the kitchen annexe of the Rectory and the stable block: the work was done by the local contractors Carroll and Cupitt for £44 9s. At the same time a bath was installed for the rector and running water was supplied to the upstairs rooms in the Rectory.[58] There was an earmarked fund of around £150 for rectory repairs and this was drawn on for unspecified work in the Rectory completed in 1898 under the supervision of the Blacket firm.[59]

If Walls Could Talk

The Rectory has seen many interesting and unexpected events between its walls. The Reverend Henry Stiles, for instance, was a 'man of large sympathies' and took a keen interest in humanitarian advocates like Caroline Chisholm who worked to assist female immigrants. He was moved to write to her from the Rectory in November 1841, some of the earliest support she received in the colony:

> Dear Madam,—
>
> Your frank and straightforward avowal of the objects you aim at, and the means you use for their attainment, disarm suspicion. The assurance in your note that you will pursue steadily the good of the whole of the emigrants who may come under your care induces me to offer you very cordially whatever support I am able to afford. I beg to enclose £2 as a donation.[60]

147. Painting by award-winning Hawkesbury artist, Greg Hansell, of the stables at St Matthew's, 1999. The arch on the left was originally for a second carriage entry, converted to groom's quarters in the 1840s. Greg Hansell, *The Rectory Stables*, booklet by Stables Task Force, 2003.

During the flood of 1864, Stiles took in some of the dispossessed and housed them in the Rectory: the minister wrote to his son about his distress at the effects of the flooding and how one of the two families sheltering in the laundry, 'consisting of a labourer, wife and children, are simply without anything'.[61] The situation in 1867 was even more dire.

S.G. Fielding, the author of several books, wrote them in the Rectory between 1893 and 1904, and according to William Freame they reached a wide audience.[62] In normal times, the ladies of the parish were busy visitors to the Rectory. They held meetings there with Mrs Fielding to make arrangements for vital fund-raising functions. There the organization for the annual Sunday school picnic which was to take place in September, to Gosper's Groves between Macquarie Street and South Creek just north of the railway line,[63] was carried out, and just before Christmas in 1898 another function was held in the rectory grounds: a Tea meeting, Moonlight Concert and Christmas tree. [64] Even more work was the annual floral fete held each October to commemorate the anniversary of the founding of St Matthew's. The money raised was for repairs and by 1903 the Wednesday afternoon meeting was still a 'well attended meeting of ladies'.[65] A lantern slide show was organized for the church hall in New Street when the Reverend F.W. Reeve, rector at Annandale, returned from Palestine.[66]

In 1898 the first Juvenile Industrial Exhibition and Floral Fete was held, opened by Lady Harris, who was accompanied to Windsor by her husband Sir Matthew Harris, the lord mayor of Sydney. In 1901, which was the third year that Lady Harris, who had been brought up on the Hawkesbury, had performed this ceremony, the Sydney visitors lunched in the Rectory with Mr J.J. Paine, the Mayor, and other guests.[67]

One of the highlights of the occasion was a message from Mr Fielding, recorded in Christchurch four weeks after his arrival, on a holiday to restore his health, and sent across to his Windsor congregation by post. The cylinder was played to the townsfolk at the fete on the new-fangled phonograph. The newspaper described the new technology:

> Unfortunately, however, something went wrong with the works, and the address was not distinctly reproduced. Later in the afternoon it was given, with much better effect, and Mr. Fielding's characteristic humorous passages, and kind and sympathetic message, delighted those present ... a private recital of the speech was given, and the record worked splendidly.[68]

In May 1906, Sydney Fielding was appointed to the Garrison Church at Millers Point and was farewelled in a full church hall, with representatives from other denominations present. Fielding was told by his parish:

> During the time Mr Fielding had been in Windsor he had made a number of improvements. In fact, some of his improvements might be called innovations. Furthermore, his idea was to teach people to be happy; and he set a good example himself. The Church of England people in this district had profited by his ministry.

Fielding left St Matthew's and its rectory well placed for the twentieth century.

148. The front and southern end of the Rectory stables, showing the carriageway, bridle room and groom's quarters on the ground level, and hay storage loft above. The chimney allowed the groom to have a fire. Photograph by Chris Jones, rector of St Matthew's, 2016

149. Back entries to the stables at St Matthew's, showing the ventilation roundels. Photograph by Chris Jones, rector of St Matthew's, 2016.

Part Three: Into the Twentieth Century and Beyond

9 Today's Rectory, Glebe and Cemetery

150. The Rectory of St Matthew's looking north-west from McQuade Park (Macquarie's 'great square') in the 1990s. Photograph supplied by John and Dorothy Butler.

Into the Twentieth Century

Sydney Fielding and his family brought in the twentieth century at the Windsor Rectory. Memorable amongst Fielding's exquisitely varied sermons there was the 1903 series on 'Poets of Love and Faith,' when 'one of the largest congregations seen in the old church' was attracted to the first sermon on British poet, Lord Alfred Tennyson. The local newspaper confidently told its readers that 'we may promise the congregation an impressive discourse' when the rector was to talk about Charles Kingsley.'[1]

When the Fieldings left almost a year later they had lived in the Rectory for eleven years. The whole of the Fielding family's valuable furniture, being unsuited to their next residence in Millers Point, was auctioned by W. Gosper in Windsor in May 1904.[2]

The Reverend Philip Dowe replaced Fielding in 1904, staying to minister two years. In reality Fielding and Dowe swapped rectorships, for Dowe had been at the Garrison Church in Millers Point for the three years previous to coming to St Matthew's. Dowe's son had been born in Sydney a year before.[3]

One of the earliest crises with which Philip Dowe had to deal occurred in November 1904 when the church was damaged. During an exceptional gale:

> sheds were unroofed, windows smashed, verandahs, fences, and trees blown down, and in some places slates and iron were torn from roofs of buildings. One of the windows of St. Matthew's Church of England, happily not one of the coloured ones, was smashed; some slates were blown off the roof, and the turret of the tower was damaged ... Many trees were laid low, one in the Park, opposite the rectory, and one at Mrs Dick's residence.[4]

The routine of the many services conducted by Hawkesbury ministers resumed uninterrupted.

One of the first officiated by Dowe was the funeral service of an old Hawkesbury resident, John Hiram Kirwan, who was connected to many other well-known Hawkesbury families like the Turnbulls, Everinghams, Arndells, Dunstans and Horderns. The funeral took place on a Thursday and was very well attended, with Thomas Primrose as the undertaker. The newspaper described the coffin as 'polished cedar, silver-mounted'. The pall-bearers were highly regarded men from families with long associations to St Matthew's: John J. Paine, JP, A.J. Berckelman, JP, S.F. Dunston, JP, and James Holmes.[5]

All these families and more remained involved in the resplendent Floral Fetes which continued to be held annually. In 1905, to commemorate the 88th anniversary of the church, the fete and entertainments opened on a Wednesday, continued through Thursday, closed on Friday, ran on Saturday afternoon and evening and finished on Monday night. Mrs Dowe opened the event in the church's New Street school hall, which was full of stalls and decorated by flags lent by David Jones, the great Sydney store. Philip Dowe thanked the ladies for their involvement, and the 'great deal of trouble' they had expended, and praised such events which he believed 'brought the people together' and gave 'goodwill and good feeling'. Some regular supporters, Mrs Paine, Mrs Pye and Mr Berckelman, were not able to be present due to ill-health. Berckelman, previously the 'secretary of church affairs', had just been obliged to restrict himself to keeping the church's accounts in order.

The ceremony opened with 'Little Miss Jean Tebbutt' presenting Mrs Dowe with a basket of flowers. Other well-known district names were present. Gertrude Cobcroft from Glenroy and Mrs William McQuade were in charge of the kitchenware stall. John Tebbutt's wife had charge of the sweets stall, with the boiled lollies a favourite, helped by the Callaghan sisters and J. Pendergast. The fancy goods stall sold pin-cushions, fans and ornaments. A produce stall selling jams, pickles, honeycomb, fruits and vegetables was popular, as well as the flower-stall in Miss Dunstan's charge, assisted by Misses Forssberg, Rubery, and Dunstan. Mrs D. Gosper and Mrs Dowe ran the stall selling children's and other clothing and Mrs Dyer's early Christmas tree was 'laden with toys of all descriptions'. The tearoom's offerings were 'very toothsome and daintily served' under the watchful eye of Mrs George Kirwan and others.[6] The entertainments ranged from a concert to a nail-driving competition for women, won by Mrs Kirwan who drove home 21 nails in three minutes.[7] The following year the fete was conducted every day from Wednesday to Saturday.[8]

The Dowes remained just two years. At their farewell there were many speeches directed to Philip Dowe, but to the community's later chagrin it seems Mrs Dowe was forgotten. One of the speakers, G.C.K. (George Colclough Kirwan, whose wife Priscilla Dunstan[9] had run the tearoom stall at the fete), was chastened enough to write to the local newspaper asking, 'Will you kindly allow me space in your valuable columns to say I am sorry the speakers [including myself] omitted to make special mention of the good work done by Mrs Dowe in the parish of St Matthew's'. His letter continued:

> Her connection with the Mothers' Union, Ladies' Working Guild, and Sunday School are all deserving of our best thanks. Mrs Dowe frequently invited lady speakers from Sydney to address the Mothers' Union at considerable expense and trouble, to try and better our social conditions. The mothers of Windsor have indeed lost a good and true friend.[10]

As had happened over the years, in the period between ministers, the Rectory was inspected and repaired while it was briefly uninhabited. Between Philip and Mrs Dowe leaving and Norman Jenkyn beginning his long tenure, the urgent repairs identified in 1906 were to the hall, the bathroom,

151. View from the Rectory as it would have been seen by Norman Jenkyn when he lived there and kept his horse in the paddock. Sketch by Lionel Lindsay, 1909, 'St Matthew's from the Rectory Window',National Library of Australia, PIC DRAWER 8945 #R7983

the kitchen and the scullery and minor works were done in all four locations.[11]

Norman Jenkyn was the first bachelor to occupy the Rectory and he remained unmarried during his tenure of thirty years. When he arrived in 1906 he soon saw that ongoing maintenance and updating continued to be necessary. So followed rather more works in 1908, done by a parishioner, Fred Cupitt. The bath was now 'unfit for use' and was replaced at the end of 1908.[12] In 1910 the hall was repainted with kalsomine, the principal bedroom was papered and the bathroom received more attention.[13] Jenkyn found the Rectory much larger than he required. He described it as standing

> in the shades of an old and wide spreading Japanese elm and huge kurrajong trees, and seemed almost to rest in the shadow of the big historic Church, with its ancient God's Acre, almost 110 years old. The Rectory is hoary with age and reeks with tradition, and to the passer-by truly suggests 'ghosts'.[14]

Jenkyn was looked after in the earlier years by an elderly housekeeper and then by a Japanese groom and a cook. The cook left abruptly after one of the periodic alarms about a ghost in the Rectory.[15] The rector himself told the story in a letter to the *Windsor and Richmond Gazette*, recalling how first he himself and then his housekeeper on separate occasions heard someone apparently rummaging in the drawer of the sideboard in the dining room. His sister was so disturbed by occurrences during her visit that she refused to stay.

One winter evening as Jenkyn and his Japanese employee were sitting by the fire in the dining room, they both heard footsteps along the back flag-stoned corridor and the noise of bricks being placed in position. The noise was ignored until at last, after twenty minutes, they went to investigate, but found nobody. After the cook had departed, Jenkyn heard footsteps on the stairs, and although he rushed out of his bedroom when they reached the top step no one was there. On many occasions he found the locked front doors opened on his return home. Norman Jenkyn was quite philosophical about sharing a rectory with ghosts for 30 years, and he commented:

> I regard them as great company ... I am not unmindful of the fact that spirits and ghosts are closely allied – especially if the former are taken within ... The visible creation is not the only creation that serves mankind. 'The things that are seen are temporal, but the things that are unseen are eternal.'[16]

Although the fabric of the house continued to deteriorate, particularly the lath-and-plaster ceilings upstairs, the next major repairs were not done until 1924, when the Adams family painted

152. Windsor Rectory in 1916. J. Steele, *Early Days of Windsor*, Tyrrell's, Sydney, 1916, after p. 88.

the interior and did general renovation, which cost £109. The task was described in the parish magazine as 'difficult'.[17] Further small repairs were done in 1927 by a parishioner, one of the Mullingers, well-known local builders.[18]

After the First World War, Jenkyn occupied only two of the rooms on the upper level. At night his bed was within an improvised cage of planks and rugs which he removed every morning. The cage was apparently an insurance against collapse of the lath-and-plaster ceiling. Downstairs, the old kitchen at the back of the house became unusable.[19]

When Jenkyn took a six-month holiday to England, the congregation gave him a temporary farewell in January 1923 and a gift of money. One of the speechmakers complimented the minister on the fact that his economic management had been so sound that: 'The committee were thankful to Mr. Jenkyn for taking a great burden off their shoulders. During his sojourn in the parish he had never lifted a penny of the Glebe rents, except a little from the Rectory, and he was entitled to do so'.

Another of those giving Jenkyn a fond bon voyage was George Philip Birk, who was to be his successor. Birk was at that time the rector at Pitt Town, and engaged in jovial banter with Jenkyn in his speech.[20] George Birk said:

> he counted it an honour to be there to join in the felicitations to the rector of St. Matthew's on the eve of his trip abroad. He is my rural dean ... and in the bigger things of the church I look to him. I feel there is a beautiful spirit among the people of this parish. ... You know we ministers are not all alike, and Mr. Jenkyn and I do not agree on some matters. For instance, we wear different size boots, and he wears spectacles, and I don't. (Laughter). Rev. N. Jenkyn: And I've got hair on top of my head, and he hasn't! (Laughter).[21]

153. Lorna as a small girl, taken with her sisters, her parents, Thomas and Ada Campbell, in the grounds of the Rectory with Vera Perry (reclining) and three of the young men from the Scheyville Training Farm and Migrant Accommodation Centre, early 1930s. Photograph in *Our Town*, Vol. 3, No. 4, Autumn 2001, p. 17, published by *Hawkesbury Gazette*.

Whilst on his extended holiday in 1923 Jenkyn rented the Rectory and its grounds to the Campbell family. Thomas Campbell, the schoolmaster appointed to Freemans Reach in 1919, found the school residence there too out of the way for convenience: there were five Campbell children, two of whom were working, while two were at high school. So the family moved in to Windsor and rented Fitzroy Cottage at 2 Tebbutt Street close to the church in the early 1920s, but the owner of the cottage decided to resume residence in 1923 and the Campbell family faced a problem, since there were very few houses for lease in Windsor.

The Campbells were strong adherents of St Matthew's. At various periods, the father served as warden and one of the daughters was choirmaster and organist. After a talk with Norman Jenkyn on his return in 1923, it was agreed that the Campbells should continue to lease the Rectory, while the minister found accommodation first in the Commercial Hotel close by (on the corner of George and Tebbutt Streets, now the Hawkesbury Hotel) and later in the Macquarie Arms at Thompson Square (then trading as the Royal Hotel). The rector retained the use of the front downstairs room on the eastern side as his office. The door separating the outer hall from the inner hall had ever since 1825 ensured that this front room could be used for pastoral purposes without trespassing on the privacy of the home.[22]

Jenkyn decided to stay on in hotel accommodation and the Campbell family continued to rent the Rectory. Nonetheless, the rector remained fascinated by the building. In 1932 Jenkyn wrote of the house: 'it is to-day haunted with weird sounds suggestive of ghosts, which can only be heard between the hours of 12 and 2 – the mystic hours when spirits walk!'[23]

Lorna, the youngest Campbell daughter, who grew up in the Rectory, remembers how in the 1930s the stairs did indeed creak one by one, as if someone unseen were walking up but the creaking always stopped at the landing.[24]

Until Jenkyn retired from St Matthew's in 1936, the Rectory remained a much loved home for the Campbells. Although Thomas Campbell had retired from teaching two years before, he stayed on in the Rectory until Jenkyn left the church.

Over their thirteen years of occupancy, the Campbells made a number of improvements and the house became a family home again, as it had not been since Victoria's reign. Mr Campbell built a tennis court in the rectory grounds and in the early 1930s there were tennis afternoons 'with lemon cheese tart, cream cakes and scones'. Boys from the Scheyville migrant camp used to come and play'.[25]

Thomas Campbell used a horse and sulky to commute to Freemans Reach as late as the 1930s. Laddie was a very well-behaved horse when he was driving Mr Campbell to school or taking the family on outings. However, in his leisure time he could be a 'very naughty' horse. Housed in the rectory stables, Laddie was remembered particularly fondly by Lorna and she loved to recount how he could undo the latch on the stable door and let himself out to roam the neighbourhood. The Campbell family's neighbour, Mrs Gow, had not appreciated his munching on her vegetables.[26]

154. Thomas Campbell's watercolour of the Rectory garden shows the position of the tennis court and garden the family built behind the rectory in the 1930s. Painting in possession of Miss Lorna Campbell, photograph by Ian Jack.

155. Lorna Campbell outside the back of the Rectory stables. Distressed by the deterioration that had gradually occurred over the years, Lorna formed a community task force to help the church conserve this important vestige of the days when the horse was the minister's most important asset. St Matthew's historic precinct remains intact because of her actions. Photograph by Jan Barkley-Jack, 1999.

The Campbell family bought a house called Balaklava at 458 George Street, South Windsor (originally the suburb of Newtown) after Thomas retired and the youngest daughter, Lorna, who lived there until recently, continued to cherish memories of both the Rectory and its stables.

Welcome Attention for the Stables

During G.P. Birk's time as minister between 1936 and 1940, the Rectory and stables were restored under the supervision of Professor Wilkinson of Sydney University with a 'baker's oven and a dripstone' to be preserved. The stables, referred to as 'the old coachhouse' were to be conserved, even to the replacing of 'several bars missing from the old hayricks', and Birk was considering using the building as an 'historical Museum'.[27] The 'partition wall in the old Coach House' was also removed.[28]

Canon Rawson's long incumbency, from 1961 until 1980, saw more activity when there was sensitive appreciation of the historic value of both the Rectory and the stables. Both Harold and his wife, Jessie, 'loved everything about the precinct, their surroundings and the history'. It was the

156. Interior of the stables of St Matthew's, showing the horse stalls, with their automatic feeds from the hay store in the loft above. Photograph by Graham and Carol Edds, 2003

unselfish and generous actions of Jessie Rawson during the 1970s which helped save the stables and kept the nineteenth-century church complex intact. When Jessie received a small inheritance, she 'quietly and unobtrusively set about installing eight timber soldier beams along the main walls of the stables where they were showing signs of acute stress after nearly forty years of neglect.'[29]

Almost thirty years later the stables were again showing the stress of neglect. In the late 1990s, their dilapidated state distressed Lorna Campbell and the high historic significance of the stables as well as the Rectory was recognized by a group of parishioners and residents who responded to her pleas. A Stables Task Force was set up by Lorna, with Ron Soper, one of the wardens, as chair. The other members of the committee were: Hon. Kevin Rozzoli, Jan Barkley-Jack, Malcolm Domars, Carol Edds, Graham Edds, Joyce Edwards, Margaret Fennell, Max Fleming, Penny Fraser, Lorna Hatherly, Max Hatherly, Ian Jack and Harry Khouri.

157. The rectory stables in the 1990s showing the supporting vertical beams installed by Mrs Rawson twenty years before. Photograph supplied by John and Dorothy Butler, 1990s.

Money from local fund-raising as well as funding from the Heritage Office of New South Wales and the Commonwealth Government was obtained and plans for the conservation of the stables were drawn up by Graham Edds & Associates. Over this time a considerable amount of documentary evidence had been gathered and specific physical analysis had been undertaken for the various conservation works to be carried out by the church. As active members of Australia ICOMOS (the International Council On Monuments and Sites),[30] Graham Edds & Associates followed the conservation philosophy outlined in the Burra Charter of 'doing only as much as is necessary and as little as possible' to preserve historic fabric. Graham recalls:

> The Rectory stables are probably the earliest remaining two-storey stable associated with a church precinct in Australia. They are also the final essential element in the superb Anglican church complex at Windsor. ... That the stables remain today reflects the contribution of three people of earlier times. The first was Professor Leslie Wilkinson, Professor of Architecture during the 1930s at the University of Sydney, who advised the Diocese against the proposal by the church to demolish the stables and build a garage for the then rector. The second was Jessie Rawson, and the third Lorna Campbell.
>
> As part of the Stables Task Force, Graham Edds & Associates was engaged as the Conservation Architect for the stables conservation in conjunction with Conservation Engineer Simon Wilshire of Hughes Truman Pty Ltd. Due to the financial constraints the work was proposed to be undertaken in a series of stages subject to funding being available. Tenders were requested to indicate the extent of work they could undertake for $35,000. Stan Hellyer, builder, tendered to provide reinstatement of the eastern wall up to the eaves level including proposed underpinning, with all joinery repaired and prime painted. Work commenced on 13 November 2000. ... It became evident that the major problem contributing to the wall failure was that the beam/lintels had been almost totally eaten out by termites which had caused the wall below to push outwards just below the first floor level.
>
> The failure of the main beam had also allowed the brick wall above to sag as it was no longer properly supported. Best fabric conservation practice was employed enabling the dismantled sandstock bricks and the original mortars

containing fragments of shells to be rejuvenated with a little modern slaked lime and sand to a workable mix. The brick walls were then reconstructed to their original form, keeping as much of the original fabric as possible. With the retirement of Stan Hellyer, further restoration work involving roof works, timber joinery both externally and internally, internal plaster repair, lath and plaster ceiling stabilisation, conservation of horse stalls and painting was undertaken by Greg Brown and Lester Salter of the Sydney Restoration Company.[31]

158. Stables loft joinery. Photograph by Carol and Graham Edds, 2002

Focus on the Rectory

159. Rectory with cocoon poultice applied to the outside of the building to reduce salt contamination in the bricks. When the poultice was removed it contained the salts that affect the walls. Photograph by Graham and Carol Edds, 2009.

The main focus of attention in the 1930s, during bad economic times, was the condition not of the church but of the Rectory, simultaneously with the work on the stables. Major works on the church did not recommence until the 1950s.

Immediately after Norman Jenkyn tendered his resignation as rector in 1936, the Campbells moved out of the Rectory.

A builder, R.B. Ashley, made a survey of the Rectory inside and out and made recommendations about extensive alterations. The architect, W. Thompson, met the Parochial Council in August and proposed some changes to Ashley's suggestions. In particular Thompson wanted to demolish the entire kitchen block and to erect instead a back verandah with a laundry at the north end. He also argued for the demolition of the stables and the construction of a brand-new garage.[32]

Professor Leslie Wilkinson was then brought in during October 1936. He reinstated Ashley's specifications.[33] Ashley was engaged to do the work.

The new minister, George Birk, had found that there was still a shortage of rental accommodation in the town, so he moved into the Rectory in September 1936 and lived there while it was still being renovated.[34] The works on the Rectory itself cost £850, and Birk saw at close quarters the substantial repairs proceeding in 1937 and 1938. To celebrate the renovations, a marble tablet was unveiled by the Archbishop on the front of the Rectory on 26 March 1938. The Municipal Council also assisted by making improvements in the roadway in front.[35] Birk remained at St Matthew's until 1940.

Charles Williams replaced Birk and was rector during the dark days of the Second World War,

160. Under the Rectory stairs, showing early lath and plaster work. Photograph by Ian Jack, 1999.

remaining until 1947. During his ministry major renovation to the Rectory was postponed throughout the war, but repairs became a major issue again in 1950, and during the interregnum after the departure of his replacement, Robert Hallahan, in June 1951. Concern for an incoming rector always focused attention back on the Rectory. The recurrent problem of damp on the ground floor walls was to the fore in 1950, as it still was in 2009.[36]

The families of subsequent ministers, D.G. McCraw and W.F. Carter, resided in the Rectory for three years and six years respectively until 1960, followed by the families of Harold Rawson, then Len Abbott, John Butler, Chris Burgess, Aleks Pinter and now Chris Jones. Conservation action has been needed in the Rectory over an extended period. This has involved placing a damp-proof course in some of the Rectory walls, together with poulticing to reduce the salt contamination levels. Graham Edds explained the details:

> Works such as the conservation of early brickwork from rising damp involved the removal of misguided cement render applications to external and internal walls along with the injection of damp-proof barrier to the kitchen wing and adjacent rooms and increasing of sub-floor ventilation. A leaking roof, the failure of gutters and downpipes and blockage of the storm-water drainage system meant that further work was programmed in stages to rectify these issues. Included also was the repair of the large chimneys, the weathered capping around the chimney pots and the replacement of chimney flashings. With the change in ministers taking up residence in the Rectory, other repairs and maintenance were undertaken at regular intervals including the repair of a leaking first-floor bathroom that had caused water damage to the ceilings and walls below. These maintenance works were undertaken by various tradespersons including parishioners.[37]

161. A glimpse of the daily life of the Campbell family at the back of the Rectory, taken to the north-west side of the kitchen at the back of the main building in the 1920s or early 1930s. Thomas Campbell and his wife are seated, and at least two daughters appear, one washing her hair in a tub, and another watching on, leaning on the tree. Photograph supplied by John and Dorothy Butler.

John and Dorothy Butler moved into the Rectory in 1988. The Butlers were to find that there were unexpected hazards of living in such a large old residence, just as Norman Jenkyn had done in September 1917. Unlike Jenkyn's challenge of a black snake, the Butlers had the more unusual: unexpected visits by ducks and bees. The ducks which liked to sit on the chimney pots often fell down the uncapped chimney flues into the open fireplace below.

The bees were a different matter. The carpets in the downstairs room used as a study by the ministers became mysteriously sticky with what turned out to be honey. With windows and doors closed, the question was how the bees were gaining

162. Bees on the inside of a Rectory window. Photograph by John and Dorothy Butler, taken *c.* 1996.

163. Honeycombs above the Rectory ceiling. Photograph by John and Dorothy Butler, taken *c.* 1996.

entry. The honey was found to be dropping from the ceiling. The bees had entered into the cavity above the ceiling and built an enormous hive there. When the floor above was ripped up, a vast amount of honeycomb was visible. It was removed and cleaned up with difficulty.

Dorothy Butler was very involved in aspects of the ministry of her husband. She became President of the Mothers' Union, a member of the Ladies Guild, a coordinator of SMILE (the St Matthew's Informal Ladies' Evening) and a leader in the Girls' Friendly Society which had been an Anglican club for girls for the past seventy years. In 1924 Mrs W.F. Green had presided at the piano for the young women.[38] There was the usual amount of entertaining, such as gathering the wives of Anglican clergy in the Hawkesbury to the Rectory to meet the bishop's wife.[39]

The stables were conserved during Chris Burgess' ministry by a community group, as already discussed, and urgent further work was

164. The dining room of the Rectory during the time that Aleks and Susannah Pinter and their family were living there. Photograph by Graham and Carol Edds, 2010.

commissioned by Aleks Pinter to the bathroom of the Rectory.

In mid-2015 a new rector, Chris Jones, and his wife Kerry arrived at the Rectory. They instantly found themselves in the midst of plans to celebrate the church's bicentenary over the years from 2017 to 2022. Chris and Kerry have begun familiarizing themselves with the heritage aspects of the Rectory and the stables and are working hard to ensure the works needed are done promptly to lessen deterioration and to reduce maintenance costs, besides being paid for by grants as much as possible; at the same time they seek to understand the pulse of the extensive parish.

The Twentieth Century in the Cemetery

By 1900 the gravemarkers in the churchyard completely encompassed the church, but there was still substantial free space along the Moses Street frontage.

As individual monumental masons were giving way to large-scale businesses using power tools and working in marble and granite, a trend towards the standardization of tombstones intensified.[40] The decorative stone and marble markers of the 1890s began to give way to smaller, minimalistic slabs in concrete-edged plots on the remaining edges of St Matthew's cemetery by the turn of the twentieth century.

Nonetheless, in the early twentieth century burials in family vaults continued and the occasional high status monuments continued to appear. By far the most impressive and largest of the turn of the century graves is the Tebbutt family vault. The prestigious site for this vault, near the early magistrates such as William Cox in the south-western sector, had been secured in 1837 for the burial of the Tebbutt matriarch. The monument itself was designed by her son, the internationally acknowledged astronomer John Tebbutt, a Fellow of the Royal Astronomical Society, just five or six years before his own death. Tebbutt's achievements have been celebrated on a recent Australian $100 note. The Tebbutt grave commands attention as a dominating square sandstone memorial topped at each corner with a marble celestial sphere. John Tebbutt himself was buried there on 1 December 1916. There are 21 members of his family in the vault, including triplets who died in 1981.[41]

The funeral of John Tebbutt was conducted in the church by Sydney Fielding, the former rector and a personal friend. Tebbutt's scientific achievements were documented by 'those best qualified for the task in Australia, in Europe and in America', but it was Tebbutt's 'great reverence for Truth, whether religious or scientific' that the minister chose to ponder.[42]

Norman Jenkyn officiated by the graveside where he addressed not only Tebbutt's large family, including his grandchildren, but a wide array of mourners, from the President of the New South Wales Branch of the British Astronomical Association, a representative of the Royal Astronomical Society of London, a representative of the Royal Society of New South Wales, the Minister for Mines representing the New South Wales Government and the Principal Librarian of the State Library of New South Wales, through to various bank managers, the Mayor of Windsor, an ex-mayor, aldermen and other leading Hawkesbury citizens to 'a number of Mr. Tebbutt's tenants'.[43]

Whilst modern graves are to be found on most edges of the graveyard, it is the four front rows of newish graves on the south-western side of the church along Moses Street that are more regular and more densely packed than the older

165. South-eastern sector of St Matthew's graveyard showing the beginnings of the use of a smaller marker, usually on a cement or stone base. Photograph by Jan Barkley-Jack, 2016.

166. The large monument designed by the astronomer John Tebbutt (who died in 1916) for himself and his family. The metal plate to the right covers the steps leading into the vault. Photograph by Ian Jack, 2016.

area immediately to the north and elsewhere. They extended the area of the active cemetery to the south of the nineteenth-century élite section. These rows with their smaller rectangular markers and simple surrounds reflect the more restrained Anglican style of the twentieth century.

The first recorded renovation of the Italian marble monument to Amelia McQuade at the front of the church was done by George Robertson himself in 1916.[44] In 1930 Mr Cupitt was engaged to clean the monument.[45] In 1931, and probably before, the maintenance of the monument was identified as the obligation of the Perpetual Trustee Company which acted for the McQuade family, and in 1932 the Trustee Company engaged a lady to keep the monument in order for an annual fee.[46]

167. The twentieth-century rows of graves between the church and Moses Street from the west. Most interments here date from the 1920s to the 1960s. Photograph by Ian Jack, 2016.

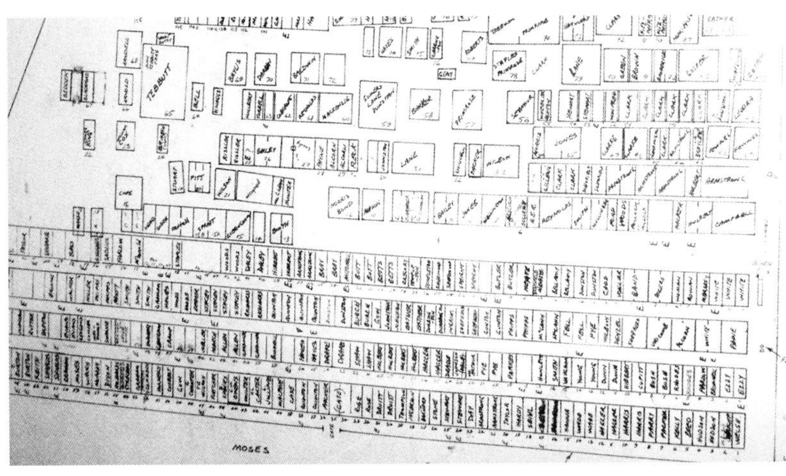

168. The south-west sector of the cemetery, with Moses Street at the bottom of the plan. The four bottom rows are much later than most of the graves immediately to the north. Photograph by Ian Jack, 2009.

Vandalism became a problem in the 1960s. After hooligans had climbed the McQuade monument and put a lamp on top, the Perpetual Trustee Company was requested to attend to the problem. The highly regarded monumental mason, Cornelis Sondermeyer, was engaged to repair the urn from the apex in February 1964. He was one of the sons of Dutch stonemason Johannes Sondermeyer whose company, J.H. Sondermeyer, had been making memorial stones at Richmond since 1959.[47] Nothing happened and in October the wardens claimed that the monument was 'being destroyed by vandals' and sought to put broken pieces into store. Dr Skinner moved that the monument be removed altogether, as long as the diocese and no individual objected. The following year, the rector, Canon Rawson, proposed that it might be re-erected in McQuade Park to become a public responsibility.[48]

The Parish Council warmed to the idea of disposing of the McQuade monument and agreed in September 1965 to dismantle it. This lead to the hope that the pieces of Carrara marble might be sold for a windfall sum, although the lawyer among them doubted whether this was lawful and another with a keen political sense warned that the church might be criticized for any such sale. A firm specializing in marble was contacted and made an offer which was regarded unfavourably and, in Dr Skinner's absence in December, the Parish Council decided to get the monument restored.[49]

Sondermeyer's quotation for over $460 was rejected and opinion lurched back to favouring removal. The broken urn became a symbol of the terminal state of the monument and Dr Skinner successfully moved to advertise the imminent removal in the *Sydney Morning Herald*. Opposition mounted and a rescission motion was passed later in March 1966.[50] Debate was finally silenced by the intervention of the McQuades.

The trustee for the late Josephine McQuade wrote a pointed letter in October 1966. Within three weeks there were two tenders for suitable repairs. In March 1967 Sondermeyer's new quotation was accepted and the McQuade Trust guaranteed money for this repair and for future upkeep. In June 1968, the Parish Council finally closed this unhappy chapter by approving that the work be completed by Sondermeyer.[51] However, it was decided that not all the urns would be returned to the monument.

The present low stone walling along Greenway Crescent was not built until 1961. In 1960 Les Quinton sold the stone from his former tannery in Mileham Street, South Windsor, to the church for £20. Quinton then helped to demolish the tannery building, which was constructed partly in stone, partly in brick. The stone blocks were carted to the cemetery by a parishioner and an engineer in the Department of Main Roads organized a crane to assist in moving the blocks. Windsor Municipal Council was then successfully approached to assist in erecting the stone wall along the eastern side of the cemetery, 'thus enabling us to beautify in a practical manner this section on Cornwallis Rd'.[52] In his annual report for 1960–1961, the Cemetery Superintendent paid tribute to the community effort involved in creating the new, low wall: 'Our Anglican Family has cause to feel very proud of our men responsible for the shaping of the many sized stones into a lasting & pleasing wall in Cornwallis Rd which when completed will be in keeping with other jobs accomplished'.[53] Although there is no mention of the final completion of the wall, it is likely that the work was brought to a satisfactory conclusion later in 1961. It is likely also that the stone gateposts at the northern end of the wall, with the double gates in iron, were erected at the same time.

Despite all the time and money spent on constructing various forms of fencing to secure the cemetery, straying stock remained a nuisance well into the twentieth century.[54]

There were other buildings in the cemetery in the nineteenth century, but little is known about them. The verger-cum-sexton had a cottage within the graveyard, probably from the 1820s onwards. This small building is shown as a simple rectangle on Galloway's 1841 plan of the church and burial ground. It lay right on the back boundary of the cemetery due north of the church tower beside a small seasonal creek which ran north-west down to Rickabys Creek. Another structure, approximately the same size as the cottage but probably a tool shed, is shown on the same 1841 plan tucked into the north-west corner of the cemetery.[55] By the time of Galloway's plan, the cottage was in need of

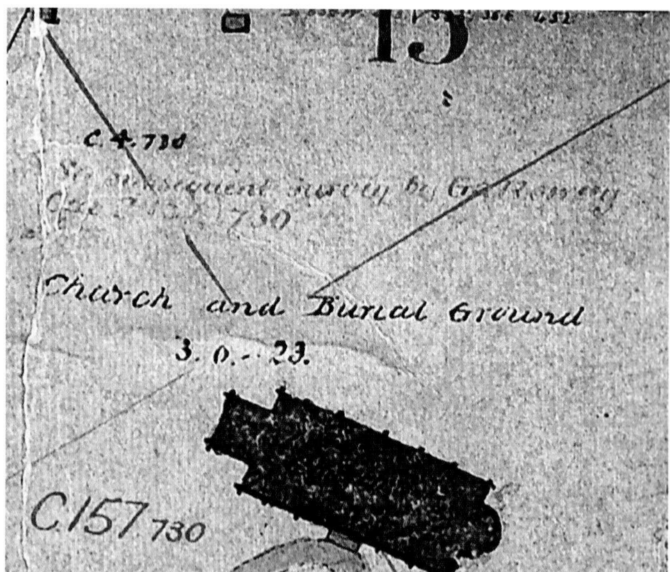

169. The location of the early nineteenth-century cottage occupied by the verger/sexton (on the back boundary within the cemetery), due north of the church tower. North is approximately at the top of the map. The building on the extreme north-west corner of the church land is probably a tool shed, perhaps later a privy. Plan by Galloway, 1841. Land and Property Information, Crown Plan, W 443a.

substantial repairs.[56] Forty years later, in 1886, the cottage was still there, but was described as 'the old verger's residence', which implies that it was by then being used as a shed rather than as a dwelling.[57] A privy had been erected in the cemetery grounds, perhaps in the original tool-shed, at an unknown date in the nineteenth century: by 1885 it was in a dilapidated condition.[58] A new ladies' toilet was constructed in weatherboard in 1925.[59] Finally brick toilets were erected by Sydney Kent in 1929.[60]

The Columbarium

The Public Health Act of 1896 included a clause permitting local government authorities and cemetery managers to build and run crematoria within cemetery reserves. By 1924, the New South Wales Crematorium Company built a crematorium at Rookwood Necropolis, conducting the first cremation in May 1925.[61] The concept reached St Matthew's in 1959, when the church committee decided to build a columbarium in two parts, one around the McQuade monument, the other along the front wall of the cemetery.[62] Two plans were submitted at the estimated cost of £1200 on 4 June

1959.[63]

Wider aspects were also discussed on 8 June 1959: 'the Graveyard was a very historic one and the Parish Council had been very concerned with the untidiness of it for a long while', the rector said. In addition to the columbarium wall, landscaping of lawns and the creation of a double driveway were envisaged.[64] In 1960 as part of this, Lloyd Rutter of Windsor laid kerbing along the front church driveways as a personal donation to the restoration, so that lawn could be grown. Shrubs were planted along the frontage and three wrought-iron gates were painted and erected.[65]

170. The columbarium encircling the McQuade monument. Photograph by Graham and Carol Edds, 2008.

The decision to build niches for ashes produced in August 1959 a document about cemetery charges and policy in general. It was reaffirmed that all burial places were reserved for Anglicans, but that parishioners should pay much less than other Anglicans for inhumations and that niches in the circular crematorium wall around the McQuade monument should be reserved for parishioners. Although there was no preferential rate for niches offered to parishioners, the 96 niches in that part of the front wall between the main entrances to the church along Moses Street would cost 50% more than the other 684 niches to be provided. There were also 420 inhumation plots created by levelling the rear part of the cemetery, with standard headstones approved by the Parish Council.

A total of 1,200 new interments was envisaged. Each would carry a fee of a guinea, while the actual niche or grave would cost an additional ten, twelve or fifteen guineas. The total potential income was £15,446. The immediate outlay totalled £1,693, which included £1,150 for the 'walls of memory', £93 for a nine-inch kerb around the McQuade monument and £75 for levelling the back part of the cemetery.[66]

Sixteen thousand bricks were purchased and building of the columbarium wall started in December 1959, with priority given to completing the circular part around the McQuade monument. The latter was completed in February 1960 after the first attempt was pulled down and restarted in an echo of the building of the church itself in Macquarie's time. The front wall with its niches was not finished until November. It was felt necessary to prohibit people from sitting on the columbarium walls.[67] *The Parish Messenger* reported in November 1960 that the first placing of ashes had taken place.[68]

At the south-eastern corner of the fence, where the columbarium brick wall meets the low stone wall erected along Greenway Crescent in 1961, there are two sandstone blocks arranged as informal steps to give access to the graveyard.

Closure of the Cemetery

A perception that the cemetery was getting full was evident as early as the 1890s. In 1893 the new rector, Sydney Fielding, thought it appropriate to propose to his first Vestry Meeting that burials should cease in St Matthew's Cemetery, except in plots already purchased.[69] The mill ground slowly, however, and more than seven decades passed before a final decision was made.

On 15 March 1969 the Parish Council, along with the gravedigger, inspected the graveyard 'to investigate the suitability of the remaining ground

171. The conjunction of the 1961 stone wall along Greenway Crescent and the brick wall of the columbarium along Moses Street. Photograph by Ian Jack, 2009.

172. Eastern side of the cemetery looking north, showing the array and density of the marked graves around St Matthew's Church. Photograph by Ian Jack, 2016.

... for interments'. They noted that 'the evidence available showed that it was difficult to choose a new grave site with any certainty', so decided 'that the cemetery be closed forthwith, except where plots have already been purchased'.[70]

The monumental mason Cornelis Sondermeyer has commented that, when a new grave was dug in what was thought from the records to be an empty spot, it was often found that someone had already been interred there.[71] Cornelis as a member of the local firm, J.H. Sondermeyer, 'Monumental and General Mason', advertised in the parish newsletter as being located in Richmond, firstly in Pitt Street in the 1960s and then in Bowman Street, during the 1980s.[72] Almost 7,000 burials were registered between 1810 and 2000: the details have been painstakingly published from the church registers by the Lake Macquarie Family History Group.[73] The number of gravemarkers is, of course, much less, because many of the early burials were unmarked and because many plots contain several members of the one family. But the scope for interpreting and illustrating the changing community of Windsor over 160 years through the iconography and style of the funeral monuments is high. There is an unfulfilled historical potential in St Matthew's graveyard for some scholar.

In 1926 a commentator wrote:

> St. Matthew's, at Windsor, is probably the most picturesque of all the churchyards in Australia. Hundreds of memorials cluster about Greenway's beautiful old church, and from the ridge on which it lies there is an utterly lovely view of all the valley of the Hawkesbury, and the long wall of the Blue Mountains across the River.[74]

In 2016, the view is no less spectacular, and attracts a wide variety of visitors, not least the relatives of those buried there.

Restoration of gravemarkers is the responsibility of the family but in an historic graveyard over 200 years old it is also of wider concern. The Cemetery Committee of the National Trust of Australia (NSW) organizes practical workshops and has published guidelines on the proper conservation of graveyards.[75] The National Trust's latest Cemetery Workshop was held at St Matthew's in May 2016 and was most informative.

Following such guidelines, many graves in the cemetery have been conserved and appropriately cleaned with material which will not damage the surface of the marker. Some have been professionally and accurately recut, paid for by families. The conservation of the gravestone of Andrew Thompson, bereft of family descendants, was paid for by the Royal Australian Historical Society in 1910 and the long inscription was made legible once more in 1961 by the Hawkesbury Historical Society. Thompson's grave is much visited, like the cemetery generally, by tourists and commercial tour groups, including a well-patronized ghost tour group. Cleaned again in 2010, however, the inscription on the marker is hard to read.[76]

The Glebe

The Parochial Council was anxious to gain capital funds from selling off the Rectory glebe. It first tried in 1930, proposing to sell off the entire Rectory glebe, except the land on which the Rectory itself was built, but prudently left the matter in abeyance for the time being.[77] Although the wardens had welcomed the leasehold revenue, they were acutely aware that the act of leasing made the land liable to local rates, and the Parish Council over many decades had been aroused to fury at the thought of paying any rates to the municipal council; alternatively, if rates had to be paid on land from which the rector was receiving the rent, then, the council argued, the rector, and not the wardens, should be paying. [78]

The capital value of the two parts of the glebe, that beside the Rectory and that remaining at Clarendon, was declared in 1935–1936 to be £325 for the Clarendon land and £25 for the Rectory glebe.[79] On 8 June 1936, one of the wardens, A.H. Wilcher, gave notice that there should be a petition to Synod to sell glebe land in the parish. The ordinance allowing such sales was uttered in October 1937 and thereafter in a protracted and messy way the area along The Terrace was sold. The church attempted to place covenants over the purchases to ensure that the houses built would be appropriate: slate or tiled roofs were specified and a minimum cost for the house.[80]

In 1938 it was agreed to ask the diocese to sell the Clarendon glebe at auction and it was sold as a single lot in December 1938 for £560.[81]

The Second World War interfered with the sale of other parts of the Rectory glebe although two allotments on Cornwallis Road were sold in 1943.[82] As soon as war was over in 1945 the new allotments numbered 9 to 15 along The Terrace were determinedly offered for sale at prices ranging from £2 to £7, with covenants now extending to the walls, which had to be of brick or stone. By August 1947 all but one of these seven lots had been sold. Lots 3 to 8 reverted to the church and thereby avoided council rates, which were still resented by the wardens.[83]

St Matthew's Anglican Parish Centre

From the beginning, there had always been a buffer zone between the church and the Rectory, afforded by the south-western section of the Rectory glebe, the paddock which was retained after the sub-divisions of the 1940s and 1950s. In the mid-1950s there was agitation to replace the 1825 rectory with a modern manse. This thrust was led by the rector, W.F. Carter, whose practical needs overwhelmed his historical scruples. Professor Wilkinson drew up plans for a new rectory, parish hall and tennis court on the vacant land to the west of the old rectory and, although these plans were approved in principle by the church in May 1957, they were dropped and nothing happened for a quarter of a century.[84] Canon Rawson, who followed Carter as rector, was 'vehemently opposed to anything being built on the land between the Rectory and the church.'[85]

In 1982 the Parochial Council decided that a parish hall should be built in the Rectory paddock and engaged Ridley Smith of Noel Bell Ridley Smith and Partners to draw up plans. The cost was estimated at $200,000, partly offset by subdivision of part of the paddock for housing, partly by the sale of the church's New Street hall in Windsor and perhaps also its Ham Street hall in South Windsor, opened in 1966.[86]

Not surprisingly, the proposal provoked vigorous debate. The National Trust claimed that 'the setting of St Matthew's Church and Rectory was of such significance that no new building, however sensitive or sympathetic, should be permitted to intrude'. It asked that the church consider alternative sites and lobbied the Heritage Council 'to preserve the integrity of this historic site, and refuse approval for the development proposal.'[87]

The church, through the rector, Len Abbott, responded with some vehemence. It claimed that

173. St Matthew's Anglican Parish Centre, with the church in the left background. Photograph by Ian Jack, 2009.

the other three possible sites were 'more likely to obstruct the view of the river or disturb historic tombs or are otherwise unacceptable because of cost or accessibility'.[88] Abbott asserted that 'the rectory paddock was reserved for a church hall nearly 50 years ago in 1936 but no hall was ever built because of lack of funds'. He also said that 'the new hall had been designed to blend in with St Matthew's and the rectory' and that 'the hall and the two proposed residences would be positioned so as not to interfere with the view of the church from the road and nearby residences'.[89]

The initial design was exchanged for 'a compromise proposal for a sub-soil structure on a portion of the rectory paddock adjacent to the stables', but this was rejected by the Heritage Council.[90] The church and the Anglican Property Trust appealed against the decision and the commissioner appointed to hear the matter decided in favour of the church. As a result the Minister for Planning and Environment gave his consent in 1984 and early in 1985 Ridley Smith produced new plans for the approval of the Heritage Council.

In March 1985 the successful tenderer was Mick Scruci, although neither the Heritage Office nor the Hawkesbury City Council had yet formally approved the plans. The cost, which was estimated to exceed $300,000, was to be met from a number of sources, the Church Property Trust, St Matthew's own funds and further sales of the glebe land. The bottom block to the north of the Rectory was to be purchased by Hawkesbury City Council, while another block would be subdivided. Meanwhile Scruci had failed to obtain the necessary support of his bank and the firm of Hinchey and Cross became the contractors instead in May 1985.[91]

Work began in June, the base slab was laid in August and the Parish Centre was dedicated by Archbishop Robinson on 22 December 1985.[92]

The tree line along Moses Street directly in front of the Parish Centre near the Rectory was famously the site of another more recent ghost sighting this time by Alex Hendrikson, a local antique dealer and well-liked member of many community organizations. One evening after the meeting of a council committee around 1993, Hendrikson left to walk across the oval in McQuade Park, to his home on the lower slopes beyond the Rectory. As he drew near the large tree growing near the footpath at the Parish Centre, an indistinct and ephemeral figure loomed in front of him dressed in the long black coat and distinctive round black beaver hat, so associated in pictures with the Reverend Samuel Marsden, who had died in the very building Hendrikson had been approaching. The apparition could only be Marsden.

Hendrikson's uncontrolled behaviour as a result of this bizarre sighting can be attested by one of the authors of this book, who was herself present at the meeting that night at Windsor Council Chambers. Alex dashed back to the gathering at breakneck speed and burst back in on the remaining members of the group, white as any lily and shaking so much in shock that he was unable to speak for several minutes. He had to be driven home. Alex's story, from his fearful countenance and uncontrollable tremors, would have been believed by the staunchest of ghost deniers.

Len Abbott incorrectly maintained that 'the only spirit Alex saw was in the Mayor's liquor cupboard',[93] for at least six people, including one

174. Mayor Wendy Sledge accepts flowers in front of the Parish Centre *c.* 1994, watched by rector John Butler who became the town crier for the day. Photograph supplied by John and Dorothy Butler.

of the authors, at the meeting that night can vouch that Alex had not been drinking at the Council Chambers.

175. The view of the Parish Centre and St Matthew's Church looking west as seen from the Rectory. Photograph by Chris Jones, rector of St Matthew's, 2016.

176. From the Rectory glebe looking west across the Rectory and stables to the Parish Centre and thence to the church. A Hercules aircraft is going in to land at the RAAF base, Richmond. Photograph by Graham and Carol Edds, 2010.

10 A Centenary and Onwards to the Bicentenary

Long Ministries

Henry Stiles had dominated the nineteenth-century history of St Matthew's, which he served for 34 years. None of the other ten rectors before 1901 was in Windsor for more than ten years and, although they all contributed to the maintenance of the church and congregation, the brevity of their association with the parish was a contrast to the 43-year period when Stiles and his son-in-law, Charles Garnsey, occupied the Rectory and enhanced the aesthetic of the church.

In the twentieth century St Matthew's benefited from two long-serving ministers, Norman Jenkyn from 1906 until 1936 and Harold Rawson from 1961 until 1980.

As in the previous century, the other rectors, eight in number, served only short terms. Two of those wrote short histories of the church. W.F. Carter's *Cathedral of the Hawkesbury*, an illustrated pamphlet published in at least two undated versions after he ceased to be rector in 1960, remains an indispensable place of first resort. Carter, while primarily concerned with informing visitors about the fabric of the buildings, reminded all who might write about St Matthew's that:

> The Church ... is not made of brick and mortar. It is a living organism made up of men and women who share the life of the risen Christ and who seek, through worship and witness, to proclaim the eternal truth of God in its day and generation.[1]

An attractively illustrated *Short Guide to the Church & its History* was published by John Butler, using text written by his predecessor, Len Abbott, and colour photographs by Ossie Emery. A second edition appeared in 2002, with a new set of Emery photographs.[2]

177. Canon John Butler and Canon Harold Rawson at St Matthew's in 1992. Photograph supplied by John and Dorothy Butler.

178. Christening of Narelle Vance by Canon Rawson with godparents Robyn and Neil Cammack, August 1977. Photograph supplied by Carol Roberts.

Norman Jenkyn

Norman Jenkyn did not write any pamphlet on his church, but he had an acute sense of history. In 1932, he contributed an attractive article to the *Windsor and Richmond Gazette*, entitled 'Historic Windsor, its Rise and Progress: a Ramble through the Town'. In this article, Jenkyn reminisced about his first experiences as rector of St Matthew's, 26 years earlier:

> In 1906, on a lovely morning in the month of May, I started out on a ramble through Windsor to find out for myself and to see the places and locate the things that had helped to make the town so historic. I first made my way to the banks of the river ... and sitting down I began to ruminate ... [Thompson] Square simply reeked with history, and I was loath to leave it. ... I then turned homeward [to the Rectory], ... fascinating brick, mellowed with the years, and its beautiful doorway, the admiration still of architects, builders and artists. Within is the spiral cedar stairway so perfect and symmetrical in design that thousands of visitors have desired to view it. Ascending it I entered the front room on the left where the celebrated Rev. Samuel Marsden passed away in 1838. ... I offered a prayer and passed quietly down and out into the street again. [Then the rector walked over to St Matthew's Church.] Surely I had kept the best until last.[3]

193. The Reverend William Carter. Photograph supplied by Beverley Hunt, taken in 1957.
179. The Doctors' House, Thompson Square, Windsor, by Hardy Wilson, 1919. H. Wilson, *Old Colonial Architecture*,

Jenkyn had come to Windsor from Bulli in the Illawarra in 1906, exchanging parishes with Philip Dowe, who had been at Windsor during the previous three years.[4] Jenkyn took the Hawkesbury to his heart. He expressed this particularly warmly in 1922, when there was a civic dinner to celebrate the opening of the reconstructed Windsor Bridge. Jenkyn delivered the toast to the Town and District. Reported in the local newspaper in indirect speech, the minister spoke eloquently about his environment and his people:

> He considered the Hawkesbury district a wonderful garden – not the Garden of Eden, because there were no fig leaves and no apples – but the very real granary of the near west. ... But its productivity and beautiful scenery were so little known ... that he was afraid [the Minister for Public Works] might have been inclined to regard the Hawkesbury as a sort of Poverty Point or Hungry Hill ... As a tourist resort it was one of the finest places in New South Wales, with its noble river and unsurpassed mountain scenery. ... There was little crime in the district, and no cause for anxiety or worry – the people were not called upon to support the helpless poor, they were all helping themselves and able to live in comfort, and were a law unto themselves.[5]

He took his civic duties as seriously as his religious and served as an alderman of Windsor Municipal Council for sixteen years and was mayor in 1932: his grandfather had been Premier of Queensland.[6] During his years in office, he presided over the Back to Windsor Week which he had instigated and collaborated with a well-known historian, William Freame, in a number of historical activities.[7]

Although benevolent, Jenkyn was a stickler for appropriate behaviour. In 1926 he was publicly censorious over the behaviour of visitors to the church and he contrasted these visitors with his own congregation:

> Some women walk in without their hats ... others laugh and talk, while some men keep their hat on. Such ignorance on the part of men is unpardonable. But [the worst] is the one who visits the church with a lighted cigar or pipe in his hand ... Thank God our own parishioners always behave most reverently in church.[8]

St Matthew's Centenary Celebrations

Much thought was given to the church's centenary, which was to be celebrated in 1917. *The Sydney Morning Herald* gave the centenary celebrations a free acknowledgement:

> The rector, Hon. Norman Jenkyn, has occupied that position during the past 11 years. To all former rectors, past parishioners, and those, who in any other way, have been associated with St. Matthew's, he has issued a cordial invitation to co-operate in making the celebrations worthy of the occasion.[9]

Because of the war, however, the centenary was a very muted event. The rector issued a simple two-page document relating to the service held on Thursday, 11 October 1917. The front page showed a photograph of the 'Cathedral of the Hawkesbury', the title first coined by Jenkyn himself in 1914. Page 2 gave historical information and specifically mentioned that the chalice and paten being used at the centenary communion were those given by George IV in 1822.[10]

There were, however, substantial and visible achievements from a protracted Centenary lasting until 1921. Over the years Jenkyn had been making significant changes and renovations to St Matthew's. As well as attending to the school hall, the Rectory and the stables, Jenkyn had reacted vigorously to a problem at the south entry to the church. The two stone steps which had been put at the south doorway in 1834 had become worn by a long procession of parishioners. As a result, in 1907 two possums got into the church between the bottom of the door and the curvature of the top step and created a nuisance, so the two stones were removed and put back upside down.[11]

Four years later, in 1911, Jenkyn turned to the greater matter of the chancel. The chancel was tiled for the first time to the design of the local architect, George Matcham Pitt, at the substantial cost of £38 10s.[12] Five years later, in 1916, electric light in the church superseded the gas-lighting of 1884 and the old gas fittings were removed.[13]

All this was in preparation for the Centenary. The diocesan architects, Robertson & Marks, were commissioned in 1917 to report on the condition of the church. One of the partners in the firm,

180. Detail of the first electric lighting in the nave of St Matthew's, installed in 1916. Photograph by Perier, *c.* 1926, State Library of New South Wales, 34355h.

G.H. Godsell, reported to Jenkyn in January 1918 in an important document which is pasted onto the back fly-leaf of the Parish Council's Minute Book. Godsell was scathing about some of the past attempts to keep the church in repair:

> the cure has often been worse than the disease, and such work now requires to be removed and reinstated as it existed when the Church was built. In this respect we refer more particularly to the Tower where the fine old Cupola has been much mutilated, to the Western Doorway where the window over the doors [to the Tower] has been walled up, and to the southern Entrance [shown in the Terry drawing] where a Porch was erected subsequent to the Main Building and a doorway formed under the original window opening [there always had been a door there]. In the latter case the lintels are now giving way, and the brickwork over same is collapsing.[14]

Godsell proceeded to give a long list of necessary works, which were the subject of protracted discussion and negotiation over the next year. The original proposal to repair the nave roof by replacing defective slates with new ones was changed after Godsell climbed the scaffolding in June 1919. This inspection alarmed the architect, who then recommended that the heavy slates be removed entirely; that the roof beams 'which were greatly sagged' be strengthened; and that mahogany shingles 'which would last well and be lighter for the roof timbers to carry' should replace the slates.[15]

The Parish Council accepted Godsell's revised advice and the Rector's Warden, Colonel Paine, agreed to seek financial assistance from the retail magnate Sir Samuel Hordern. Sir Samuel's grandmother, Harriet Hordern, had been married in St Matthew's in 1844 and had been commemorated by a stained-glass window in 1872. Sir Samuel and his brothers, Anthony and Lebbeus, agreed to pay for the new shingling at the bargain price of £415 on the understanding that it would be called the 'Horderns Memorial Roof'.[16]

Work began in April 1919, both on the tower and on the nave roof. The galvanized iron on the tower was replaced with shingles, the defective stonework in the cornices was replaced, the staircase and the 'bell floor' were repaired and the western door was replaced, along with all the wooden sashes and frames in the tower.[17] The roof took much longer. By the end of 1919 half of the slate roof had been replaced by mahogany shingles, but the supply of shingles suddenly dried up and the reroofing was not completed until late 1920.[18]

The 1857 porch was also rebuilt in 1919, revealing the original Macquarie plaque dated 1820 which was then attached to the exterior pediment. Jenkyn did not share Stiles' antipathy to 'notice-boards'.[19] When the plaque was examined it was found:

> to have a duplicate set of lettering on the back, but with only one 'T' in Matthew. Evidently Macquarie's economical mind suggested that ... it would be a pity to waste the stone, so it was turned round and the inscription you now see, engraved on the other face.[20]

It was presumably at this time in 1919 that the floor of the porch was raised so that the two old stone steps giving entry to the church, which Jenkyn had inverted in 1907, became redundant.

Other renovations completed by 1920 included the replacement of the columns which supported the gallery and the provision of enhanced ventilation of the nave by laying pipes above the ceiling, connected with existing louvre vents in the roof. All this work was to be done 'in the best possible manner, and as one of "Restoration"'. These louvres were removed when copper sheeting was applied in 1956.[21]

181. The roundel from the Hordern window, 1872. Photograph by Ian Jack, 2016.

By January 1921 the principal matters still needing attention were the removal and replacement of 'all perished bricks' and the removal of defective foundation stones. The contractor, the Parramatta builder W. Noller (who had built the new public hospital in Windsor in 1910–1911), with some assistance from the architect's firm, completed the work by June 1921.[22]

The centenary works halfway through Jenkyn's incumbency were his lasting mark on the church fabric.

A Well-Loved Rector

Although Norman Jenkyn continued as a well-loved rector until 1936, he appears to have been extremely nervous of certain situations. Added to the oft-told story of his fear of the rectory ceiling falling down on him in his sleep, was his timidity around snakes. Jenkyn had unexpectedly met a black snake entwined in the banister of the rectory stairs one night in September 1917, and although it was killed the fear there might be others in

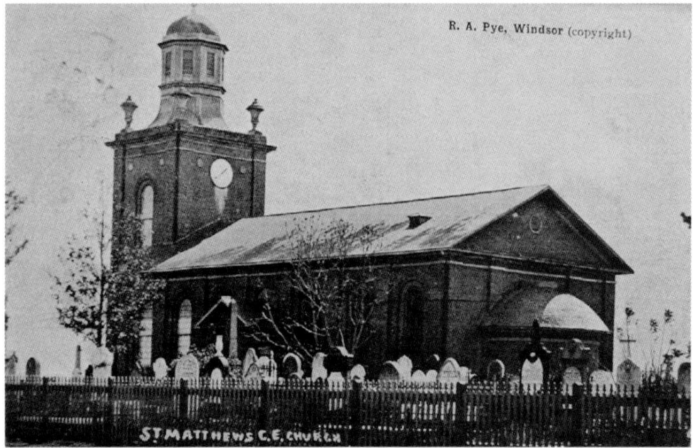

182. A louvred outlet for the ventilation system can be seen in the roof. The new system devised in 1918 seems to have used the existing louvres. Photograph no date, on a postcard produced by R.A. Pye, Windsor. Supplied by Hawkesbury Regional Museum.

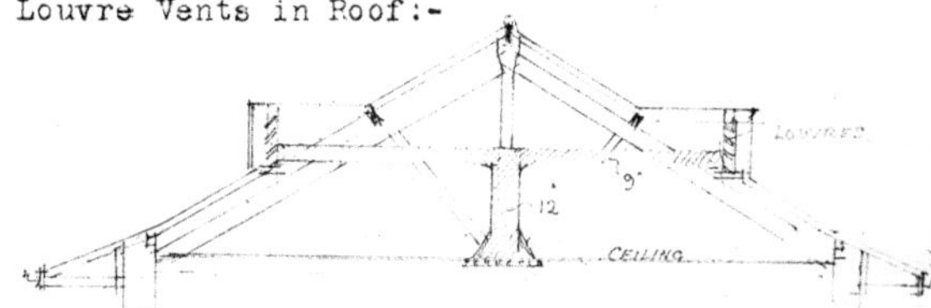

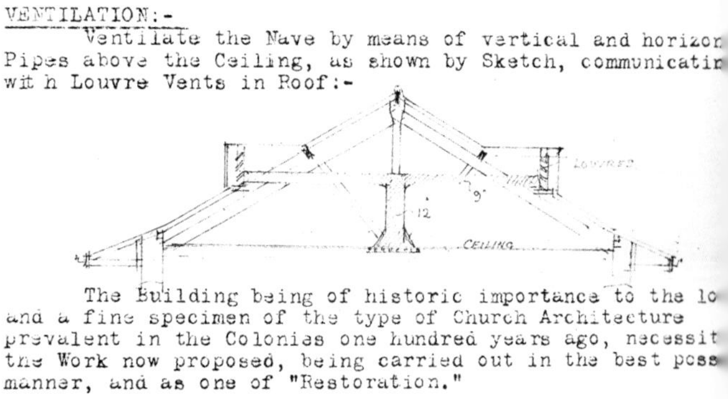

VENTILATION:-
Ventilate the Nave by means of vertical and horizon
Pipes above the Ceiling, as shown by Sketch, communicatin
with Louvre Vents in Roof:-

The Building being of historic importance to the lo
and a fine specimen of the type of Church Architecture
prevalent in the Colonies one hundred years ago, necessit
the Work now proposed, being carried out in the best poss
manner, and as one of "Restoration."

183. Plan of proposed above-ceiling ventilation for the nave, using pipes and external louvres, prepared by Robertson and Marks, Sydney architects, in January 1918. St Matthew's Archives, Minute-Book, 1886–1918, pasted onto back fly-leaf.

the house made him pack a bag and stay for an unknown period at the Macquarie Arms, then trading as the Royal Hotel. Snakes were becoming a problem in Windsor that spring, with another being killed in McQuade Park, and another at Dunn Bros cordial factory.[23]

The depth of the personal connection which Jenkyn developed with his congregation and indeed with the wider community became very obvious in 1923 when he was given a bon voyage gathering before he left for his first ever holiday. The speeches were good-humoured and full of heart-felt praise for the rector.

Jenkyn told them that Archdeacon Knox was coming to fill in for him for six months, assuring them that Knox 'had a record for vigorous work', and that Thomas Campbell had agreed to edit the church magazine in his absence. In his usual humorous way, Jenkyn added in mock seriousness and to much laughter that he hoped 'you will tell him all the news, but don't tell him any funny bits or he will get into trouble. I have got into serious trouble myself and people refused to speak to me over paragraphs in the magazine.'[24] Jenkyn told those assembled they had been 'real friends' to him and assured them he was coming back. It was quite miraculous how Jenkyn opened up to his friends, explaining that despite appearances he was a lonely man. He told how:

> When I first came to Windsor I determined to stay five years. But I grew to like the people and Windsor district. There is a fascination in Windsor, everybody gets fond of the place, and I grew to like the district, where I found a whole-hearted people ready indeed to extend the church's work and help liberally in every cause. I don't know any parish where the people help their minister so loyally. It was a revelation to me what was done. The work that was done for the material side of the church was wonderful. From the time I took charge of the parish, taking in all funds, the amount given has averaged £1200 a year. That is a tremendous sum for a parish like Windsor. There is the spiritual side, but we can't get on without money.[25]

Even more revealing were his reasons for wanting to return on a visit to England:

> When I was 13 years of age I cleared out from home. I was anxious to go aboard ship. I went to Dalgety's and got an order for a berth in a ship. When I called on the ship's officer the first thing he asked was 'Does your mother know you came?' I promptly said, 'Yes.' (Laughter). I told a lie then, but have never told one since. (Laughter) ... I went home and my mother kissed me and then whipped me. (Laughter). From that day I have looked forward to the time when I would be able to go home and see the old country.[26]

Adding another piece of humour at his own expense, Jenkyn related that 'when I told 'a lady parishioner that I would tell them all about my trip when I returned she exclaimed in dismay, "But you won't make your sermons any longer, will you?"'[27]

On his return, Norman Jenkyn resumed his drive to raise funds, and in 1924 he appealed to the entire state to fund interior works. He argued forcefully, in words still relevant today, that

> St Matthew's does not belong alone to Windsor – it is more than a parish church. It is a national asset. It belongs to Australia, to the Commonwealth ... Within

> the last 18 years we have spent over £2000 on repairs to the outside of it. Its roof will now last for years to come, but the inside is badly in need of painting. We cannot allow this historic church to grow shabby.[28]

The brickwork of the church still occasioned some alarm. The brick piers supporting the nave walls were pulled down and replaced by William Douglass in 1924.[29] Around the same time other bricks were tuck-pointed, causing one commentator to remark: 'Its [brick] colour has been toned and softened by the hand of that great craftsman, Time. A vandal architect has, however, "restored" by pointing the bricks above the windows in glaring white.'[30]

184. The 108th anniversary talk by Frank Walker on 10 October 1925, in front of St Matthew's. Photograph by F. Walker, pasted into his compilation about Windsor, Royal Australian Historical Society, Rare Book 991.3 WIN.

The gallery at the west end of the church, no longer housing the organ, now supported on fluted columns made of wood but painted to resemble marble, was described in 1924 as 'old-fashioned', and was 'out of use, owing to its condition of dangerous dilapidation'.[31]

The 108th anniversary of St Matthew's in October 1925 attracted widespread attention, probably because the church was so well cared for. Norman Jenkyn was to the fore, showing off his church to the world, and the event made the *Sydney Morning Herald*:

> Many people from all parts of the State visited Windsor during the week-end ... The visitors assembled in front of the McQuade Memorial in the cemetery on Saturday, and were welcomed to the church by Alderman W.J. Ross, Mayor of Windsor. Outside the southern porch of the church were hung two oil paintings, one of Lachlan Macquarie, Governor at the time of the erection of the church, lent by the Justice Department, and taken from the historic Windsor Court-house; the other one of the late Rev. J. Cartwright, first incumbent of the old church, lent by his great-great-granddaughter, Miss Cartwright, of Sydney.[32]

Jenkyn opened the proceedings with prayer and gave an address. He was noted as having been the clergyman of the parish and Rural Dean of the district for the past twenty years. He opened the Rectory to the guests, pausing at the room in which Samuel Marsden had died.

Frank Walker, President of the Royal Australian Historical Society, addressed the gathering in the open air in front of the porch and gave a history of the church, reported in several newspapers. This was followed by a pilgrimage to the graves of Andrew Thompson and Henry Stiles and to the foundation stone laid by Macquarie.[33]

Jenkyn, mindful of the admonition he had received two years before on the length of his sermons, remarked in his account of the proceedings in the parish magazine: 'That afternoon did more to create an interest in the Church than perhaps a hundred sermons'.[34] The public interest prompted him to have a small marble tablet added to the foundation stone later in 1925, explaining that the stone was laid in 1817.[35]

Jenkyn retired from St Matthew's in 1936, 'mainly due to his desire to search for better health and strength'.[36] His farewell banquet took place in the Royal Theatre in Windsor, attended by 500 people: his gifts were a travelling case, a dressing gown and a wallet of notes.

The newspaper regarded the turnout as 'a striking demonstration of the popularity of the guest and the respect and esteem in which he is held by the community'.[37] Jenkyn stayed on in Windsor, remaining an alderman until 1941. He died in Windsor Hospital in January 1942 and is buried at St Matthew's.[38]

185. Gravestone of the Reverend Norman Jenkyn, St Matthew's cemetery, 1942. Photograph by Jan Barkley-Jack, 1998.

Another Centenary and More Works

The new minister, G.P. Birk, found that there was a shortage of rental accommodation in the town, so he moved into the Rectory in September 1936 and lived there while it was being renovated.[39] Birk presided over the centenary of Samuel Marsden's death in July 1938, when a marble plaque was installed in the church. Twenty-two descendants of Marsden attended. The Maori bishop of Aotearoa and a large Maori choir came from New Zealand, where Marsden was still warmly remembered as a missionary parson. Afterwards the Maori visitors

> were provided with afternoon tea at the Rectory by Mrs. Birk, assisted by a number of ladies of the parish, and afterwards one of the most interesting features of the day was enacted. The Maoris made an inspection of the room at the Rectory in which Rev. Marsden passed away just over 100 years ago, and, led by Bishop and Mrs. Bennett, sang in their native tongue a lament to the memory of the founder of Christianity in New Zealand. Many were visibly affected by the solemnity of the occasion. Recognition of the importance of the occasion was given by the fact that the two Australian film and gazette companies, Fox Movietone and Cinesound News, had each sent their movable unit to Windsor to film much of what transpired. Owing to the fact that it would have been difficult to make satisfactory lighting arrangements, no pictures were taken inside the church, but a sound recording was made of the choir singing the anthem during the service. In addition, a moving picture was taken of the choir on the rectory lawn, when the Bishop spoke a message and a 'haka' was sung in Maori.[40]

Three weeks later the marble image of a ram, in token of Marsden's role in sheep-breeding, was added to the plaque and later a piece of New Zealand greenstone.[41] Soon afterwards, in 1939, the pillars supporting the former organ gallery were again under scrutiny and the local builder and parishioner, Mullinger, replaced the pillars and did repairs to the gallery itself.[42] Major renovation was postponed during the Second World War, when the seven stained-glass windows were removed for safety in 1942 and stored in the cellar of Rouse Hill House until 1945.[43]

Major works on the church did not recommence until the 1950s. A subcommittee was convened in 1951 to discuss yet again the restoration of the church, stimulated, perhaps, by the decay of some of the Hordern shingles on the roof. The first action was to install an electric motor for the organ, which had previously been pumped by hand. To accommodate the electric motor in 1952, a hole was cut through the east wall of the chancel just behind the organ and a small shed for the motor was built outside by the local contractor D'Emilio.[44] This motor shed was removed when the organ was moved back into the gallery in 1986.

In June 1962 Canon Rawson reported that the organ was 'completely stripped down, a new platform constructed [in the same place in the south-eastern corner], and the instrument renovated and rebuilt upon it by Mr Peter Rowe of Woollahra' for about £550.[45]

In 1958, Leslie Wilkinson, the dominating Professor of Architecture at the University of Sydney, among all his other involvements, supervised the repainting of the church interior. Wilkinson had designed Samuel Hordern's home at Bellevue Hill, and other important houses of the time and was the first president of the State chapter of the Royal Australian Institute of Architects in 1934. As architect to the Sydney Anglican diocese, he had charge of many churches around Sydney and was much influenced by Australia's colonial styles, as well as by medieval and Renaissance buildings in Europe. He was an artist, not a scientific conservator, as we understand the term in modern times. Otherwise the process at St Matthew's would have been to discover the earlier colours used in painting the ceiling by taking a series of paint scrapes.

The redecoration of Kemp's ceiling of exactly a hundred years before was instead done in colours selected by Wilkinson from 'a Capstan cigarette-box which he happened to have in his pocket.'[46] We still enjoy the Capstan colours today.

The most recent repainting of the interior of the church in 1924 by the Richmond decorator, J. Taylor, had excluded the sanctuary dome. He had painted the ceiling white and 'the walls in buff'.[47] During the incumbency of William Carter, Freestone, the current contractor, was ordered in May 1958 not to proceed with 'gold painting of the dome'. Instead in July the sanctuary dome was given its 'first coat of aluminium'.

186. The colours of St Matthew's ceiling as conceived by Leslie Wilkinson in 1958. Photograph by Trevor Bunning, Canberra, 2012.

In October the rector reported that the dome 'was still not successful'. Freestone claimed that he had always said that it would not be a success. Finally, in September 1958, just before the dedication service for the total restoration works, it was decided that the painting of the sanctuary would not do and that the inside of the dome should be covered with fibrous plaster.[48]

The outcome is unclear from the Minute Books, but the removal of plaster from the dome in 1984 makes it certain that Freestone acted upon the suggestion in 1958. What was revealed under the plaster in 1984 (and presumably also under the aluminium paint) was a night-sky scene of blue with gold stars which has happily been retained. Whether this starry scene was a tactful reference to John Tebbutt, the astronomer who was a keen, though disputatious, member of the congregation, is uncertain. Blue with gold stars was a popular late Victorian decoration, which could be seen in old St Stephen's Presbyterian Church in Phillip Street and can still be seen in the 1876 Library at St Andrew's College at the University of Sydney. On stylistic grounds, the date of the 1880s hazarded in 1984 is a very plausible conjecture.[49]

In the 1950s, attention was not focused on the decoration of the sanctuary dome, but rather on the divisive issue of concealing with drapes the painted texts around the sanctuary wall.

The texts were, from left to right, the Lord's Prayer, The Ten Commandments and the Apostles' Creed, and the text panels were in need of repainting in the 1950s. The cheaper alternative of hanging material over them finally won the day. Strong opinions on both sides were expressed throughout 1958 and 1959 and the necessary faculty was granted by the diocese only with reservations. The curtains were in place by November 1958. The reversibility of the decision made the occlusion more palatable, and the texts have indeed been rendered visible again today.[50]

Restoration Appeals

In 1952 under Douglas McCraw it had been decided to launch a Rectory Restoration Appeal, and in 1953 a Church Restoration Appeal Committee was formed.[51] The architectural firm of McDonald was commissioned and in June 1954 Mr Knowles from that firm reported on the state of the roof. The meeting attended by Knowles was also the first meeting chaired by the new

187. Deep blue and white drapes were hung over the painted panels of the Lord's Prayer, the Ten Commandments and the Apostles' Creed as a cheaper alternative to repainting in 1958. Photograph from June Bryant, taken *c.* 1960, supplied by Jan Barkley-Jack.

rector, W.F. Carter, who went on to write the well-researched history of his church, proudly entitled *The Cathedral of the Hawkesbury*.[52]

The state of the roof was the primary preoccupation during the first phase of work in 1955. The Parish Council itself, at the meeting attended by Knowles in 1954, on the motion of John Paine, the solicitor, had decided that the shingles should be replaced by copper and once copper became available work began in 1956. There was some concern over the appearance of the copper: the rector had wrongly understood that 'the copper sheets were to be made to represent shingles.' But the roof was completed punctually in mid-1956 by the contractors, Webb Bros, at a cost of around £10,000 and attention was focused on all the other aspects of restoration and upon the financing of the loans which had been necessary to supplement the money raised by the appeal.[53]

After some dithering, it was decided to re-lay the aisles of the nave with Hawkesbury sandstone in 1957. Many of the old flagstones were 'badly worn and pitted' and most of them were reused 'to provide weather strips outside the church, and generally to beautify the grounds.'[54] Some of the former flagstones, however, were re-laid in the church, but the rest were sold to parishioners. Alf Cammack, Carol Roberts' father, bought about 50 of them for 2s. each to make a path in his yard in Court Street.[55] The 140th anniversary celebrations held on 12 October 1957 were a day to be 'long remembered in our parish' when nearly 800 people were present to celebrate the conservation works and the re-dedication of St Matthew's by the Archbishop.

Two new vestries, panelled with cedar, were constructed under the gallery. One was for the rector, the other for the wardens.[56] A new lighting system introduced electric lamps set into the nave ceiling with concealed fluorescent tubes in the sanctuary. It also incorporated underground cabling, so that the light poles disfiguring the McQuade Memorial could be removed in 1957.[57] New ceilings were constructed for the gallery and the tower porch. The pews were moved to allow for new hardwood flooring where required and the pews themselves were reconditioned. Tiles were introduced into the chancel area at the east end, which for the first time gave the chancel a character distinctive from the nave. The apsidal sanctuary was carpeted and, after some vigorous disagreement and an appeal to the Archbishop, the curtains were finally installed and the archbishop rededicated the restored church in April 1959.[58]

In the spring of 1962, after Harold Rawson had replaced William Carter, it was noticed that the roof, especially in the tower, was leaking and the decision in principle to launch an appeal to preserve the historic fabric was taken in October. The Government Architect, E.H. Farmer, came personally to the church after one of his colleagues had climbed the tower and said: 'Either we pull it down quickly, or it will fall down.'[59]

Farmer then took two critically important steps. He persuaded the Public Works Department to divert some of its facilities and experienced architects, though not its workmen, to address the problems. Secondly, he approached the National Trust for funds.[60] As a result the Penrith firm of Irons and Hughes was quickly engaged and in December they dismantled the tower roof. They found that there was no alternative to rebuilding this roof and the belfry. Soon afterward white ants were detected or suspected in the floor timbers of the nave. By the end of the church's financial year, in March 1963, the equivalent of $2,336 had already been spent on essential repairs to the tower, as well as $1,113 on a new roof for the Rectory.[61] But this was only a beginning and in July 1963 a journalist described the church as 'like a rose apple with a rotten core'.[62] The church itself was galvanised into action under Rawson's urging. The architectural historian Morton Herman and Professor Wilkinson, a long-time friend of St Matthew's, were pressed into service on radio and television in April 1963. The National Trust set up an Appeal Committee and in June Rachel Roxburgh, one of the *grandes dames* of the National Trust, came to a meeting of the Parish Council along with another member of the committee, an architect representing Farmer, the Government Architect, and Norman Irons, the managing director of the firm doing the work. The Parish Council expressed 'great uplift' at the prospect of outside fund-raising being undertaken for the church.[63]

The public appeal for £50,000 for St Matthew's tower and rectory was announced by the National Trust in July 1963. It was the first such appeal launched by the Trust since its inauguration in 1947. Although the Council at St Matthew's appreciated the financial and moral help, relations between the Trust and the church authorities became testy at times.

The diocese tried to raise funds from Anglican parishes and St Matthew's itself had a Restoration Fund containing loan funds. There was uncertainty about who was paying whom for what. Moreover, in October 1963 the National Trust President, Justice McClemens, tried to insist that as a corollary to the restoration the church commit itself to preserving the buffer land between the church and the Rectory: the Parish Council refused to give such an undertaking (and in 1982 this again became an issue between the church and the National Trust). This led in turn to a motion on 23 October 1963 that: 'whilst we gratefully accept any monies raised by the National Trust in St Matthew's Windsor appeal, [the Parish] Council feels that it cannot allow control of Parish property out of its hands'.[64]

A weekly telecast of a church service from different venues saw morning prayer beamed from St Matthew's on 1 September, organised by Rachel Roxburgh, the honorary secretary of the Appeal, with a parishioner, Dorothy Campbell (Lorna's sister) playing the organ and the singing provided by the Junior and Senior Choirs trained by Ron Stewart.[65]

In the meantime work continued, largely controlled by the National Trust, replacing the fretted brickwork of the tower with sandstock bricks of a suitable date. As it happened, the 1838 rectory at St Thomas' Anglican Church, Mulgoa, was being demolished in 1963 and most of the bricks were salvaged for St Matthew's. The Mulgoa bricks were supplemented with other early bricks from private donors.[66] Irons and Hughes were unable to find a bricklayer experienced in this sort of conservation work but the Public Works Department, despite its initial refusal, provided a suitable Scottish bricklayer.[67]

The builders employed by Irons and Hughes seem to have resented any interference from the church. Attempts by the wardens to inspect their work resulted in October 1963 in some bad language from the tradesmen and considerable ill-feeling among some wardens.[68] But work continued. Scaffolding went up the south face of the tower and then enveloped the belfry, which was largely dismantled.[69] The timber dome was being amassed on the ground prior to its reassembly aloft. *The Parish Messenger* reported that inside the parapet out of sight, 'steel girders were being inserted and fretted bricks replaced to strengthen this portion in readiness for the timber [superstructure] being put into position'.[70]

The wooden cross and orb were not in a fit state to be returned to the tower, so a new cross was made.[71] The 1844 cross was salvaged by the Hawkesbury Historical Society during the reconstruction of the tower and belfry in 1963 and is now in the Hawkesbury Regional Museum, as part of the collection of Hawkesbury Historical Society. The large wooden cross was carved in three parts.

The National Trust cajoled the air force into providing a helicopter to lower the new cross and orb onto the top of the uncompleted tower on 2 November 1963.[72] The National Trust St Matthew's Windsor Appeal capitalized on this unique event by holding a Go to Windsor Day that Saturday, advertising that:

> About midday, if the weather is suitable, the 16 ft. tower cross will be replaced on the 32ft belfry which surrounds the 56ft. tower of St Matthew's. The belfry which has been rebuilt, is a faithful copy of the original ... This

188. The tower under repair in 1963. Photograph from the collection of Hawkesbury Historical Society, now housed in the Hawkesbury Regional Museum in Windsor, run by Hawkesbury City Council, accession no. 1977.130.3.

189. The remains of the original 1844 wooden cross from the church tower on display. Collection of Hawkesbury Historical Society, now housed in the Hawkesbury Regional Museum in Windsor, run by Hawkesbury City Council, accession no. 1977.39.

operation will be carried out by a RAAF helicopter from No. 9 Squadron, Fairbairn. The National Trust is greatly indebted to the RAAF for assisting in the rescue of St Matthew's, our finest historical monument from the Macquarie era.

190. A helicopter from RAAF No. 9 Squadron, Fairbairn, replacing the 1844 carved wooden cross with a new one in 1963. Collection of Hawkesbury Historical Society, now housed in the Hawkesbury Regional Museum in Windsor, run by Hawkesbury City Council, accession no.1977.130.1.

The day's programme included an inspection open to the public by 'kind permission of Air Commodore C.W. Pearce, CBE, DFC', of the 'RAAF station at Richmond', a band recital by the Royal Australian Navy in McQuade Park in front of the church, followed by a welcome by 'Governor and Mrs Macquarie' and Alderman V. Gillespie to Lieutenant J.B. McMillan 'and four other ranks from 1st Royal NSW Regiment (Commando), City of Sydney's Own Regiment', who had walked from Macquarie Place, Sydney to Windsor, dressed in uniforms of the NSW Corps, emulating an officer who had walked the route in 1794 for 'a trifling wager'. The Macquaries were played by Mr and Mrs Shanley of Richmond. *The Daily Mirror* newspaper donated the programmes.

Currency lads and lasses sold the programmes,

and the other local Greenway-designed building, Windsor Court House, was opened for public inspection, as was Hawkesbury Museum run by Hawkesbury Historical Society in Thompson Square. The Women's Guild of St Matthew's arranged the refreshments in the park, while the local appeal committee held a produce stall assisted by the Apex and Rotary clubs. The helicopter replaced the cross precisely as the church clock struck twelve.[73]

The rebuilding of the superstructure of the belfry was not completed until late 1964, when the scaffolding was finally removed. Tallowwood from the rainforests of Eden and Dorrigo had been felled to replace the large curved beams of stringy bark, spotted gum and blackbutt as well as tallowwood, which Greenway's builders had been able to source from the Hawkesbury woodland in Macquarie's time.[74]

Other work was done within the nave. The seven stained-glass windows were taken down late in 1964 and put back in new frames. In the following year the wooden flooring was raised and replaced by the present stone flagging on a concrete base. The pews were taken away, repaired, sanded and stained over eighteen months. The ceiling and the sanctuary arch were reinforced.[75] On 31 October 1965 Archbishop Gough presided at a Thanksgiving Service for the completion of the work (although some of the pews were not fully treated until the following year).[76] He thanked the National Trust for taking responsibility and the Government Architect for his supervision. The National Trust's Annual Report for 1965–1966 summed up the process underlying the restoration:

> While the work of restoration is complete, that of raising the money to pay for it is not. The final cost was $86,367. The Trust's Women's Committee, which had already contributed $18,750 of the $54,000 raised by the Appeal Committee, has contributed a further $8,000 towards the reduction of the debt which now stands at $24,000. The Women's Committee has agreed to devote its further efforts to the liquidation of this debt. The appeal is still open, however, and any contribution ... would be gratefully received.

The report continued:

> The National Trust feels that it has an obligation to all those who contributed towards the restoration to ensure that the historic character and architectural integrity of St. Matthew's is preserved in perpetuity and the Council [of the National Trust] is negotiating with the church authorities for an agreement that the Trust will be consulted in respect of any work or development associated with the church or its setting which may be projected in the future.[77]

To commemorate the joint venture, two plaques were erected in the church porch in 1967.[78]

The diocese, through the Archdeacon in particular, had taken a keen interest in recent events and in the latter part of 1966 Archdeacon Fillingham urged that a consultative body be created 'to take care of the material upkeep of the church fabric' and recommended that St Matthew's should cooperate with the National Trust. As a result, in November, a committee was formed, consisting of the rector, the wardens, the Archdeacon representing the Archbishop, a representative from the Church Property Trust and one member of the National Trust.[79]

Canon Rawson conducted a special service on 11 October 1967, for the 150th anniversary of the church. The Governor-General, Lord Casey, attended. A plastic cylinder containing a number of unspecified items was sealed into the church floor near the tower door as part of the sesquicentenary celebrations, and there was a re-enactment of the laying of the foundation stone (on a different site). In the paddock between the church and the Rectory, Governor Macquarie, portrayed by Kevin Rozzoli, took part in the proceedings. The other characters included members of the Richmond Players, Warden Ray Wilcher as Marsden in his distinctive black beaver hat, and Rector's Warden Len Mynett, with his daughter Beverley and granddaughter Fiona.[80]

Five years later, on Sunday 17 December 1972, in the presence of the Governor-General, Sir Paul Hasluck, and Lady Hasluck, a commemorative service was held in the church to celebrate its 150th anniversary of the consecration.[81]

Modern Works

A campaign of more thorough documentation of the organ had begun in 1978 through a grant from the Myer Foundation. David Kinsela, a prominent

191. Re-enactment of Governor Macquarie laying the foundation stone in 1817, portrayed as part of the 150th Anniversary celebrations. Photograph supplied by Beverley Hunt.

192. Len Mynett, the Rector's Warden, with daughter Beverley and granddaughter Fiona Hunt as part of the 1967 re-enactment for the 150th celebrations at the church. Photograph supplied by Beverley Hunt.

organist led the way. David explained:

> On returning to Australia in 1978 after a decade of organological activity in Europe, I was inspired by the Windsor relic to initiate and guide its restoration. The daunting eight-year project owed much to the enthusiastic support of rector Len Abbott and ... Barry Ingold [then Parish Council Secretary]. Extensive consultations with organ-builders and parish officers led to agreement that the organ be returned to its gallery with restitution of the extended Great and (most controversially) the shortened Swell.[82]

A further grant was received from the Heritage Council of New South Wales in 1981 and David Kinsela was appointed organ consultant to the church, liaising with the organist, Graeme Hunt. The result was a wide-ranging restoration scheme, which the Heritage Council approved in 1984 and funded to the extent of $28,000. The church had to find an additional $20,000. An appeal brochure was issued, entitled 'A National Treasure: the Restoration Appeal for Australia's First Locally Built Pipe Organ at the Historic Anglican St. Matthew's Church Windsor, N.S.W.'. This contained a ringing endorsement from the pianist Roger Woodward, claiming (before he had heard the organ back in the gallery) that 'I cannot find a more beautiful acoustic in Australia than in this place of worship'. The restorer was Knud Smenge Pty Ltd of Melbourne, who had extensive experience in restoring early organs in Denmark and Holland. He added an impressive trumpet stop.[83]

The gallery had required some attention. The church engaged Lowe and Hooke (Aust.) Pty Ltd, consulting engineers, to inspect the gallery in July 1983 to determine its adequacy to support the organ. Termite-affected wood was replaced by builder Mick Scruci who installed two new timber beams and new flooring before the organ could be returned. Further advice was sought from the Public Works Department. Meanwhile an early electric keyboard was used as a replacement for the organ. The fully restored organ was returned to its proper place in 1986. David Kinsela gave a concert soon after, and in 1996 recorded a CD on St Matthew's organ, the disc released the following year.[84]

It fell on the rector, John Butler, to organize yet more work on the roof when it was found that the copper roof sheeting installed 33 years earlier was failing. Graham Edds & Associates were employed in the 1990s and, with Professor Max Hatherly from the Department of Metallurgy from the School of Materials Science and Engineering at the University of NSW, analysed the causes of the copper's premature failure.[85] Graham Edds relates:

> The timber structure was also the subject of structural investigation by McBean & Crisp, structural engineers, who determined and recommended that with some prudent strengthening the roof structure would have the capability of supporting a new slate, timber shingle or metal roof. To lessen the load on the structure a metal roof was selected and programmed for installation.
>
> The appropriately named Copperform 'Greenway' design copper roof panels 600mm wide were installed during 1993–1994 covering the Nave gable roof and the domed cupola of the Sanctuary. Guttering and downpipes were also replaced.[86]

Extensive research on the project was also carried out by Ian Douglas (B.Sc.) on behalf of the Parish Council.[87]

Edds & Associates have also conducted other modern conservation measures on the church. These related to the conservation of the windows and the problem of rising damp damaging the brickwork, familiar since Joseph Docker's ministry in the late 1820s.

In summary, Graham continues that:

> Rising damp in the walls of the church has been a complex conservation issue, necessitating perimeter drainage and particularly since the 1980s following the unfortunate installation of a concrete slab floor within the nave. As the installation of a damp-proof course was not considered feasible, because of the excessive wall thickness, in part up to one metre, the use of sacrificial plasters and poultices of paper pulp and diatomaceous earth to draw out and reduce the deteriorating salt level from within the walls was instigated. The external work was done initially by Jim Scanlan of North Richmond and later by S. Edenden, plasterer. It proved to be very successful. This has resulted in a dramatic lessening of salt contamination levels to external wall surfaces of sandstone and sandstock brick and to internal plasters. An injected damp-proof course was however trialled and installed within the thinner circular wall of the apse. Similarly, rising damp in the walls of the Rectory over a long period led to conservation action involving the placement of an injected damp-proof course in some of the Rectory walls, together with poulticing to reduce the salt contamination levels. The successes of these conservation approaches to combat rising damp will depend on future ongoing monitoring and maintenance.[88]

Graham remembers the large wind storm during 2003 that began the next round of works while Chris Burgess was minister:

193. Graham Edds supervising the recladding of the roof at St Matthew's in 1993. *Windsor and Richmond Gazette,* 5 May 1993, p. 9.

> The damage to a single stained glass window, repaired in part under the church's insurance, was the catalyst for a detailed look at the nearby stained glass windows along the northern face of the church. This investigation revealed considerable damage to three other windows. Heritage assistance grant funds were successful. The four windows were the two earliest, the Terry and Rouse, dating from 1864, the joint Elias and Robinson in the late 1870s and the Lucinia Wood window in the late 1880s.[89]
>
> The restoration work completed by Rodney Marshall Stained Glass during 2004 involved the complete removal of these four windows, one at a time, their relocation to a workshop for cleaning with water, replacement of missing and broken glass, repainting individual pieces of glass where deteriorated and re-leading, then replacement into position in the window openings.
>
> The timber window frames were repaired and repainted whilst internally the plaster window surrounds had the same care. During the same year one very large window in the bell-tower was restored and another stabilised and

protected from further damage. The restored window contained two sashes, one a 25-pane rectangular sash, the upper sash rectangular with a domed top containing 35 panes. This window restored by Greg Brown and Lester Salter of the Sydney Restoration Company was

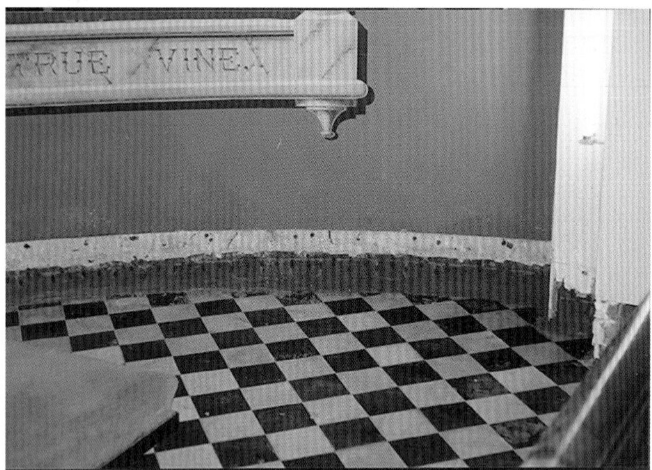

194. Inside the Sanctuary apse, a DPC (damp proof course) was inserted. Photograph by Graham and Carol Edds, 1997.

dismantled, timber sash frames repaired, painted and reassembled.[90]

Throughout the necessary bouts of church repair and conservation, the business of the church continued to be conducted. Weddings, baptisms and funerals were carried out by Reverends Carter, Rawson, Abbott, Butler, Burgess and Pinter as usual. Beverley Mynett married Neville Hunt in 1957, and the wedding of Elin Hayes of Windsor to Kenwin Alderton of Schofields was held on New Year's Day in 1958, among many more.

In late 1960 William Carter and his wife Violet reluctantly said goodbye to St Matthew's. In November 1960 Violet wrote to her 'dear friends' in the parish about the 'happy days we have spent in Windsor' and how she had enjoyed her work 'in the GFS, in the Sunday School and amongst the women in the parish and in the choir'.[91]

Harold Rawson Gets his 'Dream Parish'

Harold Rawson had spent the years of the First World War in Sheffield in England, and remained there for a few years more until he was one of the few selected from among hundreds to migrate to Australia under the Dreadnought Scheme. On arrival, along with the other new immigrants, he

195. In addition to the injected damp proof course installed within the apse, a poultice was applied externally to the rest, then removed. Photograph by Graham and Carol Edds, 1993.

196. Tower window stabilization. Graham and Carol Edds, 2008.

undertook agricultural training in the Scheyville training camp, until sent to Dapto. After some farming experience Harold joined the army and spent the Second World War in North Africa and then New Guinea. In the 2nd and 3rd Infantry Battalion, his experiences included being part of General Wavell's desert sweep as far as Tobruk. He

197 and 198. Stained glass restoration in 2004. Photograph by Graham .and Carol Edds.

marched over the mountains to Greece and was then sent to Palestine and finished on the Kokoda Track, where illness necessitated him being evacuated to Port Moresby.[92]

After the war, Harold attended Moore Theological College in Sydney and ten years later married a long-time friend Jessie McLean from Bowral. Ministry in the Blue Mountains led to St Matthew's which Harold Rawson, a lover of history, described as his 'dream parish'. He was well equipped to deal with the problems which lay ahead, including the district's highest floods since Stiles' time.[93]

199. Interior wall repair of St Matthew's. Photograph by Graham and Carol Edds. 1990.

200. Wedding of Beverley Mynett to Neville Hunt in 1957. Photograph supplied by Beverley Hunt.

201. Lynne Hayes ahead of the bride, Elin Hayes, and the groom, Kenwin Alderton, in St Matthew's on 1 January 1958. Photograph supplied by Kim Alderton.

Queen Elizabeth II, accompanied by the Duke of Edinburgh, made the first royal visit to St Matthew's during Rawson's incumbency,

The Queen was touring Australia during the celebrations for the bicentenary of James Cook and came to Windsor on 30 April 1970.[94] The Bishop of Parramatta, Gordon Begbie, was also in attendance for the visit. The parish was enthused by the royal visit and crowds queued to see the Queen.[95] Kim Alderton, daughter of Elin and Kenwin, who had been married twelve years before in the church, was one of the myriad of district schoolchildren who waited hours for a glimpse of the royal couple.[96]

202. (Left) The Queen with Bishop Begbie, and members of the parish of St Matthew's: (left to right) People's Warden Horrie Hollier, Joyce Hollier (obscured), Alice Hayes, People's Warden Bert Hayes (obscured) and Rector's Warden Len Mynett, 1970. Photograph supplied by Beverley Hunt.

203. During the visit of Queen Elizabeth II and the Duke of Edinburgh to the district on 30 April 1970, the Royal visitors examined the 1822 silver watched by rector Harold Rawson and by Bishop Begbie in the nave of St Matthew's. Photograph supplied by Chris Jones, rector of St Matthew's.

204. Schoolchildren and parishioners greeting Queen Elizabeth II on her visit to St Matthew's in 1970. Photograph supplied by Hawkesbury Regional Museum, accession no. 2014.86.2.

In retirement as required by ordinance at 71 years,[97] Harold Rawson liked to keep busy. The church's newsletter, called from 1988 onwards *The Weekly Bulletin*, shows him as an honorary assistant minister of St Matthew's who was on the roster for parishioners' duties until September 1995.[98] He cleaned the church once a month regularly from 1988 until mid-1993, when he retreated to once every two months on average. He continued on the cleaning roster on this basis until July 1995.[99] Even immediately after celebrating his 80th birthday on 25 August 1988, he was cleaning the nave.[100]

Moreover, Canon Rawson, as he was affectionately known to his parishioners and community alike, added 'Hospital Visitor' to his obligations more or less weekly from December 1990 until 1992, when the frequency declined to once a month and then after June 1994 to two-monthly. His last hospital visit was in May 1995.[101] He was unwell from September 1995 until his death in Hawkesbury Hospital in July 1996.[102] The eulogy delivered by Archbishop Marcus Loane is quoted in *The Weekly Bulletin*, No. 435, 21 July 1996:

> There was a strong and determined strain in his character. He was not a man to yield to pressure when that pressure was contrary to his own deep seated convictions. He was a man who was gentle, modest, in many ways retiring, even diffident, always courteous, always considerate.

205. Baby Kim Alderton in the arms of her mother, Mrs Elin Alderton, on 17 February 1963. Photograph supplied by Kim Alderton.

Rawson easily melded with families who had lived a long time in the area. Along the way, Harold Rawson has left a legacy without end in the number of people he served in his parish until 1980: he married almost a thousand couples and baptized two thousand babies. The latest generation of the Alcorn family was one of a great many Hawkesbury families who in their various branches had lived and farmed in the district for around two hundred years, and continued to get married in the church. In the 1950s and 1960s, Joseph Alcorn married Irene Maraga in October 1958, and Una Alcorn married Alfred Tromp in August 1960. The following October, Frederick Alcorn married Lorraine Gill. In 1963 Albert Roche married Helen Alcorn.[103]

Many babies christened by Harold Rawson in the 1960s still live in the district. The Alderton family is an example. When Kim Alderton was christened at St Matthew's in 1963, her family had long connections to the church. Her parents had been married there, and Kim Alderton's grandfather, Edward Hayes, had, for 60 years, repaired the clock in the tower.[104]

Edward was a watchmaker who had a shop on the south-western corner of the intersection of George and Catherine Streets, Windsor, where now the old, empty electricity building stands. As part of his business, Edward also sold bicycles. He and his wife lived for a while in a house attached to the shop. In 1953, when he died, his burial had been conducted by Carter's predecessor, Douglas McCraw.[105]

Holy Baptism

IN THE NAME OF THE FATHER, AND OF THE SON, AND OF THE HOLY GHOST

Kim Marie Alderton

Was Baptised at the Church of

St. Matthew, Windsor

on 17th. February, 1963.

by Harold Rawson.

PARENTS AND GODPARENTS

Ye are to take care that this Child be brought to the Bishop to be confirmed by him, so soon as the Child can say the Creed, the Lord's Prayer and the Ten Commandments, and be further instructed in the Church Catechism set forth for that purpose.

Parents should themselves teach their children the faith of the Church, and should take them to Church and also take care to send them, as soon as possible, to the Church Sunday Schools.

206. Baptismal certificate of 17 February 1963, signed by Harold Rawson. Kim Alderton.

1980s and 1990s, Continuing Celebrations

Len Abbott juggled his rectorship between 1980 and 1988 with repairs and many new challenges, and introduced the more appealing service time for young families of 10 a.m.

A pressing task was the preparations for the visit of Governor-General Sir Ninian Stephen and Lady Stephen to St Matthew's in 1988 while the nation was in full swing to commemorate 200 years since European settlement. When John Butler's ministry began in 1988, with Canon Rawson as his honorary helper, along with assistance from Neil Manuell, he arrived just in time to present Len Abbott's already planned ceremonies for the Bicentenary, and for the 150th anniversary of Samuel Marsden's death in the Rectory in 1838.[106]

207. Dignitaries at the 1988 induction of John Butler, left to right: Neville Hunt (churchwarden), Kevin Rozzoli (State parliamentarian), Dorothy Butler, John Butler, John Horrex (mayor), Alasdair Webster (Federal member of parliament). Photograph supplied by John and Dorothy Butler.

On 11 October 1992 a commemorative service was held to celebrate the 175th anniversary of the laying of the foundation stone of St Matthew's. The governor of New South Wales, Rear Admiral Peter Sinclair, and Mrs Shirley Sinclair were guests of a large congregation of present and past parishioners. The preacher was the Archbishop of Sydney, the most Reverend Donald Robinson.

On 1 October 1994 Governor Sinclair returned to Windsor to celebrate 200 years of European settlement in the district. He unveiled a statue of his predecessor Lachlan Macquarie in McQuade Park opposite the church: the statue was paid for by the Rural Press, then owners of the *Windsor and Richmond Gazette,* with a $50,000 donation. Other events were held in Thompson Square and Governor Phillip Park alongside the river, and as part of the activities the church hosted a magnificent Bicentenary of Settlement Flower Show.

208. The Governor, Rear Admiral Peter Sinclair, and his wife, Mrs Shirley Sinclair, walking past the St Matthew's cemetery with Warden Neville Hunt and his wife Beverley in 1992. Photograph supplied by John and Dorothy Butler.

210. Warden, Ron Soper, in 1992. Photograph supplied by John and Dorothy Butler.

209. Governor Peter Sinclair and his wife, Mrs Shirley Sinclair, meeting the Archbishop of Sydney, Donald Robinson, Mrs Robinson (to Archbishop's left), the rector John Butler, Dorothy Butler, and Neville and Beverley Hunt outside St Matthew's Church in 1992. Photograph supplied by Beverley Hunt.

211. (left) Kath and Peter Griffiths, Russell Reeves, Madge Green, Jan Reeves, Heather Reeves (president of Ladies' Guild) and Betty Huxley on the occasion of the visit of Governor Peter Sinclair and Mrs Sinclair in 1992. Photograph supplied by John and Dorothy Butler.

212. The communion service in St Matthew's before a large congregation, celebrating the church's 175th anniversary in 1992. Governor Peter Sinclair and Mrs Sinclair are seated in the front row. The baptismal font is in the right foreground. Photograph supplied by John and Dorothy Butler.

213. Margaret Fennell (left) and Joyce Edwards (right) outside the Rectory. Joyce was a long-term member of Parish Council and a warden. Margaret Fennell is a warden and a current member of the Parish Council, and is responsible for the management of the cemetery. Photograph supplied by Kim Alderton, from *Hawkesbury Gazette*, 11 June 1999.

Church Festivals and Parish Responsibilities

The traditional church festivals and parish responsibilities continued alongside the special occasions. Over the years St Matthew's has been richly decorated for the Harvest Festival with local produce which is then given to the various children's homes which the church has supported with financial donations, and to others in need.[107] The life of the parish within the Christian year was omnipresent.

The Butlers returned happily to these normal events. Christmas in particular was a family affair for them, with their children Janelle and David helping to set up the Nativity scene by setting the straw in place in preparation for the busy church season ahead.

214. The font of St Matthew's decorated as the centrepiece of the Bicentennial Flower Show in 1994. Photograph by Kim Alderton, 1994.

215. Narelle Vance at the Harvest Festival at St Matthew's around 1984. Photograph by Carol Roberts.

The rectory children of the Butlers were also involved in the 1990s with church activities. Janelle taught in the Sunday school, and David was a leader in the Youth Group with the Parish Stipendiary Layworker, Ruth Mahaffey, together with Muriel Gilmore.

There was an active children's program during the 1990s, largely supported by Ian and Dianne Douglas who also established a community vegetable garden in the rectory paddock. The parish later employed a children's worker, Cathy Bell, for a short time. This was in addition to the Sunday school and Sunday school picnics which were held at Warragamba Dam and other places. Scripture classes in public schools once a week continue today, taken by parish volunteers and the rector.[108]

Many children entered the special category for the young provided in the Ladies' Guild Flower Show competitions, creating floral saucers and other decorative arrangements.[109]

216. David and Janelle Butler transporting the hay bales for the Nativity scene around 1990. Photograph supplied by John and Dorothy Butler.

217. Nativity scene used in St Matthew's in the 1990s. Photograph supplied by John and Dorothy Butler.

Family Celebrations

The rites of passage of the congregation dominate the records of St Matthew's, like every other Christian church. In all of these the ministers were intimately concerned. Between 1822 and 2000 13,000 Hawkesbury babies were baptized.

218. Christening of Carol Cammack at St Matthew's in 1947. Back, left to right: Jean Hornery, Charlotte Hornery (grandmother), Reverend C.L. Williams, Dorris Hornery (Clements). Front, left to right: Enid Schneider, Iris Cammack (Hornery) holding baby Carol Cammack, June Hornery, and five-year old Neil Cammack, a brother to Carol. Photograph supplied by Carol Roberts.

Over the same period from 1822 to 2000 over 4,000 marriages were celebrated. During the nineteenth century there had never been more than 22 marriages in a single year, and this number was not exceeded until 1930, but from then on the number fluctuated in the twenties and thirties until there was a sharp increase from 1967 until 1981, with a record 104 weddings in 1974. These weddings led, of course, to christenings and subsequent marriages and confirmations too were held regularly.

The wedding of the Butlers' only daughter, Janelle, took place in 1997, complete with the popular arrival and departure in a horse-drawn open carriage.

Continuing the St Matthew's connection, John and Dorothy Butler's grandchildren were two of the 7,126 who used the stone font during the twentieth century or soon after. Although John Butler had left St Matthew's in 1999 to take up another appointment, he arranged with the then rector, Chris Burgess, that he should baptize his granddaughter Ashley in 2000 and his grandson Thomas in the church in 2004.

219. Marriage of widow Carol Vance (née Cammack) and Geoff Roberts, conducted in 1995 by John Butler. Carol's first marriage to Barry Vance in 1973 was conducted by Canon Rawson. Photograph supplied by Carol Roberts.

220. Dorothy Butler, the bridegroom Patrick O'Malley, the bride Janelle Butler, and John Butler in 1997. Photograph supplied by Dorothy and John Butler.

Into the 21st Century

In 1999 the parish welcomed a new rector, Chris Burgess. Chris, who is now Assistant to the Bishop of North Sydney, Chris Edwards, found, like many of the ministers at St Matthew's over the years, that his ministry at Windsor was necessarily:

> characterised by efforts to balance active bible based leadership, services, outreach and special events amongst the church and in the community; with efforts to address the ongoing management and restoration of historically

> significant buildings, including the church building built 1817 and the rectory built 1823–1825. Hence evangelistic services, missions, courses explaining the Christian faith occurred regularly along with the restoration of the Stables; the repointing of four of the magnificent church Stained Glass Windows; and ongoing maintenance and restoration on the Rectory.[110]

With his wife Cathy and their family, Chris Burgess spent eight years in Windsor between 1999 and 2007. He saw in the 21st century at the Rectory, making him, along with Sydney Fielding, the only minister to span different centuries. The 190th anniversary of the laying of the foundation stone was another milestone the Burgess family witnessed. Organized by Joyce Edwards and a committee, the visit of Governor Marie Bashir was a gracious highlight to the 2007 event, for during the service the governor read the lessons and gave an insightful view of Macquarie and St Matthew's Church. The morning tea and lunch were provided by the parish, and historical displays were mounted by Jan Barkley-Jack for Hawkesbury Historical Society, amid other well-supported stalls.[111]

221. A 'Cavalcade of Fashion' was held in St Matthew's in 1999. Photograph by Kim Alderton.

In 2003 the Alcorn family was celebrating 200 years in Australia (their connections to the church of St Matthew having been regularly noted in this book as representative of the numerous Anglican families descended from the pioneers in the district who are buried in St Matthew's cemetery). An Alcorn re-union was held in early June in the church's Parish Centre.[112] Equally the reunions of descendants of the Melville family in May 2004,[113] and the Moses family before them on 12 November 2000 and many others were all connected to St Matthew's cemetery during Chris Burgess' ministry.[114]

The Reverend Aleks Pinter served as the rector of St Matthew's from June 2008 until April 2015. With wife Susannah, he now lives at Maroubra, serving as senior minister of St Mary's, Waverley. The Pinter children, Amelia, Isabella and Sophia, often played musical instruments at the 10 a.m. services accompanied by Graeme Hunt, and Amelia was confirmed at St Matthew's.

Reflecting on his time as rector, Aleks said

> What I enjoyed about my time at St Matthew's were the many community connections I was able to establish and the opportunities that these afforded me for proclaiming the good news about our Saviour, Jesus Christ. St Matthew's is uniquely positioned in the Hawkesbury community. Even among those who do not have a regular church commitment, many still saw St Matthew's as their church and me as their minister. Apart from the normal day to day activities of church services, Scripture classes at the local schools, baptisms, weddings and funerals, I also took part in growing ministry to the homeless and disadvantaged in the community through emergency relief and joint activities like the Hawkesbury Hub.[115]

Aleks Pinter also participated in Memorial Services at Hawkesbury Hospital and the two major RSL remembrance days, ANZAC Day and Remembrance Day. He recalls that

> I also had the honour of serving on the Hawkesbury Council's Macquarie Bicentenary Committee which celebrated the proclamation of the five Macquarie Towns in 2010. The celebration began with a Thanksgiving Service at St Matthew's and was attended by many from the community as well as notable dignitaries including the Governor of New South Wales, Professor Marie Bashir AC CVO, the Mayor of the Hawkesbury, Councillor Bart Bassett and Bishop Paul Barnett. But the greatest thrill for me was always the one-on-one conversations, as people came to understand who Jesus is, and what he achieved for them by dying on the cross and rising again. I will always look back on my time at St Matthew's with great fondness.[116]

222. A re-enactment of the red-coated regiment of the Rum Corps, who guarded convicts in the colony up to the time of Governor Macquarie, taking part in a parade along Moses Street in front of St Matthew's for the 200th anniversary celebration of the naming of the five Macquarie towns. Photograph by Kim Alderton, 5 December 2010.

In 2010, the celebrations encompassed the entire district as part of a state remembering the 200th anniversary of the arrival in New South Wales of Governor Macquarie, who founded the main Hawkesbury towns, and gave impetus to the colony generally. Several of the events in the district were attended by Macquarie's successor, Marie Bashir. In December a parade took place to commemorate Macquarie's 1810 dinner at the Government House in Windsor, when he named the newly created towns Windsor, Richmond, Wilberforce, Pitt Town and Castlereagh.

Today's Challenge

The Ladies' Guild has been a steady supporter of St Matthew's over the years, raising money to contribute to the church's expenditure. Over fifty years between 1936 and 1986, the guild raised thousands of dollars and gave it to the Church Fund for various projects. Heather Reeves was just one of many dedicated presidents, with Suzanne Hinzmann currently serving.[117] At first almost all their energies went into the annual fete and flower show (also called a bazaar), and this event continued up until the 2000s to be their main fundraiser, especially during the war years. The fete and flower show had begun in the nineteenth century, built to the extravaganzas of 1898 to 1906 under the Fieldings and Dowes, as described in the local newspaper, and appears to have continued on uninterrupted for almost a hundred years.[118] Street stalls, afternoon teas and luncheons became more popular. The ladies of today's guild meet monthly to plan events, to chat, to make exquisite craft items for sale and to create blankets for missions. At present they are working towards air conditioning the Parish Centre.

223. Ladies' Guild meeting in the parish hall. Left to right: Janet Price, Judith Barnard, Beverley Hunt, Lyn Williams, Prue Gill, Fay Cragg and Suzanne Hinzmann. Helen Gosby, Diana Fisher and Yvonne Soper were absent. Photograph by Jan Barkley-Jack, 2016.

Other church groups which have been active in connection with the church over previous years besides the Ladies' Guild and Mothers' Union, of which Mrs Mynett had been secretary in the late 1940s until 1957,[119] have been Girls' Friendly

Society (GFS), Church of England Boys' Society (CEBS), Youth Group, Church of England Men's Society (CEMS) and Sunday school held in the parish hall in New Street for younger children. Under Dorothy Butler an informal women's evening group (SMILE) thrived too.

In the 1960s Charlie Green drove the church's bus to pick up the church and Sunday school attenders. Members of all parish organizations, in uniform where appropriate, were asked to be present on special occasions, like the 140th Anniversary Holy Communion service when Bishop Wilton gave the address. The leader of CEBS at that time was Phil Stubbs, whilst Wendy Rea led GFS. By 1960, Bruce Farlow was assisting Phil Stubbs with CEBS, and many others, over time, gave equal dedication in all groups.[120] Moves were afoot in 1958 under William Carter to have a dedicated building as a youth centre, with the current Rectory even being mooted.[121] By 1963 the plans were for a hall on a South Windsor allotment the church had bought with a bequest.[122]

The Youth Fellowship was particularly active under Doug McCraw, with up to 80 attending each meeting in one of the rooms of the Rectory, hence the group was nicknamed 'SQUASH'; as well as Bible study, outings to the river and picnics were enjoyed. Doug played the accordion and later under Harold Rawson Robert Phipps assisted with the group.[123] The Fellowship continued under later ministers, with Aleks Pinter appointing a youth worker, Roger Kingdon, to run the group.

The important individual task of ringing the bell at St Matthew's was carried out by Kevin Drake in a suit and hat through the 1960s for every service, except for the period in 1963 when the belfry was in pieces. However, Kevin continued winding the clock throughout and was also organ blower from at least 1947 until the electric motor was installed in 1952. The blower was rewired with copper wire at least once by Alf Cammack after it blew up. Kevin continued ringing the bell until the mid-1980s. He died in 1992 aged 80 years.[124]

Over the years the tower clock has been lovingly kept ticking by a dedicated few. The mechanism for the clock required winding by hand from the narrow platform inside the top of the tower once or twice a week, so that the weight which had slowly moved down towards the base of the tower could be returned to the top to keep the clock working. In more recent times, Cameron Neich, Brian Barter and Ron Soper wound the clock, with Don Mills continuing after Ron. The need to trek to the top of the tower has become less frequent since the winding mechanism was electrified around 2005, but it remains necessary to make seasonal adjustments. Small adjustments to the nut holding the pendulum do the trick.[125] When Doug Minty, a master clockmaker, was called in to carry out the electrification of the clock, it was seen that the clock face was in poor condition. However, the white painted face with Arabic numerals applied on it, as it was at that time, held an unexpected surprise. When it was being conserved, paint scrapes showed that the original layer of the clock face had been black enamel with the Roman numerals in gold leaf. Today it is seen in all its original glory thanks to Doug Minty.[126]

The communion cloth for the altar 'so beautifully made by Miss M. Holland' and laundered with loving care by her sister by the 1960s has today been replaced by another hand-made piece worked by Fay Cragg. It is an elegant cover with filet crochet of fine cotton crosses worked within, and has a scalloped border.[127]

Music in the church had been part of the services ever since Macquarie left the colony. In addition to band and then organ, a senior choir provided accomplished choral accompaniment. In 1957 when Bishop Wilton gave the Anniversary address, as an aside he told William Carter that he himself had been 'a member of St Matthew's choir for a short period during the incumbency of the Reverend S. G. Fielding.'[128]

In 1937 robes for choir members were introduced.[129] Today, Beverley Hunt remembers her days in the now disbanded choir, and relates how, as for so many other families of the parish, the varied jobs of keeping St Matthew's functioning became a family affair. Similarly, with volunteers like Kath Griffiths and Marj Noble who cleaned the church and arranged the flowers, many were from long-worshipping families. Kath's family, the Chapmans, has connections from the1800s, as have many, many others.[130]

Beverley Hunt's daughter, Fiona, like Margaret

224. The Senior Choir, *c.* 1956. Left to right: (back row): ?, Mr Appleby (People's Warden), Tom Wilcox, Len Mynett, Bernie Dean; (front row): Violet Carter, Beverley Mynett (Hunt), Jean Stubbs, Doll Ingram, Judith Mortley, Val Garnish, Margaret Burton, Melba Austin, Mavis Oldmeadow. Photograph supplied by Beverley Hunt.

Noble (Terry) and Trish Noble were in the Junior Choir, and Beverley's son, Graeme, has been a distinguished organist at St Matthew's since his teens, now having tallied up over 40 years dedication to the job. He began part time in December 1972, and became full-time organist at St Matthew's in August 1977.[131]

Organists accompanied the choirs, and from her research historian Carol Roberts has found that in 1873 the organist had been Clara Ridge, then from about 1877 Frederick Mortley, the Mayor of Windsor, who remained organist until February 1895, when Clara (now Mrs Joseph Eather) returned until 1918. Lizzie Savage, Fred Palmer and Mr E.W. Munro followed in the position until 1942, when Mrs Billings took over.[132]

225. The Junior Choir, *c.* 1973, trained by Margaret Noble (Terry) until Beverley Hunt took over in 1973, followed by Jean Burton and then Fiona Hunt (back row, second from right). Graeme Hunt, the organist, is seated in the middle row. Photograph supplied by Beverley Hunt.

From 1961 the organist and choir mistress were Dorothy Campbell, who had succeeded Mrs Billings. Between Dorothy and Graeme, the organists were Barry Gibbons, appointed in 1966, Margaret Noble (Terry) from May 1967 until 1971, Ted Chislett (playing only at the 7 p.m. service) and Carol Cammack (now Roberts) until November 1975. Don Cobcroft and Carol continue to fill in occasionally.[133]

The wardens who were in place during 1957 were the Rector's Warden, R.C. Wilcher, and People's Wardens G.R. Hannabus and Bert Hayes. In 1984 when Bert Hayes retired, he was presented with a painting for his 39 years' service, as was Len Mynett in recognition of 25 years of warden service to the parish. Speakers included second generation church supporter, John Paine, with 53 years of service to the Parish Council, former rector Harold Rawson, Archbishop Robinson and rector Len Abbott, who said: 'Attitudes to church leadership are changing and I doubt whether we will ever again pay tribute to 64 years' service in one function ... These two men have served St Matthew's solely for the glory of God in Christ.'[134]

The award was presented by the then warden, Ron Soper, to whom a plaque was erected in the cemetery for his own contribution as 'Church Warden and Cemetery Manager for 40 years' on his death in 2011. Ron had become a warden in 1976. Neville Hunt then began as a warden followed by Tony Cragg as a People's Warden from *c.* 1983 to 1993. He had served on the Parish Council since 1972.[135] During the works of the 1970s one council consisted of Ray Wilcher, Len Mynett, Reg Voller, Max Quinton, H. Thompson, Noel Robertson, O.K. Quinton, W.J. Paull jr, John Paine, G.F. Mellish, Horrie Hollier and Bruce Gardiner. Len was the secretary and John Paine (II) the treasurer. Peter Griffiths, and a host of others too have been part of the Parish Councils over the years.[136]

Others who have made long and lasting contributions to the church are Russell and Heather

Reeves and Margaret Fennell, a former warden, who continues as Manager of the Cemetery and a current member of Parish Council. Joyce Edwards was for many years a warden, was involved in the Parish Council, and with running the fete and the Arts and Craft Show: Joyce was also archivist and guided the Restoration Fund.[137] Wardens serve on the Parish Council and still every year the Rector's Warden is appointed by the minister and the People's Wardens are elected at the Vestry Meeting. Parish Council has always played a most important lay role, having responsibility for decisions about all activities and works, from 1837 onwards. The first woman on council was Doll Ingram elected in 1972.[138]

The parish newsletter, a valuable means of communication and now a major research tool, was created as the *St Matthew's Parish Magazine* by Norman Jenkyn. The earliest issues known to exist are Vol. 3, No. 3 for April 1920 in the church's possession and Vol. 7, No. 10 for December 1924, costing 3d., in the possession of Margaret Fennell.[139] This implies that it began in 1918. It seems to have appeared more or less monthly. It has continued to be compiled by each minister, sometimes with a helper, for over a hundred years. Later it was called *The Parish Messenger*, appearing monthly. The Ladies' Guild, through a donation from the family of long-serving treasurer, Marj Noble, has an almost complete set of *The Parish Messenger* from 1957.[140] It was transformed into a more frequent publication called *The Weekly Bulletin* by John Butler in 1988 and is now a weekly news-sheet called *The Bulletin.* The Ladies' Guild also preserves its Treasurer's Account books from 1936.[141]

The normal services at present are held at 8 a.m., 10 a.m. and 5 p.m. on Sundays, with another service on the first Wednesday morning of each month, as well as special services to celebrate the events of the church calendar.

Other special events are held regularly and involve many in today's parish and congregation in close camaraderie, like the much-enjoyed Christmas party. Held in December 2015 in the Parish Centre, the speaker was the new minister at St Matthew's, the Reverend Chris Jones.[142]

226. A great turnout, 90 people for the Christmas dinner in December 2015, held in the Parish Centre. Photograph by Chris Jones, rector of St Matthew's, 2015.

227. Congregation at 8 a.m. service, Sunday, 5 June 2016. Photograph by Jan Barkley-Jack.

228. Some of the 2016 Parish Council of St Matthew' members: From left to right back row: Chris Jones (rector) Heidi Barthram, Kalita Thorburn, Craig Thorburn, Margare Fennell, Diana Fisher and John Barnard. Missing fron the photo: Daniel Adrichem, Merryne Ghantous, Suzann Hinzmann, Graeme Hunt and Ian Moore.

The current Parish Council members overseeing all the work of the parish who were elected in March 2016 are: John Barnard (Rector's Warden) Diana Fisher (People's Warden), Kalita Thorburn (People's Warden), Craig Thorburn, Graeme Hunt, Merryne Ghantous, Daniel Adrichem, Ian Moore, Heidi Barthram, Margaret Fennell and Suzanne Hinzmann.

229. The 2016 wardens: Left to right: John Barnard, Kalita Thorburn and Diana Fisher. Photograph by Jan Barkley-Jack, 2016.

230. Graeme Hunt has been the distinguished organist at St Matthew's for over 40 years. Photograph taken in 2014.

The New Rector

Keeping the iconic St Matthew's in the physical condition befitting one of the most important national heritage items of Australia, stretching right back by association to the eighteenth-century beginnings of Australia, is tied into a new conundrum of fitting such a wealth of heritage into the spiritual needs and finances of a parish in the expensive 21st century. Chris Jones is the rector who has taken on this heavy challenge. He is serving as St Matthew's 24th rector and he and his wife, Kerry, have embraced the congregation and community alike. Chris and Kerry are currently prayerfully working towards rebuilding a lively church where all ages are represented.

Chris Jones feels that 'We as a church are committed to respecting our spiritual heritage and traditions but also to allowing worship which invitingly involves future generations'.

One of the major contributions Chris has made in his first year at St Matthew's, in conjunction with the Parish Council, has been to begin to address the logistical problems arising from the superintending of a unique heritage landmark which is State Heritage listed. Nimbly creating a

231. Congregation at the 5 p.m. service on 12 June 2016. Photograph by Chris Jones, rector of St Matthew's, 2016.

232. Congregation at 10 a.m. service, Sunday 5 June 2016. Photograph by Jan Barkley-Jack.

St Matthew's Precinct Advisory Committee as a subcommittee of the Parish Council has been a starting point to offer the parish some relief from the financial impositions associated with this historical privilege. The group is comprised of people with expertise to advise Parish Council on conservation issues. Members are not asked to make a faith commitment but are called to work with goodwill towards the worshipping congregation and reaching out to the officers of the New South Wales Heritage Division and to the National Trust of Australia (NSW) for expert help with the conservation of the church complex. Currently being launched is the St Matthew's Anglican Church Windsor Conservation Management Appeal in conjunction with the National Trust of Australia (NSW), remembering the very first appeal launched by the young National Trust had been for St Matthew's. Tax deductable donations will be used separate from the normal ministries of the church in the present appeal. They will enable conservation work and create a fund by which the church can match dollar for dollar all grants it may be able to attract.

233. Congregation at 10 a.m. first Wednesday of the month service on 1 June 2016. Photograph by Chris Jones, rector of St Matthew's, 2016.

234. Rector Chris Jones and wife, Kerry, outside the Rectory. Photograph supplied by Chris Jones, rector of St Matthew's, 2016.

The Future

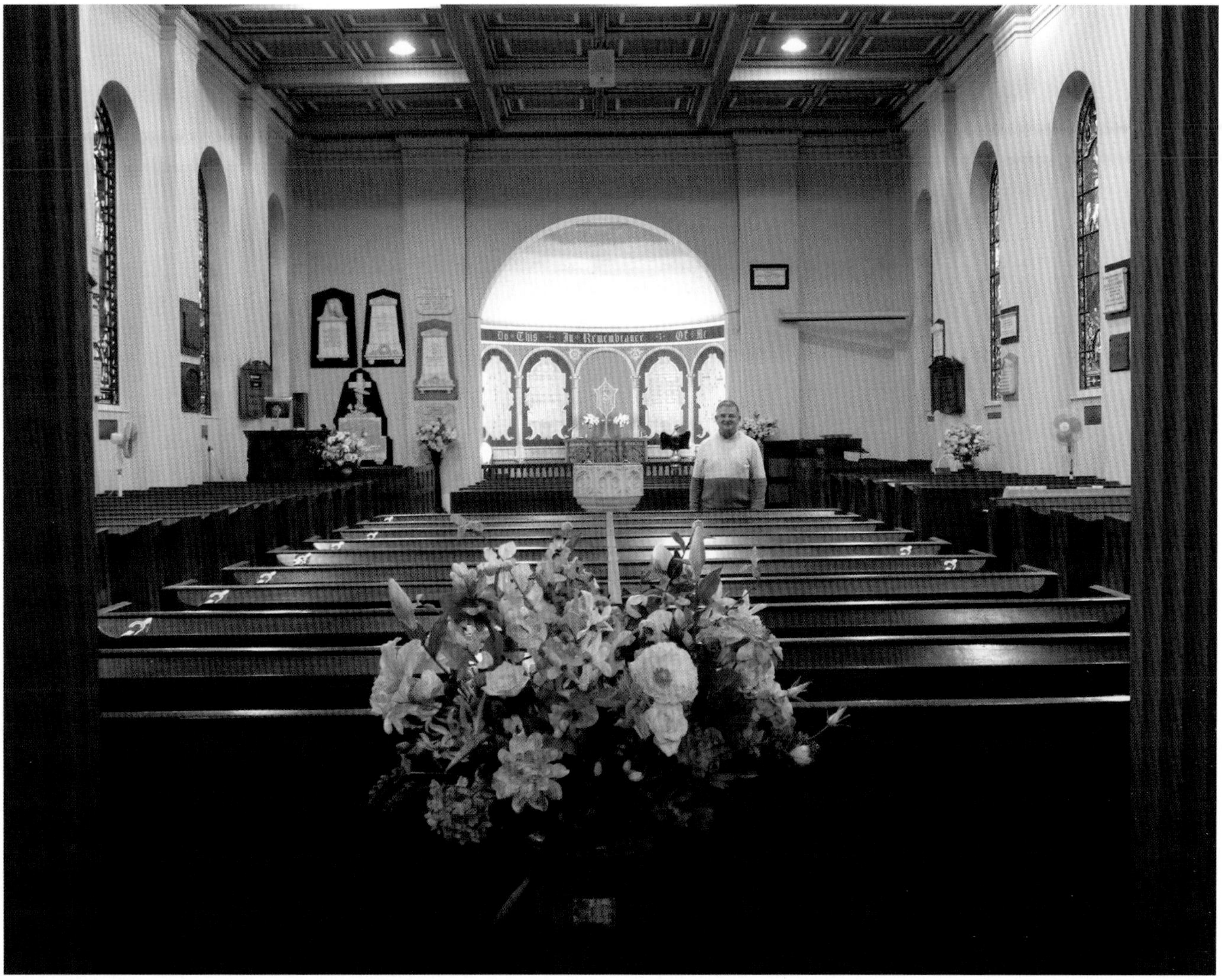

235. Rector Chris Jones, a new, vital minister in the old, but still relevant, historical St Matthew's Anglican church, Windsor. Source: Photograph by Jan Barkley-Jack, 2016.

St Matthew's Anglican church is about to celebrate proudly two hundred years of being an Anglican landmark in the Hawkesbury district and throughout Australia. Chris Jones believes 'that for a religious precinct born of both colonial struggle and glory, the parish is now emerging into a different world: one that is not only rapidly urbanizing and multicultural, but multi-ethnic as well. Seeking to be a credible presence of Jesus in today's changing Hawkesbury is how we are beginning to move forward into the next 200 years.'

Appendices

Appendix 1

Names of those who signed a petition of support as parishioners of the Reverend Joseph Docker in the districts of Windsor and Richmond, March 1833

(Taken from the list as reproduced in J. McMillan, *The Two Lives of Joseph Docker*, Spectrum, Melbourne, 1994, pp. 89–90)

[See Chapter 4]

J. Brabyn

Richd. Fitzgerald

George Loder

Thos. Tebbutt

W. Croft

John Teale

Dr Benjamin Clayton

John Wood

William Smith

Edward Robinson

J.R. Rouse

Abm. Johnston

W. Bladdey

John Wood

Charles Sommers

Edwd. Glee

Thomas Dargin

Robert Martin sr

Robert Martin jr

Wm. Price

John Town

Richd. Kippax

Richd. Dunston

Joseph W[D?]ellander

Mary Dellandre

John Sansome

Samuel Howell

Saml. Marsden [not the Reverend]

John Adell

J.L. Scarvell

John Tebbutt

Jas. Rochester

Jas. Bullock

Wm. Thos. Bayliss

John Dight

Wm. Faithfull

Robert Aull

Thos. Howell

Wm. Farlow

Thos. Cross

Joseph McAudling

Matthew Hughes

George Freeman

Thos. Freeman

George Walpole

John Tebbutt jr

Chas. Thompson

J.S. Creek

William Bowman

W. John Fitz

Paul Randall

Hy. Frat. Seymour

George Howell

Walter Howell

M. Farlow

Thos. Parnell jr

Joseph Owen

George Walpole

Appendix 2

Burials in St Matthew's (Anglican) Burial Ground, 1812

(Taken from Lake Macquarie Family History Group, *St Matthews Church of England Windsor NSW: Parish Registers 1810 to 1856*, Teralba, 2003)
(See Chapter 7)

January:	William Cartwright	3 months (son of the Rev. Robert Cartwright)
	Edward Young	39 years
	James Erwin	40 years
	Letitia Ivory	7 weeks
February	James Thompson	53 years
	Martin McEwen	4 months
	John White	46 years
	Joseph Bocock	70 years
March	William Tyrrol	42 years
	William Upten	6 months
	James Baker	70 years
	Ann Haughton	3 months
	John Smith	no details
April	John Marsden	64 years
	John Martin	40 years
May 9	John Merriott	69 years

May 11 second anniversary of consecration of St Mathew's burial ground

May 20	Richard Burke	42 years
	Edward Kelly	50 years
	Richard Alcorn	41 years
	Edward Martin	4½ years
June	John Collins	18 years
	Julianna Franklin	24 years
	Jane Watson	17 months
July	John Clarke	7 years
	Patrick Kerwin	70 years
August	Dennis Malone	no details
	Patrick Clarke	42 years
	Jonathan Holdsworthy	47 years
September	Joseph Kearns	65 years
November	James Ward	45 years
December	Henry Murray	32 years (hanged himself)
	William Allen	19 years

Appendix 3

Ministers of the Anglican chapel and of St Matthew's Church, Windsor

Dates served in Windsor

Visiting ministers

	Services in chapel, northern end of Windsor	
1795–1822 Rectory	Samuel Marsden	died 1838 at Windsor
1800–1801	Henry Fulton	to Norfolk Island
c. 1809	John Youl	at Ebenezer

Resident ministers

1810–1819	Robert Cartwright	to Liverpool
	Services in St Matthew's Church from December 1822	
1819–1828	John Cross	to Port Macquarie
1828	Elijah Smith	to Britain, later Penrith NSW
1829–1833	Joseph Docker	left ministry
1833–1867	Henry Tarlton Stiles	died 1867, buried St Matthew's
1867–1876	Charles Garnsey	to Sydney
1876–1878	Henry Archdall Langley	to Victoria
1878–1885	Frederick William Stretton	died 1885, buried St Matthew's
1885–1890	Arthur Blacket	to Victoria
1890–1893	Gerard d'Arcy-Irvine	to Bowral
1893–1904	Sydney Glanville Fielding	to Miller's Point
1904–1906	Philip William Dowe	to Bulli
1906–1936	Norman L.J. Jenkyn	retired, died 1942, buried St Matthew's
1936–1940	George P. Birk	to Burwood East
1940–1947	Charles L. Williams	retired
1947–1951	Robert T. Hallahan	to Sans Souci
1951–1954	Douglas G. McCraw	to New Guinea
1954–1960	William F. Carter	to Brisbane
1961–1980	Harold Rawson	retired, died 1996, ashes in St Matthew's
1980–1988	Len Abbott	retired
1988–1999	John Butler	to Angl. Retirement Villages, Castle Hill
1999–2007	Chris Burgess	to Eastwood
2008–2015	Aleks Pinter	to Waverley
2015–	Chris Jones	

Bibliography

1. Archives of St Matthew's Anglican Church, Windsor

Registers of Births, Deaths and Marriages. The original registers, commencing in 1810, are still held by the church, but have been microfilmed and published up to 2000 by the Lake Macquarie Family History Group (see below, under **3. Printed Primary Sources**)

The set of **Minute Books** relating to the Parochial or Parish Council is unbroken from 1837, following on the Church of England Temporalities Act of that year. The bound volumes have not been microfilmed or published. They contain the minutes of a variety of meetings, which, with the exception of the vestry meetings, change their nomenclature over time:

Vestry (a formal meeting held around Easter each year)
Minister and pew-holders
Minister and wardens
Special meetings of parishioners
Parochial Council.

Each volume has been footnoted as 'Minute Book', which is the original title blind-stamped on the foundation volume. There are no original volume numbers, so references are given by covering dates. All volumes except the first have original pagination.

Church wardens were instituted under the same 1837 Act and a magisterial volume of Wardens' Accounts, similar in appearance to the first Minute Book, survives, covering the years 1838 to 1882. Like the first Minute Book, this volume is not paginated. The record of the wardens' regular meetings with the minister are included in the Minute Books, continuing after the separate series of Wardens' Accounts ceases in 1882. The only subsequent volume of Wardens' Accounts, bound in red cloth, shows income and expenditure in detail from 1940 to 1948.

The volumes from the church archives which form the basis of this history are:

Minute Book, 1837–1885 (not paginated)
Wardens' Accounts, 1838–1882 (not paginated)
Minute Book, 1886–1918
Minute Book, 1918–1930
Minute Book, 1931–1957
Accounts, 1940–1948
Minute Book, 1957–1968
Minute Book, 1968–1977
Minute Book, 1977–1983
Minute Book, 1983–1985.

Pasted in or inserted loosely in the Minute Books are some issues of the parish magazine, many monthly and annual statements of accounts and, in the 1970s and 1980s, typescript annual reports. There are also a few significant letters loose within the Minute Books.

The archival volumes are preserved in an iron safe donated to the church for the purpose by the solicitor's office of Colonel Paine in 1931 and transferred to the rectory in 1937. Some volumes were stored in a wooden chest retrieved from the loft of the rectory stables by the wardens in the 1990s.

The church has not maintained a master set of the church magazine, which has been published under a variety of titles since 1918: *St Matthew's Parish Magazine*, *The Parish Messenger*, *The Weekly Bulletin* and *The Bulletin*. In addition to odd copies preserved in the Minute Books and a set of *The Parish Messenger* from 1957 held by the Ladies' Guild, copies have been accessed in the local and state libraries, in the collections of the Royal Australian Historical Society and in private hands. A former rector, John Butler, gave generous access to his complete set of *The Weekly Bulletin* from 1988 to 1999.

2. Other Manuscript Sources

Hawkesbury City Library, Windsor
Local Studies, Vertical Files, *sub* St Matthew's Anglican Church and Rectory.

Hawkesbury Regional Museum, Windsor
Minute Books of Hawkesbury Historical Society.

Lands and Property Information
Grants of Land Registers 1, 2, 3.
Map of parish of St Matthew, county of Cumberland, Lands, PMapMN05, Sheet 1, 14076801.
Plan of Windsor, Galloway, 1841, Crown Plan W 443a.
Plan of Clarendon glebe, Crown Plan, C909.690.

Royal Australian Historical Society
'Schedule showing various Crown Appropriations for Religious and Public Purposes in the Town of Windsor', estray from State Records, Mis.13/17465, Selkirk Collection, Manuscript Red M 186.
Walker, F., 'Windsor', unpublished MS, Rare Book 991.3 WIN.

State Library of New South Wales, Mitchell Library
Armstrong, J., 'Plan of the New & Old Glebe adjoining the Town of Windsor', 1837, ZM2 811.1122/1837/1.
Bonwick Transcripts, box 10.
Evans, G. W., 'Settlement on the Green Hills', watercolour, *c.* 1809, PXD 388, Vol. 3, fol.7.
Evans, G.W. 'Windsor, Head of Navigation, Hawkesbury', *c.* 1811, SV1B/Wind/6.
Fielding, R., 'A Johnson Family History', ML MSS 5582/5.
Fielding, S., proof sheets of *Down to the Sea in Ships*, ML MSS 7285/2/5.
Harris, S.L., 'Report and Estimates of the Value of the Improvements which have taken place in the Public Buildings of Sydney, Parramatta, Windsor, Liverpool and Campbell-town between the 25th of Decr. 1822 & the 24th of Decr. 1823 inclusive, and an Exposé of the present state of the Public Buildings in New South Wales, by Order of His Excellency Sir Thomas Brisbane K.C.B &c &c*'*, C 226, Reel CY 1035.
Hasssell family papers, A 859.
Lycett, J., 'View of Windsor upon the river Hawkesbury, New South Wales', 1824, MRB/F980.1/L.
'Plans of Buildings by John Verge', Macarthur Papers, Vol. 222, Reel CY 748, PXD 188.
'Sketch of the inundation in the neighbourhood of Windsor … 2 June 1816', watercolour by an unknown artist, panorama in four panels, PX*D 264.
Slaeger, P., artist and engraver 'The Red House Farm, Windsor in New South Wales', Absalom West, Sydney, 1814, PX*D65.
Stiles papers, A 269.

State Records NSW
Church Lands, 2/1845; 2/1846, 34/5020.
Colonial Secretary's In-Letters
Superintendent's Day-Book, signed by William Cox, Reel 6017, 4/5782.
Campbell to Marsden, 1811, Reel 6002, 4/3490D.
Lands, Old Register 2, now available digitally as L. Sabine, ed., *Old Registers 1 to 9*, NSW
Lands Department, NSW Commerce Department and State Records NSW, 2008.
Maps: SZ 529, signed by Governor Macquarie (Meehan, 1812)
1856 (Felton Mathew, 1827)
1975 (Galloway, 1843)
6216 (Ham Common parish, *c.* 1830s)

2/1846, 44/7400 (A.G. Maclean, 1844 tracing from Map 1975).
Primary Applications, 17513/43/192/36240, 17513/32/170/33287.
Returns for the Colony, Reel 1409, 4/251–255, 263–265.
Supreme Court, Criminal Jurisdiction, Reel 2651.
Surveyors' Field Book 67, Reel 2622, SZ888; 83, Reel 2623, SZ901.
Surveyors' Sketchbooks, Reel 2778 Vol. 1, B8; Reel 2778, Vol. 3, Part 1, between 0498 and 0499.

3. Printed Primary Sources

Newspapers up to 1954 were accessed through Trove and are not listed here.
'A Friend to Truth and Peace', A Letter to the Rev. Henry Tarlton Stiles, Minister of St Matthew's, Windsor, Tegg, Sydney, 1840.
Bach, J., ed., *An Historical Journal of Events at Sydney and at Sea, 1787–1792* by Captain John Hunter, Angus and Robertson in association with Royal Australian Historical Society, Sydney, 1968.
Baxter, C., ed., *Musters of New South Wales and Norfolk Island 1805–1806*, Australian Biographical and Genealogical Record in association with the Society of Australian Genealogists, Sydney, 1989.
[Broughton, W.G.], *The Journals of Visitation to the Northern and Southern Portions of his Diocese, by the Lord Bishop of Australia*, Society for Propagation of the Gospel, London, 1846.
Burton, W.W., *The State of Religion and Education in New South Wales*, Cross, London, 1840.
Collins, D., *An Account of the English Colony in New South Wales*, Vol. 1, London, 1798; ed. B.H. Fletcher, Reed and Royal Australian Historical Society, Sydney, 1975.
Historical Records of Australia, Series 1, 26 volumes, Sydney, 1914–1925.
Historical Records of New South Wales, 9 vols, Sydney, 1892–1901, reprinted Lansdowne Slattery, Sydney, 1978–1979.
Lachlan Macquarie, Governor of New South Wales: Journals of his Tours in New South Wales and Van Diemen's Land 1810–1822, Library of Australian History in conjunction with Library Council of New South Wales, Sydney, 1979.
Lake Macquarie Family History Group, eds, *St Matthews Church of England Windsor, NSW Parish Registers 1810 to 1856: 'A Complete Transcription'*, Lake Macquarie Family History Group, Teralba, 2003.
Lake Macquarie Family History Group, eds, *St Matthews Church of England Windsor Parish Registers, 1857 to 1900: 'A Complete Transcription'*, Lake Macquarie Family History Group, Teralba, 2004.
Lake Macquarie Family History Group, eds, *St Matthews Church of England Windsor Parish Registers, 1900 to 1950: 'A Complete Transcription'*, Lake Macquarie Family History Group, Teralba, 2006.
Lake Macquarie Family History Group, eds, *St Matthews Church of England Windsor Parish Registers, 1951 to 2000: 'A Complete Transcription'*, Lake Macquarie Family History Group, Teralba, 2009.
Marsden, S., Sermons, transcribed by John Pettett, 2014, Library of Moore Theological College, Sydney, at https://www.moore.edu.au/library/samuel-marsden, accessed 9 February 2016.
Read, M.J., *Aunt Spencer's Diary (1854): A Visit to Bontharambo and the North-East Victorian Goldfields*, Neptune, Newtown Victoria, 1981.
Report of Diocesan Committee of the Societies for Propagation of the Gospel in Foreign Parts and for Promotion of Christian Knowledge for 1840, Sydney, 1841.
Ritchie, J., ed., *The Evidence to the Bigge Reports*, Vol. 1, *The Oral Evidence*; Vol. 2, *The Written Evidence*, Heinemann, Melbourne, 1971.
Russell, P., ed., *This Errant Lady: Jane Franklin's Overland Journey to Port Phillip and Sydney, 1839*, National Library of Australia, Canberra, 2002.
Sainty, M.R. and K.A. Johnson, eds, *Census of New South Wales, November 1828*, Library of Australian History, Sydney, 1980.
Slaeger, P., artist and engraver, 'A View of Part of the Town of Windsor', Absalom West, Sydney, 1813.
Stiles, H., *A Sermon preached in St. John's Church, Parramatta, May 20th, 1838, on occasion of the death of the Rev. Samuel Marsden, of Parramatta, senior chaplain of the Colony of New South Wales*, Tegg, Sydney, [1838].
Stiles, H., *A Sermon preached in St Matthew's Church, Windsor, on Sunday, December 1st, 1839, previously to the Opening of a new Wesleyan Chapel in that Town*, Tegg, Sydney, 1840.
Stiles, H.T., *A Sermon, preached at St. Matthew's Church, Windsor, on Wednesday the 18th June, 1845, before the Brethren of the United Loyal Hawkesbury Lodge, No.7, of the Australian Supreme Grand Lodge, of the Independent Order of Odd Fellows*, Statham and Forster, Sydney, 1843.
Tebbutt, J., *Astronomical Memoirs*, White, Sydney, 1908, reprinted Hawkesbury City Council, Windsor, 1986.
Tench, W., *Expedition to Botany Bay* and *A Complete Account of the Settlement at Port Jackson*, annotated by L.F. Fitzhardinge, Library of Australian History in association with Royal Australian Historical Society, Sydney, 1979.
Terry, F.C., *Landscape Scenery, Illustrating Sydney, Parramatta, Richmond, Maitland, Windsor and Port Jackson, New South Wales*, also published as *Australian Keepsake*, Sands and Kenny, Sydney and Melbourne, 1855, reprinted as *New South Wales Illustrated*, Lansdowne, Sydney, 1973.
Walker, W., *Reminiscences (Personal, Social and Political) of a Fifty Years' Residence at Windsor on the Hawkesbury*, Turner and Henderson, Sydney, 1890, reprinted Library of Australian History, North Sydney 1977.
Wallis, J., *An Historical Account of the Colony of New South Wales and its Dependent Settlements*, Ackermann, London 1821.
Walsh, R., ed., *In Her Own Words: The Writings of Elizabeth Macquarie*, Exisle Press, Wollombi, 2011

4. Interviews

Alderton, Kim, 2016.
Burgess, Chris, Reverend, 2016.
Butler, Dorothy and John, Reverend, 2016.
Campbell, Miss Lorna, a daughter of Thomas Campbell, 15 August 2009.
Cragg, Fay and Tony, 2016.
Edds, Carol and Graham, 2010, 2016.
Edwards, Joyce, 2016.
Fennell, Margaret, 2016.
Griffiths, Kath and Peter, 2016.
Hogarth, Mrs Caroline (née Cobcroft), 1980s.
Hunt, Beverley, 2016.
Hunt, Graeme, 2016.
Jones, Chris, Reverend, 2016.
Mills, Don and Jill, 2016.
Minty, Doug, 2016.
Pinter, Aleks, Reverend, 2016.
Quinton, Les, and his family, August 2009.
Roberts Carol, 2016.
Ryan, Kay, 2016.
Sledge, Wendy, 2016.
Sondermeyer, Cornelis, 2016.
Terry, Margaret, 2016.
Wright, Mrs Jean, a daughter of Thomas Campbell, 10 August 1996.

5. Secondary Works

Abbott, L.M., *St Matthew's Windsor: A Short Guide to the Church & its History*, St Matthew's Church, Windsor, 1st ed., n.d., 2nd ed., 2002.
Aldrich, A., *Spanning the Centuries of Hawkesbury's History, Journal of the Hawkesbury Historical Society*, No. 2, 2011, pp. 61–62, 64–66.
Anon., 'Reminiscences of a Visit to the Hawkesbury', *Town and Country Journal*, 24 January 1874, p. 141.
Australian Dictionary of Biography, online.
Baker, H., *Historic Buildings: Windsor and Richmond*, State Planning Authority of New South Wales, Sydney, 1967.
Barkley, J., and Nichols, M., *Hawkesbury 1794–1994: The First Two Hundred Years of the Second Colonisation*, Hawkesbury City Council, Windsor, 1994.
Barkley-Jack, J., 'Celebrating 50 Years', *Spanning the Centuries of Hawkesbury's History, Journal of Hawkesbury Historical Society*, No. 1, 2006, pp. 1–5.
Barkley-Jack, J., 'Communicating History: Cultural Tourism: A Walking Tour of the Burial Ground at St Matthews Church of England, Windsor', as-

signment for BA (Hons), University of Western Sydney, 1998.

Barkley-Jack, J., 'Early Boat Building on the Upper Hawkesbury', in J. Powell, ed., *Cross Currents*, Deerubbin Press, Berowra Heights, 1997, pp. 37–64.

Barkley-Jack, J., *Hawkesbury Settlement Revealed: A New Look at Australia's Third Mainland Settlement*, Rosenberg Press, Kenthurst, 2009.

Barkley-Jack, J., *Toongabbie's Government Farm: An Elusive Vision for Five Governors, 1791–1824*, Toongabbie and District Historical Society, 2013.

Biographical Dictionary of Australia, online.

Border, R., 'Scott,Thomas Hobbes (1783–1869)', *Australian Dictionary of Biography*, http://adb.anu.edu.au/biography/scott-thomas-hobbes-2645, accessed 18 March 2016.

Bowd, D.G., *Macquarie Country: A History of the Hawkesbury*, rev. ed., author, Windsor, 1973.

Bowd, D.G., ed., *Monuments, Memorials and Plaques in the Hawkesbury Shire*, Hawkesbury Historical Society, Windsor, 1988.

Bradbury, O., *Sir John Soane's Influence on Architecture from 1791: A Continuing Legacy*, Ashgate, Farnham, 2015.

Broadbent, J., *The Australian Colonial House: Architecture and Society in New South Wales, 1788–1842*, Hordern House, Potts Point, Sydney, 1997.

Burnswoods, J., and J. Fletcher, *Sydney and the Bush: A Pictorial History of Education in New South Wales*, NSW Department of Education, Sydney, 1980.

Byrne, J.V., 'An Outcast Goat or The Life and Times of Andrew Thompson', unpublished MA thesis, University of Sydney, 1957.

Cable, K.J., 'Cartwright Robert (1771–1856)', *Australian Dictionary of Biography*, http://adb.anu.au/biography/cartwright-robert-1882/text2211, published first in hard copy 1966, accessed on line, 31 March 2016.

Cable, K.J., 'Fulton, Henry (1761–1840)', *Australian Dictionary of Biography*, http://adb.anu.edu.au/biography/crook-william-pascoe-1935/text2311, published first in hard copy 1966, accessed online 17 February 2016.

Cable, K.J., 'Garnsey, Charles Frederick (1828–1894)', *Australian Dictionary of Biography*, http://adb.anu.edu.au/biography/garnsey-charles-frederick-3593/text5569, published first in hard copy 1972, accessed online 22 April 2016.

Cable, K.J., 'Stiles, Henry Tarlton (1808–1867)', *Australian Dictionary of Biography*, http://adb.anu.edu.au/biography/stiles-henry-tarlton-2701/text3789, published first in hard copy 1967, accessed online 7 April 2016.

Cable, K., and R. Annable, *St James', 1824–1999*, Churchwardens of St James', Sydney, 1999.

Carruthers, C., 'Sgt Samuel Edgerton', *Hawkesbury Historical Society Newsletter*, No. 84, June 2009, pp. 1–3.

Carter, J., *Eyes to the Future: Sketches of Australia and her Neighbours in the 1870s*, National Library of Australia, Canberra, 2000.

Carter, W.F., *The Cathedral of the Hawkesbury: A Sketch of St. Matthew's Windsor*, n.p., n.d. [There were at least two editions of Carter, both undated, published between the 1960s and the 1980s]

Carty, M., *William Broughton and the Kennedy Connection: A Young Adventurer, his Two Families and his Pioneer Relations*, author, 1987.

Cobley, J., *Sydney Cove, 1795–1800: The Second Governor*, Angus & Robertson, North Ryde, 1986.

Colwell, J., *The Illustrated History of Methodism, Australia: 1812 to 1855. New South Wales and Polynesia: 1856 to 1902*, Brooks, Sydney, 1904.

Cox, R., *William Cox: Blue Mountains Road Builder and Pastoralist*, Rosenberg, Kenthurst, 2012.

Daily Telegraph, 27 October 1965; 6 September 1963.

d'Arcy-Irvine, D., typescript of talk about her father, Gerard d'Arcy-Irvine, to the Church of England Historical Society in Sydney, 7 February 1974, Hawkesbury Library, Local Studies, Vertical Files, *sub* St Matthew's Anglican Church, Windsor.

Dethlefsen, E., and J. Deetz, 'Death's Heads, Cherubs and Willow Trees: Experimental Archaeology in Colonial Cemeteries', *American Antiquity*, Vol. 31, 1966, pp. 52–58.

Dickey B., ed., *The Australian Dictionary of Evangelical Biography*, Evangelical History Association, Sydney, 1994.

Dow, G.M., *Samuel Terry, the Botany Bay Rothschild*, Sydney University Press, Sydney, 1974.

Ellis, M.H., *Francis Greenway: His Life and Times*, Angus & Robertson, Sydney, 3rd ed., 1973.

Fawcett, F.W., *A Brief Life of the Reverend John Cross: Forty Years a Chaplain in the Colony of New South Wales*, Hinchcliffe, Brisbane, 1898.

Fitzpatrick, J.C.L., *The Good Old Days*, Dymock, Sydney, 1900.

Fitzpatrick, J.C.L., *Those Were the Days: More Hawkesbury History*, NSW Bookstall Co, Sydney, 1923.

Flood, Fire and Fever: A History of Elwood, http://skhs.org.au/~SKHSflood/Early_Settlers.htm.

Gillen, M., *The Founders of Australia: A Biographical Dictionary of the First Fleet*, Library of Australian History, Sydney, 1989.

Gray, N., 'Howe, John (1774–1852)', *Australian Dictionary of Biography*, http://adb.anu.edu.au/biography/howe-john-2205/text2855, published first in hard copy 1966, accessed online 17 April 2016.

Gunson, N., 'Crook, William Pascoe (1775–1846)', *Australian Dictionary of Biography*, http://adb.anu.edu.au/biography/crook-william-pascoe-1935/text2311, published first in hard copy 1966, accessed online 17 February 2016.

Gunson, N., 'Harris, John (1754–1819)', *Australian Dictionary of Biography*, http://adb.anu.edu.au/biography/harris-john-2163/text2771, published first in hard copy 1966, accessed online 14 February 2016.

Hansen, I.V., 'Langley, Henry Thomas (1877–1968)', *Australian Dictionary of Biography*, http://adb.anu.edu.au/biography/langley-henry-thomas-10785/text19127, published first in hard copy 2000, accessed online 9 April 2016.

Hardwick, J., 'Anglican Church Expansion and Colonial Reform Politics in Bengal, New South Wales and the Cape Colony *c.* 1790–1850', DPhil thesis, University of York, 2008.

Hardy, B., *Early Hawkesbury Settlers*, Kangaroo Press, Kenthurst, 1985.

Havard, W.L., 'Francis Howard Greenway, Macquarie's Architect', *Journal of Royal Australian Historical Society*, Vol. 22, 1936, pp. 137–189.

Havard, W.L., 'Note on St Matthew's Church, Windsor', *Journal of Royal Australian Historical Society*, Vol. 31, 1945, pp. 125–127.

Hawkesbury Family History Group, *Hawkesbury Pioneer Register*, Vol. 2, author, Windsor, 2001.

Hawkesbury Gazette, 26 June 1957; 17 July 1985.

Herman, M., *The Early Australian Architects and their Work*, Angus & Robertson, Sydney, 1954.

Herman, M., 'Greenway, Francis (1777–1837)', *Australian Dictionary of Biography*, http://adb.anu.edu.au/biography/greenway-francis-2120/text2681, published first in hard copy 1966, accessed online 19 April 2016.

Hickson, E., 'Cox, William (1764–1837)', *Australian Dictionary of Biography*, http://adb.anu.edu.au/biography/cox-william-1934/text2309, published first in hard copy 1966, accessed online 17 April 2016.

History Australia: Convict Stockade at http://www.historyaustralia.org.au/twconvic/716.

http://arc.parracity.nsw.gov.au/blog/2015/08/07/female-factory-and-the-thwaites-and-reed-turret-clock/, accessed 2 April 2016.

http://australianroyalty.net.au/family.php?famid=F15192&gedpurnellmccord.ged, accessed 7 March 2016.

http://dictionaryofsydney.org/building/st_matthews_anglican_church_windsor.

http://en.wikipedia.org/.../List_of_Commonwealth_visits_made_by_Queen_Elizabeth.

http://hawkesburyheritage.blogspot.com.au/2013/06/hawkesbury-river floods.html, accessed 11 March 2016.

http://stoneletters.com/blog/gravestone-symbols, accessed 10 May 2016.

http://www.australiandressregister.org/garment/329/, accessed 11 March 2016.

http://www.britainexpress.com/attractions.htm?attraction=2391, accessed 16 March 2016.

http://www.clockmuseum.co.uk/english_turret_makers.html, accessed 2 April 2016.

http://www.familytreecircles.com/u/janilye/?cat=1395, accessed 7 March 2016.

http://www.whitechapelbellfoundry.co.uk/identify.htm, accessed 2 April 2016.

Jack, R. I., *Exploring the Hawkesbury*, Kangaroo Press, Kenthurst, 2nd ed., 1990.

Jackson, F., 'Windsor, N.S.W., its Monuments', *Sydney Morning Herald*, 17 May 1924.

Jahn, G., *Sydney Architecture*, Watermark Press, Sydney, 1997.

Judd, S., and K. Cable, *Sydney Anglicans*, Anglican Information Office, Sydney, 1987.

Kerr, J., ed., *The Dictionary of Australian Artists: Painters, Sketchers, Photographers and Engravers to 1870*, Oxford University Press, Melbourne, 1992.

'Kirwan, Hiram John (1819–1904)', Obituaries Australia, National Centre of Biography, Australian National University, http://oa.anu.edu.au/obituary/kirwan-hiram-john-17696/text29308, accessed 14 May 2016.

'Langley, Rt Rev. Henry Archdall', *Who Was Who*, Black, 1920–2008; online ed., Oxford University Press, December 2007, accessed 26 May 2012.

Lavelle, S., *Cemeteries: Guidelines for their Care and Conservation*, Department of Planning, Heritage Council of NSW, Sydney, 1992.

Lenehan, M., 'Rouse, Richard (1774–1852)', *Australian Dictionary of Biography*, http://adb.anu.edu.au/biography/rouse-richard-2612/text3601, published first in hard copy 1967, accessed online 26 April 2016.

'Lorna's Life at the Rectory', *Our Town*, supplement to *Windsor and Richmond Gazette*, Vol. 3 No. 4, Autumn 2001, pp. 16–17.

Lucas, C., 'Wilkinson, Leslie (1882–1973)', *Australian Dictionary of Biography*, Vol. 12, Melbourne University Press, Carlton, 1990, pp. 492–494.

Lucas-Smith, C., 'History of the Smith Family', Windsor Library, Local Studies, Vertical File *sub* St Matthew's Anglican Church, Windsor, typescript, 2002.

McCarthy, F., *Rock Carvings of the Sydney Hawkesbury District*, Part 1, Records of the Australian Museum, Vol. 24, Part 5, November 1956.

McGregor, A., *A Forger's Progress: The Life of Francis Greenway*, New South Publishing, Sydney, 2014.

McGuanne, J.P., 'Early Schools of New South Wales', *Journal of Royal Australian Historical Society*, Vol. 2, 1906–1907, pp. 70–87.

MacLaurin, E.C.B., 'Fitzgerald, Richard (1772–1840)', *Australian Dictionary of Biography*, http://adb.anu.edu.au/biography/fitzgerald-richard-2048/text2537, published first in hard copy 1966, accessed online 18 April 2016.

McMillan, J., *The Two Lives of Joseph Docker*, Spectrum Publishing, Melbourne, 1994.

Maple, C.S., 'Barker, Frederic', B. Dickey, ed., *The Australian Dictionary of Evangelical Biography*, Evangelical History Association, Sydney, 1994, p. 26.

Marshall, H., 'Cross, John (1781–1858)', *Australian Dictionary of Biography*, http://adb.anu.edu.au/biography/cross-john-1937/text2315, published first in hard copy 1966, accessed online 19 April 2016.

Melbourne, T., 'The Unexpected Chaplain: Henry Fulton and Early Colonial Evangelicalism', integrity.moore.edu.au/article/download/6/5, accessed 16 February 2016.

Mirror, 5 July 1963.

Moon, T., 'Stoned and Fallen Angels of the Hawkesbury', unpublished paper, 2008.

Murray, L., *Death and Dying in Twentieth Century Sydney*, 2013, http://dictionaryofsydney.org/entry/death_and_dying_in_twentieth_century_sydney.

National Trust of Australia (NSW), *A Guide to the Conservation of Cemeteries*, Sydney, 1982.

National Trust of Australia (NSW), *Annual Report for 1965–1966.*

Needham, A., *The Women of the Neptune*, author, Dural, 1992.

Nichols, M., *Disastrous Decade*: *Flood and Fire in Windsor, 1867–1874*, Deerubbin Press, Berowra Heights, 2001.

Normington-Rawling, J., 'Harpur, Charles (1813–1868)', *Australian Dictionary of Biography*, Vol. 1, Melbourne University Press, Carlton, 1966, pp. 514–515.

O'Neill, S., 'Fielding, Una Lucy (1888–1969)', *Australian Dictionary of Biography*, http://adb.anu.edu.au/biography/fielding-una-lucy-10178/text17983, published first in hard copy 1996, accessed online 9 April 2016.

Powell, J., *Spanning the Centuries of Hawkesbury's History*, *Journal of the Hawkesbury Historical Society*, No. 2, 2011, pp. 62–63, 66–67.

Purtell, J., 'Charles Chidley Harpur', *Windsor and Richmond Gazette*, 22 January 1986, p. 9.

Query@VintageVictorian.com, accessed 27 April 2016.

Radar, 27 October 1982.

Reeve, G., 'Our Link with Canberra and the Rev. Joseph Docker', *Windsor and Richmond Gazette*, 29 June 1928.

Robinson, P., *A Short History and Guide for St Thomas' Mulgoa*, St Thomas' Church, Mulgoa, 1988.

Roxburgh, R., *Early Colonial Houses of New South Wales*, Ure Smith, Sydney, 1974.

Rushworth, G.D., *Historic Organs of New South Wale: The Instruments, their Makers and Players, 1791–1940*, Hale & Iremonger, Sydney, 1988.

Salier, C.W., 'The Life and Writings of Charles Harpur', *Journal of Royal Australian Historical Society*, Vol. 32, 1946, pp. 89–105.

Sheumaker, H. and S.T. Wajda, eds, *Material Culture in America: Understanding Everyday Life*, ABC-CLIO, Santa Barbara, 2008.

Stancombe, G.H., 'Youl, John (1773–1827)', *Australian Dictionary of Biography*, http://adb.anu.edu.au/biography/youl-john-2827/text4055, published first in hard copy 1967, accessed online 15 February 2016.

St Matthew's Anglican Rectory Stables Task Force, *The Rectory Stables, 1825, St Matthew's Anglican Church, Windsor*, Windsor, [2003].

Steele, J., *Early Days of Windsor N.S. Wales*, Tyrrell's, Sydney, 1916, reprinted Library of Australian History, North Sydney, 1977.

Stockton, E., *Blue Mountains Dreaming: The Aboriginal Heritage*, Three Sisters, Winmalee, 1996.

Streatfeild, D., 'Transcript of Catholic Burial Ground, Windsor, 1822–1899', unpublished assignment, MA in Local History, University of Sydney, 1982.

Stubbs, R., *Ghosts and Myths of the Hawkesbury*, author, Windsor, 1982.

Sunday Telegraph, 3 November 1963.

Sydney Architecture, http://sydneyarchitecture.com/HIST-EARLY/Hist-Early006.htm, accessed 11 February 2016.

Teale, R., 'Hordern, Anthony (1819–1876)', *Australian Dictionary of Biography*, http://adb.anu.edu.au/biography/hordern-anthony-3796/text6009, published first in hard copy 1972, accessed online 27 April 2016.

Torbet, R., *The Wonderful Windows of William Wailes*, Scotforth Books, Lancaster, 2003.

Turnbull Clan Genealogy, at http://www.library.turnbullclan.com/tca_genealogy/tca_all2-o/g0/p184.htm, accessed 15 May 2016.

Walker, F., 'St Matthew's Church, Windsor, N.S.W.: A Sketch on the 108th Anniversary', *Australian Christian World,* 16 October 1925.

Wilson, H., *Old Colonial Architecture*, Union House, Sydney, 1924.

Weymark, M., *Governor Macquarie and the Case for the Court-house Portrait*, [Windsor, *c.* 1975], reprinted J. Miller and Windsor Business Group, Windsor, 2007.

Windsor and Richmond Gazette, 13 October 1982; 5 May 1993.

Yarwood, A.T., 'Marsden, Samuel (1765–1838)', *Australian Dictionary of Biography*, http://adb.anu.edu.au/biography/marsden-samuel-2433/text3237, 1967, accessed online 8 April 2016.

Yarwood, A.T., *Samuel Marsden: The Great Survivor*, Melbourne University Press, Carlton, 1977.

[

Endnotes

Chapter 1

1. J. Cobley, *Sydney Cove, 1795–1800: The Second Governor*, V, Angus & Robertson, North Ryde, 1986, p. 12.
2. A.T. Yarwood, *Samuel Marsden: The Great Survivor*, Melbourne University Press. Carlton, 1977, passim.
3. Cobley, *Sydney Cove, 1795–1800*, p. 12.
4. *Historical Records NSW* [*HRNSW*], Vol. 2, p. 238; Grants of Land Register 1, 104(1) to 145(1).
5. E. Stockton, *Blue Mountains Dreaming: The Aboriginal Heritage*, Three Sisters, Winmalee, 1996; F. McCarthy, *Rock Carvings of the Sydney Hawkesbury District*, Part 1, Records of the Australian Museum, 24 (5), November 1956 at www.australianmuseum.net.au/Uploads/Journals/17791/54_complete.pdf, accessed 2015.
6. D. Collins, *An Account of the English Colony in New South Wales*, 1798, B. Fletcher (ed.), Reed and Royal Australian Historical Society, Sydney, 1975, Vol. 1, pp. 462–463; J. Bach, ed., *An Historical Journal of Events at Sydney and at Sea, 1787–1792 by Captain John Hunter*, Angus & Robertson and Royal Australian Historical Society, Sydney, 1968, pp. 104, 106; W. Tench, *Sydney's First Four Years*, Library of Australian History and Royal Australian Historical Society, Sydney, 1979, pp. 155, 230, 234, 236.
7. J. Barkley and M. Nichols, *Hawkesbury 1794–1994: The First Two Hundred Years of the Second Colonisation*, Hawkesbury City Council, Windsor, 1994, pp. 1–3, 8; Collins, *An Account of the English Colony in New South Wales*, Vol. 1, p. 357.
8. *Historical Records of Australia* [*HRA*], Series 1, Vol. 1, pp. 13–14.
9. J. Barkley-Jack, *Hawkesbury Settlement Revealed: A New Look at Australia's Third Mainland Settlement, 1793–1802*, Rosenberg, Kenthurst, 2009, pp. 416–418.
10. Paterson to Dundas, 15 June 1795, *HRNSW*, Vol. 2, pp. 307, 309.
11. Paterson to Dundas, 16 September 1795, *HRNSW*, Vol. 2, pp. 319–320; Collins, *An Account of the English Colony in New South Wales*, Vol. 1, p. 367.
12. King v. Edward Powell *et al*, Court of Criminal Jurisdiction, State Records NSW [SRNSW], Reel 2651, p. 314, William Goodall, 17 October 1799; pp. 318–319, Neil McKellar, 18 October 1799.
13. Elizabeth Macarthur, 1 September 1795, *HRNSW*, Vol. 2, p. 510.
14. Thomson to Cooke, 28 June 1804, *HRNSW*, Vol. 5, p. 390.
15. Barkley-Jack, *Hawkesbury Settlement Revealed*, pp. 99–101.
16. Collins, *An Account of the English Colony in New South Wales*, Vol. 1, p. 371.
17. Collins, *An Account of the English Colony in New South Wales*, Vol. 1, pp. 359–361; Cobley, *Sydney Cove 1795-1808*, pp. 6–14.
18. D.G. Bowd, *Macquarie Country: A History of the Hawkesbury*, rev. ed., 1973, p. 56.
19. Elizabeth Macarthur, 1 September 1795, *HRNSW*, Vol. 2, p. 510.
20. J. Barkley-Jack, 'Early Boat Building on the Upper Hawkesbury River', *Cross Currents: Historical Studies of the Hawkesbury*, ed. J. Powell, Deerubbin Press, Berowra Heights, 1997, p. 38.
21. Land Grants Register 2, p. 172, Whitehouse Farm, 1 June 1797; p. 211, Smallwood Farm, 1 June 1797; p. 247, Catherine Farm (Thomas Rickaby), 6 February 1798; Barkley-Jack, *Hawkesbury Settlement Revealed*, p. 442.
22. Collins, *An Account of the English Colony in New South Wales*, Vol. 1, pp. 340–341.
23. Crossley v Edwards, Faithful, Baker and Baker, Court of Civil Jurisdiction, SRNSW, June–September 1804, CY1098, pp. 41, [William] Baker, Storekeeper, 7 August 1804; Land Grant Register 3, p. 51, 20 June 1800.
24. Yarwood, *Samuel Marsden*, p. 51.
25. Barkley-Jack, *Hawkesbury Settlement Revealed*, pp. 216–217, 222.
26. Barkley-Jack, *Hawkesbury Settlement Revealed*, pp. 224–226.
27. Yarwood, *Samuel Marsden*, p. 51.
28. Barkley-Jack, *Hawkesbury Settlement Revealed*, p. 140.
29. 'Sketch of the Inundation in the Neighbourhood of Windsor … 2 June 1816', State Library of New South Wales, Mitchell Library, PX*D 264.
30. Barkley-Jack, *Hawkesbury Settlement Revealed*, pp. 336–337.
31. Barkley-Jack, *Hawkesbury Settlement Revealed*, p. 371.
32. Collins, *An Account of the English Colony in New South Wales*, Vol. 1, p. 401.
33. Barkley-Jack, *Hawkesbury Settlement Revealed*, pp. 174, 177, 178.
34. Marsden, Sermon 2, p. 14, transcribed by John Pettett, 2014, Library of Moore Theological College, Sydney, at https://www.moore.edu.au/library/samuel-marsden, accessed 9 February 2016.
35. Marsden's Sermon 4, p. 3, transcribed Pettett.
36. *HRNSW*, Vol. 4, pp. 259, 467, 719.
37. T. Melbourne, 'The Unexpected Chaplain: Henry Fulton and Early Colonial Evangelicalism', p. 8, *integrity.moore.edu.au/article/download/6/5*, accessed 16 February 2016.
38. K.J. Cable, 'Fulton, Henry (1761–1840)', *Australian Dictionary of Biography*, http://adb.anu.edu.au/biography/crook-william-pascoe-1935/text2311, published first in hard copy 1966, accessed 17 February 2016.
39. Melbourne, 'The Unexpected Chaplain', *integrity.moore.edu.au/article/download/6/5*, accessed 16 February 2016, p. 14.
40. Bowd, *Macquarie Country*, p. 66.
41. N. Gunson, 'Crook, William Pascoe (1775–1846)', *Australian Dictionary of Biography*, http://adb.anu.edu.au/biography/crook-william-pascoe-1935/text2311, published first in hard copy 1966, accessed 17 February 2016;
42. Hassall Family Papers, State Library of New South Wales, Mitchell Library, http://acms.sl.nsw.gov.au/item/itemdetailpaged.aspx?itemid=411588, accessed 17 February 2016.
43. *HRNSW,* Vol. 5, p. 163.
44. *HRNSW*, Vol. 5, p. 163.
45. *Sydney Gazette*, 26 August 1804.
46. *HRNSW*, Vol. 6, p. 43.
47. Gunson, 'Harris, John (1754–1819)', *Australian Dictionary of Biography*, http://adb.anu.edu.au/biography/harris-john-2163/text2771, published first in hard copy 1966, accessed 14 February 2016.
48. *HRNSW*, Vol. 4, pp. 211, 446.
49. *Sydney Gazette,* 30 March, 13, 27 April 1806; *HRNSW*, Vol. 6, p. 69.
50. *HRA*, series 1, Vol. 6, p. 358; Steele, *Early Days of Windsor*, p. 67.
51. Gunson, 'Harris, John (1754–1819)', *Australian Dictionary of Biography*, http://adb.anu.edu.au/biography/harris-john-2163/text2771, published first in hard copy 1966, accessed 14 February 2016.
52. *HRNSW*, Vol. 5, p. 425.
53. G.H. Stancombe, 'Youl, John (1773–1827)', *Australian Dictionary of Biography*, http://adb.anu.edu.au/biography/youl-john-2827/text4055, published first in hard copy 1967, accessed 15 February 2016; *HRNSW*, Vol. 6, p. 708.
54. *Windsor and Richmond Gazette*, 6 November 1914; W. Freame, *Windsor and Richmond Gazette*, 4 November 1911.
55. Steele, *Early Days of Windsor*, p. 67

Chapter 2

1 *Sydney Morning Herald*, 23 December 1856; K.J. Cable, 'Cartwright Robert (1771–1856)', *Australian Dictionary of Biography*, http://adb.anu.au/biography/cartwright-robert-1882/text2211, first published in hard copy 1966, accessed, 31 March 2016.

2 J. Ritchie, *The Evidence to the Bigge Reports*, Vol. 1, *The Oral Evidence*, Heinemann, Melbourne, 1971, p. 147.

3 Lake Macquarie Family History Group, eds, *St Matthews Parish Registers 1810 to 1856*, '*A Complete Transcription*', Lake Macquarie Family History Group, Teralba, 2003, p. 183, item 3208; Cable, 'Cartwright', *Australian Dictionary of Biography*, accessed 31 March 2016.
4 The small volume containing the *Pocket Sermons* remained in the possession of the Cartwright family until it was presented to St Matthew's by Cartwright's great-great-grand-daughter, Mrs Quester.
5 Ritchie, ed., *The Evidence to the Bigge Reports*, Vol. 1, p. 151.
6 *Sydney Gazette*, 15 September 1810.
7 *Sydney Gazette*, 15 September 1810.
8 http://www.records.nsw.gov.au/state-archives/guides-and-finding-aids/archives-in-brief/archives-in-brief-123, accessed 7 October 2014.
9 Ritchie, ed., *The Evidence to the Bigge Reports*, Vol. 1, p. 152.
10 Ritchie, ed., *The Evidence to the Bigge Reports*, Vol. 1, p. 146.
11 Macquarie's list of public works, *Historical Records of Australia*, Series 1, Vol. 10, pp. 684–699; Ritchie, ed., *The Evidence to the Bigge Reports*, Vol. 1, p. 152; J. Steele, *Early Days of Windsor N.S. Wales*, Tyrrell's, Sydney 1916, reprinted Library of Australian History, North Sydney, 1977, pp. 117–118.
12 Ritchie, ed., *The Evidence to the Bigge Reports*, Vol. 1, p. 152.
13 Cable, 'Cartwright', *Australian Dictionary of Biography*, accessed 31 March 2016.
14 *Truth*, 21 April 1901; Cable, 'Cartwright', *Australian Dictionary of Biography* accessed 17 February 2016.
15 Ritchie, ed., *The Evidence to the Bigge Reports*, Vol. 1, p. 156.
16 Anon., 'Sketch of the Inundation in the neighbourhood of Windsor…2 June 1816', watercolour, State Library of New South Wales, Mitchell Library, PX*D 264; Ritchie, ed., *The Evidence to the Bigge Reports*, Vol. 1, p. 156.
17 *Sydney Gazette*, 9 August 1817.
18 Land Grants Register 3, p. 47, Thomas Hobby, 20 June 1800 Sutton Farm; Land Grants Register 2, p. 89, Land Grants Register 3, 114(5), Neil McKellar, 6 July 1803, McKellar Farm; Land Grants Register 2, 163, William Nash, Nashe's Farm, 30 December 1796; Land Grants Register 2, 406, William Nash, unnamed grant, 12 November 1799; State Records NSW, Lands, *Old Register of Assignments and Leases* 1 p. 18 entry 89, William Nash to Thomas Hobby 5 March 1802; Parish map of St Matthew, county of Cumberland, Land and Property Information, edition no. 0, sheet reference 3.
19 State Records NSW, Lands, *Old Register of Assignments and Leases* 4 p. 27 entry 311 Thomas Hobby to John Brabyn, 23 April 1810.
20 Ritchie, ed., *The Evidence to the Bigge Reports*, Vol. 1, p. 156.
21 *Sydney Gazette*, 9 August 1817.
22 Ritchie, ed., *The Evidence to the Bigge Reports*, Vol. 1, p. 157.
23 *Sydney Gazette*, 15 August 1818; Steele, *Early Days of Windsor*, pp. 46–47.
24 Steele, *Early Days of Windsor*, p. 68.
25 *Sydney Gazette*, 31 January 1818; Biographical Data Base online, James Birnie search, accessed 28 February 2016.
26 Cartwright to Hassall, 15 February 1815 and Hassall to Cartwright, 17 February 1815, Steele, *Early Days of Windsor*, pp. 46–47.
27 Ritchie, ed., *The Evidence to the Bigge Reports*, Vol. 1, pp. 154, 157.
28 Lachlan Macquarie, Governor of New South Wales, *Journals of his Tours in New South Wales and Van Diemen's Land 1810–1822*, Library of Australian History, Sydney, 1979, p. 28.
29 *Sydney Gazette*, 14 January 1810.
30 A. Needham, *The Women of the Neptune*, author, Dural, 1992, p. 168.
31 Cf. the watercolour of Green Hills in 1811 attributed to G.W. Evans, State Library of New South Wales, Mitchell Library, SVIB/Wind/6.
32 Macquarie, *Journals of his Tours*, p. 43.
33 *Sydney Gazette*, 24 October 1812.
34 *Sydney Gazette*, 11 July 1812.
35 *Sydney Gazette*, 3 July 1813.
36 *Sydney Gazette*, 18 July 1812.
37 *Sydney Gazette*, 30 January 1819.
38 F. Tomms, *The Land*, 21 December 1923.
39 *Sydney Gazette*, 23 October 1813.
40 *Sydney Gazette*, 5 August 1815.
41 *Sydney Gazette*, 10 September 1814.
42 Ritchie, ed., *The Evidence to the Bigge Reports*, Vol. 1, pp. 152–153.
43 *Sydney Gazette*,12 July 1817.
44 *Sydney Gazette*, 15 November 1817.
45 *Sydney Gazette*, 8 January 1814.
46 *Sydney Gazette*, 12 June 1819
47 Macquarie, *Journals of his Tours*, p. 43.
48 Ritchie, ed., *The Evidence to the Bigge Reports*, Vol. 1, p. 152.
49 Ritchie, ed., *The Evidence to the Bigge Reports*, Vol. 1, p. 153.
50 Ritchie, ed., *The Evidence to the Bigge Reports*, Vol. 1, p. 153.
51 Ritchie, ed., *The Evidence to the Bigge Reports*, Vol. 1, p. 153.
52 Macquarie, *Journals of his Tours*, pp. 41–42.
53 J. Barkley-Jack, *Hawkesbury Settlement Revealed: A New Look at Australia's Third Mainland Settlement*, Rosenberg, Kenthurst, 2009, pp. 156–160, 281.
54 J. Meehan, plan of Windsor, 1812, signed by Governor Macquarie, State Records NSW, Map SZ529.
55 *Sydney Gazette*, 26 October 1811. A court case report gives information that Thomas was given a grant in 1796 along with John Pugh, although it was not registered until 1802. This was unknown when Barkley-Jack, *Hawkesbury Settlement Revealed,* was published and consequently Thomas does not appear as a grantee for that year nor is his grant shown on the map of 1796 grants, as drawn in 2009. The *Sydney Gazette* information updates the 2009 publication.
56 Land Grants Register 3, p. 78(2), Charles Thomas, 31 March 1802; p. 101(1), Sarah Verender 15 September 1802; Barkley-Jack, *Hawkesbury Settlement Revealed*, pp. 395–397.
57 Meehan, plan of Windsor, 1812, State Records NSW SZ529; map of St Matthew parish, county Cumberland, Land and Property Information, PMapMN05, Sheet 1, 14076801.
58 Map of St Matthew parish, county of Cumberland, Land and Property Information, PMap MN05, 14076801.
59 Abstract of Returns submitted to the King's Visitor, 1825, pp. 44–45, Re payment of expenses of the public school at Windsor, pp. 95–98, ancestry.com.au *New South Wales, Australia, Colonial Secretary's Papers, 1788–1856* [database on-line], accessed 25 February 2016.
60 M.H. Ellis, *Francis Greenway: His Life and Times*, Angus & Robertson, Sydney, 3rd ed., 1973, p. 89.
61 State Records NSW, Lands, *Old Register of Assignments and Leases* 2 p. 25 entry 84. The registered deed is undated but the context is between 1808 and 1810.
62 W.L. Havard, 'Note on St Matthew's Church, Windsor', *Journal of Royal Australian Historical Society* [*JRAHS*], Vol. 31, 1945, p. 126.
63 J.C.L. Fitzpatrick, *Those Were the Days: More Hawkesbury History*, NSW Bookstall Co., Sydney, 1923, p. 208.
64 Ritchie, ed., *The Evidence to the Bigge Reports*, Vol. 1, p. 187.
65 Ritchie, ed., *The Evidence to the Bigge Reports*, Vol. 1, p. 186; Vol. 2, *The Written Evidence*, p. 31; *Sydney Gazette*, 15 January 1804.
66 E.C.B. MacLaurin, 'Fitzgerald, Richard (1772–1840)', *Australian Dictionary of Biography*, http://adb.anu.edu.au/biography/fitzgerald-richard-2048/text2537, published first in hard copy 1966, accessed 18 April 2016; Ritchie, ed., *The Evidence to the Bigge Reports*, Vol. 1, p. 186.
67 R. Walsh, ed., *In Her Own Words*, p. 191; Ritchie, ed., *The Evidence to the Bigge Reports*, Vol. 1, p. 186.
68 Ellis, *Francis Greenway*, pp. 28–31, 37, 89.
69 *Sydney Gazette*, 28 December 1816.
70 O. Bradbury, *Sir John Soane's Influence on Architecture from 1791: A Continuing Legacy*, Ashgate Publishing, 2015, p. 197.
71 Sydney Architecture, http://sydneyarchitecture.com/HIST-EARLY/Hist-Early009.htm, accessed 11 February 2016, based on M. Herman, *Early Australian Architects and Their Work,* Angus & Robertson, Sydney, 1954.
72 *Sydney Gazette*, 15 February 1817.
73 Sydney Architecture, http://sydneyarchitecture.com/HIST-EARLY/Hist-Early009.htm, accessed 11 February 2016.
74 A. McGregor, *A Forger's Progress: The Life of Francis Greenway*, NewSouth Publishing, University of New South Wales Press, Sydney, 2014, pp. 225–226.
75 Ritchie, ed., *The Evidence to the Bigge Reports*, Vol. 1, p. 136. The argument for the Greenway design is accepted by Herman, *The Early Australian Architects and their Work.*
76 Information from Graham Edds, 2010.
77 McGregor, *A Forger's Progress: The Life of Francis Greenway*, pp. 225–6

78 Ellis, *Francis Greenway*, p. 93. For the text of the committee's report, see Havard, *JRAHS*, Vol. 22, 1936, p. 159 note †; McGregor, *A Forger's Progress: The Life of Francis Greenway*, pp. 231, 228.
79 Lake Macquarie Family History Group, eds, *St Matthews Parish Registers 1810 to 1856,* p. xiv; McGregor, *A Forger's Progress: The Life of Francis Greenway*, p. 224.
80 McGregor, *A Forger's Progress: The Life of Francis Greenway*, pp. 226–7.
81 Lake Macquarie Family History Group, eds, *St Matthews Parish Registers 1810 to 1856*, p. xv.
82 *Sydney Gazette*, 11 April 1818.
83 *Sydney Gazette*, 4 February 1818, 6 June 1818; McGregor, *A Forger's Progress: The Life of Francis Greenway*, p. 232.
84 Bradbury, *Sir John Soane's Influence on Architecture from 1791*, p. 197.
85 McGregor, *A Forger's Progress: The Life of Francis Greenway*, p. 228.
86 McGregor, *A Forger's Progress: The Life of Francis Greenway*, p. 231.
87 McGregor, *A Forger's Progress: The Life of Francis Greenway*, p. 231.
88 Ellis, *Francis Greenway*, p. 93. For the text of the committee's report, see Havard, *JRAHS,* Vol. 22, 1936, p. 159 note †; McGregor, *A Forger's Progress: The Life of Francis Greenway*, pp. 231.
89 D.G. Bowd, *Macquarie Country: A History of the Hawkesbury*, rev. ed., author, Windsor, 1973, pp. 144–146; *Windsor and Richmond Gazette*, 29 October 1898.
90 McGregor, *A Forger's Progress: The Life of Francis Greenway*, p. 232.

Chapter 3

1. M. Herman, 'Greenway, Francis (1777–1837)', *Australian Dictionary of Biography*, http://adb.anu.edu.au/biography/greenway-francis-2120/text2681, published first in hard copy 1966, accessed 19 April 2016.
2.Sydney Architecture, http://sydneyarchitecture.com/HIST-EARLY/Hist-Early006.htm, accessed 11 February 2016.
3. J. Purtell, 'Charles Chidley Harpur', *Windsor and Richmond Gazette*, 22 January 1986, p. 9; J. Normington-Rawling, 'Harpur, Charles (1813–1868)', *Australian Dictionary of Biography*, http://adb.anu.edu.au/biography/harpur-charles-2158/text2759, published first in hardcopy 1966, accessed 19 April 2016.
4. C.W. Salier, 'The Life and Writings of Charles Harpur', *Journal of Royal Australian Historical Society* [*JRAHS*], Vol. 32, 1946, p. 90.
5. The original Register book is still in the custody of St Matthew's. It was microfilmed in 1980 and can be consulted in the Windsor Library and metropolitan repositories.
6. J. Steele, *Early Days of Windsor*, Tyrrell,'s Sydney 1916, reprinted Library of Australian History, North Sydney, 1977, pp. 70–73; D.G. Bowd, *Macquarie Country: A History of the Hawkesbury*, rev. ed., author, Windsor, 1973, pp. 67–68; W.F. Carter, *The Cathedral of the Hawkesbury: A Sketch of St. Matthew's Windsor,* n.d., pp. 7–9, 12.
7. Register of St Matthew's Church, Windsor, 4 June 1819.
8. J. Ritchie, ed., *The Evidence to the Bigge Reports*, Vol. 2, *The Written Evidence*, pp. 124–163.
9. M.H. Ellis, *Francis Greenway: his Life and Times*, Angus & Robertson, Sydney, 3rd ed., 1973, pp. 88–94, 211–212
10. *Sydney Gazette*, 8, 15 June 1816, 15 March 1817, 27 February 1819.
11. *Sydney Gazette*, 15 March 1817.
12.M. J. Read, *Aunt Spencer's Diary (1854): A Visit to Bontharambo and the North-East Victorian Goldfields*, Neptune, Newtown Victoria, 1981, pp. 74–75.
13. Ritchie, ed., *The Evidence to the Bigge Reports*, Vol. 1 p. 153.
14. Ritchie, ed., *The Evidence to the Bigge Reports*, Vol. 1, pp. 153–154; *Sydney Gazette*, 25 April 1812; *Sydney Gazette*, 29 October 1814.
15. Ritchie, ed., *The Evidence to the Bigge Reports*, Vol. 1, p. 154.
16. Ritchie, ed., *The Evidence to the Bigge Reports*, Vol. 1, p. 155.
17. Ritchie, ed., *The Evidence to the Bigge Reports*, Vol. 1, p. 157.
18. Ritchie, ed., *The Evidence to the Bigge Reports*, Vol. 1, p. 157.
19. ancestry.com. au *'New South Wales, Australia, Colonial Secretary's Papers, 1788–1856'* [database on-line], p. 140, 23 September 1815, pp. 305–310, 18 January 1817, accessed 20 April 2016.
20.Ritchie, ed., *The Evidence to the Bigge Reports* Vol. 1, p. 156.
21.Ancestry.com.au *'New South Wales, Australia'*, *Colonial Secretary's Papers, 1788–1856* [database on-line], p. 123, 18 December 1819, accessed 20 April 2016.
22.*Sydney Gazette*, 18 December 1819.
23.*Sydney Gazette*, 18 December 1819
24. H. Marshall, 'Cross, John (1781–1858)', *Australian Dictionary of Biography*, http://adb.anu.edu.au/biography/cross-john-1937/text2315, published first in hard copy 1966, accessed 19 April 2016; J. W. Fawcett, *A Brief Life of the Reverend John Cross: Forty Years a Chaplain in the Colony of New South Wales*, Hinchcliffe, Brisbane, 1898, http://nla.gov.au/nla.obj-52768195/view#page/n0/mode/1up, pp. 5–6, accessed 1 March 2016.
25.*Sydney Gazette*, 4 March 1820.
26. Marshall, 'Cross, John', *Australian Dictionary of Biography*, http://adb.anu.edu.au/biography/cross-john-1937/text2315, accessed 11 February 2016.
27.Marshall, 'Cross, John', *Australian Dictionary of Biography*, http://adb.anu.edu.au/biography/cross-john-1937/text2315, accessed 18 March 2016.
28.Fawcett, *A Brief Life of the Reverend John Cross*, http://nla.gov.au/nla.obj52768195/view#page/n0/mode/1up, pp. 5–6, accessed 1 March 2016.
29.Steele, *Early Days of Windsor*, p. 76.
30.*Sydney Herald*, 9 January 1834.
31.Fawcett, *A Brief Life of the Reverend John Cross*, p. 9, accessed 18 March 2016.
32. J. Hardwick, 'Anglican Church Expansion and Colonial Reform Politics in Bengal, New South Wales and the Cape Colony c. 1790–1850', DPhil thesis, University of York, 2008, pp. 88–90.
33.Marsden to Bishop Howley, 11 March 1821, in Hardwick, DPhil thesis, pp. 88, 101, 102, 126; R. Border, 'Scott, Thomas Hobbes (1783–1869)', *Australian Dictionary of Biography*, http://adb.anu.edu.au/biography/scott-thomas-hobbes-2645, accessed 18 March 2016.
34.Marsden to Bishop Howley, 11 March 1821, quoted in Hardwick, DPhil thesis, pp. 88, 101, 102, 126; Border, 'Scott, Thomas Hobbes', *Australian Dictionary of Biography*, http://adb.anu.edu.au/biography/scott-thomas-hobbes-2645, accessed 18 March 2016.
35.Fawcett, *A Brief Life of the Reverend John Cross*, http://nla.gov.au/nla.obj-52768195/view, p. 9, accessed 18 March 2016; Hardwick, DPhil thesis, p. 77.
36.Fawcett, *A Brief Life of the Reverend John Cross*, http://nla.gov.au/nla.obj-52768195/view, pp. 9, 13, accessed 18 March 2016.
37.Marsden to Howley, 11 March 1821, Hardwick, DPhil thesis, pp. 88, 101 102, 126; Border, 'Scott, Thomas Hobbes', *Australian Dictionary of Biography*, http://adb.anu.edu.au/biography/scott-thomas-hobbes-2645, accessed 18 March 2016.
38.Scott to Smith, 28 November 1828, Steele, *Early Days of Windsor*, p. 79; Marshall, 'Cross, John', *Australian Dictionary of Biography*, http://adb.anu.edu.au/biography/cross-john-1937, accessed 18 March 2016.
39.Marshall, 'Cross, John', *Australian Dictionary of Biography*, http://adb.anu.edu.au/biography/cross-john-1937, accessed 18 March 2016; Fawcett, *A Brief Life of the Reverend John Cross,* http://nla.gov.au/nla.obj-52768195/view, p. 7, accessed 18 March 2016
40.*Windsor and Richmond Gazette*, 20 January 1894\
41.Lake Macquarie Family History Group, eds, *St Matthews Church of England Windsor NSW: Parish Registers 1810 to 1856 'A Complete Transcription'*, Lake Macquarie Family History Group, Teralba, 2003, p. 219, item, 3781, 21 July 1827, John Skinner.
42.*Windsor and Richmond Gazette*, 20 January 1894, 29 October 1898.
43.*Sydney Gazette*, 11, 13 March 1819.
44.J. Powell, *Journal of the Hawkesbury Historical Society: Spanning the Centuries of Hawkesbury's History* [*JHHS*], No. 2, 2011, pp. 62–63, 66–67.
45.*Sydney Gazette*, 30 January 1819; 8 January 1820.
46.W.L. Havard, 'Note on St Matthew's Church, Windsor', *JRAHS*, Vol. 31, 1945, p. 127.
47.Havard, *JRAHS*, Vol. 31, 1945, p. 126.
48.The evidence for both plaques is their physical existence at their respective buildings.
49.St Matthew's Anglican Church Archives [SMACA], Minute Book, 1918–1930, p. 149. The 1925 plaque is reproduced in Carter, *Cathedral of the Hawkesbury*, n.d., p. 31, and in L.M. Abbott, *St Matthew's Windsor: A Short Guide to the Church and its History*, St Matthew's Church, Windsor, 2002, p. 4.

50.A. Aldrich, *JHHS*, No. 2, 2011, p. 62.
51. Aldrich, *JHHS*, No. 2, 2011, p. 64.
52.Powell, *JHHS*, No. 2, 2011, p. 67.
53.*Sydney Gazette,* 29 July 1820.
54.SRNSW, Colonial Secretary's Correspondence, Reel 6051, 4/1749, pp. 23–30; Powell. *JHHS*, No. 2, 2011, p. 67.
55. SRNSW, Colonial Secretary's Correspondence, Reel 6051, 4/1749, pp. 23–30.
56.SRNSW, Colonial Secretary's Correspondence, Reel 6008, 4/3504, p. 377.
57.*Sydney Gazett*e, 19 May 1820.
58. Lake Macquarie Family History Group, eds, *St Matthews Parish Registers 1810 to 1856,* p. xv.
59. Hardwick, DPhil thesis, p. 88.
60. C. Roberts, *JHHS*, No.2, 2011, p. 74.
61. M. Weymark, *Governor Macquarie and the Case for the Court-house Portrait*, n.d, *passim*. Note the research of Marjorie Weymark provides compelling evidence that the painting is authentic, although this is not universally accepted.
62. Marshall, 'Cross, John', *Australian Dictionary of Biography*, http://adb.anu.edu.au/biography/cross-john-1937/text2315, accessed 11 February 2016.
63. A. McGregor, *A Forger's Progress: The Life of Francis Greenway*, New-South Publishing, Sydney, 2014, p. 243.
64.McGregor, *A Forger's Progress: The Life of Francis Greenway*, p. 234.
65.A.T. Yarwood, *Samuel Marsden: The Great Survivor*, Melbourne University Press, Carlton, 1977, p. 233.
66.Lake Macquarie Family History Group, eds, *St Matthews Parish Registers 1810 to 1856*, p. xv; Steele, *Early Days of Windsor*, p. 73; *Sydney Gazette*, 27 December 1822.
67. Lake Macquarie Family History Group, eds, *St Matthews Parish Registers 1810 to 1856*, p. xv.
68.*Sydney Gazette*, 27 December 1822.
69. Steele, *Early Days of Windsor*, p. 72.
70. J.P. McGuanne, 'Early Schools of New South Wales', *JRAHS*, Vol. 2, 1906–1907, pp. 86–87; Salier, 'The Life and Writings of Charles Harpur', *JRAHS*, Vol. 32, 1946, p. 90.
71.*Sydney Gazette*, 25 December 1823; Steele, *Early Days of Windsor*, pp. 73–74.
72. Steele, *Early Days of Windsor*, p. 72.
73.SMACA, Wardens' Account Book, 1851–1852.
74. Carter, *Cathedral of the Hawkesbury*, p. 22; SMACA. Minute Book, 1931–1957, pp. 111, 116.
75.Steele, *Early Days of Windsor*, p. 76; Carter, *Cathedral of the Hawkesbury*, photographs, pp. 30, 36.
76.F. Jackson, 'Windsor, N.S.W., its Monuments', *Sydney Morning Herald*, 17 May 1924.
77.Thwaites and Reed, at http://www.clockmuseum.co.uk/english_turret_makers.html, accessed 2 April 2016.
78. Information from Doug Minty, June 2016.
79.Anon., 'Reminiscences of a Visit to the Hawkesbury', *Town and Country Journal*, 24 January 1874, p. 141; Bowd, *Macquarie Country: A History of the Hawkesbury*, rev. ed., author, Windsor, 1973, p. 70; information from Dr Rosemary Annable, former archivist to St James'.
80. Anon., 'Reminiscences of a Visit to the Hawkesbury', *Town and Country Journal*, 24 January 1874, p. 141.
81. T. Meares, Foundry, London, http://www.whitechapelbellfoundry.co.uk/identify.htm, accessed 2 April 2016.
82.S.L. Harris, 'Report and Estimates of the Value of the Improvements which have taken place in the Public Buildings of Sydney, Parramatta, Windsor, Liverpool and Campbell-town between the 25th of Decr. 1822 & the 24th of Decr. 1823 inclusive, and an Exposé of the present state of the Public Buildings in New South Wales, by Order of His Excellency Sir Thomas 1.Brisbane K.C.B &c &c', [Sydney] 1824, p. 2, State Library of New South Wales, Mitchell Library, C 226, reel CY 1035; Steele, *Early Days of Windsor*, pp. 75–76
83. P. Russell, ed., *This Errant Lady: Jane Franklin's Overland Journey to Port Phillip and Sydney, 1839*, National Library of Australia, Canberra, 2002, p. 160.

Chapter 4

1 J. Steele, *Early Days of Windsor*, Tyrrell's. Sydney, 1916, reprinted Library of Australian History, North Sydney, 1977, p. 76.
2 Lake Macquarie Family History Group, eds, *St Matthews Church of England Windsor NSW: Parish Registers 1810 to 1856 'A Complete Transcription'*, Lake Macquarie Family History Group, Teralba, 2003, pp. 203–207, October 1821 to 1 February 1823; p. 205, item 3561, 28 April 1822, Richard Fitzgerald.
3 Lake Macquarie Family History Group, eds, *St Matthews Parish Registers 1810 to 1856*, p. 27, item 0603, 2 March 1823, Sarah Deakins.
4 Joseph Harpur, in Lake Macquarie Family History Group, eds, *St Matthews Parish Registers 1810 to 1856*, p. 207, item 3596, 17 February 1823, Daniel Barnett [written as Barney in the Register].
5 Land Grants Register 1, NSW Land and Property Information 1, 109(2), registered 3 November 1794, the fourteenth Mulgrave Place grant registered.
6 Steele, *Early Days of Windsor*, p. 76; J.W. Fawcett, *A Brief Life of the Reverend John Cross: Forty Years a Chaplain in the Colony of New South Wales*, F.W. Hinchcliffe, Brisbane,1898, http://nla.gov.au/nla.obj-52768195/view#page/n0/mode/1up, p. 10, accessed 1 March 2016.
7 C. Lucas-Smith, 'History of the Smith Family', Windsor Library, Local Studies, Vertical File, 'St Matthew's Anglican Church, Windsor', typescript, 2002, unpaginated; obituary, *Sydney Morning Herald*, 2 December 1870.
8 *Sydney Gazette*, 7 December 1827; 16 January 1828. This date is confirmed by the registers.
9 Lake Macquarie Family History Group, eds, *St Matthews Parish Registers 1810 to 1856*, p. 220, item 3804, 11 February 1828, John Macarthy; p. 38, item 0855, 17 February 1828, Thomas Leak; p. 144, item 2776, 20 February 1828, Charles Knight and Elizabeth Dargin.
10 Lucas-Smith, 'History of the Smith Family'; Steele, *Early Days of Windsor*, p. 77.
11 *Sydney Gazette*, 17 October 1828.
12 Lake Macquarie Family History Group, eds, *St Matthews Parish Registers 1810 to 1856*, p. 222, item 3835, 30 December 1828, Charlotte Cross.
13 *Sydney Gazette*, 31 March 1829; *Australian*. 3 April 1829.
14 *Sydney Gazette*, 31 March 1829.
15 *Sydney Morning Herald*, 2 December 1870.
16 *Sydney Morning Herald*, 2 December 1870.
17 J. McMillan, *The Two Lives of Joseph Docker*, Spectrum Publishing, Melbourne, 1994, p. 47.
18 *Flood, Fire and Fever: A History of Elwood*, http://skhs.org.au/~SKHS-flood/Early_Settlers.htm; Steele, *Early Days of Windsor*, pp. 80–81.
19 *Sydney Gazette,* 7 February 1829.
20 G. Reeve, 'Our Link with Canberra and the Rev. Joseph Docker', *Windsor and Richmond Gazette*, 29 June 1928.
21 Lake Macquarie Family History Group, eds, *St Matthews Parish Registers 1810 to 1856*, p. 39, item 0876, 14 January 1829, Mary Jane Docker, p. 222, item 3836, 6 January 1829, John Cliffe.
22 Lake Macquarie Family History Group, eds, *St Matthews Parish Registers 1810 to 1856*, p. 43, item 0953, 1 September 1831, Charles Docker; p. 44, item 0968, 5 January 1832, Stanley Docker.
23 Lake Macquarie Family History Group, eds, *St Matthews Parish Registers 1810 to 1856*, p. 58, item 1283, 17 May 1835, Frederick Docker.
24 Lake Macquarie Family History Group, eds, *St Matthews Parish Registers 1810 to 1856*, p. 56*,* item 1237, 4 August 1837, Matthew Docker.
25 Lake Macquarie Family History Group, eds, *St Matthews Parish Registers 1810 to 1856*, p. 222, item 3836, 6 January 1829, John Cliffe; p. 39, item 0876, 14 January 1829, Mary Jane Docker; p. 145, item 2793, 27 January 1829, John Doyle and Ellen Fitz; p. 231, item 4020, 23 March 1833, Thomas Finlay; p. 151, item 2864, 25 March 1833, George Chich and Emma Smith; p. 46, item 1023, 1 July 1833, Samuel Tuckwell of Kurrajong; Docker to Broughton, 28 July 1833, McMillan, *The Two Lives of Joseph Docker*, p. 79.
26 McMillan, *The Two Lives of Joseph Docker*, pp. 59–60.
27 McMillan, *The Two Lives of Joseph Docker*, p. 60.
28 *Sydney Gazette,* 9 February, 1830; McMillan, *The Two Lives of Joseph Docker*, p. 53.
29 McMillan, *The Two Lives of Joseph Docker*, p. 61.

30 McMillan, *The Two Lives of Joseph Docker*, pp. 52, 53.
31 McMillan, *The Two Lives of Joseph Docker*, p. 61.
32 McMillan, *The Two Lives of Joseph Docker*, p. 61.
33 McMillan, *The Two Lives of Joseph Docker*, p. 56; Steele, *Early Days of Windsor*, p. 79.
34 McMillan, *The Two Lives of Joseph Docker*, p. 48.
35 J. Hardwick, 'Anglican Church Expansion and Colonial Reform Politics in Bengal, New South Wales and the Cape Colony c. 1790–1850', DPhil thesis, University of York, 2008, pp. 114, 129.
36 *Sydney Gazette*, 28 July 1832; T.H. Scott, letter, 15 October 1832, *Sydney Herald*, 22 October 1832.
37 Hardwick, DPhil thesis, p. 102.
38 Quoted in a letter signed PETO, *Sydney Herald*, 18 April 1833.
39 J. Hardwick, DPhil thesis, pp. 103–104.
40 McMillan, *The Two Lives of Joseph Docker*, p. 48; Scott to Bishop of London, quoted in Hardwick, DPhil thesis, p. 102.
41 Hardwick, DPhil thesis, p. 103.
42 McMillan, *The Two Lives of Joseph Docker*, p. 62.
43 Docker to Broughton, 2 April, 1, 24 November, 1829, 11 July 1833, McMillan, *The Two Lives of Joseph Docker*, pp. 56, 58, 75.
44 Broughton to Brabyn, 30 July 1833, McMillan, *The Two Lives of Joseph Docker*, p. 85.
45 McMillan, *The Two Lives of Joseph Docker*, pp. 49, 58.
46 McMillan, *The Two Lives of Joseph Docker*, p. 50.
47 McMillan, *The Two Lives of Joseph Docker*, pp. 48, 49, 50, 58.
48 McMillan, *The Two Lives of Joseph Docker*, pp. 49, 58.
49 Steele, *Early Days of Windsor*, p. 80.
50 McMillan, *The Two Lives of Joseph Docker*, pp. 50–51.
51 McMillan, *The Two Lives of Joseph Docker*, p. 49.
52 Docker to Broughton, 11 July 1833, McMillan, *The Two Lives of Joseph Docker*, p. 75; P. Russell, ed., This *Errant Lady: Jane Franklin's Overland Journey to Port Phillip and Sydney, 1839*, National Library of Australia, Canberra, 2002, p. 160; Lake Macquarie Family History Group, eds, *St Matthews Parish Registers 1810 to 1856*, p. 224, item 3896, 6 March 1830, William Cope.
53 Docker, journal, 14 February 1830, McMillan, *The Two Lives of Joseph Docker*, p. 62.
54 Lake Macquarie Family History Group, eds, *St Matthews Parish Registers 1810 to 1856*, p. 224, item 3896, 6 March 1830, William Cope.
55 Steele, *Early Days of Windsor*, pp. 12–13.
56 McMillan, *The Two Lives of Joseph Docker*, p. 63.
57 Steele, *Early Days of Windsor*, p. 80 McMillan, *The Two Lives of Joseph Docker*, pp. 55, 75.
58 McMillan, *The Two Lives of Joseph Docker*, pp. 55, 75.
59 McMillan, *The Two Lives of Joseph Docker*, pp. 56–57.
60 McMillan, *The Two Lives of Joseph Docker*, p. 66.
61 A.G. Austin, *Australian Education 1788–1900*, quoted in McMillan, *The Two Lives of Joseph Docker*, pp. 55, 58.
62 S. Judd and K. Cable, *Sydney Anglicans*, Anglican Information Office, Sydney, 2000, pp. 23–25; McMillan, *The Two Lives of Joseph Docker*, p. 55.
63 McMillan, *The Two Lives of Joseph Docker*, p. 56.
64 Hardwick, DPhil thesis, p. 123.
65 Docker to Broughton, 11 July 1833, McMillan, *The Two Lives of Joseph Docker*, p. 74.
66 M.J. Read, *Aunt Spencer's Diary (1854): A Visit to Bontharambo and the North-East Victorian Goldfields*, Neptune, Newtown Victoria, 1981, p. 19.
67 Reeve, *Windsor and Richmond Gazette*, 29 June 1928; Louisa Cross to John Cross, 8 January 1833, Magistrates of Windsor and Richmond to Broughton, 3 February 1833, McMillan, *The Two Lives of Joseph Docker*, pp. 70, 92.
68 Address of the inhabitants of Windsor and Richmond to Docker, March 1833, McMillan, *The Two Lives of Joseph Docker*, p. 89.
69 Docker to Broughton, 11 July 1833, McMillan, *The Two Lives of Joseph Docker*, p. 75.
70 Docker to Broughton, 11 July 1833, McMillan, *The Two Lives of Joseph Docker*, pp. 74–75.
71 Steele, *Early Days of Windsor*, p. 153 (The White Hart Inn between Kable and Fitzgerald Streets Windsor on southern side of George Street, kept by J. Baker, Byrnes and by Hall, at the earliest period of its history in the 1830s); Magistrates to Broughton, 16 July 1833, McMillan, *The Two Lives of Joseph Docker*, p. 76.
72 J. Ritchie, ed., *The Evidence to the Bigge Reports*, Vol. 1, *The Oral Evidence*, p. 175; McMillan, *The Two Lives of Joseph Docker*, p. 66.
73 Docker to Broughton, 11 July 1833, Scarvell to Docker, 9 May 1833, McMillan, *The Two Lives of Joseph Docker*, pp. 74, 87.
74 Magistrates to Broughton, 16 July 1833, McMillan, *The Two Lives of Joseph Docker*, p. 76.
75 Magistrates to Broughton, 3 February, 16 July 1833, McMillan, *The Two Lives of Joseph Docker*, pp. 70, 76.
76 Broughton to Docker, 1 March 1833, Letter, McMillan, *The Two Lives of Joseph Docker*, pp. 71–72.
77 Docker to Broughton, 11 July 1833, McMillan, *The Two Lives of Joseph Docker*, pp. 74–75.
78 Docker to Broughton, 11 July 1833, McMillan, *The Two Lives of Joseph Docker*, p. 75.
79 Docker to Broughton, 11 July 1833, Broughton to Docker, 1 March 1833, McMillan, *The Two Lives of Joseph Docker*, p. 75, 71.
80 McMillan, *The Two Lives of Joseph Docker*, pp. 74–75.
81 John Rush Petition 27/5290 7 June 1827, John Rush, Petition 27/8059 24 August 1827, NSW State Records, Colonial Secretary's Correspondence, research by Linda Emery and Kirrilly Brentnall, for *Who Do You Think You Are?*, Artemis International and Serendipity Productions, SBS Television, 2014; Ritchie, ed., *The Evidence to the Bigge Reports*, Vol. 1, pp. 175, 213; A. Aldrich, *Journal of the Hawkesbury Historical Society: Spanning the Centuries of Hawkesbury's History*, No. 2, 2011, '1820-Conflicting Views', p. 61.
82 Louisa Cross to John Cross, 8 January 1833, McMillan, *The Two Lives of Joseph Docker*, p. 92.
83 McMillan, *The Two Lives of Joseph Docker*, p. 92.
84 McMillan, *The Two Lives of Joseph Docker*, p. 70.
85 Broughton to Magistrates, 1 March 1833, McMillan, *The Two Lives of Joseph Docker*, p. 71.
86 McMillan, *The Two Lives of Joseph Docker*, pp. 77, 83–84.
87 McMillan, *The Two Lives of Joseph Docker*, p. 92.
88 McMillan, *The Two Lives of Joseph Docker*, pp. 89–90.
89 Steele, *Early Days of Windsor*, p. 81; McMillan, *The Two Lives of Joseph Docker*, pp. 74–75, 78; Lake Macquarie Family History Group, eds, *St Matthews Parish Registers 1810 to 1856*, pp. 45–46, 151–152, 231.
90 Docker to Broughton, 11, 30 July 1833, McMillan, *The Two Lives of Joseph Docker*, pp. 74–75, 83.
91 Docker to Broughton, 11, 30 July, 6 August 1833, McMillan, *The Two Lives of Joseph Docker*, pp. 74–75, 84, 86.
92 McMillan, *The Two Lives of Joseph Docker*, p. 62.
93 Docker to Broughton, 28 July 1833, McMillan, *The Two Lives of Joseph Docker*, p. 79.
94 North to Broughton, 28 July 1833, McMillan, *The Two Lives of Joseph Docker*, p. 80.
95 Broughton to Docker, 24 July 1833, in I. McMillan, *The Two Lives of Joseph Docker*, p. 77.
96 Docker to Broughton, 1 August 1833, McMillan, *The Two Lives of Joseph Docker*, p. 86.
97 Steele, *Early Days of Windsor*, pp. 94–95. A former rector, L.M. Abbott, claims that the original pews faced the long north wall, *St Matthew's Windsor: A Short Guide to the Church and its History*, St Matthew's Anglican Church, Windsor, 2002, p. 5, but this does not agree with Standish Harris' 1824 plan, nor with Steele.
98 *Windsor and Richmond Gazette*, 6 April 1917.
99 Lake Macquarie Family History Group, eds, *St Matthews Parish Registers 1810 to 1856*, pp. 39–45, 145–151, 222–231.
100 Read, *Aunt Spencer's Diary*, pp. 19, 22.
101 Scarvell to Docker, 9 May 1833, McMillan, *The Two Lives of Joseph Docker*, p. 87.
102 Docker to Broughton, 11 July 1833, McMillan, *The Two Lives of Joseph Docker*, p. 75.

Chapter 5

1 Lake Macquarie Family History Group, eds, *St Matthews Church of England Register NSW: Parish Registers 1810 to 1856 'A Complete Transcript'*, Lake Macquarie Family History Group, 2003, p. 231, 25 August 1833, entry no. 920.

2, J. Hardwick, 'Anglican Church Expansion and Colonial Reform Politics in Bengal, New South Wales and the Cape Colony c. 1790–1850', DPhil thesis, University of York, 2008, p. 136.

3 W.W. Burton, *The State of Religion and Education in New South Wales*, Cross, London, 1840, p. 189, quoted in Steele, *Early Days of Windsor*, p. 90.

4 Burton, *The State of Religion and Education*, p. 189, quoted in Steele, *Early Days of Windsor*, pp. 89–90.

5 W. Walker, *Reminiscences (Personal, Social and Political) of a Fifty Years' Residence at Windsor on the Hawkesbury*, Turner and Henderson, Sydney, 1890, reprinted Library of Australian History, North Sydney 1977, p. 9.

6 K J. Cable, 'Stiles, Henry Tarlton (1808–1867)', *Australian Dictionary of Biography*, Australian National University, Canberra, http://adb.anu.edu.au/biography/stiles-henry-tarlton-2701/text3789, published first in hardcopy 1967, accessed 7 April 2016.

7 Lake Macquarie Family History Group, eds, *St Matthews Parish Registers 1810 to 1856*, p. 48, no. 1069; 20 April [1833], Henry Stiles; p. 51, no. 1137, 23 October 1835, George Stiles; p. 60, no. 1333, 7 March 1839, Charles Stiles baptized by J.E. Keane; p. 66, no. 1462, 16 November 1840, Samuel Stiles; p. 71, no. 1560, 23 October 1842, William Stiles; p. 85, no. 1860, 27 November 1847, Clement Stiles; p. 56, no. 1244, 8 July 1837, Mary Emma; p. 88, no. 1945, 30 October 1849, Annie Jane; p. 249, no. 4405, 13 May 1841, Samuel Stiles buried by Stiles; p. 254, no. 4495, 8 December 1842, William Stiles buried by C.C. Kemp; p. 266, no. 4741, 7 November 1849, Annie Jane Stiles buried by T.C. Ewing.

8 Lake Macquarie Family History Group, eds, *St Matthews Parish Registers 1810 to 1856*, p. 240, no. 1082.

9 Charles Fraser, James Blake in J. Ritchie, ed., *The Evidence to the Bigge Reports*, Heinemann, Melbourne, 1971, Vol. 1, *The Oral Evidence*, pp. 175–180; John Blackman, evidence, 29 November 1820, State Library of New South Wales, Mitchell Library, Bonwick Transcripts, Box 10 pp. 66474–66475; A. Aldrich, '1820-Conflicting Views', *Spanning the Centuries of Hawkesbury's History, Journal of the Hawkesbury Historical Society*, No. 2, 2011, p. 61.

10 *The Colonist*, 16 May 1838.

11 A.T. Yarwood, 'Marsden, Samuel (1765–1838)', *Australian Dictionary of Biography*, http://adb.anu.edu.au/biography/marsden-samuel-2433/text3237, 1967, accessed 8 April 2016; Ritchie, ed., *Evidence to the Bigge Reports*, Vol. 1, pp. 175–185; Vol. 2, *The Written Evidence*, pp. 92–124.

12 Lake Macquarie Family History Group, eds, *St Matthews Parish Registers 1810 to 1856*, p. 240, nos. 4197, 4199.

13 Burton, *The State of Religion and Education*, p. 189, quoted in Steele, *Early Days of Windsor*, p. 89.

14 Burton, *The State of Religion and Education*, p. 189, quoted in Steele, *Early Days of Windsor*, pp. 89–90.

15 Burton, *The State of Religion and Education*, p. 189, quoted in Steele, *Early Days of Windsor*, p. 90.

16 Steele, *Early Days of Windsor*, p. 119.

17 J. Tebbutt, *Astronomical Memoirs*, White, Sydney, 1908, reprinted Hawkesbury Shire Council, Windsor, 1986, p. 3.

18 Steele, *Early Days of Windsor*, pp. 119–120.

19 *New South Wales Police Gazette*, 4 June 1862, p. 83, ancestry.com.au, accessed 7 March 2016.

20 P. Russell, ed., *This Errant Lady: Jane Franklin's Overland Journey to Port Phillip and Sydney, 1839*, National Library of Australia, Canberra, 2002, p. 160.

21 Russell, ed., *This Errant Lady*, p. 160.

22 Russell, ed., *This Errant Lady*, p. 160.

23 *Sydney Herald*, 5 June 1841, in australianroyalty.net.au/individual.php?pid=I76378&ged, accessed 6 March 2016 [note: this marriage is not listed in the Register].

24 Alcorn family, http://australianroyalty.net.au/family.php?-famid=F15192&gedpurnellmccord.ged, accessed 7 March 2016; Lake Macquarie Family History Group, eds, *St Matthews Parish Registers 1810 to 1856*, p. 152, no. 2870; Births, Deaths and Marriages, NSW, John and Isabella Alcorn, 1857, no. 2786; Birth Register John Alcorn, 1859, no. 13555; John, 1862, no. 14759; Death Register, John Alcorn, 1859, no. 5413, ancestry.com.au.

25 Alcorn family, http://australianroyalty.net.au/family.php?-famid=F15192&ged=purnellmccord.ged, accessed 7 March 2016; Lake Macquarie Family History Group, eds, *St Matthews Parish Registers 1810 to 1856*, p. 152, 17 September 1833, no. 2870; p. 244, 16 December 1838, no. 4286; p. 268, 24 April 1851, no. 4786; Births, Deaths and Marriages, NSW, John Alcorn, 1857, no. 4713.

26 Steele, *Early Days of Windsor*, p. 85.

27 S. Judd and K. Cable, *Sydney Anglicans*, Anglican Information Office, Sydney, 1987, p. 25.

28 [W.G. Broughton], *The Journals of Visitation to the Northern and Southern Portions of his Diocese, by the Lord Bishop of Australia*, Society for Propagation of the Gospel, London, 1846.

29 Lake Macquarie Family History Group, eds, *St Matthews Parish Registers 1810 to 1856*, p. 161, 7 February 1839, no. 2969; http://www.australiandress-register.org/garment/329/, accessed 11 March 2016.

30 *Sydney Gazette*, 21 November 1835, in http://www.familytreecircles.com/u/janilye/?cat=1395, accessed 7 March 2016.

31 Steele, *Early Days of Windsor*, pp. 84–85; Lake Macquarie Family History Group, eds, *St Matthews Parish Registers 1810 to 1856*, p. 233–234, September 1834; p. 49, September 1834; pp. 52, December 1835.

32 Steele, *Early Days of Windsor*, p. 84.

33 Bishop Broughton, letter to H.T. Stiles, 8 January 1840, State Library of New South Wales, Mitchell Library, Stiles Papers, A269, pp. 40a, 40c.

34 *Historical Records of Australia*, Series 1, Vol. 18, p. 956.

35 Hardwick, DPhil thesis, pp. 138–139.

36 H. Stiles, *A Sermon preached in St. John's Church, Parramatta, May 20th, 1838, on occasion of the death of the Rev. Samuel Marsden, of Parramatta, senior chaplain of the Colony of New South Wales, Tegg, Sydney*, [1838], pp. 8–9.

37 J. Colwell, *The Illustrated History of Methodism, Australia: 1812 to 1855. New South Wales and Polynesia: 1856 to 1902*, Brooks, Sydney, 1904, pp. 99, 346.

38 H. Stiles, *A Sermon preached in St Matthew's Church, Windsor, on Sunday, December 1st, 1839, previously to the Opening of a new Wesleyan Chapel in that Town*, Tegg, Sydney, 1840, pp. 1, 8, 10.

39 'A Friend to Truth and Peace', *A Letter to the Rev. Henry Tarlton Stiles, Minister of St Matthew's, Windsor*, Tegg, Sydney, 1840, p. 3.

40 Minutes of Methodist District Meeting in Hawkesbury, in Colwell, *Illustrated History of Methodism*, p. 346.

41 Colwell, *Illustrated History of Methodism*, p. 346.

42 'A Friend to Truth and Peace', *A Letter to the Rev. Henry Tarlton Stiles*, p. 22.

43 H.T. Stiles, *A Sermon, preached at St. Matthew's Church, Windsor, on Wednesday the 18th June, 1845, before the Brethren of the United Loyal Hawkesbury Lodge, No. 7, of the Australian Supreme Grand Lodge, of the Independent Order of Odd Fellows*, Statham and Forster, Sydney, pp. 14–15. For the Oddfellows in Windsor, see Steele, *Early Days of Windsor*, p. 228.

44 Steele, *Early Days of Windsor*, p. 87.

45 The only known copy of the petition is State Library of New South Wales, Dixson Library, D87/73.

46 http://www.australiaonnet.com/about-australia/famous-australians/john-tebbutt.html, accessed 7 March 2016.

47 Steele, *Early Days of Windsor*, p. 87.

48 Steele, *Early Days of Windsor*, pp. 85–86.

49 Walker, *Reminiscences*, pp. 8, 10 (Walker was an eye-witness in the late 1830s); W.F. Carter, *Cathedral of the Hawkesbury*, n.d., p. 13; Steele, *Early Days of Windsor*, pp. 141–142. For the bandmaster, see Carol Carruthers, 'Sgt Samuel Edgerton', *Hawkesbury Historical Society Newsletter*, 84, June 2009, pp. 1–3.

50 Steele, *Early Days of Windsor*, p. 86; Carter, *Cathedral of the Hawkesbury*, p. 33.

51 Steele, *Early Days of Windsor*, p. 86; Carter, *Cathedral of the Hawkes-

bury, p. 33; D. Rushworth, *Historic Organs of New South Wales: The Instruments, their Makers and Players, 1791–1940,* Hale & Iremonger, Sydney, 1988, pp. 63–66, 68. For the correct date of the Johnson-Tompson wedding, see Lake Macquarie Family History Group, eds, *St Matthews Parish Registers, 1810–1856*, p. 160, item 2954.

52 *Report of Diocesan Committee of the Societies for Propagation of the Gospel in Foreign Parts and for Promotion of Christian Knowledge for 1840*, Sydney, 1841, pp. 40, 45.

53 *Sydney Morning Herald*, 22 October 1840, quoted in Rushworth, *Historic Organs*, p. 65.

54 Quoted in Steele, *Early Days of Windsor*, pp. 75–76.

55 *Sydney Gazette*, 15 January 1824.

56 St Matthew's Anglican Church Archives [SMACA], Minute Book, 1837–1885, 17 August 1840; Wardens' Account Book, plan of interior on inside back cover.

57 Steele, *Early Days of Windsor*, p. 82.

58 SMACA, Wardens' Account Book, 20 June 1840; abstract of accounts, 1840–1841.

59 *Report of Diocesan Committee of the Societies for Propagation of the Gospel in Foreign Parts and for Promotion of Christian Knowledge for 1840*, p. 63.

60 SMACA, Wardens' Account Book, 22 November 1845.

61 *Report of Diocesan Committee of the Societies for Propagation of the Gospel in Foreign Parts and for Promotion of Christian Knowledge for 1840*, p. 63.

62 SMACA, Wardens' Account Book, 22 November 1845. Carter, *Cathedral of the Hawkesbury*, p. 13, gives the date as 1846 and the information about the earlier wooden font. The placement of the stone font is shown on the plan of the church drawn on the inside back cover of the Wardens' Account Book some time between 1845 and 1857.

63 Peter Robinson, *A Short History and Guide for St Thomas' Mulgoa*, St Thomas' Church, Mulgoa, 1988. The author gives no information about any font at St Thomas' Church.

64 Information from St Thomas' Church, Mulgoa.

65 SMACA, Wardens' Account Book, 22 November 1845.

66 Judd and Cable, *Sydney Anglicans*, pp. 70–73; G.S. Maple, 'Barker, Frederic', in B. Dickey, ed., *The Australian Dictionary of Evangelical Biography*, Evangelical History Association, Sydney, 1994, pp. 22–24.

67 Russell, ed., *This Errant Lady*, p. 160.

68 SMACA, Wardens' Account Book, 23 July 1844 (Panton), 1 May, 29 November 1844, 12 February 1845 (Atkinson); Minute Book, 1837–1885, 29 July 1844 (Churchwardens).

69 Steele, *Early Days of Windsor*, p. 86.

70 Steele, *Early Days of Windsor*, p. 86.

71 Stiles to Colonial Secretary, 3 February 1834, SRNSW, Colonial Secretary's correspondence, Reel 726, 4/2226.5, 34/77.

72 SMACA, Minute Book, 1837–1885, 16 January 1854.

73 SMACA, Wardens' Account Book, 16 January 1855.

74 SMACA, Minute Book, 1837–1885, Easter Tuesday [10 April] 1855.

75 SMACA, Minute Book, 1837–1885, April 1855.

76 SMACA, Minute Book, 1837–1885, 9, 28 May 1855.

77 SMACA, Minute Book, 1837–1885, 5 August, 5 November, 21 November, 17 December 1855, 5 January 1856.

78 SMACA, Minute Book, 1837–1885, 21 November 1855; Wardens' Account Book, 1, 31 August 1855.

79 Carter, *Cathedral of the Hawkesbury*, p. 13.

80 SMACA, Minute Book, 1837–1885, Subscription list 1857; 6 February, 26 September 1857, 18 January 1858; Wardens' Account Book, 6 February, 8 March 1857. For Fitzgerald, see D.G. Bowd, *Macquarie Country: A History of the Hawkesbury*, rev. ed. 1973, pp. 112–113.

81 *Town and Country Journal*, 24 January 1874, p. 141; Lake Macquarie Family History Group, eds, *St Matthews Parish Registers 1810 to 1856*, p. 272, no. 4883 (Catherine Roxburgh). Louisa Fitzgerald, an infant, was buried at St Matthew's on 31 January 1854 (p. 273, no. 4900)

82 F. Walker, letter to the editor, *Daily Telegraph*, 16 August 1919, p. 8; Steele. *Early Days of Windsor*, p. 86.

83 J. Burnswoods and J. Fletcher, *Sydney and the Bush: A Pictorial History of Education in New South Wales*, NSW Department of Education, Sydney, 1980, p. 103; Graham Jahn, *Sydney Architecture*, Watermark Press, Sydney, 1997, pp. 58, 66, 216.

84 SMACA, Minute Book, 1837–1885, 3, 7 April, 7 May, 21 June 1858; Wardens' Account Book, 22 June, 7 September, 7, 17 November 1858.

85 SMACA, Wardens' Account Book, 19, 24 July, 28 August, 10 September, 12 October 1858.

86 SMACA, Minute Book, 1837–1885, Easter Tuesday 1855; 24 April, 9, 28 May 1855; 15 March, 23 June 1858; Wardens' Account Book, plan of church before the alterations of 1858, inside back cover.

87 SMACA, Minute Book, 1837–1885, 23 January 1860; Wardens' Account Book, 10 April 1860, abstract 1861–1862.

88 *The Maitland Mercury and Hunter River General Advertiser*, 21 June 1864; R. Roxburgh, *Early Colonial Houses of New South Wales*, Ure Smith, Sydney, 1974, p. 268.

89 *Sydney Morning Herald*, 15 June 1864.

90 *Australian Almanac, 1867* in *Windsor and Richmond Gazette*, 7 October 1911.

91 *Sydney Morning Herald*, 2 July 1867.

92 *Sydney Morning Herald*, 2 July 1867.

93 *Sydney Morning Herald*, 2 July 1867.

94 *Sydney Morning Herald*, 28 February 1936.

95 *Sydney Morning Herald*, 28 February 1936.

96 *Windsor and Richmond Gazette*, 7 April 1922.

97 *Windsor and Richmond Gazette*, 7 April 1922; *Sydney Morning Herald*, 16 June 1865, 12 July 1867.

98 *Windsor and Richmond Gazette*, 25 November 1932.

99 Steele, *Early Days of Windsor*, pp. 90–91, 192; Bowd, *Macquarie Country*, pp. 19–20.

Chapter 6

1 C.S. Maple, 'Barker, Frederic', B. Dickey, ed., *The Australian Dictionary of Evangelical Biography*, Evangelical History Association, Sydney, 1994, p. 26.

2 K.J. Cable 'Garnsey, Charles Frederick (1828–1894)', *Australian Dictionary of Biography*, http://adb.anu.edu.au/biography/garnsey-charles-frederick-3593/text5569, published first in hard copy 1972, accessed 22 April 2016.

3 J. Steele, *Early Days of Windsor*, Tyrrell's, Sydney, 1916, reprinted Library of Australian History, North Sydney, 1977, p. 127; *Empire*, 19, 20 September 1860.

4 Cable. 'Garnsey, Charles'. *Australian Dictionary of Biography*.

5 Cable, 'Garnsey, Charles', *Australian Dictionary of Biography*.

6 *Sydney Morning Herald*, 12 June 1875.

7 St Matthew's Anglican Church Archives [SMACA], Minute Book, 1837–1885, 23 August, 29 October 1866.

8 *Sydney Morning Herald*, 12 July 1867; *Windsor and Richmond Gazette*, 7 April 1922; Cable, 'Garnsey, Charles', *Australian Dictionary of Biography*.

9 SMACA, Wardens' Account Book, 28 February1867.

10 SMACA, Minute Book, 1837–1885, 11 October 1870.

11 SMACA, Minute Book, 1837–1885, 11 October 1870; Wardens' Account Book, 1870, 1871.

12 G.M. Dow, *Samuel Terry, the Botany Bay Rothschild*, Sydney University Press, Sydney, 1974, pp. 230–231; Steele, *Early Days of Windsor*, p. 93. The name of the maker of the first five windows at St Matthew's is known from a garbled account naming the firm as 'Wills, Son, and Strong' in the local Windsor newspaper, the *Australian*, 24 January 1874. For Wailes and his son-in-law Thomas Strang, see R. Torbet, *The Wonderful Windows of William Wailes*, Scotforth Books, Lancaster, 2003.

13 Marjorie Lenehan, 'Rouse, Richard (1774–1852)', *Australian Dictionary of Biography*, http://adb.anu.edu.au/biography/rouse-richard-2612/text3601, published first in hard copy 1967, accessed 26 April 2016; Steele, *Early Days of Windsor*, p. 93.

14 Steele, *Early Days of Windsor*, p. 93.

15 R. Teale, 'Hordern, Anthony (1819–1876)', *Australian Dictionary of Biography*, http://adb.anu.edu.au/biography/hordern-anthony-3796/text6009, published first in hard copy 1972, accessed 27 April 2016; Steele, *Early Days*

of Windsor, p. 93; *Australian*, 24 January 1874; Lake Macquarie Family History Group, eds, *St Matthews Church of England Windsor NSW: Parish Registers 1810 to 1856 'A Complete Transcription'*, Lake Macquarie Family History Group, Teralba, 2003, p. 165, item 3010.
16 W. Walker, *Reminiscences (Personal, Social and Political) of a Fifty Years' Residence at Windsor on the Hawkesbury*, Turner and Henderson, Sydney, 1890, reprinted Library of Australian History, North Sydney, 1977, p. 26.
17 SMACA, Minute Book, 1931–1957, pp. 239, 241, 24, 244, 274; Paine to Ashwin, 14 August 1944, inserted between pp. 352 and 353.
18 D.G. Bowd, ed., *Monuments, Memorials and Plaques in the Hawkesbury Shire*, Hawkesbury Historical Society, Windsor, 1988, pp. 39–40.
19 Bowd, ed., *Monuments, Memorials and Plaques in the Hawkesbury Shire*, pp. 39–40.
20 Statutory Declaration by Arthur Clifton Hoskisson, in State Records NSW, Primary Application, 17513/43/192/36240, item 27.
21 Quoted in W.F. Carter, *The Cathedral of the Hawkesbury: A Sketch of St. Matthew's Windsor*, n.d., p. 27.
22 J. Carter, *Eyes to the Future: Sketches of Australia and Her Neighbours in the 1870s*, pp. 89–90, copyright to National Library of Australia, at https://books.google.com.au/books?id=92EwAgAAQBAJ&pg=PT106&lpg=PT106&dq=Reverend+Garnsey+Windsor&source=bl&ots=LQ4djr2R-6j&sig=N51dRb92g1qrsxvGM0e71YTOqBE&hl=en&sa=X&ved=0ahUKEwixqsvywPzLAhWoFaYKHTNkB4I4ChDoAQgfMAE#v=onepage&q=Reverend%20Garnsey%20Windsor&f=false, accessed 7 April 2016.
23 *Protestant Standard*, 4 March 1871.
24 *Sydney Morning Herald*, 24 December 1874; Protestant Standard, 4 March 1871.
25 Steele, *Early Days of Windsor*, pp. 91–92.
26 Cable, 'Garnsey, Charles'. *Australian Dictionary of Biography*.
27 Steele, *Early Days of Windsor*, pp. 91–92.
28 'Langley, Rt Rev. Henry Archdall', *Who Was Who*, Black, 1920–2008; online edn, Oxford University Press, December 2007, accessed 26 May 2012: I.V. Hansen, 'Langley, Henry Thomas (1877–1968)', *Australian Dictionary of Biography*, http://adb.anu.edu.au/biography/langley-henry-thomas-10785/text19127, published first in hard copy 2000, accessed 9 April 2016; Macquarie Family History Group, eds, *St Matthews Parish Registers 1857 to 1900*, p. 59 item 1309.
29 Steele, *Early Days of Windsor*, p. 92.
30 Steele, *Early Days of Windsor*, pp. 83, 92; Bowd, Macquarie Country, p. 67; SMACA, Minute Book, 1886–1918, pp. 268–269.
31 Steele. *Early Days of Windsor*, p. 92.
32 *Hawkesbury Gazette*, 22 June 1974.
33 Steele, *Early Days of Windsor*, p. 93; Hawkesbury Family History Group, *Hawkesbury Pioneer Register*, Vol. 2, p. 186, nos 479, 480; Macquarie Family History Group, eds, *St Matthews Parish Registers 1857 to 1900*, pp. 168, item 1270; p. 179, item 3357; p. 283, item 5054.
34 SMACA, Minute Book, 1837–1885, 4 November 1883; Carter, *Cathedral of the Hawkesbury*, p. 21.
35 SMACA, Minute Book, 1837–1885, 21, 23 January, [July], 3 November 1884.
36 *Hawkesbury Chronicle and Farmers' Advocate*, 2 February 1884.
37 SMACA, Minute Book, 1837–1885, 21 January 1884.
38 Steele, *Early Days of Windsor*, p. 92; Macquarie Family History Group, eds, *St Matthews Parish Registers 1857 to 1900*, p. 63, item 1388; p. 76, item 1694; p. 256, item 4519; p. 259, item 4581.
39 SMACA, Minute Book, 1886–1918, pp. 46–53, 113;
40 Steele, *Early Days of Windsor*, p. 94.
41 Dorothy d'Arcy-Irvine, typescript of talk about her father, Gerard d'Arcy-Irvine, to the Church of England Historical Society in Sydney, 7 February 1974, Hawkesbury Library, Local Studies, Vertical Files, sub St Matthew's Anglican Church.
42 SMACA, Minute Book, 1886–1918, pp. 112–114; letter from Sulman, 30 September 1891 inserted between pp. 113 and 114; Carter, *Cathedral of the Hawkesbury*, p. 21.
43 SMACA, Minute Book, 1886–1918, pp. 116, 120, 122–123, 136.
44 SMACA, Minute Book, 1886–1918, pp. 134–135.
45 SMACA, Minute Book, 1931–1957, p. 414.
46 SMACA, Minute Book, 1886–1918, pp. 90–93, 95.
47 D. d'Arcy-Irvine, talk 1974.
48 *Hawkesbury Herald*, 9 January 1903, https://www.elephind.com, accessed 8 May 2016.
49 SMACA, Minute Book, 1886–1918, pp. 168–170; Steele, *Early Days of Windsor*, pp. 94–95.
50 *Windsor and Richmond Gazette*, 29 October 1898
51 *The Colonist*, Vol. 46, issue 10627, 28 January 1903, http://paperspast.natlib.govt.nz/cgi-bin/paperspast?a=d&d=TC19030128.2.8, accessed 8 May 2016.
52 Ruth Fielding, 'A Johnson Family History', State Library of New South Wales, Mitchell Library, ML MSS 5582/5.
53 Steele, *Early Days of Windsor*, p. 95; Sally O'Neill, 'Fielding, Una Lucy (1888–1969)', *Australian Dictionary of Biography*, http://adb.anu.edu.au/biography/fielding-una-lucy-10178/text17983, published first in hard copy 1996, accessed 9 April 2016
54 *Windsor and Richmond Gazette*, 1 September 1900; page proofs of *Down to the Sea in Ships*, State Library of New South Wales, Mitchell Library, ML MSS 7285/2/5. http://acms.sl.nsw.gov.au/item/itemdetailpaged.aspx-?itemid=431433, accessed 8 May 2016.
55 Wikipedia, https://en.wikipedia.org/wiki/Down_to_the_Sea_in_Ships_(1922_film, accessed 7 May 2016.
56 King James version, Psalm 107, verses 23, 24.
57 *Windsor and Richmond Gazette*, 20 October 1900.
58 Caroline Hogarth (née Cobcroft), interview by Jan Barkley-Jack, 1980s.
59 *Hawkesbury Herald*, 9 January 1903.
60 *Hawkesbury Herald*, 11 September 1903; transcription, janilye 2014
61 *Hawkesbury Herald*, 19 June 1903.
62 *Hawkesbury Herald*, 27 May 1904.
63 'New Zealand Tablet', *Intercolonial*, Vol. 32, Issue 26, 30 June 1904, http://paperspast.natlib.govt.nz/cgi-bin/paperspast?a=d&d=NZT19040630.2.66, accessed 8 May 2016.
64 *Sydney Morning Herald*, 26 December 1904, p. 5.
65 *Hawkesbury Herald*, 13 May 1904.

Chapter 7

1 *Historical Records NSW* [*HRNSW*], Vol. 7, p. 530.
2 Ellis Bent to his mother, 4 March 1809, in J.V. Byrnes, 'An Outcast Goat or the Life and Times of Andrew Thompson', MA thesis, University of Sydney, 1957, p. 245.
3 Lachlan Macquarie, Governor of New South Wales, *Journals of his Tours in New South Wales and Van Diemen's Land 1810–1822*, Library of Australian History, Sydney, 1979, pp. 23, 27–28, 30–31.
4 Macquarie, *Journals*, pp. 27–28.
5 Government and General Orders, 7 January 1810, in *Sydney Gazette,* 14 January 1810.
6 Sydney Gazette, 3 November 1810; Lake Macquarie Family History Group, eds, *St Matthew's Church of England Register NSW: Parish Registers 1810 to 1856 'A Complete Transcript'*, Lake Macquarie Family History Group, 2003, p. 181, item 3172, 25 October 1810.
7 *Sydney Gazette*, 3 November 1810.
8 Macquarie, *Journals*, pp. 27–28.
9 J. Barkley and M. Nichols, *Hawkesbury 1794–1994: 200 Years of the Second Colonisation*, Hawkesbury City Council, Windsor, 1994, p. 42.
10 State Records NSW, extracts from Superintendent's Day book, signed by William Cox,
Colonial Secretary's Correspondence, Reel 6017, 4/5782, pp. 54–55.
11 Hawkesbury Regional Museum, Minute Book of Hawkesbury Historical Society, 1960.
12 *Sydney Gazette*, 3 November 1810.
13 Macquarie. *Journal*, p. 42, 12 January 1811.
14 Edna Hickson, 'Cox, William (1764–1837)', *Australian Dictionary of Biography*, Australian National University, http://adb.anu.edu.au/biography/cox-william-1934/text2309, published first in hard copy 1966, accessed 17 April 2016; Old Register of Assignments and other Legal Instruments, in L. Sabine, ed., Old Register 1 to 9, NSW Lands Department, NSW Commerce

Department and State Records NSW, 2008, 27 March 1802, Book 1, p. 18, item 91; Grants of Land Register 3, 136(2) William and James Cox, 16 July 1804; R. Cox, *William Cox: Blue Mountains Road Builder and Pastoralist,* Rosenberg, Kenthurst, 2012, pp. 73–74.

15 Macquarie, *Journals*, pp. 41–42.

16 Macquarie, *Journals*, p. 42.

17 State Records NSW, Reel 2623, SZ901, Field Book 83.

18 State Records NSW, Reel 6002, 4/3490D, 2 February 1811, 56, 26 December 1810.

19 *HRNSW*, Vol. 7, p.530.

20 *HRNSW*, Vol. 7, p. 530.

21 Lake Macquarie Family History Group, eds, *St Matthew's Church of England Windsor NSW: Parish Registers 1810 to 1856*, pp. 181–182.

22 Lake Macquarie Family History Group, eds, *St Matthews Parish Registers 1810 to 1856*, p. 181; *HRNSW*, Vol. 7, p. 530.

23 *Sydney Gazette*, 22 December 1810.

24 Macquarie, *Journals*, pp. 23, 28, 30–31; R. Ian Jack, *Exploring the Hawkesbury*, Kangaroo Press, Kenthurst, 2nd ed., 1990, p. 87.

25 Lake Macquarie Family History Group, eds, *St Matthews Parish Registers 1810 to 1856*, pp. 182–184.

26 Lake Macquarie Family History Group, eds, *St Matthews Parish Registers 1810 to 1856,* p. 183, item 3208, 7 January 1812.

27 Lake Macquarie Family History Group, eds, *St Matthews Parish Registers 1810 to 1856,* p. 183, items 3207, 3218; p. 184, item 3223.

.28 Lake Macquarie Family History Group, eds, *St Matthews Parish Registers 1810 to 1856*, pp. 182–184; p. 183, item 3206, 27 December 1811 Austin Forrest; p. 183, item 3212, 8 February 1812, James Thompson.

29 Lake Macquarie Family History Group, eds, *St Matthews Parish Registers 1810 to 1856*, p. 183, item 3212, 8 February 1812 James Thompson.

30 J. Barkley-Jack, *Hawkesbury Settlement Revealed: A New Look at Australia's Third Mainland Settlement*, Rosenberg, Kenthurst, 2009, pp. 51–52, 178, 181–182, 184; Lake Macquarie Family History Group, eds, *St Matthews Parish Registers, 1810–1856*, p. 184, item 3223, 9 May 1812, John Merriott.

31 All transcriptions, grave descriptions and grave details, Jan Barkley-Jack, June 2009–2016.

32 *Biographical Dictionary of Australia* [*BDA*] online, search for John Marrott and John Merritt, accessed 13 July 2016.

33 Land Grants Register 2, p. 385, James Cunningham and Land Grant Register 3, p. 19, 1 May 1797, Lewis Curry and James Payne, Land and Property Information, reproduced in Barkley-Jack, *Hawkesbury Settlement Revealed*, p. 435.

34 C. Baxter, ed., *Musters of New South Wales and Norfolk Island 1805–1806*, Australian Biographical and Genealogical Record in association with the Society of Australian Genealogists, Sydney, 1989, pp. 138–139, John Marriott BO568 'Sherrard's Farm Caddi'; pp. 132–133 James Sherrard BO345 'Purchase Bradley Hawkesbury'; State Records NSW, Primary Application 17513/32/170/33287-01, items 5 and 6, 12 October 1808, signed by William Baker, and witnessed by Thomas Broadhurst; BDAonline, at http://www.bdaonline.org.au, accessed 13 July 2015;

35 John Marrott, History Australia: Convict Stockade at http://www.historyaustralia.org.au/ twconvic/716.

36 See Appendix 2.

37 Lake Macquarie Family History Group, eds, *St Matthews Parish Registers 1810 to 1856*, p. 184, no. 3226, 22 May1812, Richard Alcorn; p. 139, no. 2719, 8 February 1825, Richard Alcorn and Charlotte Gullidge; p. 152, no. 2870, 17 September 1833, John Alcorn and Mary Ann Cross; p. 141, no. 2742, 14 November 1825, John Brown and Elizabeth Alcorn; p. 229, no. 3981, 2 May 1832, Sarah Alcorn.

38 Lake Macquarie Family History Group, eds, *St Matthews Parish Registers, 1810–1856*, p. 184, item 3227, 25 May 1812, Edward Martin.

39 Lake Macquarie Family History Group, eds, *St Matthews Parish Registers, 1810–1856*, pp. 184–185; p. 184, item 3229, 16 June 1812, Julianna Franklin.

40 Lake Macquarie Family History Group, eds, *St Matthews Parish Registers, 1810–1856*, pp. 185–186; p. 185, item 3244, 20 January 1813, Margaret Ralph; p. 186, item 3263, 8 October 1813 Elizabeth Waring; Barkley-Jack, *Hawkesbury Settlement Revealed*, pp. 58–59.

41 Lake Macquarie Family History Group, eds, *St Matthews Parish Registers, 1810–1856*, p. 186, item 3269, 27 December 1813, John Smith; p. 186, item 3270, 27 December 1813, Sarah Barnes.

42 Lake Macquarie Family History Group, eds, *St Matthews Parish Registers, 1810–1856*, p. 189, item 3317, 19 September 1815, Mary Hollis; p. 190, item 3330, February 1816, 18 February 1816, Patrick Brady; p. 191, item 3345, 24 October 1816, Benjamin Hookham (in South Creek); p. 181, item 3349, 26 December 1816, Moses Davis; p. 192, item 3352, 3 March 1817, Simon Carney; pp. 185–192; p. 192, item 3353, 3 March 1817, Thomas Hassing; p. 191, item 3344, 19 October 1816, October 1816, Mary Ezzy.

43 Lake Macquarie Family History Group, eds, *St Matthews Parish Registers, 1810–1856*, p. 191, item 3346, 30 November 1816, Robert White; p. 191, item 3337, 1 April 1816, James Bennett; p. 190, item 3335, 19 March 1816, Charles White (snakebite); p. 191, item 3339, 12 April 1816, Patrick Grady; p. 189, item 3317, 22 September 1815, Mary Hollis (drowned); p. 190, item 3332, n.d. February 1816, John Anderson (murdered); p. 191, item 3342, 5 September 1816, Thomas Wright (murdered); p. 189, item 3306, 14 March 1815, Charles Williams; Barkley-Jack, *Hawkesbury Settlement Revealed*, pp. 80–88.

44 Lake Macquarie Family History Group, eds, *St Matthews Parish Registers, 1810–1856*, p. 187, item 3275, 15 January 1814, Thomas West; p. 190, item 3334, 7 March 1816, George Smith; p. 189, item 3320, 18 November 1815, Phoebe Cussley.

45 Lake Macquarie Family History Group, eds, *St Matthews Parish Registers, 1810–1856*, p. 190, item 3322, 12 December 1815, John Benn; p. 249, item 4396, 12 April 1841, John Griffin; J. Barkley-Jack, 'Early Boat Building on the Upper Hawkesbury', in J. Powell, ed., *Cross Currents*, Deerubbin Press, Berowra Heights, 1997, p. 43.

46 William Gaudry at australianroyalty.net.au/individual.php?pid=I52519&ged...ged, accessed 17 April 2016; *Sydney Gazette*, 15 December 1810; p. 190, item 3324, 5 January 1815, William Gaudry.

47 Lake Macquarie Family History Group, eds, *St Matthews Parish Registers, 1810–1856*, pp. 192–194.

48 Lake Macquarie Family History Group, eds, *St Matthews Parish Registers, 1810–1856*, p. 196, item 3429,7 March 1819, Rebecca Cox; p. 240, item 4198, 20 March 1837, William Cox.

49 Lake Macquarie Family History Group, eds, *St Matthews Parish Registers, 1810–1856*, p. 202, item 3522, 6 May 1821, Thomas Arndell.

50 Lake Macquarie Family History Group, eds, *St Matthews Parish Registers, 1810–1856*, p. 200, item 3488, 5 September 1820, Ann Bladdey; Barkley-Jack, *Hawkesbury Settlement Revealed*, pp. 151, 259, 390–391, 395.

51 Lake Macquarie Family History Group, eds, *St Matthews Parish Registers, 1810–1856*, p. 199, item 3475, 4 June 1820, George Loder; 1834, George Loder; p. 264, item 4701, 20 August 1848, George Loder; p. 233, item 4063, 14 August, George Loder at Australian Royalty, http://australianroyalty.net.au/individual.php?pid=I52145&ged=purnellmccord.ged, accessed 20 April 2016.

52 Lake Macquarie Family History Group, eds, *St Matthews Parish Registers, 1810–1856*, p. 211, item 3653, 10 July 1824, Thomas Dargin.

53 Lake Macquarie Family History Group, eds, *St Matthews Parish Registers, 1810–1856*, p. 200, item 3491, 14 September 1820, George Black.

54 Lake Macquarie Family History Group, eds, *St Matthews Parish Registers, 1810–1856*, p. 204, item 3561, 28 April 1822, Richard Fitzgerald jr; J. Barkley-Jack, *Toongabbie's Government Farm: An Elusive Vision for Five Governors 1791–1824*, Toongabbie and District Historical Society, 2013, pp. 14–15, 17–18, 53–54.

55 Lake Macquarie Family History Group, eds, *St Matthews Parish Registers, 1810–1856*, p. 207, item 3596, 17 February 1823.

56 Transcription by Jan Barkley-Jack, 1998.

57 Lake Macquarie Family History Group, eds, *St Matthews Registers, 1810 to 1856*, p. 239, no. 4193.

58 Nancy Gray, 'Howe, John (1774–1852)', *Australian Dictionary of Biography*, National Centre of Biography, Australian National University, http://adb.anu.edu.au/biography/howe-john-2205/text2855, published first in hard copy 1966, accessed 17 April 2016.

59 Australian Royalty at http://australianroyalty.net.au/individual.php?pid=I52345&ged =purnellmccord.ged, accessed 17 April 2016.

60 Lake Macquarie Family History Group, eds, *St Matthews Registers, 1810 to 1856*, p. 217, no. 3735 (Sovereign 1795 Gentleman 72 years).
61 M. Carty, *William Broughton and the Kennedy Connection: A Young Adventurer, his Two Families and his Pioneer Relations*, author, 1987, 66–69; Lake Macquarie Family History Group, eds, *St Matthews Parish Registers, 1810 to 1856*, p. 217, item 3735.
62 B. Hardy, *Early Hawkesbury Settlers*, Kangaroo Press, Kenthurst, 1985, pp. 153–154; Lake Macquarie Family History Group, eds, *St Matthews Registers, 1810 to 1856*, p. 215, item 3707.
63 Lake Macquarie Family History Group, eds, *St Matthews Registers, 1810 to 1856*, p. 205, item 3561, p. 254, item 4492; J. Barkley-Jack, unpublished study of St Matthew's cemetery, 1998.
64 Lake Macquarie Family History Group, eds, *St Matthews Registers, 1810 to 1856*, p. 279, item 5030.
65 Lake Macquarie Family History Group, eds, *St Matthews Registers, 1810 to 1856*, p. 222, item 3854; p. 223, item 3865; p. 230, item 4000; p. 249, item 4385; p. 231, item 4025; p. 244, item 4294.
66 Lake Macquarie Family History Group, eds, *St Matthews Registers, 1810 to 1856*, p. 204, item 355; p. 269, items 4801, 4811; p. 277, item 4970; p. 304, item 3551.
67 Lake Macquarie Family History Group, eds, *St Matthews Registers, 1901 to 1950*, p. 300, item 4350.
68 Lake Macquarie Family History Group, eds, *St Matthews Register1857 to 1900*, p. 264, item 4669; p. 265, item 4706.
69 https://stoneletters.com/blog/gravestone-symbols, accessed 10 May 2016; list is provided by The International Association of Cemetery Preservationists, http://www.thecemeteryclub.com/symbols.html, accessed 10 May 2016.
70 E. Dethlefsen and J. Deetz, 'Death's Heads, Cherubs and Willow Trees: Experimental Archaeology in Colonial Cemeteries', *American Antiquity*, Vol. 31, 1966, pp. 502–508.
71 Trish Moon, 'Stoned and Fallen Angels of the Hawkesbury', unpublished paper, 2008, pp. 1–7.
72 Lake Macquarie Family History Group, eds, *St Matthews Registers 1810 to 1856*, p. 279, item 5017; *St Matthews Registers 1857 to 1900*, p. 268, item 4757; Barkley-Jack transcription, 1998.
73 Steele, *Early Days of Windsor*, pp. 220–222; Bowd, *Macquarie Country*, pp. 117, 178; Lake Macquarie Family History Group, eds, St Matthews Registers, 1810 to 1856, p. 278, item 5007.
74 St Matthew's Anglican Church Archives [SMACA], Minute Book,1837–1885, 9 January 1863.
75 State Records NSW, Map 1975.
76 *HRNSW*, Vol. 7, pp. 530, 531.
77 *Sydney Gazette*, 11, 18 May 1811.
78 *Sydney Gazette*, 27 October 1811.
79 *Sydney Gazette*, 30 January 1813.
80 *Sydney Gazette*, 11 May 1811; Bowd, *Macquarie Country*, p. 71.
81 *Historical Records of Australia*, Series 1, Vol. 10, p. 693, 27 July 1822.
82 Royal Australian Historical Society, manuscript Red M 186.
83 SMACA, Minute Book, 1837–1885, 22 August 1882.
84 Barkley-Jack, 'Communicating Tourism', item 6.
85 SMACA, Wardens' Accounts.
86 SMACA, Wardens' Accounts, 30 July, 1 December 1849.
87 SMACA, Minute Book, 1837–1885, 22 August 1882, 27 March 1883, 7 January, [July] 1884.
88 Hawkesbury City Library, photograph 006418.
89 State Library of New South Wales, Mitchell Library, C 226, reel CY 1035.
90 Land and Property Information, Crown Plan, W 443a.
91 Harris, 'Report and Estimates', State Library of New South Wales, Mitchell Library, C 226, reel CY 1035, Windsor p. 4.
92 Frederic Terry, *Landscape Scenery, Illustrating Sydney, Paramatta, Richmond, Maitland, Windsor and Port Jackson, New South Wales*, also known as *Australian Keepsake*, Sands and Kenny, Sydney and Melbourne, 1855, plate 30, reprinted as *New South Wales Illustrated*, Lansdowne, Sydney, 1973.
93 *Windsor and Richmond Gazette*, 21 April 1900.

Chapter 8

1 Lachlan Macquarie, Governor of New South Wales, *Journals of his Tours in New South Wales and Van Diemen's Land 1810–1822*, Library of Australian History, Sydney, 1979, p. 42.
2 State Records NSW, Church Lands, 2/1845, 5 May 1828; Land Titles, Register 10 p. 98.
3 J. Steele, *Early Days of Windsor*, Tyrrell's, Sydney, 1916, reprinted Library of Australian History, North Sydney, 1977, p. 3.
4 State Records NSW, Map 1856.
5 Land and Property Information, Crown Plan, C909.690.
6 Steele, *Early Days of Windsor*, p. 68. The buildings on Cartwright's farm are shown on the watercolour panorama of the Hawkesbury at Windsor during the 1816 flood, State Library of New South Wales, Mitchell Library, PX*D 264.
7 Evidence of Robert Cartwright, J. Ritchie, ed., *The Evidence to the Bigge Reports*, Vol. 1, *The Oral Evidence*, Heinemann, Melbourne, 1971, p. 156.
8 Evidence of Samuel Marsden, Ritchie, ed., *The Evidence to the Bigge Reports*, Vol. 1, p. 119.
9 State Records NSW, Returns of Colony, reel 1409, 4/251, pp. 51–53; 4/252, pp. 172–175.
10 State Records NSW, Returns of Colony, reel 1409, 4/251, pp. 51–53; 4/252, pp. 172–175; 4/253, pp. 82–85; 4/254, pp. 66–69; 4/255, pp. 66–69.
11 *Historical Records of Australia* [*HRA*], Series 1, Vol. 9, p. 354.
12 *HRA*, Series 1, Vol. 10, p. 691.
13 *Sydney Gazette*, 30 October 1823.
14 State Records NSW, Church Lands, 2/1846, 42/5500.
15 Government land in Windsor, c.1828, State Records NSW, Surveyors' Sketchbooks, reel 2778, Vol. 1, B8; Church Lands, 2/1846, 34/5020.
16 State Records NSW, reel 1409, 4/252, pp. 122–125.
17 *Sydney Gazette*, 7 October 1824.
18 *Sydney Gazette*, 3 October 1825 (the statement of receipts and disbursements for the colony for the year ending 31 December 1824); State Records NSW, Colonial Secretary's Correspondence, reel 6070, 4/6038, p. 52.
19 'Plans of Buildings by John Verge', Macarthur Papers, Vol. 222, Mitchell Library, reel CY 748, PXD 188.
20 *Sydney Gazette*, 30 October 1823, 3, 7 October 1824.
21 Rachel Roxburgh, *Early Colonial Houses of New South Wales,* Ure Smith, Sydney, 1974, pp. 266–267.
22 James Broadbent, *The Australian Colonial House: Architecture and Society in New South Wales, 1788–1842*, Sydney, 1997, p. 207.
23 State Records NSW, Returns of the Colony, reel 1409, 4/253, pp. 82–85.
24 Roxburgh, *Early Colonial Houses*, p. 267.
25 Minutes of the Church and Schools Committee, quoted in Steele, *Early Days of Windsor.*
26 State Records NSW, Stiles to Colonial Secretary, 17 February 1834, 34/1135.
27 Steele, *Early Days of Windsor*, p. 81; State Records NSW, Returns of the Colony, reel 1410, 4/265, p. 144.
28 State Records NSW, Stiles to Colonial Secretary, 17 February 1834, 34/1135.
29 State Records NSW, Stiles to Colonial Secretary, 17 February 1834, 34/1135.
30 P. Russell, ed., *This Errant Lady: Jane Franklin's Overland Journey to Port Phillip and Sydney, 1839*, National Library of Australia, Canberra, 2002, p. 160.
31 See above, chapter 5.
32 Roxburgh, *Early Colonial Houses*, p. 270.
33 State Records NSW, Returns of Colony, reel 1409, 4/263; Reel 1410, 4/264, p. 146.
34 J. Armstrong, 'Plan of the New & Old Glebe adjoining the Town of Windsor', 1837, Mitchell Library, ZM2 811.1122/1837/1.
35 St Matthew's Anglican Church Archives [SMACA], Minute Book, 1837–1885, parish statistics for 1880–1 and 1881–2 attached to minutes, 11 April 1882. The income from the glebe does not appear in the Wardens' Accounts.
36 SMACA, Minute Book. 1918–1930, p. 153.
37 SMACA, Minute Book, 1837–1885, after 9 October 1882; Diocesan Articles of Enquiry, 1936, inserted in Minute Book, 1918–1930, after p. 99.
38 *Windsor and Richmond Gazette*, 26 February 1898.

39 State Records NSW, Church Lands, 2/1846, 34/122 and 35/935; Windsor, 1835, Surveyors' Sketchbooks, reel 2778, Vol. 3, Part 1, between 0498 and 0499; Steele, *Early Days of Windsor*, p. 111.
40 Armstrong, 'Plan of the New & Old Glebe adjoining the Town of Windsor', 1837, Mitchell Library, ZM2 811.1122/1837/1.
41 A.G. Maclean, 1844 tracing from Galloway's map of Windsor, 1843, State Records NSW, 2/1846, 44/400.
42 SMACA, Wardens' Accounts, 29 November 1844.
43 *Windsor and Richmond Gazette*, 2 September 1899.
44 SMACA, Wardens' Accounts, 30 June 1838.
45 State Records NSW, 2/1846, 44/7400.
46 SMACA, Wardens' Accounts, 4 October 1842, 14 August 1847, 16 June 1849.
47 SMACA, Wardens' Accounts, 30 November 1846, 5 April 1847, 1846–1847 Abstract, 11 May, 16 April, 4 June, 14, 23 August 1847, 9 April 1848, 1847–1848 Abstract, 20 September, 25 October 1848.
48 SMACA, Minute Book, 1837–1885, 24 April 1855.
49 SMACA, Wardens' Accounts, 1 December 1862, 7, 19 January1863.
50 SMACA, Minute Book, 1837–1885, 31 March 1872.
51 State Records NSW, 2/1846, 44/7400.
52 *New South Wales Police Gazette*, 1885, p. 85, No. 10, 8 March 1865, ancestry.com.au
53 SMACA, Minute Book, 1886–1918, p. 96.
54 SMACA, Wardens' Accounts,13 March 1877; Minute Book, 1918–1930, p. 69.
56 SMACA, Minute Book, 1837–1885, 1, 26 September 1881.
57 SMACA, Minute Book, 1886–1918, pp. 3, 13.
58 SMACA, Minute Book, 1886–1918, pp. 90–93, 95.
59 *Windsor and Richmond Gazette*, 26 February 1898.
60 William Freame, 'Old St Matthew's Revived', *Windsor and Richmond Gazette*, 12 March, 1904.
61 Roxburgh, *Early Colonial Houses*, p. 268.
62 Freame, *Windsor and Richmond Gazette*, 12 March 1904.
63 *Windsor and Richmond Gazette*, 27 September 1902.
64 *Windsor and Richmond Gazette*, 10 December 1898.
65 *Hawkesbury Herald*, 14 August 1903.
66 *Windsor and Richmond Gazette*, 2 September 1899.
67 *Windsor and Richmond Gazette*, 19 October 1901.
68 *Windsor and Richmond Gazette*, 19 October 1901.

Chapter 9

1 *Hawkesbury Herald*, 14 August 1903.
2 *Windsor and Richmond Gazette*, 21 May 1904.
3 *Sydney Morning Herald*, 31 January 1903.
4 *Windsor and Richmond Gazette*, 5 November 1904.
5 *Windsor and Richmond Gazette*, 16 July 1904; 'Kirwan, Hiram John (1819–1904)', Obituaries Australia, National Centre of Biography, Australian National University, http://oa.anu.edu.au/obituary/kirwan-hiram-john-17696/text29308, accessed 14 May 2016.
6 *Windsor and Richmond Gazette,* 14 October 1905.
7 *Windsor and Richmond Gazette*, 21 October 1905.
8 *Windsor and Richmond Gazette*, 13 October 1906.
9 Turnbull Clan Genealogy, at http://www.library.turnbullclan.com/tca_genealogy/tca_all2-o/g0/p184.htm, accessed 15 May 2016.
10 *Windsor and Richmond Gazette*, 22 September 1906.
11 St Matthew's Anglican Church Archives [SMACA], Minute Book, 1886–1918, p. 364.
12 SMACA, Minute Book, 1886–1918, pp. 395, 396, 400, 403.
13 SMACA, Minute Book, 1886–1918, p. 429.
14 *Windsor and Richmond Gazette*, 3 March 1939.
15 Rex Stubbs, *Ghosts and Myths of the Hawkesbury*, author, Windsor, 1982, p. 5.
16 *Cessnock Eagle and South Maitland Recorder,* 21 March 1939.
17 SMACA, Minute Book, 1918–1930, pp. 106, 107, 111, 113; page from parish magazine inserted after p111.
18 SMACA, Minute Book, 1918–1930, p. 183.
19 Interview by Jan Barkley-Jack with Mrs Jean Wright, a daughter of Thomas Campbell, 10 August 1996.
20 *Windsor and Richmond Gazette*, 19 January 1923.
21 *Windsor and Richmond Gazette*, 19 January 1923.
22 Interview by Jan Barkley-Jack and Ian Jack with Miss Lorna Campbell, the youngest daughter of Thomas Campbell, 15 August 2009.
23 *Windsor and Richmond Gazette*, 25 November 1932.
24 Interview by Jan Barkley-Jack with Lorna Campbell.
25 'Lorna's Life at the Rectory', *Our Town*, magazine published by *Hawkesbury Gazette*, Vol. 3, No. 4, Autumn 2001, p. 17.
26 'Lorna's Life at the Rectory', *Our Town*, Vol. 3, No. 4, Autumn 2001, p. 17; SMACA, Minute Book, 1931–1957, pp. 61–62.
27 *Windsor and Richmond Gazette*, 18 September 1936; 10 December 1937.
28 SMACA, Minute Book, 1931–1957, pp. 103, 117, 139, 145, 147.
29 Graham and Carol Edds from Graham Edds & Associates, 2016.
30 ICOMOS is a non-governmental international organization dedicated to the conservation of the world's monuments and sites.
31 Graham Edds from Graham Edds & Associates, 2016.
32 SMACA, Minute Book, 1913-1957, pp. 96, 97.
33 SMACA, Minute Book, 1931-1957, p. 106.
34 SMACA, Minute Book, 1931-1957, p. 103.
35 SMACA, Minute Book, 1931-1957, pp. 103, 117, 139, 145, 147.
36 SMACA, Minute Book, 1931-1957, pp. 352, 353.
37 Graham Edds from Graham Edds & Associates, 2016.
38 *Windsor and Richmond Gazette*, 5 September, 1924; information from John and Dorothy Butler, May 2016.
39 Information from John and Dorothy Butler, May 2016.
40 H. Sheumaker and S.T. Wajda, eds, *Material Culture in America: Understanding Everyday Life*, ABC-CLIO, Santa Barbara, 2008, p. 77.
41 Macquarie Family History Group, eds, *St Matthews Church of England Windsor NSW: Parish Registers 1901–1950 'A Complete Transcription'*, Lake Macquarie Family History Group, Teralba, 2006, p. 283 item, 4031; J. Tebbutt, *Astronomical Memoirs*, 1908, reprinted Hawkesbury City Council, Windsor, 1986, p. xiv; *Sydney Morning Herald,* 2 December 1916.
42 Tebbutt, *Astronomical Memoirs*, p. 148.
43 Tebbutt, *Astronomical Memoirs*, p. 149; *Sydney Morning Herald*, 2 December 1916.
44 SMACA, Minute Book, 1886–1918, p. 517.
45 SMACA, Minute Book, 1918–1930, p. 243.
46 SMACA, Minute Book, 1931–1957, pp. 18, 20.
47 Information from Cornelis Sondermeyer, 2 June 2016.
48 SMACA, Minute Book, 1957–1968, pp. 383–384, 422, 423, 429.
49 SMACA, Minute Book, 1957–1968, pp. 456, 467.
50 SMACA, Minute Book, 1957–1968. pp. 473, 476, 480.
51 SMACA, Minute Book, 1957–1968, pp. 507, 510–511, 528; Minute Book, 1968–1977, pp. 10, 22.
52 SMACA, Minute Book, 1957–1968, pp. 154–155, 157; interview by Jan Barkley-Jack with Les Quinton and his family, August 2009.
53 SMACA, Minute Book, 1957–1968, p. 223.
54 SMACA, Minute Book 1918–1930, p. 201 (a complaint of 1928).
55 State Records NSW, Map 1975.
56 SMACA. Wardens' Accounts, 19 November 1842.
57 SMACA, Minute Book 1886–1918, p. 3.
58 SMACA, Minute Book, 1837–1885, 28 December 1885.
59 SMACA, Minute Book, 1918–1930, p. 139.
60 SMACA, Minute Book, 1918–1930, pp. 217, 217.
61 L. Murray, *Death and dying in twentieth century Sydney*, 2013, http://dictionaryofsydney.org/entry/death_and_dying_in_twentieth_century_sydney
62 SMACA, Minute Book, 1957–1968, pp. 103 ff.
63 SMACA, Minute Book, 1957–1968, p. 105.
64 SMACA, Minute Book, 1957–1968, pasted on p. 107.
65 *The Parish Messenger*, Vol. 22, No. 7, November 1960.
66 SMACA, Minute Book, 1957–1968, pasted on p. 115.
67 SMACA, Minute Book, 1957–1968, pp. 129, 134, 141, 152, 153, 194, 203.
68 *The Parish Messenger*, Vol. 22, No. 7, November 1960.
69 SMACA, Minute Book, 1886–1918, p. 147.

70 SMACA, Minute Book, 1968–1977, p. 61.
71 Information to Jan Barkley-Jack, from C. Sondermeyer.
72 *The Parish Messenger*, December 1966, Vol. 28, No.12 and July 1980, Vol. 42, No. 7, supplied by Carol Roberts.
73 Macquarie Family History Group, eds, *St Matthews Parish Registers, 1810–1856; 1857–1900; 1901–1950; 1951–2000.*
74 J.H.M. Abbott, in *The World's News*, 11 September 1926.
75 National Trust of Australia (NSW), *A Guide to the Conservation of Cemeteries*, Sydney, 1982 and subsequent editions; S. Lavelle, *Cemeteries: Guidelines for their Care and Conservation,* Department of Planning, Heritage Council of NSW, Sydney, 1992 and subsequent editions.
76 J. Barkley-Jack, 'Celebrating 50 Years', *Spanning the Centuries of Hawkesbury History: Journal of Hawkesbury Historical Society*, No.1, 2006, p. 3.
77 SMACA, Minute Book, 1918–1930, p. 239.
78 SMACA, Minute Book, 1931–1957, pp. 30–32.
79 SMACA, Minute Book, 1931–1957, printed balance sheet 1935–1936, pasted between pp. 86 and 87.
80 SMACA, Minute Book, 1931–1957, pp. 93, 132, 134.
81 SMACA, Minute Book, 1931–1957, pp. 165, 169.
82 SMACA, Minute Book, 1931–1957, pp. 242, 255, 260.
83 SMACA, Minute Book, 1931–1957, pp. 280, 286, 288–289, 314.
84 SMACA, Minute Book, 1957–1968, pp. 3, 5, 10, 100.
85 Information from Carol Roberts, May 2016.
86 SMACA, Minute Book, 1977–1983, Reports to Annual Vestry Meeting, 5 March 1982, 7 March 1983. For completion of the South Windsor hall, see Minute Book, 1957–1968, p. 466.
87 *Windsor and Richmond Gazette*, 13 October 1982.
88 *Radar,* 27 October 1982.
89 *Windsor and Richmond Gazette*, 13 October 1982.
90 SMACA, Minute Book, 1977–1983, Report to Annual Vestry Meeting, 7 March 1983.
91 SMACA, Minute Book, 1983–1985, between pp. 127 and 128, 133, 139, 165, 169, 179–180.
92 SMACA, Minute Book, 1983–1985, p. 183; *Hawkesbury Gazette*, 17 July 1985; plaque at entrance to the Parish Centre.
93 Information from Carol Roberts, May 2016.

Chapter 10

1 W.F. Carter, *The Cathedral of the Hawkesbury: A Sketch of St. Matthew's Windsor*, n.d., p. 3 of later edition.
2 Information from John Butler, May 2016.
3 *Windsor and Richmond Gazette*, 25 November 1932.
4 J. Steele, *The Early Days of Windsor*, Tyrrell's, Sydney, 1916, reprinted Library of Australian History, North Sydney, 1977, p. 96.
5 *Windsor and Richmond Gazette*, 20 January 1922.
6 *Windsor and Richmond Gazette*, 30 January 1942.
7 *Windsor and Richmond Gazette*, 16 October 1925.
8 *Windsor and Richmond Gazette*, 22 October 1926.
9 *Sydney Morning Herald*, 6 October 1917.
10 *Windsor and Richmond Gazette*, 16 November 1917; Copy of 'The Centenary of St Matthew's Church of England, Windsor, NSW, 1917, Hawkesbury Library vertical file, 'St Matthew's Church'.
11 St Matthew's Anglican Church Archives [SMACA], Minute Book, 1886–1918, p. 370. The stones were removed from the doorway when the porch was remodelled in 1919.
12 SMACA, Minute Book, 1886–1918, pp. 437–438; Carter, *Cathedral of the Hawkesbury*, p. 26.
13 SMACA, Minute Book, 1886–1918, pp. 507–508, 511, 514.
14 SMACA, Robertson & Marks to Jenkyn, 14 January 1918, pasted to back fly-leaf of Minute Book, 1886–1918.
15 SMACA, Minute Book, 1918–1930, p. 26.
16 SMACA, Minute Book, 1918–1930, pp. 26–27, 29–35, 38. For Harriet Hordern, see chapter 6 above.
17 *St Matthew's Parish Magazine*, Vol. 3, No. 3, April 1920, p. 2; SMACA, Robertson & Marks to Jenkyn, 14 January 1918, pasted onto back fly-leaf of Minute Book, 1886–1918.
18 *St Matthew's Parish Magazine*, Vol. 3, No .3, April 1920; SMACA, Minute Book, 1918–1930, pp. 48, 58.
19 *Daily Telegraph*, 16 August 1919; Steele, *Early Days of Windsor*, p. 86.
20 F. Walker, 'St Matthew's Church, Windsor, N.S.W.: A Sketch on the 108th Anniversary', *Australian Christian World*, 16 October 1925, cutting in Walker's compilation on Windsor, Royal Australian Historical Society, Rare Book 991.3 WIN.
21 SMACA, Robertson & Marks to Jenkyn, 14 January 1918, pasted onto back fly-leaf of Minute Book, 1886–1918; Minute Book, 1918–1930, p. 56.
22 SMACA, Minute Book, 1918–1930, pp. 58–59, 64, 65. For Noller, see Steele, *Early Days of Windsor*, p. 166.
23 *Windsor and Richmond Gazette*, 28 September 1917.
24 *Windsor and Richmond Gazette*, 19 January 1923.
25 *Windsor and Richmond Gazette*, 19 January 1923.
26 *Windsor and Richmond Gazette*, 19 January 1923.
27 *Windsor and Richmond Gazette*, 19 January 1923.
28 *Cessnock Eagle and South Maitland Recorder*, 19 December 1924.
29 SMACA, Minute Book, 1918–1930, p. 116.
30 F. Jackson, 'Windsor, N.S.W., its Monuments', *Sydney Morning Herald*, 17 May 1924.
31 Jackson, *Sydney Morning Herald*, 17 May 1924.
32 *Sydney Morning Herald*, 12 October 1925.
33 *Daily Telegraph*, 13 October 1925; *Sydney Morning Herald*, 12 October 1925; *Australian Christian World*, 16 October 1925.
34 *St Matthew's Parish Magazine*, Vol. 8, No. 9, October [1925]. This survives pasted into Walker's compilation on Windsor, Royal Australian Historical Society, Rare Book 991.3 WIN.
35 *St Matthew's Parish Magazine*, Vol. 8, No. 9, October [1925].
36 *Windsor and Richmond Gazette*, 7 August 1936.
37 *Windsor and Richmond Gazette*, 7 August 1936.
38 *Sydney Morning Herald*, 26 January 1942; *Windsor and Richmond Gazette*, 30 January 1942.
39 SMACA, Minute Book, 1931–1957, p. 103.
40 *Windsor and Richmond Gazette*, 22 July 1938.
41 *Windsor and Richmond Gazette*, 12 August 1938, 19 November 1939.
42 SMACA, Minute book, 1931–1957, p. 185.
43 SMACA, Minute Book, 1931–1957, pp. 239, 241, 23, 244, 274; Paine to Ashwin, 14 August 1944, loose between pp. 352 and 353.
44 SMACA, Minute Book, 1931–1957, pp. 407, 411.
45 *The Parish Messenger*, Vol. 24, No. 7, July 1962.
46 C. Lucas, 'Wilkinson, Leslie (1882–1973)', *Australian Dictionary of Biography*, Vol. 12, Melbourne University Press, Carlton, 1990, p. 493.
47 SMACA, Minute Book,1918–1930, pp. 119, 122, 123; *St Matthew's Parish Magazine*, Vol. 7, No. 10, December 1924, in the possession of Margaret Fennell.
48 SMACA, Minute Book, 1957–1968, pp. 56, 62, 71, 73.
49 *Hawkesbury Gazette*, 22 June 1974. The church minute books give no hint of the date of the original blue-and-gold paintwork.
50 SMACA, Minute Book, 1958–1968, pp. 52, 65–67; *The Parish Messenger*, Vol. 20, No. 10, November 1958.
51 SMACA, Minute Book, 1931–1957, pp. 390, 437.
52 SMACA, Minute Book, 1931–1957, pp. 447, 448, 456; Carter, *Cathedral of the Hawkesbury*, p. 32.
53 SMACA, Minute Book, 1931–1957, pp. 447, 448, 456; Carter, *Cathedral of the Hawkesbury*, p. 32; *Hawkesbury Gazette*, 26 June 1957.
54 *Hawkesbury Gazette*, 26 June 1957.
55 Information from Carol Roberts, May 2016.
56 Carter, *Cathedral of the Hawkesbury*, p. 32.
57 *Hawkesbury Gazette*, 26 June 1957.
58 Carter, *Cathedral of the Hawkesbury*, p. 32; *The Parish Messenger*, Vol. 17, No. 9, October 1957.
59 SMACA, Minute Book, 1957–1968, p. 308; *Daily Telegraph*, 27 October 1965.
60 *Daily Telegraph*, 27 October 1965.
61 SMACA, Minute Book, 1957–1968, pp. 316, 321–322, 340.
62 *Mirror*, 5 July 1963.
63 SMACA, Minute Book, 1957–1968, pp. 328, 344–345.
64 SMACA, Minute Book, 1957–1968, pp. 357–358, 370–371.

65 *The Parish Messenger*, October 1963, Vol. 25, No. 10, supplied by Carol Roberts.

66 P. Robinson, *Short History and Guide for St Thomas' Mulgoa*, St Thomas' Church, Mulgoa, 1988; *Daily Telegraph*, 6 September 1963.

67 SMACA, Minute Book, 1957–1968, p. 362.

68 SMACA, Minute Book, 1957–1968, pp. 371, 374.

69 Hawkesbury Library, photograph 003246.

70 *The Parish Messenger*, Vol. 25, No. 10, October 1963.

71 *Sunday Telegraph*, 3 November 1963.

72 *Sunday Telegraph*, 3 November 1963.

73 Programme for National Trust St Matthew's Windsor Appeal, 'Go to Windsor' Day, Saturday, November 2, 1963, printed by the *Mirror* newspaper, supplied by Carol Roberts.

74 *Daily Telegraph*, 27 October 1965; Hawkesbury Library, photograph 013918.

75 SMACA, Minute Book, 1957–1968, pp. 406, 420, 447; Carter, *Cathedral of the Hawkesbury*, p. 33.

76 Carter, *Cathedral of the Hawkesbury*, p. 33.

77 National Trust of Australia (NSW), *Annual Report for 1965–1966.*

78 SMACA, Minute Book, 1957–1968, pp. 544, 553.

79 SMACA, Minute Book, 1957–1968, pp. 495, 513, 533.

80 SMACA, Minute Book, 1957–1968, pp. 61, 563; information from Beverley Hunt, 2016; *Windsor and Richmond Gazette*, 11 October 1967.

81 *The Program for the Order of Service, for the 150th Anniversary of St Matthew's Church, Windsor, 2.30 p.m. Sunday, 17 December 1972.*

82 D. Kinsela, in booklet for CD, *Ancestral Spirit: Music of the Augustan Age*, Great Organs of Australia Series, St Matthew's Anglican Church, Windsor, NSW, The First Australian Organ, Walsingham Classics, 1997, recorded at St Matthew's, Windsor in April 1996; information from Graeme Hunt, May 2016.

83 G. Rushworth, *Historic Organs of New South Wales*, Hale & Iremonger, Sydney, 1988.

84 SMACA, Minute Book, 1983–1985, pp. 168, 174, 182; information from Graeme Hunt, June 2016.

85 Graham and Carol Edds, Graham Edds & Associates, 2016.

86 Graham and Carol Edds, Graham Edds & Associates, 2016.

87 Information from John Butler, May 2016.

88 Graham Edds, Graham Edds & Associates, 2016.

89 Graham Edds, Graham Edds & Associates, 2016.

90 Graham and Carol Edds, Graham Edds & Associates, 2016.

91 Violet Carter, 15 November 1960, in *The Parish Messenger*, Vol. 22, No. 7, November 1960.

92 Unidentified newspaper cutting held by Local Studies at Hawkesbury Library, probably *Windsor and Richmond Gazette*, 1996.

93 Unidentified newspaper cutting held by Local Studies at Hawkesbury Library, probably *Windsor and Richmond Gazette*, 1996.

94 Unidentified newspaper cutting held by Local Studies at Hawkesbury Library, probably *Windsor and Richmond Gazette*, 1996.

95 Unidentified newspaper cuttings held by Local Studies at Hawkesbury Library, probably from *Windsor and Richmond Gazette*.

96 Information from Kim Alderton, April 2016.

97 Unidentified newspaper cuttings held by Local Studies at Hawkesbury Library, probably both from *Windsor and Richmond Gazette*, 1996.

98 St Matthew's newsletter, *The Weekly Bulletin*, nos.12 to 382; information from John Butler, May 2016.

99 St Matthew's newsletter, *The Weekly Bulletin*, No. 382.

100 St Matthew's newsletter, *The Weekly Bulletin*, No. 30.

101 St Matthew's newsletter, *The Weekly Bulletin*, Nos 147–372.

102 St Matthew's newsletter, *The Weekly Bulletin*, Nos 392–435.

103 *The Parish Messenger*, Vol. 20, No. 10, November 1958; Vol. 22, No. 7, November 1960; Vol. 23, No. 1, December 1960; Vol. 25, No. 6, June 1963.

104 Information from Kim Alderton, April 2016.

105 *Windsor and Richmond Gazette*, 15 July 1953.

106 St Matthew's newsletter, *The Weekly Bulletin*, No. 9; information from John and Dorothy Butler, 2016.

107 *The Parish Messenger*, Vol. 23, No. 3, April–May 1961; Vol. 23, No. 5, July 1961.

108 Information from John and Dorothy Butler, May 2016; information from Beverley Hunt, May 2016.

109 Information from Beverley Hunt, May 2016.

110 Information from Chris Burgess, June 2016.

111 Information from Joyce Edwards, June 2016.

112http://www.xroyvision.com.au/drake/chilcott/alcorn/alcorn.html, accessed 2 June 2016.

113archiver.rootsweb.ancestry.com/th/read/AUS-NSW-SYDNEY/2004-02/1077407099, accessed 2 June 2016.

114 www.rodstorie.com.au/html/moses_family.html, accessed 2 May 2016.

115 Information from Aleks Pinter, June 2016.

116 Information from Aleks Pinter, June 2016.

117 St Matthew's Ladies' Guild Windsor, Treasurer's Account Book, 1936–1968; information from Beverley Hunt, May 2016.

118 Information from members of Ladies' Guild and from Margaret Fennell, May 2016.

119 *The Parish Messenger*, Vol. 17, No. 10, October–November 1957.

120 *The Parish Messenger*, Vol. 17, No. 9, October 1957; Vol. 20, No. 10, November 1958.

121 *The Parish Messenger*, Vol. 23, No. 3, April–May 1961.

122 *The Parish Messenger*, Vol. 25, No. 6, June 1963; information from Margaret Fennell, May 2016.

123 Information from Beverley Hunt, May 2016.

124 Information from Beverley Hunt, May 2016; *The Parish Messenger*, Vol. 25, No. 6, June 1963; information from Carol Roberts, June 2016; information from John Butler, April 2016.

125 Information from Margaret Fennell and Don and Jill Mills, June 2016.

126 Information from Doug Minty, June 2016.

127 *The Parish Messenger*, Vol. 25, No. 6, June 1963; information by Fay Cragg, June 2016.

128 *The Parish Messenger*, Vol. 17, No. 10, October–November 1957.

129 C. Roberts, 'Long Tradition of Organists at St Matthew's Church in Windsor', written for Kurrajong-Comleroy Historical Society, and published in *Hawkesbury Gazette*, 4 June 2014.

130 Information from Kath Griffiths, June 2016; information from Margaret Terry, June 2016.

131 Information from Beverley Hunt, May 2016; information from Margaret Terry, June 2016.

132 Roberts, 'Long Tradition of Organists at St Matthew's Church in Windsor', *Hawkesbury Gazette*, 4 June 2014.

133 Information from Beverley Hunt, May, 2016; information from Carol Roberts, June 2016.

134 *Hawkesbury Gazette*, 6 April 1984.

135 *Hawkesbury Gazette*, 6 April 1984; plaque on the front lawn of St Matthew's Church; information from Tony Craig, May 2016; information from Beverley Hunt, May 2016.

136 Information from Peter Griffiths, June 2016.

137 Information from Beverley Hunt, Margaret Fennell and Joyce Edwards, May 2016.

138 Information from Beverley Hunt, May 2016.

139 *St Matthew's Parish Magazine*, Vol. 3 No. 3, April 1920, pasted into the SMACA Minute Book, 1918–1930; the only copy of Vol. 7, No. 10, December 1924, is held by Margaret Fennell.

140 Information from Ladies' Guild, May 2016; and from Fay Cragg, June 2016.

141 Information from Ladies' Guild, May 2016; information from Kay Ryan, June 2016.

142 Information from Chris Jones, June 2016.

Index